Fodor's 22nd Edition

W9-CDJ-796

Chicago

The Guide
for All Budgets

Completely
Updated

Where to Stay, Eat,
and Explore

On and Off
the Beaten Path

When to Go,
What to Pack

Maps, Travel Tips,
and Web Sites

Fodor's Travel Publications • New York, Toronto, London, Sydney, Auckland
www.fodors.com

Fodor's Chicago

EDITOR: Mary Beth Bohman

Editorial Contributors: Laura Baginski, Joanne Cleaver, Elaine Glusac, Satu Hummasti, Elisa Kronish, Robin Kurzer, JoAnn Milivojevic, Roberta Sotonoff, Judy Sutton Taylor

Editorial Production: Tom Holton

Maps: David Lindroth, *cartographer*; Bob Blake and Rebecca Baer, *map editors*

Design: Fabrizio La Rocca, *creative director*; Guido Caroti, *art director*; Jolie Novak, *senior picture editor*; Melanie Marin, *photo editor*

Cover Design: Pentagram

Production/Manufacturing: Angela L. McLean

Cover Photo (Chicago River): Robert Glusic/PhotoDisc/Getty Images

Copyright

Copyright © 2003 by Fodors LLC

Fodor's is a registered trademark of Random House, Inc.

All rights reserved under International and Pan-American Copyright Conventions. Published in the United States by Fodor's Travel Publications, a unit of Fodors LLC, a subsidiary of Random House, Inc., New York, and simultaneously in Canada by Random House of Canada Limited, Toronto. Distributed by Random House, Inc., New York.

No maps, illustrations, or other portions of this book may be reproduced in any form without written permission from the publisher.

Twenty-second Edition

ISBN 1–4000–1085–3

ISSN 0743–9326

Important Tip

Although all prices, open times, and other details in this book are based on information supplied to us at press time, changes occur all the time in the travel world, and Fodor's cannot accept responsibility for facts that become outdated or for inadvertent errors or omissions. So **always confirm information when it matters,** especially if you're making a detour to visit a specific place.

Special Sales

Fodor's Travel Publications are available at special discounts for bulk purchases for sales promotions or premiums. Special editions, including personalized covers, excerpts of existing guides, and corporate imprints, can be created in large quantities for special needs. For more information, contact your local bookseller or write to Special Markets, Fodor's Travel Publications, 1745 Broadway, New York, NY 10019. Inquiries from Canada should be directed to your local Canadian bookseller or sent to Random House of Canada, Ltd., Marketing Department, 2775 Matheson Blvd., East, Mississauga, Ontario L4W 4P7. Inquiries from the United Kingdom should be sent to Fodor's Travel Publications, 20 Vauxhall Bridge Road, London SW1V 2SA, England.

PRINTED IN THE UNITED STATES OF AMERICA

10 9 8 7 6 5 4 3 2 1

CONTENTS

9   Background and Essentials   218

Index   227

Maps and Charts

ON THE ROAD WITH FODOR'S

A trip takes you out of yourself. Concerns of life at home completely disappear, driven away by more immediate thoughts—about, say, what marvels will beguile the next day, or where you'll have dinner. That's where Fodor's comes in. We make sure that you know all your options, so that you don't miss something that's around the next bend just because you didn't know it was there. Mindful that the best memories of your trip might have nothing to do with what you came to Chicago to see, we guide you to sights large and small all over town. You might set out to shop 'til you drop on the Magnificent Mile, but back at home you find yourself unable to forget strolling along Lake Michigan with that fantastic skyline laid out before you. With Fodor's at your side, serendipitous discoveries are never far away.

About Our Writers

Our success in showing you every corner of Chicago is a credit to our extraordinary writers. Although there's no substitute for travel advice from a good friend who knows your style, our contributors are the next best thing—the kind of people you would poll for travel advice if you knew them.

Laura Baginski has lived in Chicago her entire life. Clearly she's taken her grandfather's favorite saying to heart: "If you're not in Chicago, you're only camping out." When she's not checking out the latest cultural happenings around town, she's writing for an e-learning company and moonlighting as a travel writer. She doesn't plan on camping out anytime soon.

Joanne Cleaver has been exploring the outer reaches of the Chicago metro area for nearly 20 years. Sometimes she does it on assignment for the *Chicago Tribune* or while researching her three family-travel guidebooks. The rest of the time, she is just having fun. She is particularly partial to Naper Settlement.

Elaine Glusac writes about food and travel for the *International Herald Tribune, Travel + Leisure, American Way, Southwest Spirit, National Geographic Traveler,* and *Cooking Light.* Her Chicago dining

reviews appear in both print and electronic editions of the *Chicago Tribune.*

Elisa Kronish is a resident expert on her home town of Chicago. She was an editor and now writes reviews for Chicago Citysearch.com, covering shopping, attractions, hotels and restaurants. She particularly enjoys visiting new hotels and trying out new restaurants. Her articles have also appeared in *Illinois Meetings and Events, Concierge Preferred, Windy City Sports,* and *Chicago* magazine.

Robin Kurzer is a Chicago-based travel writer with a penchant for what's hot and what's not in the wide world of Windy City sports. One of her lifelong goals is to visit every baseball park in the country; so far she's been to about 10.

Longtime Fodor's contributor Chicagoan **JoAnn Milivojevic** loves exploring art, food, and culture in the many ethnic neighborhoods around the city. Her food, fitness, and travel stories appear in magazines nationwide.

Roberta Sotonoff is a confessed travel junkie who writes to support her habit. Over 30 domestic and international newspapers, magazines, on-line sites and guidebooks have published her work. One of her favorite destinations is her hometown, Chicago.

Judy Sutton Taylor has lived in Chicago for 10 years and loves to scour shops for bargains and treasures for her husband and two dogs. Her work has appeared in the *Chicago Tribune, Self, Sports Illustrated for Women, Chicago* magazine, and other publications.

You can rest assured that you're in good hands—and that no property mentioned in the book has paid to be included. Each has been selected strictly on its merits, as the best of its type in its price range.

How to Use This Book

Up front is Smart Travel Tips A to Z, arranged alphabetically by topic and loaded with tips, Web sites, and contact information. Destination: Chicago helps get you in the mood for your trip. The Exploring chapter is divided into neighborhood sections arranged in logical geographical order; each recommends a good tour and lists local sights alphabetically. The chapters that follow Exploring are arranged alphabetically. At the end of the book you'll find Background and Essentials, including a Portrait. The Books and Movies section suggests enriching reading and viewing.

Icons and Symbols

★   Our special recommendations
✕   Restaurant
🏠   Lodging establishment
🐤   Good for kids (rubber duck)
☞   Sends you to another section of the guide for more information
✉   Address
☎   Telephone number
🕐   Opening and closing times
💰   Admission prices (those we give apply to adults; substantially reduced fees are almost always available for children, students, and senior citizens)

Numbers in white and black circles ③ ❸ that appear on the maps, in the margins, and within the tours correspond to one another.

Don't Forget to Write

Your experiences—positive and negative—matter to us. If we have missed or misstated something, we want to hear about it. We follow up on all suggestions. Contact the Chicago editor at editors@fodors.com or c/o Fodor's at 1745 Broadway, New York, New York 10019. And have a fabulous trip!

Karen Cure

Karen Cure
Editorial Director

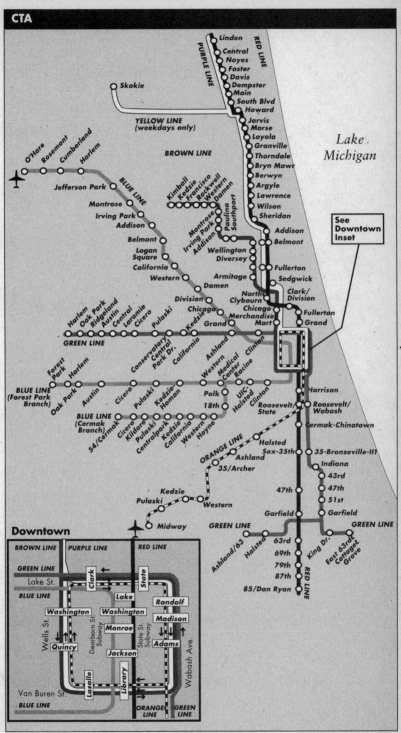

CTA

PURPLE LINE

RED LINE

Linden
Central
Noyes
Foster
Davis
Dempster
Main
South Blvd
Howard

Skokie

YELLOW LINE
(weekdays only)

Jarvis
Morse
Loyola
Granville
Thorndale
Bryn Mawr
Berwyn
Argyle
Lawrence
Wilson
Sheridan

Lake Michigan

O'Hare
Rosemont
Cumberland
Harlem

BROWN LINE

Jefferson Park

BLUE LINE

Kimball
Kedzie
Francisco
Rockwell
Western
Damen

See Downtown Inset

Montrose
Irving Park
Addison

Belmont

Logan Square
California

Western

Montrose
Irving Park
Addison

Paulina
Southport

Wellington
Diversey

Armitage
Damen

North/Clybourn

Division
Chicago

Kedzie

Grand

Addison
Belmont

Fullerton
Sedgwick

Clark/Division

Chicago
Merchandise Mart

Fullerton
Grand

Harlem
Oak Park
Ridgeland
Austin
Central
Laramie
Cicero

Pulaski
Kedzie

Conservatory
Central
Park Dr.

California

Ashland
Western
Medical Center
Racine

Clinton

GREEN LINE

Forest Park
Harlem

BLUE LINE
(Forest Park Branch)

Oak Park
Austin
Cicero
Pulaski
Kedzie
Homan

Polk
18th

UIC-Halsted
Clinton

Harrison

Roosevelt/State
Roosevelt/Wabash

BLUE LINE
(Cermak Branch)

54/Cermak
Cicero
Kildare
Pulaski
Centralpark
Kedzie
California
Western
Hoyne

Cermak-Chinatown

ORANGE LINE

Halsted
Sox-35th
35-Bronzeville-IIT

Ashland
35/Archer

Indiana
43rd
47th
51st

Kedzie
Pulaski
Western

47th

Garfield

Garfield

Midway

GREEN LINE

GREEN LINE

Ashland/63
Halsted

63rd
69th
79th
87th
85/Dan Ryan

King Dr.

East 63rd-Cottage Grove

RED LINE

Downtown

BROWN LINE | PURPLE LINE | RED LINE

GREEN LINE

Lake St.

BLUE LINE

Clark

State

Lake

Randolf

Washington
Washington
Madison

Monroe

Wells St.

Dearborn St. Subway

State St. Subway

Wabash Ave.

Quincy

Jackson

Adams

Lasalle

Library

Van Buren St.

BLUE LINE

ORANGE LINE | GREEN LINE

The Midwest and Great Lakes

MANITOBA

Lake of the Woods

NORTH DAKOTA

Thief River Falls

International Falls

Voyageurs Nat'l Park

53

Grand Forks

Red Lake

59

Ely

Virginia

Grand Portage

61

Isle R Nat'l

Mesabi Iron Range

LEECH LAKE INDIAN RES.

Eveleth

Keweenaw Peninsula

75

WHITE EARTH INDIAN RES.

Leech Lake

Hibbing

Apostle Islands National Lakeshore

Houghton

Fargo

Moorhead

MINNESOTA

Duluth

Detroit Lakes

Brainerd

Superior

Ashland

Ironwood

Fergus Falls

Mille Lacs

2

51

94

St. Cloud

Rice Lake

WISCONSIN

Willmar

35

SOUTH DAKOTA

Minneapolis

Eau Claire

Wausau

Mari

Gree Ba

St. Paul

94

Stevens Point

Marshall

New Ulm

Red Wing

Wisconsin Rapids

Appleton

39

Mankato

Rochester

61

Worthington

Fairmont

Albert Lea

Winona

90

Wisconsin Dells

Oshkosh

Fond du Lac

Sioux Falls

90

Austin

La Crosse

Spring Green

Baraboo

Platte River

IOWA

Wyoming

Madison

W

Prairie du Chien

Blue Mounds

New Glarus

94

Ro

Sioux City

Waterloo

Galena

Rockford

Stockton

Arlir He

NEBRASKA

Cedar Rapids

Savanna

Elmh

Des Moines

Sterling

Davenport

Aurora Jo

80

Omaha

La Salle

Kar

Galesburg

39

Peoria

Canton

Bloomington

7

MISSOURI

Macomb

Champa

KANSAS

Kansas City

Springfield

Decatur

Hannibal

Jacksonville

55

51

Columbia

ILLINOIS

Jefferson City

St. Louis

E. St. Louis

57

Belleville

Cent

Mount Vernon

Carb

N

2

0   150 miles

0   225 km

Chicago

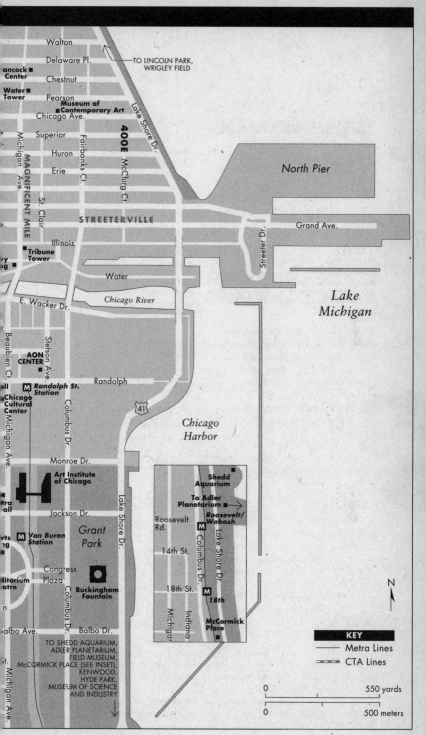

ESSENTIAL INFORMATION

ADDRESSES

Chicago streets generally follow a grid pattern, running north–south or east–west and radiating from a center point at State and Madison streets in the Loop. East and west street numbers go up as you move away from State Street; north and south street numbers rise as you move away from Madison Street. Each block is represented by a hundred number.

AIR TRAVEL TO AND FROM CHICAGO

BOOKING

When you book **look for nonstop flights** and **remember that "direct" flights stop at least once.** Try to avoid connecting flights, which require a change of plane. Two airlines may operate a connecting flight jointly, so ask if your airline operates every segment of the trip; you may find that the carrier you prefer flies you only part of the way. To find more booking tips and to check prices and make on-line flight reservations, log on to www.fodors.com.

CARRIERS

➤ MAJOR AIRLINES: **Air Canada** (☎ 888/247–2262, WEB www.aircanada. ca). **American** (☎ 800/433–7300, WEB www.aa.com). **Continental** (☎ 800/525–0280, WEB www.continental. com). **Delta** (☎ 800/221–1212, WEB www.delta.com). **Northwest** (☎ 800/225–2525, WEB www.nwa.com). **United** (☎ 800/241–6522, WEB www. united.com). **US Airways** (☎ 800/428–4322, WEB www.usairways.com).

➤ SMALLER AIRLINES: **America Trans Air** (☎ 800/225–2995, WEB www.ata. com). **America West** (☎ 800/235–9292, WEB www.americawest.com). **Southwest Airlines** (☎ 800/435–9792, WEB www.southwest.com).

CHECK-IN AND BOARDING

Always **ask your carrier about its check-in policy.** Plan to arrive at the airport about two hours before your scheduled departure time for domestic flights and 2½ to 3 hours before international flights. Assuming that not everyone with a ticket will show up, airlines routinely overbook planes. When everyone does, airlines ask for volunteers to give up their seats. In return, these volunteers usually get a certificate for a free flight and are rebooked on the next flight out. If there are not enough volunteers, the airline must choose who will be denied boarding. The first to get bumped are passengers who checked in late and those flying on discounted tickets, so **get to the gate and check in as early as possible,** especially during peak periods.

Always **bring a government-issued photo I.D. to the airport;** even when it's not required, a passport is best. If you are flying on an electronic ticket, remember to bring a paper receipt and the credit card used to purchase the flight.

CUTTING COSTS

The least expensive airfares to Chicago are priced for round-trip travel and must usually be purchased in advance. Airlines generally allow you to change your return date for a fee; most low-fare tickets, however, are nonrefundable. It's smart to **call a number of airlines and check the Internet;** when you are quoted a good price, **book it on the spot**—the same fare may not be available the next day. Always **check different routings** and look into using alternate airports. Also, price off-peak flights, which may be significantly less expensive than others. Travel agents, especially low-fare specialists (☞ Discounts and Deals), are helpful.

Consolidators are another good source. They buy tickets for scheduled international flights at reduced rates from the airlines, then sell them at prices that beat the best fare available directly from the airlines. Sometimes you can even get your money back if you need to return the ticket. Carefully read the fine print detailing penalties for changes and cancellations, purchase the ticket with a credit card, and **confirm your consolidator reservation with the airline.**

When you **fly as a courier,** you trade your checked-luggage space for a ticket deeply subsidized by a courier service. There are restrictions on when you can book and how long you can stay. Some courier companies list with membership organizations, such as the Air Courier Association and the International Association of Air Travel Couriers; these require you to become a member before you can book a flight.

➤ CONSOLIDATORS: **Cheap Tickets** (☎ 800/377–1000 or 888/922–8849, WEB www.cheaptickets.com). **Discount Airline Ticket Service** (☎ 800/576–1600). **Unitravel** (☎ 800/325–2222, WEB www.unitravel.com). **Up & Away Travel** (☎ 212/889–2345, WEB www.upandaway.com). **World Travel Network** (☎ 800/409–6753).

➤ COURIER RESOURCES: **Air Courier Association** (☎ 800/282–1202, WEB www.aircourier.org). **International Association of Air Travel Couriers** (☎ 352/475–1584, WEB www.courier.org).

FLYING TIMES

Approximate flying times are: two hours from New York, four hours from San Francisco, seven hours from London, and 17 hours from Sydney.

HOW TO COMPLAIN

If your baggage goes astray or your flight goes awry, complain right away. Most carriers require that you **file a claim immediately.** The Aviation Consumer Protection Division of the Department of Transportation publishes *Fly-Rights,* which discusses airlines and consumer issues and is available on-line. At PassengerRights. com, a Web site, you can compose a

letter of complaint and distribute it electronically.

➤ AIRLINE COMPLAINTS: **Aviation Consumer Protection Division** (✉ U.S. Department of Transportation, Room 4107, C-75, Washington, DC 20590, ☎ 202/366–2220, WEB www. dot.gov/airconsumer). **Federal Aviation Administration Consumer Hotline** (☎ 800/322–7873).

RECONFIRMING

Check the status of your flight before you leave for the airport. You can do this on your carrier's Web site, by linking to a flight-status checker (many Web booking services offer these), or by calling your carrier or travel agent.

AIRPORTS AND TRANSFERS

The major gateway to Chicago is **O'Hare International Airport (ORD).** One of the world's busiest airports, it is 20 mi from downtown, in the far northwest corner of the city. **Midway Airport (MDW),** which is about 7 mi southwest from downtown, added a terminal as part of an $800 million renovation in 2001. It primarily serves budget airlines. **Meigs Field,** just south of downtown, serves commuter airlines with flights to downstate Illinois.

➤ AIRPORT INFORMATION: **O'Hare International Airport** (☎ 773/686–2200, WEB www.ohare.com). **Midway Airport** (☎ 773/838–0600, WEB www. chicago-mdw.com). **Meigs Field** (☎ 312/922–5454).

AIRPORT TRANSFERS

Ground transport to or from both O'Hare and Midway airports can be slow, so consider taking public transportation.

BY BUS: Shuttle buses run between O'Hare and Midway airports and to and from either airport and various points in the city. When taking an airport shuttle bus to O'Hare to catch a departing flight, be sure to allow at least 1½ hours. If you're going from the South Side to Midway, call 24 hours in advance. Airport Express coaches provide service from both airports to major downtown and Near North hotels; call for reserva-

Smart Travel Tips A to Z

tions. The trip downtown from O'Hare takes a half hour or longer, depending on traffic conditions and your destination; the fare is $20, $36 round-trip. The trip downtown from Midway takes about a half hour; the fare is $15, $27 round-trip. Omega Shuttle vans travel between O'Hare and Midway, with departures every hour and a fare of $20. Travel time is roughly an hour. Omega also departs from both airports to locations in Hyde Park and the South Side. The fare is $20 from O'Hare to Hyde Park and $15 from Midway to Hyde Park.

BY TRAIN: Chicago Transit Authority (CTA) trains are the cheapest way to and from the airports; they can also be the most convenient transfer. TRAINS TO CITY signs will guide you to the subway or elevated train line. In O'Hare Airport the Blue line station is in the underground concourse between terminals. Travel time to the city is about 45 minutes. Get off at the station closest to your hotel, or from the first stop in the Loop (Washington and Dearborn streets) you can take a taxi to your hotel or change to other transit lines. At Midway Airport the Orange line El runs to the Loop. The stop at Adams Street and Wabash Avenue is the closest to the hotels on South Michigan Avenue; for others, the simplest strategy is to get off anywhere in the Loop and hail a cab to your final destination. Train fare is $1.50, which you will need in either dollar bills (turnstiles don't give change) and/or coins. A fare card is another option. Pick up brochures outside the entrances to the platforms that detail the stops of the train lines; the "Downtown Transit Sightseeing Guide" is also helpful.

BY TAXI: Metered taxicab service is available at both O'Hare and Midway airports. Trips to and from O'Hare incur a $1 surcharge. Expect to pay about $25–$35 plus tip from O'Hare to Near North and downtown locations, about $17–$27 plus tip from Midway. Some cabs participate in a share-a-ride program in which each cab carries two or three individuals going from the airport to downtown; the cost per person, $15, is substantially lower than the full rate.

BY CAR: Driving to and from O'Hare takes about an hour; the drive to and from Midway Airport takes at least 45 minutes. From O'Hare, follow the signs to I–90 east (Kennedy Expressway), which merges with I–94 (Edens Expressway). Take the eastbound exit at Ohio Street for Near North locations, the Washington or Monroe Street exit for downtown. After you exit, continue east about a mile to get to Michigan Avenue. From Midway, follow the signs to I–55 east, which leads to I–90.

➤ TAXIS AND SHUTTLES: **Airport Express** (☎ 312/454–7800 or 800/654–7871, WEB www.airportexpress.com). **American United Cab Co.** (☎ 773/248–7600). **Checker Taxi** (☎ 312/243–2537). **Flash Cab** (☎ 773/561–1444). **Omega Shuttle** (☎ 773/483–6634, WEB www.omegashuttle.com). **Yellow Cab Co.** (☎ 312/829–4222).

➤ PUBLIC TRANSIT INFORMATION: **CTA** (☎ 312/836–7000, WEB www.transitchicago.com).

BUSINESS HOURS

MUSEUMS AND SIGHTS

Chicagoland museums are generally open daily 9–5, closing only on major holidays; some larger attractions keep later hours (until about 8 PM) one weeknight per week. A number of smaller museums keep limited hours; it's always advisable to phone ahead for details.

PHARMACIES

Most pharmacies are open regular business hours, starting as early as 8 AM and closing at 5 PM.

➤ 24-HOUR PHARMACIES: **Osco** (☎ 800/654–6726 for nearest location). **Walgreens** (✉ 757 N. Michigan Ave., at Chicago Ave., ☎ 312/664–8686).

SHOPS

Most businesses in Chicago are open 9–5 Monday through Saturday; many are open Sunday, too, but often with shorter hours (i.e., noon to 4 or 5).

BUS TRAVEL TO AND FROM CHICAGO

Greyhound has nationwide service to its main terminal in the Loop and to neighborhood stations, at the 95th Street and Dan Ryan Expressway CTA station and at the Cumberland CTA station, near O'Hare Airport. The Harrison Street terminal is far from most hotels, so plan on another bus or a cab to your hotel.

➤ BUS INFORMATION: **Greyhound Lines** (✉ 630 W. Harrison St., ☎ 312/408–5970 or 800/231–2222, WEB www.greyhound.com).

CAMERAS AND PHOTOGRAPHY

With its striking architectural landscape, Chicago is a great city to photograph. Take a trip up to a skyscraper's observatory deck for a panoramic shot of the city. Or point your lens back at the unique skyline seen only from a trip out on Lake Michigan. You may also want to check with the Chicago Architecture Foundation; it occasionally leads special photographers' tours of the Loop.

The *Kodak Guide to Shooting Great Travel Pictures* (available at bookstores everywhere) is loaded with tips.

➤ PHOTO HELP: **Kodak Information Center** (☎ 800/242–2424, WEB www.kodak.com).

EQUIPMENT PRECAUTIONS

Remember that the weather is unpredictable in Chicago, so if you plan on taking photographs, make sure to protect your equipment from the perils of unexpected rain or snow. **Don't pack film and equipment in checked luggage,** where it is much more susceptible to damage. X-ray machines used to view checked luggage are becoming much more powerful and therefore are much more likely to ruin your film. Try to **ask for hand inspection of film,** which becomes clouded after repeated exposure to airport X-ray machines, and **keep videotapes and computer disks away from metal detectors.** Always

keep film, tape, and computer disks out of the sun. Carry an extra supply of batteries, and **be prepared to turn on your camera, camcorder, or laptop** to prove to airport security personnel that the device is real.

CAR RENTAL

Rates in Chicago begin at $46 a day and $170 a week for an economy car with air-conditioning, automatic transmission, and unlimited mileage. This does not include the car-rental tax of 18%.

➤ MAJOR AGENCIES: **Alamo** (☎ 800/327–9633, WEB www.alamo.com). **Avis** (☎ 800/331–1212; 800/879–2847 in Canada; 0870/606–0100 in the U.K.; 02/9353–9000 in Australia; 09/526–2847 in New Zealand; WEB www.avis.com). **Budget** (☎ 800/527–0700; 0870/156–5656 in the U.K.; WEB www.budget.com). **Dollar** (☎ 800/800–4000; 0124/622–0111 in the U.K.; where it's affiliated with Sixt; 02/9223–1444 in Australia; WEB www.dollar.com). **Hertz** (☎ 800/654–3131; 800/263–0600 in Canada; 020/8897–2072 in the U.K.; 02/9669–2444 in Australia; 09/256–8690 in New Zealand; WEB www.hertz.com). **National Car Rental** (☎ 800/227–7368; 020/8680–4800 in the U.K.; WEB www.nationalcar.com).

CUTTING COSTS

For a good deal, **book through a travel agent who will shop around.** Also, **price local car-rental companies—** whose prices may be lower still, although their service and maintenance may not be as good as those of major rental agencies—and **research rates on-line.** Remember to ask about required deposits, cancellation penalties, and drop-off charges if you're planning to pick up the car in one city and leave it in another. If you're traveling during a holiday period, also make sure that a confirmed reservation guarantees you a car.

➤ LOCAL AGENCIES: **Enterprise** (✉ 303 W. Lake St., ☎ 312/332–7783). **Paragon Auto Leasing Co.** (✉ 2550 N. Cicero Ave., ☎ 773/622–7660). **Rent A Wreck** (✉ Lincoln Park, ☎ 773/281–1111).

INSURANCE

When driving a rented car you are generally responsible for any damage to or loss of the vehicle. You may also be liable for any property damage or personal injury that you may cause while driving. Before you rent, see what coverage you already have under the terms of your personal auto-insurance policy and credit cards.

For about $15 to $20 a day, rental companies sell protection, known as a collision- or loss-damage waiver (CDW or LDW), that eliminates your liability for damage to the car; it's always optional and should never be automatically added to your bill. In most states you don't need a CDW if you have personal auto insurance or other liability insurance. Some states, including Illinois, have capped the price of the CDW and LDW. However, **make sure you have enough coverage to pay for the car.** If you do not have auto insurance or an umbrella policy that covers damage to third parties, purchasing liability insurance and a CDW or LDW is highly recommended.

REQUIREMENTS AND RESTRICTIONS

In Chicago you must be 21 to rent a car, and rates may be higher if you're under 25.

SURCHARGES

Before you pick up a car in one city and leave it in another, **ask about drop-off charges or one-way service fees,** which can be substantial. Note, too, that some rental agencies charge extra if you return the car before the time specified in your contract. To avoid a hefty refueling fee, **fill the tank just before you turn in the car,** but be aware that gas stations near the rental outlet may overcharge. It's almost never a deal to buy the tank of gas in the car when you rent it; the understanding is that you'll return it empty, but some fuel usually remains. Surcharges may apply if you're under 25. You'll pay extra for child seats (about $6 a day), which are compulsory for children under five, and for additional drivers (about $5 per day).

CAR TRAVEL

Chicago's network of buses and rapid transit rail is extensive, and taxis and limousines are readily available (the latter often priced competitively with metered cabs), so **rent a car only to visit the outlying suburbs that are not accessible by public transportation.** Chicago traffic is often heavy, on-street parking is nearly impossible to find, parking lots are expensive, congestion creates frustrating delays, and other drivers may be impatient with those who are unfamiliar with the city and its roads. **Expect snarled traffic during rush hours.** In these circumstances you may find a car to be a liability rather than an asset. The Illinois Department of Transportation gives information on expressway congestion travel times, and lane closures and directions on state roadways.

EMERGENCY SERVICES

Dial 911 in an emergency to reach police, fire, or ambulance services.

PARKING

Most of Chicago's streets have metered parking, but during peak hours it's hard to find a spot. Most meters take quarters, buying as little as 15 minutes in high-traffic areas, up to an hour in less crowded neighborhoods. Some neighborhoods, such as the area of Lake View known as Wrigleyville, enforce restricted parking and will tow cars without a permit. Many major thoroughfares restrict parking during peak travel hours, generally 9–11 AM heading towards downtown and 4–6 PM heading away. **Read street signs carefully** to determine whether a parking spot is legal.

ROAD CONDITIONS

Chicago drivers can be reckless, zipping through red lights and breaking posted speed limits. **Check both ways after a light turns green** to make sure that the cross traffic has stopped.

RULES OF THE ROAD

Speed limits in Chicago vary, but on most city roads it's 35 mph. Most interstate highways, except in congested areas, have a speed limit of 65 mph. In Chicago, you may turn right at a red light after stopping if there are no oncoming traffic and no posted restrictions. When in doubt, wait for the green. There are many one-way streets in Chicago, particularly in and around the Loop, so be alert to signs and other cars.

Passengers are required to wear seat belts. Always **strap children under age 5 into approved child-safety seats.**

CHILDREN IN CHICAGO

There's no need to hire a baby-sitter on this trip—Chicago offers plenty of diversion for youngsters, so be sure to plan ahead and **involve your kids** as you outline your trip. Museums have special rates for children, and Navy Pier—with its games, IMAX movies, and Ferris wheel—is like an amusement park in the middle of the city. Many restaurants provide children's menus. When packing, include items that will keep your children busy en route. On sightseeing days try to schedule activities of special interest to your children. When you arrive, pick up a copy of *Chicago Parent,* a monthly publication with events and resource listings, available free at locations throughout the city. *Fodor's Around Chicago with Kids* (available in bookstores everywhere) can help you plan your days together.

If you are renting a car don't forget to **arrange for a car seat** when you reserve. For general advice about traveling with children, consult *Fodor's FYI: Travel with Your Baby* (available in bookstores everywhere).

➤ LOCAL INFORMATION: *Chicago Parent* (⊠ 139 S. Oak Park Ave., Oak Park 60302, ☎ 708/386–5555, WEB www.chicagoparent.com).

BABY-SITTING

➤ AGENCIES: **American Registry for Nannies and Sitters** (☎ 800/240–1820, WEB www.american-registry.com).

FLYING

Experts agree that it's a good idea to use safety seats aloft for children weighing less than 40 pounds. Airlines set their own policies: U.S. carriers usually require that the child be ticketed, even if he or she is young enough to ride free, since the seats must be strapped into regular seats. Do **check your airline's policy about using safety seats during takeoff and landing.** Safety seats are not allowed everywhere in the plane, so get your seat assignments as early as possible.

When reserving, **request children's meals or a freestanding bassinet** (not available at all airlines) if you need them. But note that bulkhead seats, where you must sit to use the bassinet, may lack an overhead bin or storage space on the floor.

LODGING

Most hotels in Chicago allow children under a certain age to stay in their parents' room at no extra charge, but others charge for them as extra adults; be sure to **find out the cutoff age for children's discounts.**

➤ BEST CHOICES: **Best Western River North** (⊠ 125 W. Ohio St., 60610, ☎ 312/467–0800 or 800/727–0800). **Summerfield Suites Hotel** (⊠ 166 E. Superior St., 60611, ☎ 312/787–6000 or 800/833–4353).

SIGHTS AND ATTRACTIONS

Places that are especially appealing to children are indicated by a rubber-duckie icon (🦆) in the margin.

CONCIERGES

Concierges, found in many hotels, can help you with theater tickets and dinner reservations: a good one with connections may be able to get you seats for a hot show or prime-time dinner reservations at the restaurant of the moment. You can also turn to your hotel's concierge for help with travel arrangements, sightseeing plans, services ranging from aromatherapy to zipper repair, and emergencies. Always, **always tip** a concierge who has been of assistance (☞ Tipping).

CONSUMER PROTECTION

Whether you're shopping for gifts or purchasing travel services, **pay with a major credit card** whenever possible, so you can cancel payment or get reimbursed if there's a problem (and you can provide documentation). If you're doing business with a particular company for the first time, **contact your local Better Business Bureau and the attorney general's offices** in your state and (for U.S. businesses) the company's home state as well. Have any complaints been filed? Finally, if you're buying a package or tour, always **consider travel insurance** that includes default coverage (☞ Insurance).

➤ BBBs: **Council of Better Business Bureaus** (✉ 4200 Wilson Blvd., Suite 800, Arlington, VA 22203, ☎ 703/276–0100, FAX 703/525–8277, WEB www.bbb.org). **Better Business Bureau Chicago** (✉ 330 N. Wabash Ave., Suite 2006, Chicago, IL 60611, ☎ 312/832–0500, FAX 312/832–9985, WEB www.chicago.bbb.org).

CUSTOMS AND DUTIES

IN AUSTRALIA

Australian residents who are 18 or older may bring home A$400 worth of souvenirs and gifts (including jewelry), 250 cigarettes or 250 grams of tobacco, and 1,125 ml of alcohol (including wine, beer, and spirits). Residents under 18 may bring back A$200 worth of goods. Prohibited items include meat products. Seeds, plants, and fruits need to be declared upon arrival.

➤ INFORMATION: **Australian Customs Service** (Regional Director, ✉ Box 8, Sydney, NSW 2001; ☎ 02/9213–2000 or 1300/363263; 1800/020504 quarantine-inquiry line; FAX 02/9213–4043; WEB www.customs.gov.au).

IN CANADA

Canadian residents who have been out of Canada for at least seven days may bring in C$750 worth of goods duty-free. If you've been away fewer than seven days but more than 48 hours, the duty-free allowance drops to C$200. If your trip lasts 24 to 48 hours, the allowance is C$50. You may not pool allowances with family members. Goods claimed under the C$750 exemption may follow you by mail; those claimed under the lesser exemptions must accompany you. Alcohol and tobacco products may be included in the seven-day and 48-hour exemptions but not in the 24-hour exemption. If you meet the age requirements of the province or

territory through which you reenter Canada, you may bring in, duty-free, 1.5 liters of wine *or* 1.14 liters (40 imperial ounces) of liquor *or* 24 12-ounce cans or bottles of beer or ale. If you are 19 or older you may bring in, duty-free, 200 cigarettes and 50 cigars. Check ahead of time with the Canada Customs and Revenue Agency or the Department of Agriculture for policies regarding meat products, seeds, plants, and fruits.

You may send an unlimited number of gifts (only one gift per recipient, however) worth up to C$60 each duty-free to Canada. Label the package UNSOLICITED GIFT—VALUE UNDER $60. Alcohol and tobacco are excluded.

➤ INFORMATION: **Canada Customs and Revenue Agency** (✉ 2265 St. Laurent Blvd. S, Ottawa, Ontario K1G 4K3, ☎ 204/983–3500, 506/636–5064, or 800/461–9999, WEB www.ccra-adrc.gc.ca/).

IN NEW ZEALAND

All homeward-bound residents may bring back NZ$700 worth of souvenirs and gifts; passengers may not pool their allowances, and children can claim only the concession on goods intended for their own use. For those 17 or older, the duty-free allowance also includes 4.5 liters of wine or beer; one 1,125-ml bottle of spirits; and either 200 cigarettes, 250 grams of tobacco, 50 cigars, *or* a combination of the three up to 250 grams. Meat products, seeds, plants, and fruits must be declared upon arrival to the Agricultural Services Department.

➤ INFORMATION: **New Zealand Customs** (Head office: ✉ The Customhouse, 17–21 Whitmore St., Box 2218, Wellington, ☎ 09/300–5399 or 0800/428–786, WEB www.customs.govt.nz).

IN THE U.K.

From countries outside the European Union, including the United States, you may bring home, duty-free, 200 cigarettes or 50 cigars; 1 liter of spirits or 2 liters of fortified or sparkling wine or liqueurs; 2 liters of still table wine; 60 ml of perfume;

250 ml of toilet water; plus £145 worth of other goods, including gifts and souvenirs. Prohibited items include meat products, seeds, plants, and fruits.

➤ INFORMATION: **HM Customs and Excise** (✉ Portcullis House, 21 Cowbridge Rd. E, Cardiff CF11 9SS, ☎ 029/2038–6423 or 0845/010–9000, WEB www.hmce.gov.uk).

DINING

The restaurants we list are the cream of the crop in each price category. Restaurant price categories are based on the cost per person, for a main course at dinner.

In general, when you order a regular coffee, you get coffee with milk and sugar.

RESERVATIONS AND DRESS

Reservations are always a good idea; we mention them only when they're essential or not accepted. Book as far ahead as you can, and reconfirm as soon as you arrive. (Large parties should always call ahead to check the reservations policy.) We mention dress only when men are required to wear a jacket or a jacket and tie.

SPECIALTIES

Chicago is well known for its cuisine, and it specializes in several tasty items. Visitors will want to try the deep-dish pizza and ribs to taste the local flavor, but there are also some world-class restaurants featuring French, Italian, Indian, and Asian menus.

WINE, BEER, AND SPIRITS

Goose Island Beer is brewed locally and is featured in many restaurants and stores.

DISABILITIES AND ACCESSIBILITY

The Chicago Mayor's Office for People with Disabilities maintains an information and referral service for disability resources. The office publishes guides, including *Access Chicago,* which contains more than 200 pages of detailed information about Chicago's airports, accessible ground transportation, hotels, restaurants, sights, shopping, and resources regarding medical equipment and supplies.

➤ LOCAL RESOURCES: **Mayor's Office for People with Disabilities** (✉ 121 N. LaSalle St., Room 1104, ☎ 312/744–7050; 312/744–4964 TTY).

LODGING

Despite the Americans with Disabilities Act, the definition of accessibility seems to differ from hotel to hotel. Some properties may be accessible by ADA standards for people with mobility problems but not for people with hearing or vision impairments, for example.

If you have mobility problems, ask for the lowest floor on which accessible services are offered. If you have a hearing impairment, check whether the hotel has devices to alert you visually to the ring of the telephone, knock at the door, and a fire/emergency alarm. Some hotels provide these devices without charge. Discuss your needs with hotel personnel if this equipment isn't available, so that a staff member can personally alert you in the event of an emergency.

If you're bringing a guide dog, get authorization ahead of time and write down the name of the person you spoke with.

RESERVATIONS

When discussing accessibility with an operator or reservations agent, **ask hard questions.** Are there any stairs, inside *or* out? Are there grab bars next to the toilet *and* in the shower/tub? How wide is the doorway to the room? To the bathroom? For the most extensive facilities meeting the latest legal specifications, **opt for newer accommodations.** If you reserve through a toll-free number, consider also calling the hotel's local number to confirm the information from the central reservations office. Get confirmation in writing when you can.

SIGHTS AND ATTRACTIONS

Chicago's major sights and attractions all provide accessibility to people using wheelchairs, including ramps and bathrooms. Most stores and restaurants also welcome disabled visitors by providing access.

TRANSPORTATION

Although some subway stations might be difficult to reach, many Chicago Transit Authority (CTA) buses are specially equipped to handle the specific needs of customers who are physically challenged.

At O'Hare Airport, American and United airlines have specially designated lounges to provide assistance to travelers with disabilities. If needed, **ask for a wheelchair escort,** available from all airlines at O'Hare. O'Hare's CTA Blue line train station is equipped with an elevator; downtown stops with elevators are at Clark/Lake and Jackson Boulevard.

The RTA Travel Information Center's Chicago Transit Map includes information on more than 70 lift-equipped bus routes and accessible subway and El stations. The CTA offers a paratransit program with curb-to-curb service for those unable to use conventional mainline bus or rail services. To use this service, out-of-town visitors must make travel arrangements at least one week in advance.

➤ COMPLAINTS: **Aviation Consumer Protection Division** (☞ Air Travel) for airline-related problems. **Departmental Office of Civil Rights** (for general inquiries, ⊠ U.S. Department of Transportation, S-30, 400 7th St. SW, Room 10215, Washington, DC 20590, ☎ 202/366–4648, FAX 202/366–3571, WEB www.dot.gov/ost/docr/index.htm). **Disability Rights Section** (⊠ NYAV, U.S. Department of Justice, Civil Rights Division, 950 Pennsylvania Ave. NW, Washington, DC 20530; ☎ ADA information line 202/514–0301, 800/514–0301, 202/514–0383 TTY, 800/514–0383 TTY, WEB www.usdoj.gov/crt/ada/adahom1.htm).

➤ TRANSPORTATION INFORMATION: **Chicago Transit Authority paratransit program** (☎ 312/432–7025; 312/432–7140 TTY). **RTA Travel Information Center** (☎ 312/836–7000; 312/432–7025 TTY).

TRAVEL AGENCIES

In the United States, the Americans with Disabilities Act requires that travel firms serve the needs of all travelers. Some agencies specialize in working with people with disabilities.

➤ TRAVELERS WITH MOBILITY PROBLEMS: **Access Adventures** (⊠ 206 Chestnut Ridge Rd., Scottsville, NY 14624, ☎ 716/889–9096, dltravel@prodigy.net), run by a former physical-rehabilitation counselor. **Accessible Vans of America** (⊠ 9 Spielman Rd., Fairfield, NJ 07004, ☎ 877/282–8267; 888/282–8267 reservations; FAX 973/808–9713, WEB www.accessiblevans.com). **CareVacations** (⊠ No. 5, 5110–50 Ave., Leduc, Alberta T9E 6V4, Canada, ☎ 780/986–6404 or 877/478–7827, FAX 780/986–8332, WEB www.carevacations.com), for group tours and cruise vacations. **Flying Wheels Travel** (⊠ 143 W. Bridge St., Box 382, Owatonna, MN 55060, ☎ 507/451–5005, FAX 507/451–1685, WEB www.flyingwheelstravel.com).

DISCOUNTS AND DEALS

To save money on sightseeing, **buy a Chicago CityPass,** which costs $39. The passes are good for nine days from the day of first use and include admission to the Art Institute of Chicago, the Field Museum, the Museum of Science and Industry, the Adler Planetarium, the Shedd Aquarium, and the Sears Tower Skydeck. You can buy the pass at any one of the participating attractions.

For savings on bus fare, **purchase a Fun Pass** for $5. It's good for unlimited rides.

DISCOUNT RESERVATIONS

To save money, **look into discount reservations services** with Web sites and toll-free numbers, which use their buying power to get a better price on hotels, airline tickets, even car rentals. When booking a room, always **call the hotel's local toll-free number** (if one is available) rather than the central reservations number—you'll often get a better price. Always ask about special packages or corporate rates.

➤ AIRLINE TICKETS: ☎ **800/AIR-4LESS.**

➤ HOTEL ROOMS: **Accommodations Express** (☎ 800/444–7666, WEB www.accommodationsexpress.com).

Hotel Reservations Network (☎ 800/964–6835, WEB www.hoteldiscount.com). **Quikbook** (☎ 800/789–9887, WEB www.quikbook.com). **RMC Travel** (☎ 800/245–5738, WEB www.rmcwebtravel.com). **Steigenberger Reservation Service** (☎ 800/223–5652, WEB www.srs-worldhotels.com). **Travel Interlink** (☎ 800/888–5898, WEB www.travelinterlink.com). **Turbotrip.com** (☎ 800/473–7829, WEB www.turbotrip.com).

PACKAGE DEALS

Don't confuse packages and guided tours. When you buy a package, you travel on your own, just as though you had planned the trip yourself. Fly/drive packages, which combine airfare and car rental, are often a good deal. In cities, ask the local visitor's bureau about hotel packages that include tickets to major museum exhibits or other special events.

GAY AND LESBIAN TRAVEL

Gay and lesbian travelers will find Chicago a very welcoming, progressive city with a vibrant gay scene. Bars, coffeehouses, and publications serving the interests of gays and lesbians exist citywide, particularly in the adjoining neighborhoods of Lake View and New Town (aka "Boys Town"), bordered by Irving Park Road, Lincoln Avenue, Belmont Avenue, and Lake Shore Drive, and Andersonville, which is bordered by Devon Avenue, Ridge Avenue, Sheridan Road, and Lawrence Avenue).

Pick up the following publications to find out more information: *Gay Chicago Magazine* (☎ 773/327–7271, WEB www.gaychicagomag.com), the *Windy City Times* (☎ 773/871–7610, WEB www.wctimes.com), and *Outlines* (☎ 773/871–7610, WEB www.outlineschicago.com); the latter paper also publishes gay/lesbian papers specifically on nightlife (*Nightlines*), the African-American community (*Blacklines*), and the Latin-American community (*En La Vida*).

For details about the gay and lesbian scene, consult *Fodor's Gay Guide to the USA* (available in bookstores everywhere).

➤ GAY- AND LESBIAN-FRIENDLY TRAVEL AGENCIES: **Different Roads Travel** (✉

8383 Wilshire Blvd., Suite 902, Beverly Hills, CA 90211, ☎ 323/651–5557 or 800/429–8747, FAX 323/651–3678, lgernert@tzell.com). **Kennedy Travel** (✉ 314 Jericho Turnpike, Floral Park, NY 11001, ☎ 516/352–4888 or 800/237–7433, FAX 516/354–8849, WEB www.kennedytravel.com). **Now, Voyager** (✉ 4406 18th St., San Francisco, CA 94114, ☎ 415/626–1169 or 800/255–6951, FAX 415/626–8626, WEB www.nowvoyager.com). **Skylink Travel and Tour** (✉ 1006 Mendocino Ave., Santa Rosa, CA 95401, ☎ 707/546–9888 or 800/225–5759, FAX 707/546–9891), serving lesbian travelers.

GUIDEBOOKS

Plan well and you won't be sorry. Guidebooks are excellent tools—and you can take them with you. You may want to check out color-photo-illustrated *Compass American Guide: Chicago,* thorough on culture and history, and *Fodor's CITYGUIDE Chicago,* for residents. *Flashmaps Chicago* has full-color theme maps, and pocket-size *Citypack Chicago* includes a foldout map. All are available at on-line retailers and bookstores everywhere.

HOLIDAYS

Major national holidays include New Year's Day (Jan. 1); Martin Luther King, Jr., Day (3rd Mon. in Jan.); President's Day (3rd Mon. in Feb.); Memorial Day (last Mon. in May); Independence Day (July 4); Labor Day (1st Mon. in Sept.); Thanksgiving Day (4th Thurs. in Nov.); Christmas Eve and Christmas Day (Dec. 24 and 25); and New Year's Eve (Dec. 31).

INSURANCE

The most useful travel-insurance plan is a comprehensive policy that includes coverage for trip cancellation and interruption, default, trip delay, and medical expenses (with a waiver for preexisting conditions).

Without insurance you will lose all or most of your money if you cancel your trip, regardless of the reason. Default insurance covers you if your tour operator, airline, or cruise line goes out of business. Trip-delay covers expenses that arise because of bad weather or mechanical delays.

Study the fine print when comparing policies.

U.K. residents can buy a travel-insurance policy valid for most vacations taken during the year in which it's purchased (but check preexisting-condition coverage).

Always **buy travel policies directly from the insurance company**; if you buy them from a cruise line, airline, or tour operator that goes out of business, you probably will not be covered for the agency's or operator's default, a major risk. Before making any purchase, **review your existing health and home-owner's policies** to find what they cover away from home.

➤ TRAVEL INSURERS: In the United States: **Access America** (✉ 6600 W. Broad St., Richmond, VA 23230, ☎ 800/284–8300, FAX 804/673–1491 or 800/346–9265, WEB www.accessamerica.com). **Travel Guard International** (✉ 1145 Clark St., Stevens Point, WI 54481, ☎ 715/345–0505 or 800/826–1300, FAX 800/955–8785, WEB www.travelguard.com).

FOR INTERNATIONAL TRAVELERS

For information on customs restrictions, *see* Customs and Duties, *above*.

CAR RENTAL

When picking up a rental car, non–U.S. residents need a reservation voucher for any prepaid reservations that were made in the traveler's home country, a passport, a driver's license, and a travel policy that covers each driver.

CAR TRAVEL

In Chicago, gas costs averaged around $1.65 per gallon at press time. Highways are well paved. Interstate highways—limited-access, multilane highways whose numbers are prefixed by "I–"—are the fastest routes. Interstates with three-digit numbers encircle urban areas, which may have other limited-access expressways, freeways, and parkways as well. Tolls may be levied on limited-access highways. So-called U.S. highways and state highways are not necessarily limited-access but may have several lanes.

Along larger highways, roadside stops with rest rooms, fast-food restaurants, and sundries stores are well spaced. State police and tow trucks patrol major highways and lend assistance. If your car breaks down on an interstate, pull onto the shoulder and wait for help, or have your passengers wait while you walk to an emergency phone. If you carry a cell phone, dial *55, noting your location on the small green roadside mileage markers.

Driving in the United States is on the right. Do **obey speed limits** posted along roads and highways. Watch for lower limits in small towns and on back roads.

Bookstores, gas stations, convenience stores, and rest stops sell maps (about $3) and multiregion road atlases (about $10).

CONSULATES AND EMBASSIES

➤ AUSTRALIA: (✉ 123 N. Wacker St., Suite 1330, 60606, ☎ 312/419–1480 or 312/419–1499, WEB www.austemb.org/Consulates/Chicago.htm).

➤ CANADA: (✉ 2 Prudential Plaza, 180 N. Stetson, 60601, ☎ 312/616–1860 or 312/616–1877).

➤ NEW ZEALAND: (✉ 18600 Bryn Mawr Ave., Suite 500N, 60631, ☎ 773/714–9461 or 773/714–9483).

➤ UNITED KINGDOM: (✉ The Wrigley Building, 400 N. Michigan Ave., 60611, ☎ 312/970–3800, FAX 312/970–3852, WEB www.britainusa.com/chicago).

CURRENCY

The dollar is the basic unit of U.S. currency. It has 100 cents. Coins include the copper penny (1¢); the silvery nickel (5¢), dime (10¢), quarter (25¢), and half-dollar (50¢); and the golden $1 coin, replacing a now-rare silver dollar. Bills are denominated $1, $5, $10, $20, $50, and $100, all green and identical in size; designs vary. At present time, the exchange rate for the U.S. dollar was $1.41 to the British pound, 67¢ per Canadian dollar, 54¢ per Australian dollar, and 42¢ per New Zealand dollar.

ELECTRICITY

The U.S. standard is AC, 110 volts/60 cycles. Plugs have two flat pins set parallel to each other.

EMERGENCIES

For police, fire, or ambulance, **dial 911** (0 in rural areas).

INSURANCE

Britons and Australians need extra medical coverage when traveling overseas.

➤ INSURANCE INFORMATION: In the United Kingdom: **Association of British Insurers** (✉ 51 Gresham St., London EC2V 7HQ, ☎ 020/7600–3333, FAX 020/7696–8999, WEB www. abi.org.uk). In Australia: **Insurance Council of Australia** (✉ Level 3, 56 Pitt St., Sydney, NSW 2000, ☎ 02/ 9253–5100, FAX 02/9253–5111, WEB www.ica.com.au). In Canada: **RBC Insurance** (✉ 6880 Financial Dr., Mississauga, Ontario L5N 7Y5, ☎ 905/816–2400 or 800/668–4342, FAX 905/813–4704, WEB www.rbcinsurance. com). In New Zealand: **Insurance Council of New Zealand** (✉ Level 7, 111–115 Customhouse Quay, Box 474, Wellington, ☎ 04/472–5230, FAX 04/473–3011, WEB www.icnz. org.nz).

MAIL AND SHIPPING

You can buy stamps and aerograms and send letters and parcels in post offices. Stamp-dispensing machines can occasionally be found in airports, bus and train stations, office buildings, drugstores, and the like. You can also deposit mail in the stout, dark blue, steel bins at strategic locations everywhere and in the mail chutes of large buildings; pickup schedules are posted.

For mail sent within the United States, you need a 37¢ stamp for first-class letters weighing up to 1 ounce (23¢ for each additional ounce) and 23¢ for postcards. You pay 80¢ for 1-ounce airmail letters and 70¢ for airmail postcards to most other countries; to Canada and Mexico, you need a 60¢ stamp for a 1-ounce letter and 50¢ for a postcard. An aerogram—a single sheet of lightweight blue paper that folds into its own envelope, stamped for overseas airmail—costs 70¢.

To receive mail on the road, have it sent c/o General Delivery at your destination's main post office (use the correct five-digit ZIP code). You must pick up mail in person within 30 days and show a driver's license or passport.

PASSPORTS AND VISAS

When traveling internationally, **carry your passport** even if you don't need one (it's always the best form of I.D.) and **make two photocopies of the data page** (one for someone at home and another for you, carried separately from your passport). If you lose your passport, promptly call the nearest embassy or consulate and the local police.

Visitor visas are not necessary for Canadian citizens, or for citizens of Australia and the United Kingdom who are staying fewer than 90 days.

➤ AUSTRALIAN CITIZENS: **Australian State Passport Office** (☎ 131–232, WEB www.passports.gov.au). **United States Consulate General** (✉ MLC Centre, 19–29 Martin Pl., 59th floor, Sydney, NSW 2000, ☎ 02/9373–9200; 1902/941–641 fee-based visa-inquiry line; WEB www.usis-australia. gov/index.html).

➤ CANADIAN CITIZENS: **Passport Office** (to mail in applications: ✉ Department of Foreign Affairs and International Trade, Ottawa, Ontario K1A 0G3, ☎ 819/994–3500 or 800/ 567–6868, WEB www.dfait-maeci.gc. ca/passport).

➤ NEW ZEALAND CITIZENS: **New Zealand Passport Office** (☎ 04/474–8100 or 0800/22–5050, WEB www. passports.govt.nz). **Embassy of the United States** (✉ 29 Fitzherbert Terr., Thorndon, Wellington, ☎ 04/462–6000, WEB usembassy.org.nz). **U.S. Consulate General** (✉ Citibank Bldg., 3rd floor, 23 Customs St. E, Auckland, ☎ 09/303–2724, WEB usembassy. org.nz).

➤ U.K. CITIZENS: **London Passport Office** (☎ 0870/521–0410, WEB www. passport.gov.uk). **U.S. Consulate General** (✉ Queen's House, 14 Queen St., Belfast, Northern Ireland

BT1 6EQ, ☎ 028/9032–8239, WEB www.usembassy.org.uk). **U.S. Embassy** (enclose a SASE to ✉ Consular Information Unit, 24 Grosvenor Sq., London W1 1AE, for general information; Visa Branch, 5 Upper Grosvenor St., London W1A 2JB, to submit an application via mail; ☎ 09068/200–290 recorded visa information or 09055/444–546 operator service, both with per-minute charges; WEB www.usembassy.org.uk).

TELEPHONES

All U.S. telephone numbers consist of a three-digit area code and a seven-digit local number. Within most local calling areas, you dial only the seven-digit number. Within some area codes, you must dial "1" first for calls outside the local area. To call between area-code regions, dial "1" then all 10 digits; the same goes for calls to numbers prefixed by "800," "888," and "877"—all toll-free. For calls to numbers preceded by "900" you must pay—usually dearly.

For international calls, dial "011" followed by the country code and the local number. For help, dial "0" and ask for an overseas operator. The country code is 61 for Australia, 64 for New Zealand, 44 for the United Kingdom. Calling Canada is the same as calling within the United States. Most local phone books list country codes and U.S. area codes. The country code for the United States is 1.

For operator assistance, dial "0." To obtain someone's phone number, call directory assistance, 555–1212 or occasionally 411 (free at public phones). To have the person you're calling foot the bill, phone collect; dial "0" instead of "1" before the 10-digit number.

At pay phones, instructions are usually posted. Usually you insert coins in a slot (10¢–50¢ for local calls) and wait for a steady tone before dialing. When you call long distance, the operator tells you how much to insert; prepaid phone cards, widely available in various denominations, are easier. Call the number on the back, punch in the card's personal identification number when prompted, then dial your number.

LODGING

The lodgings we list are the cream of the crop in each price category. We always list the facilities that are available—but we don't specify whether they cost extra: when pricing accommodations, always ask what's included and what costs extra. Properties are assigned price categories based on the range from their least-expensive standard double room at high season (excluding holidays) to the most expensive.

Assume that hotels operate on the **European Plan** (EP, with no meals), unless we specify that they use the **Continental Plan** (CP, with a Continental breakfast daily) or **Breakfast Plan** (BP, with a full breakfast daily).

APARTMENT RENTALS

Rental apartments are available in the Loop for temporary business lodging. Try Bridgestreet Corporate Housing or Smith Corporate Living.

➤ LOCAL AGENTS: **Bridgestreet Corporate Housing** (✉ 10 E. Ontario St., ☎ 847/564–3000). **Smith Corporate Living** (✉ 440 N. Wabash Ave., ☎ 888/726–6560).

BED-AND-BREAKFASTS

➤ RESERVATION SERVICES: **Bed & Breakfast/Chicago** (✉ Box 14088, 60614, ☎ 773/394–2000 or 800/375–7084, FAX 773/394–2002, WEB www.chicago-bed-breakfast.com)

HOME EXCHANGES

If you would like to exchange your home for someone else's, **join a home-exchange organization,** which will send you its updated listings of available exchanges for a year and will include your own listing in at least one of them. It's up to you to make specific arrangements.

➤ EXCHANGE CLUBS: **HomeLink International** (✉ Box 47747, Tampa, FL 33647, ☎ 813/975–9825 or 800/638–3841, FAX 813/910–8144, WEB www.homelink.org; $106 per year). **Intervac U.S.** (✉ 30 Corte San Fernando, Tiburon, CA 94920, ☎ 800/756–4663, FAX 415/435–7440, WEB www.intervacus.com; $90 yearly fee for a listing, on-line access, and a catalog; $50 without catalog).

HOSTELS

No matter what your age, you can **save on lodging costs by staying at hostels.** In some 4,500 locations in more than 70 countries around the world, Hostelling International (HI), the umbrella group for a number of national youth-hostel associations, offers single-sex, dorm-style beds and, at many hostels, rooms for couples and family accommodations. Membership in any HI national hostel association, open to travelers of all ages, allows you to stay in HI-affiliated hostels at member rates; one-year membership is about $25 for adults (C$35 for a two-year minimum membership in Canada, £13 in the United Kingdom, A$52 in Australia, and NZ$40 in New Zealand); hostels run about $10–$30 per night. Members have priority if the hostel is full; they're also eligible for discounts around the world, even on rail and bus travel in some countries.

➤ ORGANIZATIONS: **Hostelling International—American Youth Hostels** (✉ 733 15th St. NW, Suite 840, Washington, DC 20005, ☎ 202/783–6161, 𝖥𝖠𝖷 202/783–6171, 𝖶𝖤𝖡 www.hiayh.org). **Hostelling International—Canada** (✉ 400–205 Catherine St., Ottawa, Ontario K2P 1C3, ☎ 613/237–7884 or 800/663–5777, 𝖥𝖠𝖷 613/237–7868, 𝖶𝖤𝖡 www.hihostels.ca). **Youth Hostel Association Australia** (✉ 10 Mallett St., Camperdown, NSW 2050, ☎ 02/9565–1699, 𝖥𝖠𝖷 02/9565–1325, 𝖶𝖤𝖡 www.yha.com.au). **Youth Hostel Association of England and Wales** (✉ Trevelyan House, Dimple Rd., Matlock, Derbyshire DE4 3YH, U.K., ☎ 0870/870–8808, 𝖥𝖠𝖷 0169/592–702, 𝖶𝖤𝖡 www.yha.org.uk). **Youth Hostels Association of New Zealand** (✉ Level 3, 193 Cashel St., Box 436, Christchurch, ☎ 03/379–9970, 𝖥𝖠𝖷 03/365–4476, 𝖶𝖤𝖡 www.yha.org.nz).

HOTELS

There are more than 1,000 conventions and trade shows scheduled in the Chicago area throughout the year. During the Comdex spring show in April, the National Restaurant Association show in May, the manufacturing technology show in September, the Radiological Society of America show in late November, and the National Housewares Manufacturing show in January, rooms are very difficult to find.

➤ TOLL-FREE NUMBERS: **Adam's Mark** (☎ 800/444–2326, 𝖶𝖤𝖡 www.adamsmark.com). **Baymont Inns** (☎ 800/428–3438, 𝖶𝖤𝖡 www.baymontinns.com). **Best Western** (☎ 800/528–1234, 𝖶𝖤𝖡 www.bestwestern.com). **Choice** (☎ 800/424–6423, 𝖶𝖤𝖡 www.choicehotels.com). **Clarion** (☎ 800/424–6423, 𝖶𝖤𝖡 www.choicehotels.com). **Comfort Inn** (☎ 800/424–6423, 𝖶𝖤𝖡 www.choicehotels.com). **Days Inn** (☎ 800/325–2525, 𝖶𝖤𝖡 www.daysinn.com). **Doubletree and Red Lion Hotels** (☎ 800/222–8733, 𝖶𝖤𝖡 www.hilton.com). **Embassy Suites** (☎ 800/362–2779, 𝖶𝖤𝖡 www.embassysuites.com). **Fairfield Inn** (☎ 800/228–2800, 𝖶𝖤𝖡 www.marriott.com). **Four Seasons** (☎ 800/332–3442, 𝖶𝖤𝖡 www.fourseasons.com). **Hilton** (☎ 800/445–8667, 𝖶𝖤𝖡 www.hilton.com). **Holiday Inn** (☎ 800/465–4329, 𝖶𝖤𝖡 www.sixcontinentshotels.com). **Howard Johnson** (☎ 800/654–4656, 𝖶𝖤𝖡 www.hojo.com). **Hyatt Hotels & Resorts** (☎ 800/233–1234, 𝖶𝖤𝖡 www.hyatt.com). **Inter-Continental** (☎ 800/327–0200, 𝖶𝖤𝖡 www.intercontinental.com). **La Quinta** (☎ 800/531–5900, 𝖶𝖤𝖡 www.laquinta.com). **Le Meridien** (☎ 800/543–4300, 𝖶𝖤𝖡 www.lemeridien-hotels.com). **Marriott** (☎ 800/228–9290, 𝖶𝖤𝖡 www.marriott.com). **Omni** (☎ 800/843–6664, 𝖶𝖤𝖡 www.omnihotels.com). **Quality Inn** (☎ 800/424–6423, 𝖶𝖤𝖡 www.choicehotels.com). **Radisson** (☎ 800/333–3333, 𝖶𝖤𝖡 www.radisson.com). **Ramada** (☎ 800/228–2828; 800/854–7854 international reservations; 𝖶𝖤𝖡 www.ramada.com or www.ramadahotels.com). **Renaissance Hotels & Resorts** (☎ 800/468–3571, 𝖶𝖤𝖡 www.renaissancehotels.com/). **Ritz-Carlton** (☎ 800/241–3333, 𝖶𝖤𝖡 www.ritzcarlton.com). **Sheraton** (☎ 800/325–3535, 𝖶𝖤𝖡 www.starwood.com/sheraton). **Sleep Inn** (☎ 800/424–6423, 𝖶𝖤𝖡 www.choicehotels.com). **Westin Hotels & Resorts** (☎ 800/228–3000, 𝖶𝖤𝖡 www.starwood.com/westin). **Wyndham Hotels & Resorts** (☎ 800/822–4200, 𝖶𝖤𝖡 www.wyndham.com).

MAIL AND SHIPPING

Chicago post offices are open 8–5 during the week and 8–1 on Saturday. They are closed on Sundays.

➤ POST OFFICES: **Cardiss Collins Postal Store** (✉ 433 W. Harrison St., 60607, ☎ 312/983–8182). **Nancy B. Jefferson (Midwest Station)** (✉ 2419 W. Monroe St., 60612, ☎ 312/243–2560). **Wacker Drive Postal Store** (✉ 233 S. Wacker Dr., Suite Ll1a, 60606, ☎ 312/876–1024).

OVERNIGHT SERVICES

➤ MAJOR SERVICES: **FedEx** (☎ 800/463–3339). **UPS** (☎ 800/742–5877).

MEDIA

NEWSPAPERS AND MAGAZINES

Chicago is served by two daily metro newspapers, the *Chicago Tribune* and the *Chicago Sun-Times.* Also be sure to check out the two alternative newsweeklies, *Chicago Reader,* which comes out on Thursday, and *New City,* which is available on Wednesday. Two features-oriented monthly periodicals, *Chicago Magazine* and *Chicago Social,* are sold at most newsstands.

RADIO AND TELEVISION

Local radio stations include: Q101 101.1 FM and WXRT 93.1 FM for alternative rock; WFMT 98.7 FM and WNIB 97.1 FM for classical music; WUSN 99.5 FM for country; WCKG 105.9 FM and WLUP 97.9 FM for rock; WGCI 107.5 FM for R&B; B-96 96.3 FM for Top-40 hits; and WNUA 95.5 FM for jazz. The National Public Radio affiliate is WBEZ 91.5 FM. WBBM 780 AM and WMAQ 670 AM are both news stations. For talk radio and local sports turn to WGN 720 AM.

Local television stations include WBBM Channel 2 (CBS), WMAQ Channel 5 (NBC), WLS Channel 7 (ABC), WGN Channel 9 (WB), and WFLD Channel 32 (Fox). WTTW Channel 11 and WYCC Channel 20 are public television stations.

MONEY MATTERS

Costs in Chicago are quite reasonable compared to other large cities such as San Francisco and New York. Restaurants, events, and parking costs are markedly higher in the Loop than in any other area of the city.

Prices throughout this guide are given for adults. Substantially reduced fees are almost always available for children, students, and senior citizens. For information on taxes, *see* Taxes, *below.*

CREDIT CARDS

Throughout this guide, the following abbreviations are used: **AE,** American Express; **D,** Discover; **DC,** Diners Club; **MC,** MasterCard; and **V,** Visa.

➤ REPORTING LOST CARDS: **American Express** (☎ 800/441–0519). **Discover** (☎ 800/347–2683). **Diners Club** (☎ 800/234–6377). **MasterCard** (☎ 800/622–7747). **Visa** (☎ 800/ 847–2911).

PACKING

In your carry-on luggage, **pack an extra pair of eyeglasses or contact lenses and enough of any medication** you take to last a few days longer than the entire trip. You may also ask your doctor to write a spare prescription using the drug's generic name, since brand names may vary from country to country. In luggage to be checked, **never pack prescription drugs or valuables.** And don't forget to carry with you the addresses of offices that handle refunds of lost traveler's checks. Check *Fodor's How to Pack* (available in bookstores everywhere) for more tips.

To avoid customs and security delays, carry medications in their original packaging. Don't pack any sharp objects in your carry-on luggage, including knives of any size or material, scissors, manicure tools, and corkscrews, or anything else that might arouse suspicion.

CHECKING LUGGAGE

You are allowed one carry-on bag and one personal article, such as a purse or a laptop computer. Make sure that everything you carry aboard will fit under your seat or in the overhead bin. Get to the gate early, so you can board as soon as possible, before the overhead bins fill up.

If you are flying internationally, note that baggage allowances may be determined not by piece but by weight—generally 88 pounds (40 kilograms) in first class, 66 pounds (30 kilograms) in business class, and 44 pounds (20 kilograms) in economy.

Airline liability for baggage is limited to $2,500 per person on flights within the United States. On international flights it amounts to $9.07 per pound or $20 per kilogram for checked baggage (roughly $640 per 70-pound bag) and $400 per passenger for unchecked baggage. You can buy additional coverage at check-in for about $10 per $1,000 of coverage, but it excludes a rather extensive list of items, shown on your airline ticket.

Before departure, **itemize your bags' contents** and their worth, and label the bags with your name, address, and phone number. (If you use your home address, cover it so potential thieves can't see it readily.) Inside each bag, **pack a copy of your itinerary.** At check-in, **make sure that each bag is correctly tagged** with the destination airport's three-letter code. If your bags arrive damaged or fail to arrive at all, file a written report with the airline before leaving the airport.

PUBLIC TRANSPORTATION

Chicago's extensive public transportation network includes buses and rapid transit trains, both subway and elevated (the latter known as the El).

Each of the seven Chicago Transit Authority (CTA) lines has a color name as well as a route name: Blue (O'Hare–Congress–Douglas), Brown (Ravenswood), Green (Lake–Engle-wood–Jackson Park), Orange (Mid-way), Purple (Evanston), Red (Howard–Dan Ryan), Yellow (Skokie–Swift). In general, the route names indicate the first and last stop on the train. Chicagoans refer to trains both by the color and the route name. Most, but not all, rapid transit lines operate 24 hours; some stations are closed at night. Pick up the brochure "Downtown Transit Sight-seeing Guide" for hours, fares, and other pertinent information. In general, late-night CTA travel is not

recommended. Note that the Red and Blue lines are subways; the rest are elevated. This means if you're heading to O'Hare and looking for the Blue line, look for a stairway down, not up.

Exact fares must be paid in cash (dollar bills or coins; no change given by turnstiles on train platforms or fare boxes on buses) or by transit card. Transit cards are flimsy plastic and credit-card size and can be purchased from machines at CTA train stations as well as at Jewel and Do-minicks grocery stores and currency exchanges. These easy-to-use cards are inserted into the turnstiles at CTA train stations and into machines as you board CTA buses; directions are clearly posted. Use them to transfer between CTA vehicles. To transfer between the Loop's elevated lines and the subway or between rapid transit trains and buses, you must either use a transit card with at least 30¢ stored on it, or, if you're not using a transit card, **buy a transfer when you first board.** If two CTA train lines meet, you can **transfer for free.** You can also **obtain free train-to-train transfers** from specially marked turnstiles at the Washington/State subway station or the State/Lake El station, or ask for a transfer card, good on downtown trains, at the ticket booth.

Buses generally stop on every other corner northbound and southbound (on State Street they stop at every corner). Eastbound and westbound buses generally stop on every corner. Buses from the Loop generally run north–south. Principal transfer points are on Michigan Avenue at the north side of Randolph Street for north-bound buses, Adams Street and Wabash Avenue for westbound buses and the El, and State and Lake streets for those southbound.

Pace runs suburban buses in a six-county region; these connect with the CTA and use CTA transit cards, transfers, and passes.

Commuter trains serve the city and surrounding suburbs. The Metra Electric railroad has a line close to Lake Michigan; its trains stop in Hyde Park. The Metra commuter rail system has 11 lines to suburbs and surrounding cities including Aurora, Elgin, Joliet, and Waukegan; one line serves the North Shore suburbs, and another has a stop at McCormick Place. Trains leave from a number of downtown terminals.

The CTA publishes an excellent map of the transit system, available at subway or El fare booths or on request from the CTA. The RTA Travel Information Center provides information on how to get around on city and suburban (including Metra and Pace) transit and bus lines. **Call for maps and timetables.**

FARES AND SCHEDULES

The CTA fare structure is as follows: The basic fare for rapid transit trains and buses is $1.50, and transfers are 30¢. Transit cards can be purchased in preset denominations of $10 ($11 worth of rides) or $20 ($22 worth of rides) at many local grocery stores, currency exchanges, and stations. You can also purchase a transit card of any denomination over $1.50 at any CTA stop. If you pay cash and do not use a transit card, you must buy a transfer when you first board the bus or train. Transfers can be used twice within a two-hour time period. Transfers between CTA train lines are free—no transfer card is needed. Transit cards may be shared.

Visitor passes are another option. For $5 a one-day Fun Pass offers 24 hours of unlimited CTA riding from the time you first use it. Visitor passes are sold at hotels, museums, and other places tourists frequent, plus all transit card booths. A two-day pass is $9, a three-day pass is $12, and a five-day pass is $18.

Metra trains use a fare structure based on the distance you ride. A Metra weekend pass costs $5 and is valid for rides on any of the eight operating lines all day on weekends, except for the South Shore line.

➤ CTA INFORMATION: **CTA** (✉ Merchandise Mart, 350 N. Wells St., 60654, ☎ 312/836–7000; 888/968–7282 for advance sales of visitor passes; WEB www.transitchicago.com). **Metra information line** (☎ 312/322–6777, WEB www.metrarail.com). **RTA**

Travel Information Center (☎ 312/836–7000, WEB www.rtachicago.com).

SAFETY

The most common crimes in public places are pickpocketing, purse snatching, jewelry theft, and gambling scams. Men: keep your wallet in a front coat or pants pocket. Women: close your purse securely and keep it close to you. Also **beware of someone jostling you and of loud arguments;** these could be ploys to distract your attention while another person grabs your wallet. **Leave unnecessary credit cards at home and hide valuables and jewelry** from view.

Although crime on CTA buses and trains has declined, several precautions can reduce the chance of your becoming a victim: Look alert and purposeful; **know your route** ahead of time; have your fare ready before boarding; and **keep and eye on your purse or packages** during the ride. Avoid taking public transit late at night.

SENIOR-CITIZEN TRAVEL

The Chicago Department on Aging provides information and referrals to seniors 60 years of age and older. The department's Renaissance Court offers free programs for senior citizens every weekday, including exercise classes, arts and crafts, and games. Trips and tours are available at additional cost.

To qualify for age-related discounts, **mention your senior-citizen status up front** when booking hotel reservations (not when checking out) and before you're seated in restaurants (not when paying the bill). Be sure to have identification on hand. When renting a car, ask about promotional car-rental discounts, which can be cheaper than senior-citizen rates.

➤ LOCAL RESOURCES: **Chicago Department on Aging** (✉ 121 N. LaSalle St., ☎ 312/744–4016; 312/744–2940 TTY). **Renaissance Court** (✉ 77 E. Randolph St., ☎ 312/744–4550).

➤ EDUCATIONAL PROGRAMS: **Elderhostel** (✉ 11 Ave. de Lafayette, Boston, MA 02111-1746, ☎ 877/426–8056, FAX 877/426–2166, WEB www.elderhostel.org).

SIGHTSEEING TOURS

BOAT TOURS

Get a fresh perspective on Chicago by taking a water tour or cruise. Boat tour schedules vary by season; be sure to **call for exact times and fares.** The season usually runs from May 1 through October 1. Two cruises stand out, though they're a bit more expensive than the rest: The Chicago Architecture Foundation river cruise and a trip on the *Windy*. The CAF tour highlights more than 50 sights. The cost is $21 from Monday through Friday, $23 on Saturday, Sunday, and holidays; reservations are recommended. You can get a blast from the past on the *Windy,* a 148-ft ship modeled on old-time commercial vessels. Passengers may help the crew or take a turn at the wheel as you sail Lake Michigan. The cost is $25.

You can also use the Shoreline Water Taxi to see some of Chicago's favorite destinations: Sears Tower, Navy Pier, and Shedd Aquarium. The fleet of taxis makes frequent departures from 10:30 until 6 daily from Memorial Day to Labor Day. The fare is just $6.

➤ BOAT TOURS: **Chicago Architecture Foundation river cruise** (☎ 312/922–3432 for information; 312/902–1500 for tickets; WEB www.architecture.org). **Mercury Chicago Skyline Cruiseline** (☎ 312/332–1353 for recorded information). **Shoreline Marine** (☎ 312/222–9328, WEB www.shorelinesightseeing.com). **Wendella Sightseeing Boats** (✉ 400 N. Michigan Ave., ☎ 312/337–1446, WEB www.wendellaboats.com). **Windy of Chicago Ltd.** (☎ 312/595–5555).

BUS AND TROLLEY TOURS

A narrated bus or trolley tour can be a good way to orient yourself among Chicago's main sights. Tours cost roughly $15 and normally last 1½–2 hours. American Sightseeing offers two routes; combined, they cover the city quite thoroughly. The double-decker buses of Chicago Motor Coach Company tour downtown Chicago and the lakefront.

Chicago Trolley Charters schedules stops at all the downtown attractions. You can get on and off the open-air trolleys as you like; these tours vary in price, so call for details. The Chicago Architecture Foundation's bus tours often go farther afield, exploring everything from cemeteries to movie palaces.

➤ BUS AND TROLLEY TOURS: **American Sightseeing** (☎ 312/251–3100). **Chicago Architecture Foundation** (Tour Centers: ✉ Santa Fe Bldg., 224 S. Michigan Ave.; John Hancock Center, 875 N. Michigan Ave., ☎ 312/922–3432, WEB www.architecture.org). **Chicago Motor Coach Co.** (☎ 312/666–1000). **Chicago Trolley Charters** (☎ 312/648–5000, WEB www.chicagotrolley.com).

FOREIGN-LANGUAGE TOURS

➤ FOREIGN-LANGUAGE TOURS: **Chicago Tour Guides Institutes, Inc.** (☎ 773/276–6683, WEB www.chicagoguide.net).

SPECIAL-INTEREST TOURS

➤ AERIAL SIGHTSEEING: **Chicago by Air** (☎ 708/524–1172).

➤ AFRICAN-AMERICAN: **Black Coutours** (☎ 773/233–8907). **Tour Black Chicago** (☎ 312/332–2323, WEB www.tourblackchicago.com).

➤ ARCHITECTURE: ☞ Walking Tours.

➤ BANKING: **Chicago Mercantile Exchange** (☎ 312/930–8249, WEB www.cme.com).

➤ GANGSTERS: **Untouchable Tours** (☎ 773/881–1195, WEB www.gangstertour.com).

➤ GHOSTS: **Chicago Supernatural Ghost Tours** (☎ 708/499–0300, WEB www.ghosttours.com).

➤ HORSE AND CARRIAGE RIDES: **Antique Coach and Carriage** (☎ 773/735–9400, WEB www.antiquecoach-carriage.com). **Chicago Horse & Carriage Ltd.** (☎ 312/944–9192). **Noble Horse** (☎ 312/266–7878).

➤ HISTORIC NEIGHBORHOODS: **Black Metropolis Convention and Tourism Council** (☎ 773/548–2579). **Chicago Office of Tourism** (☎ 312/744–2400, WEB www.ci.chi.il.us/CulturalAffairs/Tourism/). **A Day in Historic Beverly Hills/Morgan Park** (☎ 773/881–1831). **Willie Dixon's Blues Heaven** (☎ 312/808–1286).

➤ NEWSPAPER: The **Chicago Tribune** (☎ 312/222–2116, WEB www. chicagotribune.com) gives tours of its Freedom Center production facility; note that this is *not* at the Tribune Tower.

WALKING TOURS

The Chicago Architecture Foundation has by far the largest selection of guided tours, with more than 50 itineraries covering everything from department stores to Frank Lloyd Wright's Oak Park buildings. Especially popular walking tours of the Loop are given daily throughout the year. Friends of the Chicago River has Saturday-morning walking tours along the river. The organization also has maps of the walking routes, available for a small donation.

➤ INFORMATION: **Chicago Architecture Foundation** (Tour Centers: ✉ Santa Fe Bldg., 224 S. Michigan Ave.; ✉ John Hancock Center, 875 N. Michigan Ave., ☎ 312/922–3432, WEB www.architecture.org). **Friends of the Chicago River** (✉ 407 S. Dearborn St., Suite 1580, ☎ 312/939–0490, WEB www.chicagoriver.org).

STUDENTS IN CHICAGO

Most museums and attractions offer special rates to persons with valid student IDs. Ask if the special rate is not posted.

➤ I.D.S AND SERVICES: **STA Travel** (☎ 212/627–3111 or 800/781–4040, FAX 212/627–3387, WEB www.sta. com). **Travel Cuts** (✉ 187 College St., Toronto, Ontario M5T 1P7, Canada, ☎ 416/979–2406 or 888/ 838–2887, FAX 416/979–8167, WEB www.travelcuts.com).

TAXES

At restaurants, you'll pay an 9.5% meal tax (fractionally higher in some parts of town, thanks to special taxing initiatives).

The hotel tax in Chicago is 14.9%, and slightly less in suburban hotels.

SALES TAX

In Chicago, an 8.75% state and county sales tax is added to all purchases except groceries and prescription drugs.

TAXIS

You can hail a cab on just about any busy street in Chicago. Hotel doormen will hail a cab for you as well. Available taxis are sometimes indicated by an illuminated rooftop light. Chicago taxis are metered, with fares beginning at $1.60 upon entering the cab and $1.40 for each additional mile. A charge of 50¢ is made for each additional passenger between the ages of 12 and 65. There is no extra baggage charge. Taxi drivers expect a 15% tip.

➤ TAXI COMPANIES: **American United Cab Co.** (☎ 773/248–7600). **Checker Taxi** (☎ 312/243–2537). **Flash Cab** (☎ 773/561–1444). **Yellow Cab Co.** (☎ 312/829–4222).

TIME

Chicago is in the Central Standard Time zone. It's one hour behind New York, two hours ahead of Los Angeles, six hours behind London, and 16 hours behind Sydney.

TIPPING

You should tip 15% for adequate service in restaurants and up to 20% if you feel you've been treated well. At higher-end restaurants, where there are more service personnel per table who must divide the tip, up these measures by a few percentage points. An especially helpful wine steward should be acknowledged with $2 or $3. It's not necessary to tip the maître d' unless you've been done a very special favor and you intend to visit again. Tip $1 per checked coat.

Taxi drivers, bartenders, and hairdressers expect about 15%. Bellhops and porters should get about 50¢ per bag; valet-parking attendants $1 or $2 (but only after they bring your car to you, not when they park it), and hotel maids about $1 per person per day of your stay. On package tours, conductors and drivers usually get about $2–$3 per day from each group member. Concierges should get tips of $5–$10 for special service.

TOURS AND PACKAGES

Because everything is prearranged on a prepackaged tour or independent vacation, you spend less time planning—and often get it all at a good price.

BOOKING WITH AN AGENT

Travel agents are excellent resources. But it's a good idea to collect brochures from several agencies, as some agents' suggestions may be influenced by relationships with tour and package firms that reward them for volume sales. If you have a special interest, **find an agent with expertise in that area**; the American Society of Travel Agents (ASTA; ☞ Travel Agencies) has a database of specialists worldwide.

Make sure your travel agent knows the accommodations and other services of the place being recommended. Ask about the hotel's location, room size, beds, and whether it has a pool, room service, or programs for children, if you care about these. Has your agent been there in person or sent others whom you can contact?

Do some homework on your own, too: local tourism boards can provide information about lesser-known and small-niche operators, some of which may sell only direct.

BUYER BEWARE

Each year consumers are stranded or lose their money when tour operators—even large ones with excellent reputations—go out of business. So **check out the operator.** Ask several travel agents about its reputation, and try to **book with a company that has a consumer-protection program.** (Look for information in the company's brochure.) In the United States, members of the National Tour Association and the United States Tour Operators Association are required to set aside funds to cover your payments and travel arrangements in the event that the company defaults. It's also a good idea to choose a company that participates in the American Society of Travel Agents' Tour Operator Program (TOP); ASTA will act as mediator in any disputes between you and your tour operator.

Remember that the more your package or tour includes the better you can predict the ultimate cost of your vacation. Make sure you know exactly what is covered, and **beware of hidden costs.** Are taxes, tips, and transfers included? Entertainment and excursions? These can add up.

➤ TOUR-OPERATOR RECOMMENDATIONS: **American Society of Travel Agents** (☞ Travel Agencies). **National Tour Association** (NTA; ✉ 546 E. Main St., Lexington, KY 40508, ☎ 859/226–4444 or 800/682–8886, ᴡᴇʙ www.ntaonline.com). **United States Tour Operators Association** (USTOA; ✉ 275 Madison Ave., Suite 2014, New York, NY 10016, ☎ 212/599–6599 or 800/468–7862, ꜰᴀx 212/599–6744, ᴡᴇʙ www.ustoa.com).

TRAIN TRAVEL

Amtrak offers nationwide service to Chicago's Union Station, at 225 South Canal Street. Some trains travel overnight, and you can sleep in your seat or book a sleeper car at an additional cost. Train schedules and payment options are available by calling Amtrak directly or consulting its Web site. Amtrak trains tend to fill up, so if you don't purchase a ticket in advance at least **make a reservation.**

➤ TRAIN INFORMATION: **Amtrak** (☎ 800/872–7245, ᴡᴇʙ www.amtrak.com).

TRANSPORTATION
AROUND CHICAGO

Considering the difficulties of driving in Chicago, try other means of exploring the city. Public transit is inexpensive and convenient; taxis are generally easy to come by. And many areas of the city are a pleasure to walk through, even in unpredictable weather conditions.

Convention goers can **take advantage of several alternatives to cabs or shuttle buses.** CTA trains do not serve McCormick Place, but CTA Bus 3 (King Drive), Bus 4 (Cottage Grove), and Bus 21 (Cermak) stop at 23rd Street and Martin Luther King Drive and travel north to downtown Chicago. Another option is the Metra commuter train, which has a 23rd Street stop, accessible from the North Building, on the Metra Electric and South Shore lines. Visitors going downtown can get off at one of two stations: Van Buren Street or the northernmost and final stop, Randolph Street. On weekdays Metra trains run fairly often, but weekend service is less frequent.

TRAVEL AGENCIES

A good travel agent puts your needs first. Look for an agency that has been in business at least five years, emphasizes customer service, and has someone on staff who specializes in your destination. In addition, **make sure the agency belongs to a professional trade organization.** The American Society of Travel Agents (ASTA)—the largest and most influential in the field with more than 24,000 members in some 140 countries—maintains and enforces a strict code of ethics and will step in to help mediate any agent-client disputes involving ASTA members if necessary. ASTA (whose motto is "Without a travel agent, you're on your own") also maintains a Web site that includes a directory of agents. (If a travel agency is also acting as your tour operator, *see* Buyer Beware *in* Tours and Packages, *above*.)

➤ LOCAL AGENT REFERRALS: **American Society of Travel Agents** (ASTA; ✉ 1101 King St., Suite 200, Alexandria, VA 22314, ☎ 800/965–2782 24-hr hot line, FAX 703/739–3268, WEB www.astanet.com). **Association of British Travel Agents** (✉ 68–71 Newman St., London W1T 3AH, ☎ 020/7637–2444, FAX 020/7637–0713, WEB www.abtanet.com). **Association of Canadian Travel Agents** (✉ 130 Albert St., Suite 1705, Ottawa, Ontario K1P 5G4, ☎ 613/237–3657, FAX 613/237–7052, WEB www.acta.ca). **Australian Federation of Travel Agents** (✉ Level 3, 309 Pitt St., Sydney, NSW 2000, ☎ 02/9264–3299, FAX 02/9264–1085, WEB www.afta.com.au). **Travel Agents' Association of New Zealand** (✉ Level 5, Tourism and Travel House, 79 Boulcott St., Box 1888, Wellington 6001, ☎ 04/499–0104, FAX 04/499–0827, WEB www.taanz.org.nz).

VISITOR INFORMATION

➤ TOURIST INFORMATION: **Chicago Office of Tourism** (✉ 78 E. Washington St., 60602, ☎ 312/744–2400; 800/226–6632; 312/744–2947 TTY; 800/406–6418 TTY; WEB www.ci.chi.il.us/CulturalAffairs/Tourism). **Chicago Convention and Tourism Bureau** (✉ 2301 S. Lake Shore Dr., 60616, ☎ 312/567–8500 or 800/226–6632, FAX 312/567–8533; 312/567–8528 for automated Fax Back Information Service; WEB www.choosechicago.com). **Chicago Office of Tourism Welcome Center** (✉ 811 N. Michigan Ave.). **Chicago Cultural Center Welcome Center** (✉ 77 E. Randolph St.). **Illinois Bureau of Tourism** (✉ 100 W. Randolph St., Suite 3-400, 60601, ☎ 800/226–6632 for brochures, WEB www.enjoyillinois.com). **Mayor's Office of Special Events, General Information, and Activities** (✉ 121 N. LaSalle St., Room 703, 60602, ☎ 312/744–3315, FAX 312/744–8523). **Navy Pier Welcome Center** (✉ 700 E. Grand Ave.).

➤ U.S. GOVERNMENT ADVISORIES: **U.S. Department of State** (✉ Overseas Citizens Services Office, Room 4811, 2201 C St. NW, Washington, DC 20520, ☎ 888/407–4747; 202/647–5225 interactive hot line; WEB www.travel.state.gov); enclose a business-size SASE.

WEB SITES

Do check out the World Wide Web when planning your trip. You'll find everything from weather forecasts to virtual tours of famous cities. Be sure to **visit Fodors.com** (www.fodors.com), a complete travel-planning site. You can research prices and book plane tickets, hotel rooms, rental cars, vacation packages, and more. In addition, you can post your pressing questions in the Travel Talk section. Other planning tools include a currency converter and weather reports, and there are loads of links to travel resources.

Find out more about cultural and sightseeing offerings at the Exploring Chicago site, **www.ci.chi.il.us/tourism.** The Chicago Convention and Tourism Bureau's site, **www.choosechicago.com,** has plenty of general tips on the city and local events, plus helpful information on convention facilities. To sort out the public-transit system, log on to the CTA's site at **www.transitchicago.com.** The Web sites of the city's daily newspapers, the *Tribune* (**www.chicagotribune.com**) and the *Sun-Times* (**www.suntimes.com/index**) are great sources for reviews and events listings. The *Chicago Reader*'s site, **www.chireader.com,** is rich in arts, entertainment, and dining reviews. *Chicago* magazine's www.chicagomag. com carries a few Web-exclusive features along with articles from the monthly. Metromix's www.metromix. com thoroughly covers Chicago's entertainment scene, from arts festivals to TV. Get the scoop on clubs at the Chicago Nights Web page, www. chicagonights.com/start.htm.

WHEN TO GO

If your principal concern is comfortable weather for touring the city, **consider a visit in spring or fall,** when moderate temperatures make it a pleasure to be out and about. The city really comes alive in late fall as stores dress up for the holiday season along the Magnificent Mile and State Street.

Summertime temperatures will climb into the 90°s in hot spells, and the humidity can be uncomfortably high.

Winters can see very raw weather and the occasional news-making blizzard, and temperatures in the teens are to be expected; **come prepared for the cold.** There are January sales to reward those who venture out, and many indoor venues allow you to look out on the cold in warm comfort.

➤ FORECASTS: **Weather Channel Connection** (☎ 900/932–8437), 95¢ per minute from a Touch-Tone phone.

The following are the average daily maximum and minimum temperatures for Chicago.

Jan.	32F	0C	May	65F	18C	Sept.	73F	23C
	18	– 8		50	10		58	14
Feb.	34F	1C	June	75F	24C	Oct.	61F	16C
	20	– 7		60	16		47	8
Mar.	43F	6C	July	81F	27C	Nov.	47F	8C
	29	– 2		66	19		34	1
Apr.	55F	13C	Aug.	79F	26C	Dec.	36F	2C
	40	4		65	18		23	– 5

FESTIVALS AND SEASONAL EVENTS

➤ FEB.: **African-American Heritage Month** celebrations at the Museum of Science and Industry (✉ 57th St. and S. Lake Shore Dr., ☎ 773/684–1414, WEB www.msichicago.org), the Du-Sable Museum (✉ 740 E. 56th Pl., ☎ 773/947–0600), the **South Shore Cultural Center** (✉ 7059 S. Lake Shore Dr., ☎ 312/747–2536), the **Chicago Cultural Center** (✉ 78 E. Washington St., ☎ 312/346–3278), the **Field Museum** (✉ Roosevelt Rd. at S. Lake Shore Dr., ☎ 312/922–9410, WEB www.fmnh.org), the **Art Institute of Chicago** (✉ Michigan Ave. at Adams St., ☎ 312/443–3600, WEB www.artic.edu), and other Chicago cultural institutions include arts-and-crafts exhibitions and theater, music, and dance performances.

➤ EARLY FEB.: The **3 on 3 Basketball Tournament** is the largest indoor event of its kind (✉ Navy Pier, ☎ 773/404–0554).

➤ MID-FEB.: The **Azalea and Camellia Show** at Lincoln Park Conservatory (✉ 2400 N. Stockton Dr., ☎ 312/742–7736) and **Garfield Park Conservatory** (✉ 300 N. Central Park Ave., ☎ 312/746–5100) provides a welcome early glimpse of spring.

➤ MID-FEB.: **Winterbreak Festival** (☎ 312/744–3315) is a series of concerts, skating exhibitions, and other entertainment events in various locations; discount packages are available at many hotels.

➤ MID-FEB.–EARLY MAR.: The **Medinah Shrine Circus** at Medinah Temple (✉ 600 N. Wabash Ave., ☎ 312/266–5050) delights children of all ages each year.

➤ MAR. 11: The **St. Patrick's Day parade** (☎ 312/942–9188) turns the city on its head: The Chicago River is dyed green, shamrocks decorate the street, and the center stripe of Dearborn Street is painted the color of the Irish from Wacker Drive to Van Buren Street.

➤ LATE MAR.–EARLY APR.: The **Spring Flower Show** blooms at the Lincoln Park and Garfield Park conservatories.

➤ MID-APR.: Celebrate Latino culture during the **15th Annual Chicago Latino Film Festival** (☎ 312/663–1600) at various locations around the city.

➤ MAY 1–OCT. 1 (SOMETIMES EARLIER): **Buckingham Fountain,** in Grant Park, flows day and night. On summer evenings, from 8 until 11, the Fountain features a light and sound show on the hour.

➤ MID-MAY: The **Art 2000 Chicago** exhibition at the Navy Pier (✉ 600 E. Grand Ave., ☎ 312/587–3300) showcases modern and contemporary art with 200 international exhibitors.

➤ MID-MAY: The **Wright Plus House Walk** (☎ 708/848–1976) gives you a look at masterpieces in suburban Oak Park by Frank Lloyd Wright and other Prairie School architects.

➤ LATE MAY–EARLY JUNE: The **Printer's Row Book Fair** (✉ Dearborn St. between Congress Pkwy. and Polk St., ☎ 312/987–9896) is a two-day event in the historic Printer's Row district, with programs and displays on the printer's and binder's arts.

➤ EARLY JUNE: The **Chicago Blues Festival** (☎ 312/744–3315), in Grant Park, is a popular four-day, three-stage event starring blues greats from Chicago and around the country.

➤ EARLY JUNE: The **57th Street Art Fair,** in Hyde Park's Ray School yard (✉ 57th St. and Kimbark Ave., ☎ 773/493–3247), is the oldest juried art fair in the Midwest, with paintings, sculpture, jewelry, ceramics, clothing, and textiles.

➤ EARLY–MID-JUNE: The **Chicago Gospel Fest** (☎ 312/744–3315) brings its joyful sounds to Grant Park.

➤ MID-JUNE: The **Old Town Art Fair** (✉ Lincoln Park W and Orleans St., ☎ 312/337–1938), one of the top summer art fairs, draws people from around the region to historic Old Town.

➤ MID-JUNE: The **Boulevard-Lakefront Bicycle Tour** (☎ 312/427–3325) brings 6,000 cyclists to the city's network of boulevards and parks for a 35-mi ride.

➤ MID-JUNE: Summer fun with a Swedish flair can be found at the **34th Annual Andersonville Midsommarfest** (☎ 773/348–6784).

➤ MID-JUNE–MID-AUG.: The **Grant Park Symphony Orchestra and Chorus** (☎ 312/742–7638) gives free concerts Wednesday–Sunday.

➤ LATE JUNE–EARLY JULY: **Taste of Chicago** (✉ Grant Park, Columbus Dr. between Jackson and Randolph Sts., ☎ 312/744–3315) dishes out pizza, cheesecake, and other Chicago specialties to 3½ million people over a 10-day period that includes entertainment.

➤ LATE JUNE–LABOR DAY: The **Ravinia Festival** (☎ 847/266–5100), in Highland Park, hosts a variety of jazz, classical, and popular musical artists in a pastoral setting north of the city.

➤ ALL SUMMER: **Noontime music and dance performances** are held outdoors weekdays at the Daley Center Plaza (✉ Washington St. between Dearborn and Clark Sts.) and at the First National Bank of Chicago Plaza (✉ Dearborn St. at Madison St.).

➤ JULY 3: **Fireworks along the lakefront** draw a crowd at dusk; bring a blanket and a portable radio to listen to the *1812 Overture* from Grant Park (☎ 312/744–3315).

➤ MID-JULY: The **Chicago to Mackinac Island Boat Race** originates at Belmont Harbor (☎ 312/861–7777).

➤ MID-JULY: The **World's Largest Block Party,** at Old St. Pat's Church (✉ Madison and Des Plaines Sts., ☎ 312/648–1021), has nationally recognized bands, food, drinks, and swarms of people.

➤ LATE JULY: The **Newberry Library Book Fair** (✉ 60 W. Walton St., ☎ 312/255–3510) sells thousands of good used books at low prices; the park across the street holds the Bughouse Square Debates the same weekend.

➤ LATE JULY: **Venetian Night** (✉ Monroe St. Harbor, Grant Park, ☎ 312/744–3315) features fireworks and boats festooned with lights.

➤ LATE AUG.: The **Air and Water Show** (☎ 312/744–3315) along North Avenue Beach thrills viewers with precision flying teams and antique and high-tech aircraft going through their paces.

➤ LATE AUG.: **Chicago Triathlon** (☎ 773/404–2372) participants plunge in at Ohio Street on the lakefront for a 1-mi swim, followed by a 25-mi bike race on Lake Shore Drive, and a 10-km run in the world's largest triathlon.

➤ LATE AUG.: The **Chicago Jazz Festival** (☎ 312/744–3315) holds sway for four days during Labor Day weekend at the Petrillo Music Shell in Grant Park.

➤ LATE AUG.–EARLY SEPT.: You'll get more than food at **Taste of Polonia** (✉ Lawrence and Milwaukee Aves., ☎ 773/777–8898), which also features carnival games, polka bands, and Polish handicrafts.

➤ EARLY SEPT.: The **Around the Coyote** (☎ 773/342–6777) festival in Wicker Park and Bucktown features theater performances, poetry and fiction readings, dance, film, and a gallery walk that begins at the intersection of Milwaukee, North, and Damen avenues.

➤ SEPT.: The **Dia de los Muertos** celebration at the Mexican Fine Arts Center Museum (✉ 1852 W. 19th St., ☎ 312/738–1503) displays the work of Mexican and Mexican-American artists.

➤ EARLY–MID-SEPT.: **Viva Chicago** (☎ 312/744–3315) is a festival of Latin music in Grant Park.

➤ MID-SEPT.–EARLY OCT.: **Oktoberfest** brings out the best in beer and German specialties at the Berghoff Restaurant (✉ 17 W. Adams St., ☎ 312/427–3170) and Chicago area pubs.

➤ MID-OCT.: The **Chicago Marathon** (☎ 312/243–3274) starts in Grant Park at Columbus and Balbo streets and follows a course through the city.

➤ MID-OCT.: The **Columbus Day Parade** follows Dearborn Street from Wacker Drive to Congress Parkway.

➤ MID-OCT.: The **Chicago International Film Festival** (☎ 312/425–9400) brings new American and foreign films to various Chicago theaters.

➤ SAT. BEFORE THANKSGIVING: The **Magnificent Mile Lights Festival** (☎ 312/642–3570) kicks off the holiday season with a block-by-block illumination of hundreds of thousands of tiny white lights along Michigan Avenue and Oak Street.

➤ THANKSGIVING WEEKEND: The **lighting of Chicago's Christmas tree** takes place on Friday in the Daley Center Plaza (✉ Washington St. between Dearborn and Clark Sts.); the **Christmas Parade,** with balloons, floats, and Santa, travels down Michigan Avenue on Saturday.

➤ MID-NOV.–DEC.: The **Goodman Theatre** (✉ 200 S. Columbus Dr., ☎ 312/443–3800) presents *A Christmas Carol,* and *The Nutcracker* is performed at the **Arie Crown Theatre at McCormick Place** (✉ 2301 S. Lake Shore Dr., ☎ 312/791–6190).

➤ LATE NOV.: The **Chrysanthemum Show** holds center stage at the Lincoln Park and Garfield Park conservatories.

➤ LATE NOV.–DEC.: The **Christmas Around the World** display at the Museum of Science and Industry (✉ 57th St. and Lake Shore Dr., ☎ 773/684–1414) brings together trees decorated in the traditional styles of more than 40 countries.

➤ NOV. 28–JAN. 1: **Zoo Lights Festival** at the Lincoln Park Zoo (✉ 2200 N. Cannon Dr., ☎ 312/742–2000) shows off zoo animals, dinosaurs, and holiday themes with more than 100,000 lights.

➤ MID- TO LATE DEC.: At the **South Shore Cultural Center** (✉ 7059 S. Shore Dr., ☎ 312/747–2536), the city's largest **Pre-Kwanzaa Celebration,** a two-day family-oriented event, with performances, workshops, crafts, and food, is held in advance of the African-American cultural holiday Kwanzaa, which runs from December 26 to January 1; other Kwanzaa-related events are held at the **New Regal Theatre** (✉ 1645 E. 79th St., ☎ 773/721–9301), DuSable Museum of African-American History, Chicago Cultural Center, Art Institute of Chicago, and other cultural institutions in the city.

➤ LATE DEC.–EARLY JAN.: The **Winter Festival Flower Show** at the Lincoln Park and Garfield Park conservatories provides welcome color.

1 DESTINATION: CHICAGO

Windy City, Warm Heart

What's Where

Pleasures and Pastimes

Fodor's Choice

Great Itineraries

WINDY CITY, WARM HEART

DON'T TRY TO HANG a clever moniker on Chicago—the city moves too fast to be pinned down. What was once considered a gangster's paradise has evolved into an eclectic amalgam of transcendent architecture, world-class theater, and rabid sportsmanship.

Chicago's image has changed. No longer the "second city," America's midwestern metropolis has acquired a first-class reputation around the world, particularly when it comes to the arts. Carl Sandburg's City of the Big Shoulders is now also City of the Big Limos on opening nights.

Exhibitions at the Art Institute of Chicago have drawn worldwide acclaim. You could spend days there drinking in the Impressionist paintings alone, then be happily transported into the 21st century by eye-popping works at the bold Museum of Contemporary Art, which overlooks Lake Michigan.

Gutsy Steppenwolf Theater productions, from *True West* to *The Libertine,* have jolted critics on both coasts. The city's scores of other theaters, including the Victory Gardens, the Goodman, the Court, and the Shakespeare Repertory, regularly showcase the talents of remarkable local actors who just might turn out to be the next John Malkovich or Gary Sinise.

The Grammy-laden Chicago Symphony Orchestra wins standing ovations both at home and abroad. At the other end of the Loop, the Lyric Opera's lavish productions boast world-class singers and conductors. Chicago's staggeringly varied architecture is lauded (and occasionally lambasted) around the globe. And don't forget film criticism and TV talk. The thumbs of Roger Ebert and the late Gene Siskel weighed heavily in the movie-review scale. And who doesn't know Oprah, Jenny Jones, or Jerry Springer?

This is also the home of the ground-breaking Second City improvisation and comedy club whose talented performers have included the brilliantly funny Mike Nichols and Elaine May, Jim and the late John Belushi, Bill Murray, and George Wendt. And Chicagoans like to recall that one of Hollywood's nuttiest car chases took place in their city. In the *Blues Brothers,* John Belushi and Dan Aykroyd as Jake and Elwood Blues crash through the Daley Center, just missing the controversial Picasso sculpture in the plaza. Even city hall, headed by no-nonsense mayor Richard M. Daley, lightens up in March and dyes the Chicago River green in honor of St. Patrick.

Perhaps one reason Chicagoans have a sense of humor is the weather. As local film director Joel Sedelmaier contends, "Colder-than-hell winters saved this city." In an essay in the handsome book *Great Chicago Stories,* he wrote, "If Chicago had weather like Florida, we'd be L.A. and I wouldn't wish that on anybody." Though residents complain that the city's four seasons are "winter, winter, winter, and the Fourth of July," at least on a winter day, when the snow is blowing horizontally across the Michigan Avenue Bridge, Chicagoans can duck into such popular clubs as Andy's, where there's hot jazz even at noon.

TO GET A GRIP ON CHICAGO, take a trip along the lakefront, smack dab against the city's jagged, jazzy skyline. Walk the shoreline or drive along Lake Shore Drive, one of the most appealing roadways in town. Zooming along the Drive, as Chicagoans call it, from as far north as Hollywood Avenue or as far south as Hyde Park, you'll watch downtown Chicago grow gradually larger and larger, rising like Oz in the distance.

You'll also want to do a little Chicago-style time traveling to a period when horses clip-clopped downtown. You'll see firsthand that among America's big cities, Chicago is still remarkable for its downtown mélange of very new buildings and very old ones that are bustling, not boarded up. Walk down canyonlike LaSalle Street, Chicago's busy boulevard of high finance, to a rugged gem of a 19th-century building called the Rookery. Step inside the dazzling skylighted lobby, redesigned in 1905 by Frank Lloyd Wright. Climb the grand staircase with its white marble steps and lacy ironwork and you'll feel as though you're in turn-of-the-20th-century Chicago. Then walk a block south, two blocks west, and 100 years forward to the 110-story Sears Tower. Gawk upward, and then ride to the 103rd-floor Skydeck to see Chicago laid out like a tantalizing toy city.

Back down on the ground, a musical trip is also in order. The House of Blues, in the Marina City complex on Wacker Drive, has big-time acts and big-time prices. Visitors in search of the heart and soul of Chicago should not overlook smaller clubs such as Buddy Guy's Legends in the South Loop and Blue Chicago on North Clark Street. Sit at a table a few feet from some of the city's great bluesmen and listen long into the night to the music labeled "the facts of life" by legendary Chicago blues bassist and songwriter Willie Dixon. Like the city itself, Chicago blues is gritty and aggressive, with edgy, eloquent electric slide guitar and a rock-solid beat that will make you want to dance. And that's just the thing to do at a Chicago blues club, even if your only space is cramped between two tables.

At the Sears Tower and at blues clubs, you'll be bumping into other out-of-towners. So where can you go to encounter a richly diverse mix of native Chicagoans? Stroll State Street ("that great street"), preferably at lunchtime on a weekday when the sidewalks are elbow to elbow with Loop secretaries and lawyers, shoppers and messengers, police officers, street musicians, city sweepers, and the occasional ragtag urban philosopher orating noisily on a corner. Though Chicago remains woefully segregated in its neighborhoods, in the Loop everyone mingles easily, fostering hope that someday residential barriers may break down.

If you happen to be in the city on a steamy summer day, grab a ticket at ivy-webbed Wrigley Field—the National League's oldest ballpark. Sit with the "bleacher bums," ever loyal to their Cubs. You may catch a fly, you may catch a little sloshed beer, and you'll certainly catch a good glimpse of Chicago.

As actor William Petersen, co-founder of the city's innovative Remains Theater,

has said, "Chicago is a place to take risks, a place to fail, a place to grow. It's a place where you're not judged as being unworthy."

In other words, a Cubs kind of town.

–Anne Taubeneck

WHAT'S WHERE

The Chicago most visitors see first is the commercial and cultural heart of the city, the downtown and Near North areas, so that's where we start. The world-famous architecture, impressive skyline, museums, department stores, major hotels, and fine restaurants together define a great American city. Yet there is another, equally interesting Chicago, vibrant with neighborhoods and their distinctive populations. We head farther north to experience this diversity, from stately Lincoln Park to funky Wicker Park, from the art galleries of River North to the ethnic mosaic of North Clark Street. And finally, for a little bit of everything from distinctive museums to architectural gems, we turn south to Hyde Park and Kenwood. The organization of this book mirrors this geographical progression, so orient yourself (Lake Michigan is a handy landmark on the east) and get ready to experience Chicago.

The Loop

The heart of Chicago is the downtown area loosely bounded by elevated train lines, also known as the Loop. Constantly evolving, the area in and around the tracks is stacked with handsome old landmark buildings and shimmering new ones. These are the centers of business and the mainstays of culture; they also provide new residential areas and are the anchors of renewed older districts.

Downtown South

Just south of the Loop, old forms take on new functions that merge with the life of the central city. Once thriving, this area decayed as its core business—the printing industry—moved out. Since the 1980s, however, a gradual revival led by an aspiring restaurateur and ambitious investors has turned Downtown South into a thriving urban neighborhood enclave.

South Lake Shore Drive

After exploring the canyons of downtown Chicago up close, step back (way back) to admire the view. Driving north on South Lake Shore Drive (toward downtown) is a great way to appreciate the panorama angle. Chicago's skyline unfolds around every turn, and you can pick out many of the individual skyscrapers that towered above as you walked the streets of the Loop. On the north end of the drive is a dazzling trio of museums—the Shedd Aquarium, the Field Museum, and the Adler Planetarium—makes the most of its dramatic location on the lakefront just south of downtown.

Near North

For many, Chicago high life is the Near North, just across the Chicago River from the Loop. Glitzy shops along both sides of Michigan Avenue compose what's known as the Magnificent Mile, and the side streets of Streeterville aren't lacking in riches, either. To the east are the thriving Navy and North piers.

River North

Just west of Near North is River North. Rehabilitation has transformed an area of factories and warehouses into a neighborhood of upscale shopping strips and more than 65 art galleries.

Lincoln Park

The campuses of the old McCormick Seminary and De Paul University, the historic Biograph Theatre, and shopping districts on Halsted Street and North Lincoln Avenue are all part of Lincoln Park. The neighborhood shares its name and part of its boundaries with the oldest park in Chicago's "emerald necklace," itself encompassing many wonders. Old Town Triangle, another section of the neighborhood, contains some of the most historic and appealing streets in town.

Bucktown and Wicker Park

Two hot, hip adjoining neighborhoods meet at the intersection of diagonal Milwaukee Avenue, Damen Avenue (2000 W.), and North Avenue (1600 N.), west of the south end of Lincoln Park. Wicker Park lies south of Milwaukee Avenue, Bucktown to the north. Musicians, artists, and aspiring yuppies have staked their claims in these working-class areas. Rents are rising, and there's a profusion of restaurants, coffee bars, rock clubs, galleries, and shops.

North Clark Street

A ride up Clark Street, particularly north of Lincoln Park, is an urban tour through time and the waves of ethnic migration. Like north Milwaukee Avenue, which has gone from Polish to Hispanic to Polish again as new immigrants have arrived, Clark Street is a microcosm of the city of Chicago and the continuing ebb and flow of its populations, including Scandinavian, Asian, and Middle Eastern.

Devon Avenue

Along Devon Avenue, on the city's far north side, immigrants from the Indian subcontinent live virtually side by side with Orthodox Jews newly arrived from Russia. Here you can witness different customs and cultures in juxtaposition and sample ethnic wares and cuisines.

Hyde Park and Kenwood

Site of the World's Columbian Exposition of 1893 and today's Museum of Science and Industry, home of the University of Chicago, and locale of five houses designed by Frank Lloyd Wright, Hyde Park and the adjoining Kenwood are important historically, intellectually, and culturally. Turn-of-the-20th-century mansions and working-class cottages are still there for the looking, along with museums, churches, and bookstores. All around are signs of the process of urban renewal and the changes it has wrought in this exceptionally stable, racially integrated neighborhood.

Beyond the City

Among the highlights of the western suburbs are Oak Park, with its rich architectural legacy from Frank Lloyd Wright; the Brookfield Zoo in Brookfield; and Lisle's Morton Arboretum. A drive north along the manicured shores of Lake Michigan can take in a lighthouse in Evanston, the Baha'i House of Worship in Wilmette, and the Chicago Botanical Garden in Glencoe.

PLEASURES AND PASTIMES

Architecture

The destruction wrought by the Chicago Fire of 1871 cleared a path for architectural experimentation. Architects flocked to rebuild the city, using new technology to develop the foundations of modern architecture. Louis Sullivan, William Holabird, John Wellborn Root, Frank Lloyd Wright, and Daniel Burnham are among the builders whose creations influenced Chicago as well as cities around the world. They developed the skyscraper, and this type of structure fills the downtown skyline in hundreds of incarnations, from the crenellated Wrigley Building (Graham Anderson Probst and White) to the boxlike Federal Center and Plaza (Mies van der Rohe). Chicago and its environs also inspired Wright's low-lying Prairie School, exemplified in many Oak Park houses. The city still buzzes with new construction, though today's architects often favor the postmodern, as in Helmut Jahn's James R. Thompson Center and the Harold Washington Public Library.

Blues

In the years following World War II, Chicago-style blues grew into its own musical form, flourishing during the 1950s, then fading during the 1960s with the advent of rock 'n' roll. Today Chicago blues is coming back, although more strongly on the trendy North Side than on the South Side, where it all began. Isaac Tigrett's palatial House of Blues in the Marina City complex downtown hosts both local and nationally known musicians, though smaller clubs such as B.L.U.E.S. and Buddy Guy's Legends are still the best places to hear real Chicago-style blues.

Dining

In Chicago immigrants and their traditions give the dining scene impressive variety and spice, and their influence is felt not just in ethnic storefront eateries but in bastions of cutting-edge contemporary cuisine. You can sample cuisine from all over the food universe—Polish sausage, Swedish pancakes, Thai curry, Greek *mezes* (appetizers), and more. There are also plenty of temples to the all-American steak and to the city's trademark deep-dish pizza.

The Lake

Lake Michigan acts as Chicago's compass. You can always orient yourself in the city by finding the lake—if you're facing the lake, you're facing east. It's also a great place for outdoor activities, with harbors, beaches, and more than 20 mi of trails for walkers, skaters, and cyclists. It's easy to appreciate the lake from nearby, but it's also a beautiful backdrop to the view from city skyscrapers.

Outdoor Sculpture

You don't have to go indoors to see some of Chicago's finest art. Strolling in the Loop, you'll encounter arresting pieces, such as Picasso's beady-eyed sculpture in the Daley Plaza, Alexander Calder's arching red Flamingo in the Federal Center Plaza, and Marc Chagall's monolithic mosaic *The Four Seasons* in the Bank One Plaza. Wander on to Michigan Avenue to see Jerry Peart's wild and whimsical *Splash* at the Boulevard Towers Plaza or—for something entirely different—Edward Kemeys's magnificent bronze lions in front of the Art Institute. Children have fun sliding down the base of the Picasso and petting the lions, who wear wreaths at holiday time.

Theater

In Chicago you can find lavishly staged musicals presented in such magnificent settings as Adler and Sullivan's Auditorium Theatre as well as taut dramas in intimate settings with bare-bones scenery. Tickets can be outrageously expensive at downtown theaters, but prices are lower beyond the Loop. Not every small theater (and there are at least 75 around the city) may achieve the success of Steppenwolf—where John Malkovich, Gary Sinise, and Joan Allen got their start—but take a chance on a small production that sounds enticing. There's a wealth of talent here in the heartland.

FODOR'S CHOICE

Architecture

Citicorp Center. Hordes of commuters rush through every day; step apart from the throng for a moment to appreciate the modern train station–office tower outside and in.

James R. Thompson Center. Love it or hate it, you're sure to find the red, white, and blue postmodern, wedge-shape structure intriguing.

Monadnock Building. Take one look at the thick base walls to see why the steel frame was such an innovation.

Reliance Building. Now reborn as the Hotel Burnham, this building has the best early examples of the Chicago window.

Robie House. The cantilevered roof, leaded-glass windows, and lack of a basement exemplify Frank Lloyd Wright's Prairie style.

Rookery. The exterior is imposing, but inside is an airy marble and gold-leaf lobby remodeled by Frank Lloyd Wright in 1905.

333 West Wacker Drive. The shimmering green glass curves alongside the river that inspired it.

Dining

Arun's. The finest Thai restaurant in Chicago (some say in the country) presents multicourse, custom-designed menus. Expect the freshest of ingredients and beautiful presentations. $$$$

Charlie Trotter's. This small dining room can barely accommodate all the people who'd like to try Trotter's experimental American cuisine. $$$$

TRU. The stunning food presentation, flawless kitchen, and superb waitstaff allow for a true fine dining experience. $$$$

Spiaggia. Luxury Italian dining combines brilliantly with the views of Lake Michigan. $$$–$$$$

Keefers. This steak house defies expectations by offering bistro fare and lots of fish in addition to its top-quality beef. $$–$$$$

MK. Sleek decor and an elegant contemporary menu pull in a trendy crowd. $$–$$$$

North Pond. Head into the woods (of Lincoln Park) to enjoy contemporary cuisine that highlights organic ingredients. $$$

Frontera Grill. A cheery ambience, a constantly changing but always innovative and delicious Mexican menu, and the right price make this festive River North spot a winner. $$–$$$

Spring. Artistic but unfussy fish preparations—from tuna tartare with quail egg to cod in crab and sweet pea sauce—distinguish the sophisticated Spring from the seasonal restaurant crop. $$–$$$

Fortunato. This stylish Wicker Parker updates Italian country cooking with contemporary flare. $–$$

Lodging

Four Seasons. Ponder the panoramic views while enjoying the little pampering touches that only first-class service can provide. $$$$

The Peninsula Chicago. This elegant retreat is only steps away from the Chicago Water Tower and the shops of the Magnificent Mile. $$$$

Sofitel Chicago Water Tower. Chicago's newest luxury hotel emphasizes hospitality and personal service. $$$$

Hotel Inter-Continental Chicago. This historic building now houses a thoroughly modern hotel; be sure to check out the fabulous pool—a relic from the building's days as the Medinah Athletic Club. $$$–$$$$

Hotel Burnham. Sleep in an architectural landmark which was transformed from an office building into a lavish hotel in 1999. $$–$$$$

Hotel Allegro Chicago. You can walk to dinner and a show from this stylish spot in the heart of the theater district. $$–$$$

Days Inn Lincoln Park North. Free access to the health club next door and complimentary continental breakfast sweeten the deal at this Lincoln Park hotel. $$

Special Moments

Stroll, bike, or in-line skate along the lakefront. On a sunny summer day, hundreds of Chicagoans will join you by the shores of Lake Michigan.

Art Institute of Chicago. Be awed by the truly magnificent collection of Impressionist and other masterpieces.

Visit "Sue." The largest and most complete T. rex skeleton ever found, Sue holds court at the Field Museum.

Wrigley Field. Put your heart into (and fondly remember the late Harry Caray) singing "Take Me Out to the Ball Game" during the seventh-inning stretch, regardless of who's winning.

Second City Comedy Club. Bust a gut at the club which has launched some of the funniest comedians around.

Walk in Frank Lloyd Wright's footsteps in his Oak Park neighborhood.

Experience real roots music at a crowded, smoky blues bar, even if it's full of other out-of-towners trying to get soulful.

Views

Michigan Avenue Bridge. Get a good look at the Chicago River, with the wedding-cake-like Wrigley Building on one side, the Loop on the other.

South Lake Shore Drive. Drive north from Hyde Park to take in the Chicago skyline—each curve provides a unique vista.

Navy Pier's Ferris Wheel. It's a beautiful, breezy view of the skyline from an open-air car 15 stories off the ground.

Sears Tower Skydeck. Ride an elevator up dozens of stories for a panorama of the city.

GREAT ITINERARIES

Chicago in 5 Days

Day One. Start at the top. Hit the heights of the John Hancock Center or the Sears Tower Skydeck for a grand view of the city and the lake. Then walk to Michigan Avenue and Adams Street for a morning of culture at the Art Institute. Either grab a bite at one of the museum's eateries or stroll back west for lunch at the venerable Berghoff Restaurant. Then wander north to the Michigan Avenue Bridge, where you can pick up a boat tour of the Chicago River. Enjoy the architecture as you float by, resting your museum-weary feet.

☺ *Works any day, but note that not all boat tours are available in winter.*

Day Two. On your second day, head for Chicago's museum campus for a full day of exploring land, sea, and sky. Start with the dinosaurs, ancient Egyptians, and other wonders at the Field Museum. Then stroll over to the Shedd Aquarium and Oceanarium, where you can see marine mammals and exotic water dwellers. Gaze at the lake while lunching at the Oceanarium's restaurant; then fix your eyes heavenward on the Adler Planetarium's Sky Show. If the weather's nice, take time to stroll along the lakefront outside the Adler—it has one of the loveliest skyline views in the city. For dinner, head north to Pizzeria Uno or Pizzeria Due for authentic Chicago-style pizza. Then amble over to the House of Blues for some after-dinner entertainment.

☺ *Works any day.*

Day Three. On day three, begin with a long walk (or run) along the lakefront. Or rent a bike and watch the waves on wheels. Then catch an El train north to Wrigley Field for a little Cubs baseball; grab a dog at the seventh-inning stretch. Afterward, soak up a little beer and atmosphere at one of the local sports bars. Then head back to River North for dinner at one of the restaurants bearing the name of a past or present Chicago sports luminary: Harry Caray's or Mike Ditka's Restaurant. Finish up with a night at the theater—check out a performance at the Goodman Theatre or the Steppenwolf.

☺ *Schedule this day around the sporting events or performances of your choice.*

Day Four. On day four, do the zoo. Spend the morning at the free Lincoln Park Zoo and Conservatory. Then, in the afternoon, stroll through the park to the Chicago Historical Society for an intriguing look at Chicago's yesterdays. If you'd like to stay in Lincoln Park for dinner, you'll have plenty of terrific restaurants to choose from. Then head for Second City, home of the famous local comedy troupe.

☺ *Try to avoid a Friday: Second City offers free improvisation following the last performance every night but Friday.*

Day Five. Finally, on day five, grab your bankroll and stroll the Mag Mile in search of great buys and souvenirs of Chicago. Walking north from around the Michigan Avenue Bridge, window-shop your way along the many upscale stores. (Dedicated shoppers will want to detour to State Street for a walk through the landmark

Marshall Field's.) If you need a culture buzz, check out the Terra Museum of American Art and the Museum of Contemporary Art, both in the neighborhood. Hang a left on Oak Street for the most elite boutiques. If shopping's not your bag, head out early in the day to the suburb of Oak Park to see the exceptional grouping of Prairie School buildings, including architect Frank Lloyd Wright's home and studio. After making that tough last-night restaurant choice, consider a nightcap at the Signature Room at the 95th bar at the top of the John Hancock Center—it's a heady place to kiss the city good-bye.

☉ *Don't plan on doing Day Five on a Monday, when both the Terra and the Museum of Contemporary Art are closed.*

So that you don't show up somewhere and find the doors locked, shuffle the itinerary segments with closing days in mind.

If You Have More Time

Spend a day on and around campus—either at Northwestern University to the north of the city or at the University of Chicago in historic Hyde Park to the south. If you have children, you could spend at least half a day at the Museum of Science and Industry in Hyde Park. Another option is to visit Pullman, the late 19th-century, planned industrial community that is now a national historic landmark.

If You Have Three Days

Follow the suggestions for the first day. Then split the second day between a morning at Museum Campus and an afternoon spent cheering on the Cubs at Wrigley Field. Catch some local theater or a Second City performance in the evening. On the third day you can shop 'til you drop along Michigan Avenue. If you're not a shopper, head to Oak Park or Lincoln Park for a day of exploring. Bid farewell to the Windy City with a drink in the Signature Room Bar on the 95th.

2 EXPLORING CHICAGO

Rising at the southern edge of Lake Michigan, Chicago is a beautiful city of both quiet ponds and roaring concrete highways—not to mention a stunning skyline, world-famous museums, glorious houses of worship, and tempting galleries and shops. Its spacious parks stretch along the shores of a lake that rages in winter and seduces in summer. You might start exploring in the energetic Loop, then travel as far south as Hyde Park, home of the Nobel-studded University of Chicago, or as far north as Devon Avenue, where scents of exotic Indian spices waft into the street.

CHICAGO'S VARIETY IS DAZZLING. The canyons of the Loop bustle with bankers, lawyers, traders, brokers, politicians, and wheeler-dealers of all kinds transacting their business in buildings that make architecture buffs swoon. Equally busy but sunnier is Near North (near the Loop, that is), where the smart shops of Michigan Avenue give way to the headquarters of myriad trade associations, advertising agencies, one of the nation's leading teaching hospitals, and cathedrals of the Roman Catholic and Episcopal churches.

Updated by
JoAnn
Milivojevic and
Roberta
Sotonoff

The city's skyline is one of the most exciting in the world. Since the 1960s, the Sears Tower, the Aon Center, the John Hancock Center, the Smurfit-Stone Building, NBC Tower, the James R. Thompson Center, 333 West Wacker, Lake Point Tower, and others have joined such legendary structures as the Chicago Board of Trade, the Rookery, and the Wrigley Building. Chicago is a virtual primer of modern architecture; for some background and a who's who, read Barbara Shortt's essay, "The Builders of Chicago," in Chapter 9 before you start exploring.

Leave downtown and the lakefront, however, and you soon encounter a city of neighborhoods made up mostly of bungalows, two-flats, three-flats, and six-flats (as two-, three-, and six-story apartment buildings are called here). Churches and shopping strips with signs in Polish, Spanish, Chinese, Arabic, Hebrew, or Korean stand as symbols of vibrant ethnic community life. Visitors rarely venture to these neighborhoods, yet it is here that you may encounter people enjoying great ethnic feasts for a pittance; and you can visit the museums and churches that house cultural artifacts reflecting the soul and spirit of their communities. The hardscrabble Chicago of immigrant enterprise may seem worlds away from Chicago the glitzy megalopolis, but for a real understanding of the city you should experience both.

THE LOOP

Downtown Chicago is full of treasures for city lovers. Known as the Loop since the cable cars of the 1880s looped around the central business district, downtown comprises the area south of the Chicago River, west of Lake Michigan, and north of the Congress Parkway–Eisenhower Expressway. Downtown Chicago's western boundary used to be the Chicago River, but the boundary continues to push westward. Handsome skyscrapers now line every foot of South Wacker Drive east of the river, and investors have sent construction crews across the bridges in search of more land to fuel the expansion.

The dynamic area known as the Loop is a living architectural museum, where you can stroll past shimmering modern towers side by side with painstakingly renovated 19th-century buildings that snap you back in time. (Much of Chicago's impressive architecture can be credited to the Great Chicago Fire of 1871, which leveled the city and cleared the way for the building of skyscrapers using steel-frame construction.) There are striking sculptures by Picasso, Miró, Chagall, and others; wide plazas lively with music and other entertainment in summer; noisy, mesmerizing trading centers; gigantic department stores that amazingly have avoided death-by-mall; and globally known museums that soothe the senses. (For immediate stress reduction, check out the Impressionists at the Art Institute.) And, of course, there is the rattling overhead train Chicagoans call the El, which loops the Loop.

The **Chicago Architecture Foundation** (⊠ 224 S. Michigan Ave., Loop, ☎ 312/922–3432, WEB www.architecture.org) conducts excellent tours

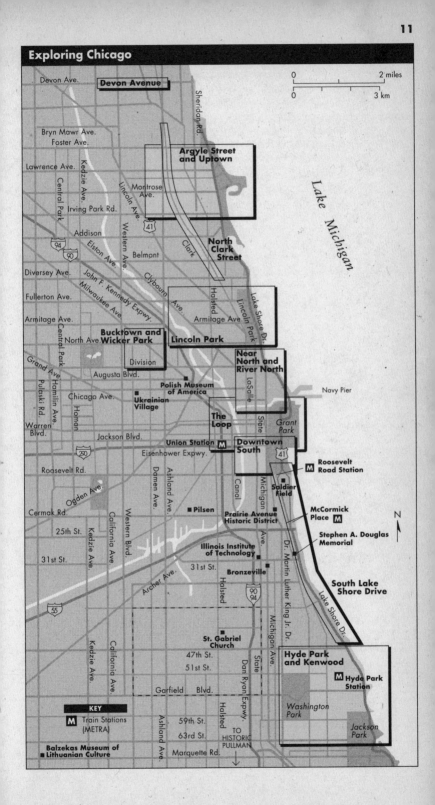

Exploring Chicago

Devon Ave.

Devon Avenue

Bryn Mawr Ave.
Foster Ave.

Lawrence Ave.

Sheridan Rd.

Argyle Street and Uptown

Montrose Ave.

Central Park

Kedzie Ave.

Irving Park Rd.

Addison

Western Ave.

Lincoln Ave.

41

Belmont

Clark

North Clark Street

Lake Michigan

Diversey Ave.

Elston Ave.

94

90

Fullerton Ave.

John F. Kennedy Expwy

Milwaukee Ave.

Clybourn

Halsted Ave.

Lincoln Park

Lake Shore Dr.

Lincoln Park

Armitage Ave.

Armitage Ave.

Grand Ave

Central Park

Hamlin Ave.

Pulaski Rd.

North Ave.

Bucktown and Wicker Park

Division

Augusta Blvd.

Near North and River North

LaSalle

Navy Pier

Warren Blvd.

Homan

Chicago Ave.

Polish Museum of America

Ukrainian Village

State

The Loop

Grant Park

Jackson Blvd.

Union Station M

Eisenhower Expwy.

Downtown South

41

290

Roosevelt Rd.

Damen Ave.

Ashland Ave.

Canal

Michigan

Soldier Field

Roosevelt Road Station M

Ogden Ave.

Cermak Rd.

■ **Pilsen**

Prairie Avenue Historic District

McCormick Place M

Stephen A. Douglas Memorial

25th St.

Kedzie Ave.

California Ave.

Western Blvd.

31st St.

Illinois Institute of Technology

Michigan Ave.

Dr. Martin Luther King Jr. Dr.

Lake Shore Dr.

Archer Ave.

31st St.

Bronzeville

90

94

South Lake Shore Drive

55

Halsted

St. Gabriel Church

Dan Ryan Expwy

Hyde Park and Kenwood

California Ave.

Kedzie Ave.

47th St.

51st St.

State

Michigan Ave.

Hyde Park Station M

KEY

M Train Stations (METRA)

Garfield Blvd.

Ashland Ave.

59th St.

63rd St.

Halsted

TO HISTORIC PULLMAN

Washington Park

Jackson Park

Balzekas Museum of
■ **Lithuanian Culture**

Marquette Rd.

0 ——— 2 miles

0 ——— 3 km

N

The Loop

400N
Kinzie St.
Union Ave.
Milwaukee Ave.
Chicago River
Orleans St.
W. Wacker Dr.
Fulton St.
15
John F. Kennedy Expwy.
Lake St.
Lake St.
Go
14
Randolph St.
Palace
Theatre
TO
MUSEUM OF
HOLOGRAPHY
13
Social
Seciurity
■ Building
M
Citicorp
Center
Washington St.
16
1W/S
Madison St.
Madison St.
Desplaines St.
Jefferson St.
Clinton St.
Canal St.
17
90
94
Monroe St.
S. Wacker Dr.
Franklin St.
Wells St.
LaSalle St.
Clark St.
Halsted St.
Adams St.
Union
Station M
31
Quincy St.
28 **27**
Old
St. Patrick's
Church
29
Jackson Blvd.
32
30
TO
PILSEN
LaSalle
400S
Van Buren St.
Van Buren St.
33
800W
500W
Dwight D. Eisenhower Expwy.
290
LaSalle St
M Station
Financial Pl.
Harrison St.

Aon Center **5**	Carson Pirie Scott **20**	Chicago Mercantile Exchange **17**	Fine Arts Building **38**
Art Institute of Chicago **22**	Chicago Athenaeum **2**	Chicago Temple **12**	Harold Washington Library Center **36**
Auditorium Theatre **37**	Chicago Board of Trade **30**	Civic Opera House **16**	Inland Steel Building **19**
Bank One Plaza **18**	Chicago City Hall–Cook County Building **13**	Daley Center **11**	James R. Thompson Center **14**
Berghoff Restaurant **24**	Chicago Cultural Center **6**	Federal Center and Plaza **26**	Marquette Building **25**
Carbide and Carbon Building **1**		Federal Reserve Bank **29**	

Kinzie St.

1 E/W

N. Water St.

Chicago River

E. Wacker Dr.

W. Wacker Dr.　S. Water St.

1

2

Lake St.

Michigan Ave.

Beaubien Ct.

Two Prudential Plaza

Page Brothers Building

Film Center

Chicago Theatre

Oriental Theatre

5

Prudential Building

3

Randolph St.

Randolph Dr.

M **Randolph St. Station**

6

4

11

Block 37

8

9

7

Washington St.

Millennium Park

2

10

Madison St.

Dearborn St.

18

20

19

Monroe St.

Xerox Center

21

25

State St.

Wabash Ave.

Adams St.

22

23

Columbus Dr.

Lake Shore Dr.

24

39

Jackson Blvd.

26

KEY

— Metro Lines

35

Fisher Building

Van Buren St.

M **Van Buren Station**

Grant Park

0　　440 yards

0　　400 meters

4

36

38

Congress

Plymouth Ct.

37

Congress Pkwy.

Plaza

Federal St.

100 E

N

of the Loop on foot, bus, or boat; highlights are an "Early Skyscrapers" tour and a "Modern and Beyond" tour, which trace the city's historic beginnings and soaring buildings. The CAF shop also has an extensive selection of books and gifts relating to Chicago architecture.

North Loop

Numbers in the text correspond to numbers in the margin and on the Loop map.

A Good Walk

To get to the walk's starting point, take a bus to Michigan Avenue and Wacker Drive. From the north, you can take Bus 3, 145, 147, or 151. Coming from the south, you can take Bus 3, 6, 145, 146, 147, or 151. If you arrive by car, you can park it in the subterranean Grant Park North Garage, with an entrance south on Michigan Avenue. Most streets in the Loop prohibit parking weekdays from 6 AM to 6 PM.

Begin your walk on North Michigan Avenue at South Water Street, one block south of the Michigan Avenue Bridge. This is the far northeast corner of the Loop. The walk will take you a few blocks south on Michigan Avenue, across the north part of the Loop, west to the Chicago River, and back east on Monroe Street.

On the southwest corner of Michigan Avenue and South Water Street stands the elegant art deco **Carbide and Carbon Building** ①. Across Michigan Avenue is the **Chicago Athenaeum** ②, a small museum with exhibits about art, architecture, and design. Head south on Michigan Avenue for two blocks to Randolph Street. On the northwest corner, the office building with the distinctively angled face is the **Smurfit-Stone Building** ③. Yaacov Agam's sculpture, *Communication X9*, sits in its plaza.

As you head east on Randolph Street, on your right is the city's 24.6-acre **Millennium Park** ④ which, at press time, was still in the final stages of construction. Continue to the soaring 1,136-ft **Aon Center** ⑤, formerly named the Amoco Building, the second-tallest building in Chicago. The odd sounds that fill the plaza emanate from a wind-chime sculpture. Directly west of the Aon Center is the **Prudential Building**, Chicago's tallest building until the late 1960s. Behind it rises the rocket ship–like **Two Prudential Plaza**, affectionately nicknamed Pru Two.

Head back west on Randolph Street to Michigan Avenue and the **Chicago Cultural Center** ⑥, with an ornate interior that includes a splendid Tiffany dome, as well as a Chicago Office of Tourism Visitor Information Center and the **Museum of Broadcast Communications** ⑦. Walk through the Cultural Center, taking the time to peruse its many splendors, and exit from the Washington Street side. Turn right on Washington Street, cross under the El tracks and enter **Marshall Field's** ⑧, the well-known department store's flagship in the landmark turn-of-the-20th-century building. After you're done shopping, exit Field's to **State Street** ⑨, the Loop's most famous thoroughfare. Across the street, on the southwest corner of State and Washington streets, is the **Reliance Building** ⑩. This National Landmark, a forerunner of the modern skyscraper, now houses the **Hotel Burnham**.

Continue west on Washington to the **Daley Center** ⑪. In the plaza is Picasso's controversial sculpture, known simply as "The Picasso." Directly opposite the Daley Center is the **Chicago Temple** ⑫, a Methodist church whose beautiful spire is so tall that it is best seen at some distance. Also on the south side of the street is Joan Miró's giant figure, *Chicago*. Continue a half block west on Washington Street to Clark

Street and turn right. Across from the Daley Center is the handsome, neoclassical **Chicago City Hall–Cook County Building** ⑬, where the city's legislators shout each other down.

Continue north on Clark Street for one block and turn right on Randolph Street. In the past few years, Chicago has revitalized its theater district, with many historic Loop theaters restored to their original ornate grandeur. Walk east on Randolph to State Street. Note the markers tagged CHICAGO'S THEATRE DISTRICT, embedded in the sidewalk pavement. On State Street, just north of Randolph Street, is the ornate, 1921 Beaux Arts **Chicago Theatre,** a former movie palace that now hosts live performances. Next door at 177 N. State Street is the 1872 **Page Brothers Building,** one of only two buildings in Chicago known to have a cast-iron facade. The handsome building directly across State Street, formerly the State-Lake Theatre, houses WLS-TV, Chicago's ABC affiliate. Turn back and head south along State Street. At the southwest corner of State and Randolph is the **Gene Siskel Film Center,** as well as the School of the Art Institute's residence hall. Turn right onto Randolph Street. Just west is the **Ford Center for the Performing Arts–Oriental Theatre,** with its long, glitzy neon sign that rivals the Chicago Theatre's world-famous marquee. On Dearborn Street, just north of Randolph Street, admire the **Goodman Theatre,** a state-of-the-art complex wrapped in the 1923 art deco facades of the Harris & Selwyn theaters.

Continue west on Randolph to reach the much-discussed **James R. Thompson Center** ⑭, a predominantly glass, red-white-and-blue government building that has been likened to a spaceship. The fiberglass sculpture in the Center's plaza is Jean Dubuffet's *Monument with Standing Beast.* Walk one block west on Randolph Street to see one more theater, the **Cadillac Palace Theatre.** Though the 1926 vaudeville theater has been modernized, its elegant marble lobby remains.

Keep walking west on Randolph Street, turn right on Franklin Street and walk two blocks north to Wacker Drive. Cross Wacker Drive and turn left before the river to get a good view of the graceful, curving, green-glass **333 W. Wacker Drive** ⑮. Follow the bend of Wacker Drive three blocks south to the art deco **Civic Opera House** ⑯, where Chicago's Lyric Opera gives its performances. Cross Madison Street to the pale-grape-color twin towers of the **Chicago Mercantile Exchange** ⑰, where action on the trading floors is frenetic.

Turn east on Monroe Street and walk about five blocks. The sunken, bi-level **Bank One Plaza** ⑱ has room to rest in the shadow of the sweeping Bank One building that curves skyward in the shape of the letter "A." The Chagall mosaic, *The Four Seasons,* is at the northeast end of the plaza. From the plaza, glance across Dearborn Street to the turquoise-tinted **Inland Steel Building** ⑲.

Leave the plaza by turning right onto Madison Street, walk one block east and then turn right on State Street to see some classic older buildings. On the left side of the street is the department store **Carson Pirie Scott** ⑳, an outstanding example of Louis Sullivan's work. The **Palmer House Hilton** ㉑, one of Chicago's grand old hotels, is one block south of Carson's, between State and Wabash streets; enter from Monroe Street.

TIMING

At a leisurely pace, figure two hours for this walk, not including any State Street shopping. That will give you enough time to study the diversity of the architecture and not only to enjoy, but also to try to decipher some of the outdoor sculptures. It will take at least an extra hour to see the Off the Beaten Track sites across the river and at least another hour for the Museum of Holography.

Sights to See

⑤ Aon Center. This stark, soaring skyscraper, with its strong vertical lines, shoots up over Millennium Park and the Chicago skyline. It would have stood out even more, according to original plans that clad the 80-story shaft in glossy white marble from the same quarry Michelangelo used. Unfortunately, the thin slabs of marble, unable to withstand Chicago's harsh climate, began to warp and fall off soon after the building was completed. The marble was replaced with light-color granite. The building's massive presence is best viewed from a distance. It sits on a handsome (if rather sterile) plaza, and Harry Bertoia's wind-chime sculpture in the reflecting pool makes interesting sounds when the wind blows. ⊠ *200 E. Randolph Dr., Loop.*

⑱ Bank One Plaza. When you stand against the side of the Bank One building, the sloping structure looks like it hangs over your head. The inward-curving shape results from sound planning: more floor space is needed at the street levels for commercial banking facilities, but tenant office space at higher levels requires less floor area. Musicians and dancers perform in the plaza in summer, and picnickers and sunbathers hang out, too. Like the Daley Center and Federal Center plazas, this area fronts on Dearborn Street and gives the street a more open feeling than many urban canyons. In any season you can visit the 70-ft-long Chagall mosaic *The Four Seasons* (1974) at the northeast end of the plaza. It is said that when Chagall arrived in Chicago to install the mosaic, he found it a more vigorous city than he had remembered, and he immediately modified the work to reflect the stronger and more vital elements he found around him. ⊠ *Bounded by Dearborn, Clark, Monroe, and Madison Sts., Loop.*

① Carbide and Carbon Building. A deep-green terra-cotta tower and a sleek gold-and-black exterior accented by curving, almost lacy brass work mark this significant art deco building, designed in 1929 by the Burnham Brothers, sons of city planner Daniel H. Burnham. Inside, the lobby is splendid, with bronze trim, glass ornamentation, and black marble. ⊠ *230 N. Michigan Ave., Loop.*

⑳ Carson Pirie Scott. Extraordinary cast-iron swirls and curls, as well as flower and leaf motifs, adorn the cylindrical entrance to this large department store. Look for the letters "LHS" in the rotunda ornamentation, initials of Louis H. Sullivan, the architect of the original 1899 building and one of its later expansions. The building is also a prime example of the "Chicago window," typical of the so-called Chicago School of architects: a large, fixed central pane with smaller movable windows on each side. The picture windows let in light, and the small double-hung windows let in the Lake Michigan breeze. Sullivan thought display windows were like pictures and merited elaborate frames, thus the ornamental patterns surrounding them. ⊠ *1 S. State St., Loop,* ☎ *312/641–7000.*

② Chicago Athenaeum. Good design can be evidenced in products ranging from a toaster to a television. This small museum, founded in 1988, has a big scope: to examine international art, architecture, and design with an emphasis on industrial design objects, as well as graphic design, product design, and urban planning. The exhibits present everyday products—from a cell phone to a coat rack to a couch—in a different light. Each year, the museum hosts the Good Design Awards, which recognize and display the work of design luminaries from some 50 countries. Its Good Design store sells many distinctive, high-design objects. You can also try the Schaumburg office (☎ 847/895–3950). ⊠ *307 N. Michigan, Loop,* ☎ *312/372–1083,* WEB *www.chi-athenaeum. org.* ⊡ *$3.* ☉ *Mon.–Sat. 9–7, Sun. 10–5.*

⑬ **Chicago City Hall–Cook County Building.** The heavy Corinthian columns of this stately 1911 building stand in sharp contrast to the high-rising Daley Center across the street. Inside are spacious halls, plenty of marble, and lots of hot air—as this is where the Chicago City Council holds its infamous meetings. City council meetings are open to the public; call for times. ⊠ *121 N. LaSalle St., Loop,* ☎ *312/744–3081.*

★ ⑥ **Chicago Cultural Center.** Elegant, ornamental details abound in this building, including sparkling mosaic tiles, sculptured ceilings, inscribed literary quotations, and a sweeping white Carrara marble staircase. The beautiful Preston Bradley Hall, on the third floor, has the world's largest Tiffany stained-glass dome. Another magnificent stained-glass dome is on the second floor in the GAR rotunda. The Randolph Street and Washington Street sides have different characters, because in 1897 the structure was built to meet two needs: to serve as the city's central library and as home of the Grand Army of the Republic museum. The Cultural Center houses splendid public spaces, with acclaimed free concerts and performances of all kinds, including live music every weekday at 1 in the Randolph Cafe, exhibitions, family programming, and a **Chicago Office of Tourism Visitor Information Center** near the Randolph Street entrance. The **Museum of Broadcast Communications,** also housed here, displays TV and radio exhibits and has a large archive of programs and commercials. Building tours are offered Tuesday–Saturday at 1:15 PM. ⊠ *78 E. Washington St., Loop,* ☎ *312/346–3278,* WEB *www.cityofchicago.org/Tourism/CulturalCenter.* ☼ *Mon.–Wed. 10–7, Thurs. 10–9, Fri. 10–6, Sat. 10–5, Sun. 11–5.*

⑰ **Chicago Mercantile Exchange.** Traders exhibit an endless display of creative hand and body movements as they negotiate for the purchase and sale of billions in pork-belly futures (these relate to the supermarket price of bacon), soybeans, currency rates, and other commodities on national and international markets. The upper visitor gallery, on the eighth floor, overlooks currency and interest-rate-product trading, while the fourth-floor gallery overlooks agricultural and index-product trading. At press time, both galleries were closed to the public due to increased security measures. Call or check the Web site for updated information. ⊠ *10 and 30 S. Wacker Dr., Loop,* ☎ *312/930–8249,* WEB *www.cme.com.*

NEED A BREAK? **Rebecca's Cafe** (⊠ 10 S. Wacker Dr., Loop, ☎ 312/993–3500), on the first floor of the Chicago Mercantile Exchange, serves up specialties that include Mediterranean grilled chicken and roasted Portobello sandwiches.

⑫ **Chicago Temple.** The Gothic-inspired headquarters of the First United Methodist Church of Chicago is the world's tallest church. Built in 1923 by Holabird and Roche, it has a first-floor sanctuary, 21 floors of office space, a sky-high chapel, and an eight-story spire (best viewed from the bridge across the Chicago River at Dearborn Street). Outside, along the building's east wall at ground level, several stained-glass windows relate the history of the church in Chicago. Joan Miró's sculpture *Chicago* (1981) is in the small plaza just east of the church. ⊠ *77 W. Washington St., Loop.*

OFF THE BEATEN PATH ★ **CITICORP CENTER** – Across the Chicago River from the Civic Opera House, the functions of commuter train station and office building unite in one stunning structure. The center combines a boxlike office tower with glass half-cylinders piled one atop the other at the lower levels. Broad contrasting horizontal and vertical bands of mirrored and smoked glass alternate up the building for a ribbon effect that is reminiscent of a similar theme—by the same architects, Murphy/Jahn—at the James R. Thompson Center. Inside, the marble floors and exposed girders, painted a soft greenish blue, remind you of the grand old railroad stations in this country and in Europe. The gates to the tracks, elevated above street level to allow traffic to proceed east and west via underpasses, are reached by going up one level and heading to the north end of the building. Go up another flight for a view looking northward out over the tracks; at this level you'll also find the entrance to the building's office spaces.

Look two blocks west to the chunky-looking **Social Security Building.** Claes Oldenburg's jokey pop-art sculpture *Batcolumn*, a 100-ft-high baseball bat, erupts from its plaza. ✉ *500 W. Madison St., Near West Side.*

⑯ Civic Opera House. The handsome Art Nouveau and art deco home of the Lyric Opera is grand indeed, with pink and gray Tennessee marble floors, pillars with carved capitals, crystal chandeliers, and a sweeping staircase to the second floor. The Opera House opened six days after the 1929 stock-market crash, shortly preceding the financial ruin of the building's visionary, Samuel Insull, a utilities magnate and manipulator. In addition to the 3,500-seat theater, the building also houses commercial office space. Lyric Opera performances sell out every year, but the hopeful may be able to purchase returned tickets. ✉ *20 N. Wacker Dr., Loop,* ☎ *312/372–7800 Civic Opera House; 312/332–2244 Lyric Opera.*

★ ⑪ Daley Center. Named for the late mayor Richard J. Daley, the father of the current holder of the office, this boldly plain high-rise is the headquarters of the Cook County court system, but it also draws visitors' attention because of what stands outside: a sculpture by Picasso. Known simply as **"The Picasso,"** it provoked an outcry when it was installed in 1967. Speculation about what it is meant to represent (knowledgeable observers say it is the head of a woman, especially when viewed in profile; others have suggested it is an Afghan dog) has diminished but not ended. Still, the sculpture has become a recognized symbol of the city. The building was constructed in 1965 of a steel known as Cor-Ten, which was developed as a medium that would weather naturally and attractively to a bronzed color; the Picasso is made of the same material. In summer, the building's plaza is the site of concerts, political rallies, dance presentations, and a weekly farmers' market (Thursday); in November, the city's official Christmas tree is erected here. ✉ *Bounded by Washington, Randolph, Dearborn, and Clark Sts., Loop,* WEB *www.ci.chi.il.us/tourism/Picasso.*

⑲ Inland Steel Building. This building can claim several "firsts" in this city of superlatives. Designed by Skidmore, Owings & Merrill in 1957, this classic skyscraper was the city's first fully air-conditioned building, and, more significantly, it was one of the first buildings to use supporting steel columns outside the glass-curtain wall, so office spaces are completely open. All the elevators, stairs, and service areas are in the taller structure behind the building proper. ✉ *30 W. Monroe St., Loop.*

★ ⑭ James R. Thompson Center. People either intensely like or dislike the center: former governor James Thompson, who selected the Helmut Jahn design for this state government building, hailed it in his dedication speech in 1985 as "the first building of the 21st century." Those who work here, and many other Chicagoans as well, have groaned in response, "I hope not!" The building's postmodern design presents multiple shapes and faces. Many features, such as the exposed elevator mechanics inside and the sections of the exterior wall that decrease in size as you near the intersection of Randolph and Dearborn streets, were meant to break down barriers between the government and the people. Instead of being red, white, and blue, the building has salmon, silver, and smoky blue hues. And, since many good government buildings are capped by a dome, the entire building, instead, is roughly shaped like a giant glass dome, with an enormous, 17-story atrium. All that glass, however, has made it a nightmare to cool and heat. The **Illinois Artisans Shop** (☎ 312/814–5321), on the second level, sells crafts and folk art by Illinois artists. The sculpture in the plaza is Jean Dubuffet's *Monument with Standing Beast.* It's nearly as controversial as the building itself. The curved shapes, in white with black traceries, have been compared to a pile of melting snow or to Snoopy in a blender. ✉ *100 W. Randolph St., Loop.*

⑧ Marshall Field's. The original site of Chicago's best-known department store holds some 500 departments to please all shoppers. Designed by D. H. Burnham & Co. and built between 1892 and 1907, the mammoth emporium has a spectacular Tiffany dome in the southwest corner above the cosmetics area near State and Washington streets. The building, with decorated columns and a spacious interior, has a classic turn-of-the-20th-century charm—except for a modern escalator atrium in the middle. Field's is a great place for a meal or a snack; for the former, check out the grand Walnut Room on the seventh floor (especially around Christmas); for the latter try the "7 on State" dining area on the seventh floor or Hinky Dink Kenna's in the basement. Don't miss the landmark clock outside the entrance at State and Randolph streets. ✉ *111 N. State St., Loop,* ☎ *312/781–1000.*

★ ❹ Millennium Park. Largely built on top of a former rail yard, the approximately 24½-acre Millennium Park, at the northwest corner of Grant Park, is in the process of turning an eyesore into another of the city's jewels. Only the McCormick Tribune Ice Rink has been completed, but renowned architect Frank Gehry's stunning music pavilion will be the showstopper here. Its design will incorporate dramatic ribbons of stainless steel that look like petals wrapping the stage. The sound system is suspended by a trellis that spans the great lawn, promising to give concert-hall sound in the great outdoors.

The pavilion, which replaces Grant Park's Petrillo band shell, will host the Grant Park Music Festival—a free classical music series—as well as the city's popular free summer concerts, including the jam-packed blues fest and jazz fest. The high-tech, sand-based lawn is designed to handle the hordes and shed rain quickly. Another good addition is the indoor 1,500-seat Music and Dance Theater Chicago, a long-needed space for midsize performing-arts companies. Soon to grace the park between Washington and Madison streets is Anish Kapoor's 60-ft-long, 30-ft-high elliptical sculpture of gleaming seamless polished steel, which has been likened to a giant jelly bean. Park plans also include a 2½-acre garden and a 400-space indoor bicycle parking facility. ✉ *Bounded by Michigan Ave., Columbus Dr., Randolph Dr., and Monroe St., Loop.*

☝ ❼ Museum of Broadcast Communications. Relive great moments in radio and television or watch or listen to your favorite hit shows from the past. The museum, which includes the Radio Hall of Fame, educates and entertains with unique, hands-on exhibits, broadcasting memorabilia, and an extensive public archives collection of more than 75,000 hours of television and radio programs and commercials. In the MBC Television Center, you can don anchor jackets, read from teleprompters, and anchor your own newscast—with a professional-quality videotape to prove it (the first tape costs $21.70, including tax; additional tapes cost $10.06, including tax). The museum is housed in the Chicago Cultural Center. ☒ *78 E. Washington St., Loop,* ☏ *312/629–6000,* WEB *www.museum.tv.* ☒ *Free.* ☉ *Mon.–Sat. 10–4:30, Sun. noon–5. Archives closed Sun.*

OFF THE
BEATEN PATH

MUSEUM OF HOLOGRAPHY – Though holography is a technical science that has furthered advances in medicine and engineering, the temptation to reach out and touch elusive, three-dimensional pictures escapes no one. Permanent exhibits delve into medicine and mathematics at this offbeat museum, located just one block west of Oprah Winfrey's Harpo Studios. ☒ *1134 W. Washington Blvd., Near West Side,* ☏ *312/226–1007,* WEB *www.holographiccenter.com.* ☒ *$4.* ☉ *Wed.–Sun. 12:30–4:30.*

㉑ **Palmer House Hilton.** Patterned marble floors and antique lighting fixtures adorn the ground-floor-level arcade of this bustling, beautiful old hotel. The original Palmer House was built in 1871 on Quincy and State. It burned down two weeks later during the Chicago fire. The second, a state-of-the-art structure at the present location, the first hotel to have electricity and elevators, was built in 1873. The current structure, a Holabird and Roche creation, dates from 1927. In the arcade are shops, restaurants, and service establishments. However, it's the lobby—up one flight of stairs—that you must see: richly carpeted, outfitted with fine furniture, and lavishly decorated (look at the ceiling murals), this room is one of the few remaining examples of the opulent elegance that was once de rigueur in Chicago's fine hotels. ☒ *17 E. Monroe St., Loop,* ☏ *312/726–7500.*

★ ⑩ **Reliance Building.** This structure, with large, airy expanses of glass, is now the **Hotel Burnham,** a boutique hotel that takes advantage of the building's architectural legacy. Completed in 1895 by D. H. Burnham & Co., the building ushered in a new era as a precursor of the modern skyscraper. The flat and projecting bays of windows are the best early example of the Chicago window, in which a picture window is flanked by narrow double-hung windows. Cream-color glazed terracotta graces the facade. The elevator lobby takes ornamentation to new heights with ornate metal elevator grilles and stairwell railings, Italian marble walls, and a mosaic floor modeled after the original. ☒ *1 W. Washington St., Loop.*

❸ **Smurfit-Stone Building.** Some wags have said this shaft, with its diamond-shape sliced-off top, looks like a giant pencil sharpener. The diagonal top slices through 10 floors of this 1984 building. The painted aluminum sculpture in the plaza that looks like someone folded it is Yaacov Agam's *Communication X9.* You'll see different patterns, depending on the angle from which you view the sculpture. ☒ *150 N. Michigan Ave., Loop.*

❾ **State Street.** "On State Street, that great street," as Frank Sinatra once sang, lies Chicago's older shopping district, which is being revitalized, albeit slowly. State Street wasn't so great after the city spent $17.2 million in 1979 to turn it into a pedestrian mall in an attempt to attract shoppers. The dreary area failed, and city planners found out that if suburbanites couldn't drive there, they wouldn't come. As a result, in 1996 the city spent more money—$24.5 million this time—to "de-mall" nine blocks of the famous street from Wacker Drive on the north to Congress Parkway on the south, allowing auto traffic to return. They widened streets, added trees and shrubs, and installed old-fashioned streetlights and subway kiosks with a 1920s look. The firm Skidmore, Owings & Merrill oversaw the makeover. ☒ *Loop.*

★ ⑮ **333 W. Wacker Drive.** The green-glass skin of this striking building mirrors the Chicago River (often a lovely shade of green, and not just on St. Patrick's Day), and its graceful, curved facade mimics the river's bend. It also reflects the grandeur of the Merchandise Mart, on the opposite bank of the river. The dark-green marble and black granite octagonal entrance columns are inspired by the towers on the Mart. On the building's south side, the facade is sliced and notched to fit in with its grittier neighbors there. This 1983 Kohn Pedersen Fox design is roughly contemporary to the James R. Thompson Center but has had a much more positive public reception. ⊠ *333 W. Wacker Dr., Loop.*

South Loop

Numbers in the text correspond to numbers in the margin and on the Loop map.

A Good Walk

To get started in the South Loop, take a bus to the Art Institute of Chicago. From the north, you can take Bus 3, 145, 147, or 151. Coming from the south, you can take Bus 3, 6, 145, 146, 147, or 151. If you arrive by car, you can park it in the subterranean Grant Park North Garage, with an entrance south on Michigan Avenue. Most streets in the Loop prohibit parking weekdays from 6 AM–6 PM.

This walk will get you acquainted with the southern reaches of the Loop. It begins and ends at the imposing entrance of one of the world's most famous museums, the **Art Institute of Chicago** ㉒. The grand-looking **Symphony Center** ㉓, across the street and just south of the Art Institute, is home to the internationally acclaimed Chicago Symphony Orchestra.

Proceed west on Adams Street toward Dearborn Street where you will encounter the Old Chicago atmosphere at the **Berghoff Restaurant** ㉔, housed in a rare cast-iron fronted building. Now turn right on Dearborn to see the terra-cotta bas-relief exterior of the **Marquette Building** ㉕. Take a peek inside to examine the sparkling mosaics in the rotunda lobby. Across the street, the new **Dearborn Center**, which is scheduled for completion in September 2003, is designed in two halves, with a 37-story office tower facing Dearborn Street and an 11-story office and retail space facing State Street. On the southwest corner of Dearborn and Monroe streets, the modern **Xerox Centre** has an unusual wraparound aluminum-and-glass wall, with larger windows on the north side to let in more light.

Retrace your steps on Dearborn to **Federal Center and Plaza** ㉖. On the right-hand side of the street is the 42-story Kluczynski Building; across the street to the east is the similar 30-story Dirksen Building. Both are part of a complex designed by Mies van der Rohe. Alexander Calder's *Flamingo*, a red mobilelike sculpture, sits in the plaza.

Travel west on Adams to LaSalle to see the beautiful **Rookery** ㉗, an imposing red-stone building that is one of the city's 19th-century showpieces; make sure to see the Frank Lloyd Wright lobby. Diagonally across from the Rookery is Phillip Johnson's **190 S. LaSalle** ㉘, with striking gold-leaf ceilings. Across Quincy Street is the massive **Federal Reserve Bank** ㉙ and its twin, Bank of America. The Corinthian capitals on the Federal Reserve Bank show that it outranks its neighbor, which used to be called the Illinois Merchants Bank Building. Continue south along LaSalle Street to Jackson Boulevard, where the street seems to disappear in front of the commanding **Chicago Board of Trade** ㉚, which sits like a throne reigning over the financial district.

Take a left on Jackson Boulevard, continuing west to the hulking, 110-story **Sears Tower** ㉛, where the 103rd-floor Skydeck provides grand views. Across Jackson Boulevard from the Sears Tower is **311 South Wacker Drive** ㉜, with a spectacular atrium and a castlelike top. Take a left on Van Buren and walk east to **One Financial Place** ㉝, where the Chicago Board Options Exchange and the Chicago Stock Exchange are located.

Walk back to Van Buren Street and turn right, heading east. Just past Clark Street, the odd, triangular, poured-concrete building looming up on your right-hand side is the **Metropolitan Correctional Center** ㉞, the high-rise jail with 5-inch windows that look like slits in the concrete. The massive, darkly handsome **Monadnock Building** ㉟ is on the north side of the street, a little farther east. Enter on Van Buren Street, and walk through the corridor to see its vintage light fixtures at the north end. On the northeast corner of Van Buren and Dearborn streets, Daniel Burnham's beautifully ornamented **Fisher Building**, has become luxury rental apartments.

Walk east to Plymouth Court, take a right and head south to Congress Parkway. The **Harold Washington Library Center** ㊱, a postmodern homage to classical-style public buildings, takes up the entire block. Cross the street to get a better view, then head east on Congress Parkway toward Michigan Avenue.

The massive granite-sheathed structure on the north side of the street houses the **Auditorium Theatre** ㊲. Take a left at Michigan Avenue and walk past the **Fine Arts Building** ㊳, an atmospheric edifice that has long housed artists and musicians. Continue walking and notice the Railway Exchange Building, better known as the **Santa Fe Building** ㊴ because of the rooftop SANTA FE sign. It is right next door to Symphony Center and across the street from the Art Institute and completes the circle of the South Loop.

TIMING

Allow about three hours for this walk, including a visit to the Sears Skydeck. If you plan to explore the Art Institute at this time, add another two hours. If possible, do the walk on a weekday, when the Loop is bustling and the lobbies of office buildings are open. If you want to explore the Off the Beaten Track destinations—Union Station and Old St. Patrick's Church—figure in another hour.

Sights to See

★ ☺ ㉒ **Art Institute of Chicago.** Some of the world's most famous paintings are housed in this museum, including an incredibly strong collection of Impressionist and post-Impressionist paintings, with seminal works by Monet, Renoir, Gauguin, and van Gogh, among others. Some of these images are so familiar in popular culture, that when you see the originals at the museum, it's like meeting a dear pen pal face-to-face for the first time. A few of the museum's best-known paintings in the permanent collection are Grant Wood's *American Gothic,* Edward Hopper's *Nighthawks,* Pablo Picasso's *The Old Guitarist,* and Georges Seurat's *A Sunday Afternoon on La Grande Jatte–1884.*

The museum also has impressive collections of medieval, Renaissance, and modern art. Less well-known are its fine holdings in Asian art and photography. Be sure to visit the Rubloff paperweight collection; a Chicago real-estate magnate donated these shimmering, multicolor objects. The Thorne Miniature Rooms show interior decoration in every historical style; they'll entrance anyone who's ever furnished a dollhouse or built a model. And don't miss the Stock Exchange Room, a splendid reconstruction of the trading floor of the old Chicago Stock

Exchange, which was demolished in 1972. The Daniel F. and Ada L. Rice Building has three floors of exhibition galleries, a large space for temporary exhibitions, and a skylighted central court dotted with sculpture and plantings. The Galleries of Contemporary Art showcase post–WWII era paintings, sculptures, and videos. The museum store has an outstanding collection of art books, calendars, and merchandise related to current exhibits, as well as gift items.

The two lion statues flanking the museum's main entrance are probably the most well-known, and photographed, in the world. And the museum capitalizes on that fact, festooning the mighty creatures with wreaths at Christmas and Chicago Bears helmets when the football team is on a winning streak. The lions have been here ever since 1893 when the institute's main building was constructed for the Columbian Exposition by Shepley, Rutan, and Coolidge.

A map of the museum, available at the information desk, will help you find your way to the works or periods you want to visit. Especially helpful for first-time visitors is the 45-minute Introduction to the Collections tour, Tuesday and Saturday at 2. If you have a youngster with you, make an early stop at the **Kraft Education Center** downstairs. Your child can choose from an assortment of 25 or so gallery games, some of which come with picture postcards. The delightful and informative games will keep children from becoming hopelessly bored as you tramp through the galleries. ⊠ *111 S. Michigan Ave., Loop,* ☎ *312/443–3600,* WEB *www.artic.edu.* ⊡ *$10, free Tues.* ☉ *Mon., Wed.–Fri. 10:30–4:30; Tues. 10:30–8; weekends 10–5.*

㊲ **Auditorium Theatre.** One of the city's architectural and cultural landmarks, this glorious Dankmar Adler and Louis Sullivan building has stunning ornamentation in plaster, wood, cast iron, art glass, and mosaics. The structure—built in 1889 to house a hotel, theater, and office space—was used as a Servicemen's Center during World War II (there was a bowling alley on the stage). The breathtaking lobby facing Michigan Avenue has marble wainscoting, a truly grand staircase, and arched rows of lights along the ceiling. Another beautiful (though less well-known) space is the barrel-vaulted library on the 10th floor of the building, originally the hotel's dining room. The theater seats 4,000 people and has unobstructed sight lines and near-perfect acoustics. Though the theater is normally closed to the public unless there's a show or concert, you can call to arrange a one-hour tour. The building is occupied by Roosevelt University, which is fighting with the Auditorium Theatre Council about who has control over the theater. ⊠ *50 E. Congress Pkwy., Loop,* ☎ *312/922–2110; 312/431–2354 tour information;* WEB *www.auditoriumtheatre.org.* ⊡ *Tour $5.*

㉔ **The Berghoff.** Only two buildings in Chicago are known to have cast-iron facades: this building, constructed in 1872; and the Page Brothers Building on State Street, built in the same year. The practice of using iron panels cast to imitate stone was common in the latter part of the 19th century, but it fell out of favor after the Great Chicago Fire when the iron melted in the heat, bringing down structures with it. Another interesting historical fact: the Berghoff is proud owner of the city's liquor license No. 1. This German restaurant is a longtime city favorite. ⊠ *17 W. Adams St., Loop,* ☎ *312/427–3170,* WEB *www.berghoff.com.*

★ ㉚ **Chicago Board of Trade.** Atop this art deco building at the foot of LaSalle Street is a gilded statue of Ceres, the Roman goddess of agriculture, an apt overseer of the frenetic commodities and financial trading that goes on within. In the pits, traders make deals for corn, wheat, soybeans, soybean meal and oil, futures on the Dow Jones Industrial

Index and on U.S. Treasury Bonds. The building was designed in 1930 by Holabird and Root and—along with the Civic Opera House and the Carbide and Carbon Building—is the city's most significant example of the art deco style. A sleek three-story lobby with dramatic lighting is finished in several types of contrasting marble. The use of light and dark marbles and rectilinear designs leaves a powerful impression. A 24-story glass-and-steel addition, facing south, was completed in 1980. There are two galleries overlooking the agricultural and the financial trading floors, but both were closed to the public at press time due to heightened security measures. Call or check the Web site for updated information. ⊠ *141 W. Jackson Blvd., Loop,* ☎ *312/435–3590,* WEB *www.cbot.com.*

㉖ Federal Center and Plaza. The Kluczynski and Dirksen federal buildings, both designed by Mies van der Rohe in 1964, are classic examples of his trademark glass-and-steel boxes. His attention to order and structural detail is astounding: the lines in the plaza pavement line up perfectly with the steel beams in the buildings. In the plaza you can't miss Alexander Calder's *Flamingo,* an arching red stabile (a sculpture that looks like a mobile), which flagrantly contrasts the disciplined matte-black buildings around it. The piece was dedicated on the same day in 1974 as Calder's *Universe* at the Sears Tower. It is said that Calder had a grand day, riding through Chicago in a brightly colored circus bandwagon accompanied by calliopes, as he headed from one dedication to the other. ⊠ *Dirksen: 219 S. Dearborn St., Loop; Kluczynski: 230 S. Dearborn St., Loop.*

㉙ Federal Reserve Bank. Though they don't hand out money here, they sure do handle a lot of the green stuff. The facility processes currency and checks, scanning bills for counterfeit, destroying unfit currency, and repackaging fit currency. A visitor center in the lobby has permanent exhibits of old bills, counterfeit money, and a million dollars in $1 bills. One-hour tours explain how money travels and show a high-speed currency-processing machine. Call two months in advance for tour reservations, since it's often booked in spring and fall with school groups. ⊠ *230 S. LaSalle St., Loop,* ☎ *312/322–2400,* WEB *www.chicagofed.org.* 🎦 *Free.*

㊳ Fine Arts Building. This fascinating, creaky old building was constructed in 1895 to house the showrooms of the Studebaker Company, then makers of carriages and later automobiles. It still evokes a time long past. Publishers, artists, and sculptors have used its spaces; today the principal tenants are professional musicians and those who cater to musicians' needs. Notice first the handsome exterior details; then step inside to see the marble and the woodwork in the lobby. The motto engraved in the marble as you enter says, ALL PASSES—ART ALONE ENDURES. The building has an interior courtyard, across which strains of piano music and soprano voices compete with tenors as they run through exercises and arias. ⊠ *410 S. Michigan Ave., Loop,* ☎ *312/427–7602.*

★ 🖑 **㊱ Harold Washington Library Center.** The country's largest public library, an imposing granite and brick structure, is part of the Chicago Public Library system. It is a unique postmodern homage to Chicago's great architecture legacy, with exterior elements that pay tribute to other Chicago structures. The shape and scale of the library recalls Daniel Burnham's 1909 Plan of Chicago; the heavy rusticated ground level recalls the Rookery; the stepped-back arched windows are a reference to the Auditorium Theatre; the swirling terra-cotta design is from the Marquette Building; the large roof acroteria and pediments are an exaggeration of the Art Institute's roof; the glass curtain wall on the west side is a nod to 1950s modernism. The building has some of the most spectacular terra-cotta work seen in Chicago since the 19th century: ears of corn, faces with puffed cheeks (representing the Windy City), and the logo of the Chicago Public Library are a few of the building's embellishments. In its final stages of construction, the library looked so much like the vintage skyscrapers around it was often mistaken for a renovation project. The library was named for the first African-American mayor of Chicago, and the primary architect was Thomas Beeby, of the Chicago firm Hammond, Beeby and Babka.

The center's holdings include the Chicago Blues Archives, the Jazz/Blues/Gospel Hall of Fame, and the Balaban and Katz Theater Orchestra Collection, all available for reference use. The excellent **children's library** on the second floor, an 18,000-square-ft haven, has vibrant wall-mounted figures by Chicago imagist Karl Wirsum. Works by noted Chicago artists are displayed along a second-floor walkway above the main lobby. There is also an impressive Winter Garden with skylights on the ninth floor used for special events. Free programs and performances are offered regularly at the center. ⊠ *400 S. State St., Loop,* ☎ *312/747–4300,* WEB *www.chipublib.org.* ⏰ *Mon. 9–7, Tues. and Thurs. 11–7, Wed. and Fri.–Sat. 9–5, Sun. 1–5. Tours Mon.–Sat. at noon and 2, Sun. at 2.*

㉕ **Marquette Building.** The lobby of this 1894 Holabird and Roche–designed building is an amazing little gem, with rich Tiffany glass mosaics depicting scenes from the journal of priest Jacques Marquette, an early explorer of the Illinois Country, for whom the building is named. In every corner of the lobby, it seems, there are details that illustrate Marquette's trek. Bronze panels tell the story of his expedition, and brass reliefs over the elevators depict French explorers and important Native American chiefs of the time. The building is a clear example of the Chicago style, with a steel skeleton, decorative terra-cotta ornament, two light wells, and recessed spandrels framing wide Chicago windows. ⊠ *140 S. Dearborn St., Loop.*

㉞ **Metropolitan Correctional Center.** This 27-story triangular high-rise, erected in 1975, is the holding area for those awaiting trial as well as convicted felons awaiting transfer to penitentiaries. The building was designed by Harry Weese, who later echoed the triangular form with his 1989 Swissôtel Chicago. The structure's shape allows jail cells to be centered around a loungelike common area on each floor. With its long slit windows (5 inches wide), the jail looks like a postmodern reconstruction of a medieval fort. You can sometimes see inmates in orange jumpsuits on the rooftop basketball and volleyball court that's covered in wire mesh. ⊠ *71 W. Van Buren St., Loop.*

★ ㉟ **Monadnock Building.** This huge, imposing 16-story structure is the tallest building ever constructed with weight-bearing walls. Burnham and Root built the northern section in 1891; the southern half, which has some vertical steel supports in the outer walls, was the work of Holabird and Roche in 1893. The problem with all-masonry buildings is that the higher they go, the thicker the base's walls must be to support the upper stories; the Monadnock's walls at the base are 6 ft thick. Look at the unornamented windows to see the wall's depth. The building has been tastefully renovated inside, with the original wrought-iron banisters and a freestanding staircase that spirals down from the 16th floor to the lobby. ⊠ *53 W. Jackson Blvd., Loop.*

NEED A
BREAK?   In the Monadnock Building, discover a lunchtime hideaway where everyone seems to know your name. **Cavanaugh's** (⊠ 53 W. Jackson Blvd., Loop, ☎ 312/939–3125) green and white awnings welcome

you in from the alley. Once inside, grab a green leather bar stool, grasp a beer and burger, gab on your cell and feel right at home.

OFF THE
BEATEN PATH
OLD ST. PATRICK'S CHURCH – Chicago's oldest church, built from 1852 to 1856, withstood the great fire of 1871. Just west of Union Station and the Loop redevelopment area, the church towers, one Romanesque- and one Byzantine-style, are symbolic of West and East. Tours are available by appointment. This house of worship is just off the I–90/94 Kennedy Expressway—drive by it too quickly, and you'll miss the statue of Jesus who watches over poor souls stuck in rush-hour traffic. Exit at Monroe Street, head east a block, and turn right onto Des Plaines Street to reach it. Or, from the Loop, head west down Adams Street. ⊠ *700 W. Adams St., Near West Side,* ☎ *312/648–1021.*

33 **One Financial Place.** Rushing traffic on the Congress Parkway–Eisenhower Expressway flows right under an arched section of this 1985 building by Skidmore, Owings & Merrill. The two windows straddling the highway light the fitness area of **LaSalle Club,** which offers hotel accommodations to the public and health club and dining facilities to members. One Financial Place also houses the **Chicago Board Options Exchange,** which is the largest securities options exchange in the world; the **Chicago Stock Exchange,** which trades equity stocks; and the superb **Everest** restaurant. Both exchanges have visitor galleries that explain the history of the exchanges and overlook the trading floors, but they were closed to the public at press time due to heightened security measures. Call or check the Web site for more updated information. ⊠ *440 S. LaSalle St., Loop,* ☎ *312/663–2980 CBOE; 312/663–2980 CSE.* ⊠ *Free.* ☉ *CBOE: weekdays 8:30–3:15; CSE: weekdays 8:30–3:30.*

28 **190 S. LaSalle.** This 40-story Postmodern office building was designed by John Burgee and Phillip Johnson in the mid-1980s. The grand, gold-leaf vaulted lobby is spectacular. ⊠ *Loop.*

★ **27** **Rookery.** Called the Rookery for the crowlike birds that used to nest here, as well as for politicians who had a reputation of "rooking" or swindling, this building was designed by Burnham and Root in 1885 using both masonry and the more modern steel-frame construction. The bird motif is incorporated into the building's exterior, with rooks carved into the front arched entrance. Frank Lloyd Wright renovated the two-story lobby and light court in 1905, redoing the mezzanine stairway in white marble with intricate incising and gold-leaf gild, as well as adding custom light fixtures. In 1931, the skylight was tarred over, along with other detrimental alterations, but it has since been restored and recovered its resplendent grandeur. A cantilevered cast-iron staircase partially hangs over the west side of the lobby. The second-floor mezzanine has a charming walkway made out of glass block from an ashtray manufacturer. ⊠ *209 S. LaSalle St., Loop.*

39 **Santa Fe Building.** Also known as the Railway Exchange Building, this structure was designed in 1904 by Daniel Burnham, who later had his office here. Its rooftop SANTA FE sign was put up early in the 20th century by the Santa Fe Railroad, one of several railroads that had offices here when Chicago was the rail center of the country. ⊠ *224 S. Michigan Ave., Loop.*

★ ☪ **31** **Sears Tower.** In Chicago, size matters. This soaring 110-story skyscraper, designed by Skidmore, Owings & Merrill in 1974, was the world's tallest building until 1996 when the Petronas Towers in Kuala Lumpur, Malaysia, claimed the title. However, the folks at the Sears Tower are quick to point out that the Petronas Towers counts its spire as part of the building. But if you were to measure the 1,454-ft-high Sears Tower in terms of highest occupied floor, highest roof, or highest antenna, the Sears Tower would win hands down.

Those bragging rights aside, the **Skydeck** is really something to boast about. Enter on Jackson Boulevard to take the ear-popping ride to the 103rd-floor observatory. Video monitors turn the 70-second elevator ride into a fun-filled, thrilling trip. On a clear day you can see to Michigan, Wisconsin, and Indiana. (Check the visibility ratings at the security desk before you decide to ride up and take in the view.) At the top, interactive exhibits tell about Chicago's dreamers, schemers, architects, musicians, writers, and sports stars. Computer kiosks in six languages help international travelers key into Chicago hot spots. Knee-High Chicago, a 4-ft-high exhibit, should entertain the kids. The Sears Tower also has spruced up the lower level with a food court, new exhibits, and an interesting, eight-minute movie about the city. Security is very tight, so figure in a little extra time for your visit to the Skydeck. Before you leave, don't miss the spiraling Calder mobile sculpture *The Universe* in the ground-floor lobby on the Wacker Drive side. ⊠ *233 S. Wacker Dr., Loop,* ☎ *312/875–9696,* ᴡᴇʙ *www.theskydeck.com.* 🖃 *$9.50.* ☉ *May–Sept., daily 10–10; Oct.–Apr., daily 10–8.*

㉓ **Symphony Center.** Orchestra Hall, home to the acclaimed Chicago Symphony Orchestra, lies at the heart of this music center. The hall was built in 1904 under the supervision of architect Daniel Burnham, a logical choice for the job since he was a CSO trustee. The Georgian building has a symmetrical facade of pink brick with limestone quoins, lintels, and other decorative elements. Orchestra Hall has been beautifully restored and acoustically renovated. The larger entity of Symphony Center, which also includes rehearsal and performance space, Rhapsody restaurant, and administrative offices. Free backstage tours are available by appointment. ⊠ *220 S. Michigan Ave., Loop,* ☎ *312/294–3000.*

㉜ **311 South Wacker Drive.** The first of three towers intended for the site, this pale pink building was the work of Kohn Pedersen Fox, also designers of 333 West Wacker Drive, a few blocks north. The 1991 building's most distinctive feature is its White Castle–type crown, blindingly lighted at night. During migration season so many birds crashed into the illuminated tower that the building management was forced to tone down the lighting. The building has an inviting atrium, with palm trees and a splashy, romantic fountain. ⊠ *Loop.*

OFF THE BEATEN PATH
UNION STATION – A 10-story skylighted waiting room, Corinthian columns, and gilded statues grace a grand old station that was completed in 1925. Steep steps leading from Canal Street into the waiting area became the bumpy path for a baby carriage caught in a shoot-out in director Brian De Palma's 1987 film, *The Untouchables.* ⊠ *210 S. Canal St., Near West Side.*

DOWNTOWN SOUTH

The Downtown South area, bounded by Congress Parkway–Eisenhower Expressway on the north, Michigan Avenue on the east, Roosevelt Road on the south, and the Chicago River on the west, presents a striking and often fascinating contrast to the Loop. Once a thriving commercial area and the center of the printing trades in Chicago, it fell into disrepair as the printing industry moved to other areas in the city because of changing needs for space. Sleazy bars, pawnbrokers, and pornography shops filled the area behind what was then the Conrad

Hilton Hotel, crowding one another on Wabash Avenue and State Street and on the side streets between.

Toward the end of the 20th century, investors became interested in renovating the run-down yet sturdy loft and office buildings in the old printing district. In 1981 Michael Foley, a young restaurateur from an old Chicago restaurant family, opened a restaurant on the edge of the redevelopment area. The innovative cuisine at Printer's Row proved a success. Soon other restaurants, shops, and businesses moved in, and today the Printer's Row district is a thriving urban neighborhood enclave. In late May or early June the area attracts large crowds during the Printer's Row Book Fair, a weekend event. Dealers sell books and prints, craftspeople give demonstrations of papermaking and bookbinding, and noted authors appear as guest speakers.

At about the time that the first renovations were being undertaken in Printer's Row, a consortium of investors, aided by preferential interest rates from downtown banks, obtained a large parcel of land in the old railroad yards to the south and put up an expansive development. This was Dearborn Park, affordable housing targeted at young middle-class families. Since then, development has only spread, with town houses and condos revitalizing the area. Some have termed it a "lofts and latte" phenomenon, with coffee-swilling urbanites moving to the area for its cheaper housing prices and proximity to downtown.

To the west, the architect and developer Bertrand Goldberg (of Marina City fame) acquired a sizable tract of land between Wells Street and the Chicago River. Driven by a vision of an innovative, self-contained city within a city, Goldberg erected the futuristic River City, the massed, almost cloudlike complex that seems to rise from the river at Polk Street.

Spurred by signs of revitalization, the owners of the Conrad Hilton scrapped plans to abandon and even demolish the hotel and instead mounted a major renovation. A beautifully appointed hotel, the Hilton Chicago once again attracts the convention business it needs to fill its 1,543 rooms.

There are still gritty, undeveloped areas in Downtown South. But the entire area near South Side, as far south as 26th Street, is attracting more and more residents who like its ethnic and racial mix, its proximity to the Loop and great museums (the Field Museum, Adler Planetarium, and Shedd Aquarium), and its growing community feeling.

Numbers in the text correspond to numbers in the margin and on the Downtown South map.

A Good Walk

Begin at Congress Street and Columbus Drive. You can drive to this point—traffic and parking conditions are far less congested in the Downtown South area than they are in the Loop, though it still can be hard to find an on-street parking space—or you can take Bus 1, 3, 4, 6, or 146 from the north or from Hyde Park.

Start your walk with a splash at **Buckingham Fountain** ①, which is set in its own plaza near the lakefront. This romantic fountain's central jet shoots up to 150 ft and, blown by lake breezes, regularly cools off summertime visitors. Walk south (left) toward Balbo Drive. East of the intersection of Balbo Drive and Michigan Avenue is the heart of beautiful **Grant Park** ②, a lovely mix of gardens, tennis courts, and softball diamonds. From Grant Park you can see what appears as a cliff of buildings, old and new, lining Michigan Avenue. The once-grand **Blackstone Hotel** ③, on the northwest corner of Michigan Avenue and Balbo Drive, has seen better days. Behind the hotel, on Balbo Drive, is the **Merle Reskin Theatre**, another vintage building, where Broadway-bound shows were once booked. The theater is now owned and run by De-Paul University. Head north on Michigan Avenue (left) to the small **Spertus Museum** ④, with a permanent collection of Jewish art, a Holocaust memorial, themed temporary exhibits, and a hands-on children's museum. Continue to the southwest corner of Michigan Avenue and Harrison Street and check out Columbia College Chicago's **Museum of Contemporary Photography** ⑤.

Turn left on Harrison Street, and follow it about three blocks to Plymouth Court. Turn right and walk down Congress Parkway to Dearborn Street (left). You will see the **Hyatt on Printer's Row** ⑥, which occupies a group of interconnected renovated buildings; on the corner is the excellent **Prairie** restaurant. Continue walking down Dearborn Street to the **Pontiac Building** ⑦, an early skyscraper from 1891. The pioneering **Printer's Row** restaurant, on the northwest corner of Dearborn and Harrison streets, is a wonderful place for an elegant (and not inexpensive) lunch during the week.

When you reach Harrison Street, take a left. One short block later, turn left onto Federal Street in front of the massive, beige-gray brick apartment complex, **Printer's Square,** which joins together buildings designed in 1909, 1912, and 1928.

Retrace your steps back to Dearborn Street and turn right. On the east side is the rehabbed brick building, **Grace Place** ⑧, creatively adapted for use by four religious congregations. Down the block, the **Donohue Building** ⑨, another handsome commercial structure, houses condominiums. On the west side of the street, **Sandmeyer's Bookstore** ⑩ has a fine selection of books about Chicago. Next door, the grand old **Franklin Building** ⑪, originally THE FRANKLIN CO.: DESIGNING, ENGRAVING, ELEC-TROTYPING, as its sign says, is now condominium apartments.

In the historic **Dearborn Station** ⑫, at the foot of Dearborn Street, shops, offices, and an airy galleria have replaced the train station's waiting room. If you are interested in a short detour, River City is about a four-block walk west on Polk Street to Wells Street, but this area can be deserted, so be cautious. Apartments, all with curving exterior walls (making it a bit difficult to place square or rectangular furniture), ring the circumference of the building. To continue your walk from Dearborn Station, turn east on Polk Street (left) and head to Plymouth Court. At the intersection, turn right and head south into the northern reaches of **Dearborn Park** ⑬, a mix of high-rise, low-rise, and single-family units, some in red brick and some in white.

Continue down Plymouth Court to 9th Street and turn left. Walk two blocks to Wabash Avenue and turn left again. At the corner of Wabash Avenue and 8th Street is the club of blues great Buddy Guy, the aptly named **Buddy Guy's Legends**; you can hear Chicago's signature sound nightly. Turn right on 8th Street and, one block later, turn left on Michigan Avenue. Enter the **Hilton Chicago** ⑭ and stroll through the opulent lobby, complete with gilded horses flanking the walls.

TIMING

Allow about three hours to complete the walk. You could spend 45 minutes or more in the Spertus Museum, especially if you have children, who might enjoy the Rosenbaum ARTiFACT Center (open in the afternoon only). The area west of South Michigan Avenue tends to empty out on weekends and especially in the evenings, so it's best to visit during the daytime on weekdays. Be sure to exercise caution, as you would in any big city.

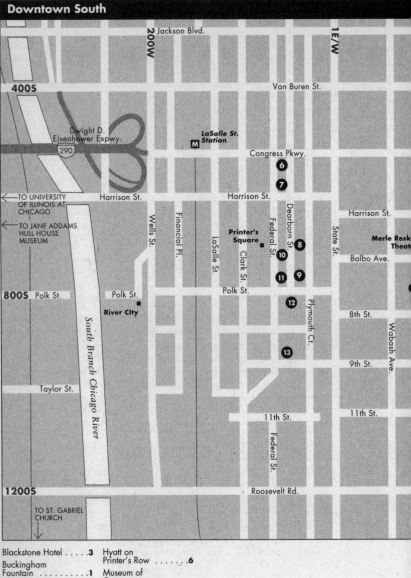

Downtown South

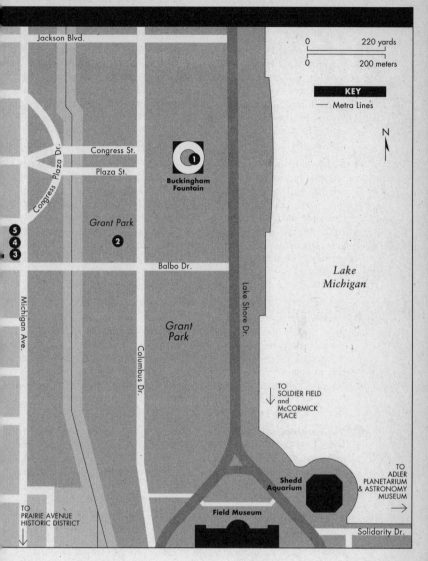

Jackson Blvd.

Congress Plaza Dr.

Congress St.

Plaza St.

Buckingham Fountain

①

Grant Park

②

⑤
④
③

Balbo Dr.

Michigan Ave.

Columbus Dr.

Grant Park

Lake Shore Dr.

Lake Michigan

TO
SOLDIER FIELD
and
McCORMICK
PLACE

TO
ADLER
PLANETARIUM
& ASTRONOMY
MUSEUM

Shedd Aquarium

Field Museum

Solidarity Dr.

TO
PRAIRIE AVENUE
HISTORIC DISTRICT

0   220 yards
0   200 meters

KEY
— Metra Lines

N

Sights to See

❸ Blackstone Hotel. An excellent example of modern Beaux-Arts architecture, the hotel has fallen on hard times. It was shut down in late 1999 for violating city building codes, but the owners say they have plans to open it back up. Designed by Marshall and Fox, the architects who also designed the Drake Hotel on Michigan Avenue, the 1910 Blackstone was once one of Chicago's most elegant hotels. Teddy Roosevelt, Jimmy Carter, and a string of presidents in between stayed here. It was also the site of the famous "smoke-filled rooms," now a political cliche, where Warren G. Harding was chosen as Republican nominee for president in 1920. ⊠ *636 S. Michigan Ave., Downtown South.*

❶ Buckingham Fountain. A centerpiece in Grant Park, this decorative, tiered fountain has intricate designs of pink marble seashells, water-spouting fish, and bronze sculptures of sea horses. It was patterned after a fountain at Versailles but is about twice as large as its model. Thanks to its size, the 25-ft-tall fountain can propel water 150 ft high and circulate 14,000 gallons a minute. Dedicated in 1927, the fountain was given to Chicago by philanthropist Kate Sturges Buckingham in memory of her brother Clarence. See it in all its glory between May 1 and October 1, when it's elaborately illuminated at night and sprays colorfully lighted waters. ⊠ *Grant Park between Columbus and Lake Shore Drs. east of Congress Plaza, Downtown South.*

❸ Dearborn Park. Begun in the 1970s on the site of abandoned rail yards in the South Loop, this planned neighborhood of high-rises, low-rises, town houses, and single-family homes has a tidy suburban look. Cul-de-sacs, parks, and landscaping, along with the absence of offices or entertainment complexes, add to the suburban effect. But make no mistake: the stunning view of the skyline and the Sears Tower is pure city living. The 1,800 housing units make it a key residential area. ⊠ *Bounded by Polk, 15th, State, and Clark Sts., Downtown South.*

❷ Dearborn Station. Chicago's oldest standing passenger train station, a South Loop landmark, now serves as a boutique-filled galleria. Designed in Romanesque Revival style in 1885 by the New York architect Cyrus L. W. Eidlitz, it has a wonderful tall clock tower and a red-sandstone and redbrick facade ornamented with terra-cotta. Striking features inside are the white, rust, and jade marble floor; a handsome wraparound walkway with brass railings and attractive grillwork; and arching wood-frame doorways. Since its opening in 1985, Dearborn Station has been successful in attracting office tenants but less so in attracting retailers. ⊠ *47 W. Polk St., Downtown South.* ☉ *Daily 7 AM–9 PM.*

❾ Donohue Building. This building has two important "firsts" to its credit: built in 1883, it was the first major printing facility in Printer's Row; and, after its 1979 renovation, it became the first of Chicago's factory lofts to undergo condo conversion. The main entrance is flanked by marble columns topped by ornately carved capitals, with tile work over the entrance set into a splendid granite arch. Note the beautiful ironwork and woodwork in the doors and frames of the first-floor retail establishments. ⊠ *711 S. Dearborn St., Downtown South.*

NEED A BREAK? 'Da Mare' himself, Richard M. Daley, has stood up for the turkey burgers at the tiny **Standing Room Only (SRO Chicago)** (⊠ 610 S. Dearborn St., Downtown South, ☎ 312/360–1776). The inexpensive deli is a favorite with locals and sports fans who feel at home amidst the Bulls and White Sox memorabilia.

⓫ Franklin Building. Built in 1888 and initially the home of the Franklin Company, a printing concern, this condominium building has intricate decoration. The tile work on the facade leads up to *The First Impression*—a medieval scene illustrating the first application of the printer's craft. Above the entryway is a motto: THE EXCELLENCE OF EVERY ART MUST CONSIST IN THE COMPLETE ACCOMPLISHMENT OF ITS PURPOSE. ⊠ *720 S. Dearborn St., Downtown South.*

⑧ Grace Place. Grace Episcopal Church of Chicago, which owns this building, shares facilities with Loop Christian Ministries, the World Outreach Conference Center, and Makom Shalom/The Community. This former printers building, built in 1915 and renovated in 1985, has a parish hall on the first floor and a modest sanctuary on the second with pointed arch windows and a skylight that illuminates the altar. ⊠ *637 S. Dearborn St., Downtown South.*

★ ② Grant Park. Here you'll find two of Chicago's greatest treasures—the Art Institute and Buckingham Fountain. This is also where the Chicago Bulls thanked fans during huge rallies after winning the NBA Championship six times. Bordered by Lake Michigan to the east and a spectacular skyline to the west, the ever-popular Grant Park hosts many of the city's outdoor events, including the annual Taste of Chicago, a vast picnic featuring foods from more than 70 restaurants that precedes a fireworks show around the Fourth of July.

Grant Park has been the site of violence, too. On a hot summer night during the last week of August 1968, the park was filled with people protesting the Vietnam War and the Democratic presidential convention that was taking place at the Conrad Hilton Hotel down the street. Rioting broke out; heads were cracked, protesters were dragged away screaming, and the late Mayor Richard J. Daley gave police the order to "shoot to kill." Later investigations into the events of that evening determined that a "police riot"—not the misbehavior of the protesters, who had been noisy but not physically abusive—was responsible for the violence that erupted. ⊠ *Downtown South*, ☎ *312/747–1534.*

⑭ Hilton Chicago. This showplace hotel has a grand history, from its ornate ballroom and beautiful gold frescoes to the 11 presidents who have stayed here. Built in 1927 as the Stevens Hotel with its own in-house hospital, theater, bowling alley, and ice rink, it later became the Conrad Hilton Hotel and then, in 1985, the Chicago Hilton and Towers. When it was first built, it had 3,000 guest rooms; because the rooms have been enlarged, there are 1,543 guest rooms today. The Grand Ballroom, at the top of a sweeping stairway near the Michigan Avenue entrance, is one of the most spectacular rooms in the city. On opening night at the Lyric Opera, when a midnight supper and dance is held here, a brass quintet stationed at the top of this stairway plays fanfares as the guests arrive. ⊠ *720 S. Michigan Ave., Downtown South.*

⑥ Hyatt on Printers Row. This sleek hotel is housed in not one but three adjoining buildings, two of them built during the late 19th century. The hotel's entrance is in the 1896 Morton Building; north of that is the simpler redbrick Duplicator Building, which dates to 1886. The two are connected to a third and newer building, which also houses the **Prairie** restaurant. ⊠ *500 S. Dearborn St., Downtown South,* ☎ *312/986–1234.*

⑤ The Museum of Contemporary Photography. This museum, part of Columbia College Chicago, focuses on American-born and American-resident photographers. "Contemporary" is defined as anything after 1959, the date of Robert Frank's seminal work *The Americans,* which is on display here and portrays Americans in a way that they had not seen themselves—or wanted to see themselves—before. Rotating exhibits range in techniques and themes from photojournalism to scientific photos; the permanent collection contains works from Dorothea Lange, Ansel Adams, and Nicholas Nixon. ✉ *600 S. Michigan Ave., Downtown South*, ☎ *312/663–5554.* ✏ *Free.* ☉ *Mon.–Wed., Fri. 10–5, Thurs. 10–8, Sat. noon–5.*

❼ Pontiac Building. An early Chicago School skyscraper—note its classic rectangular shape and flat roof—the simple, redbrick, 14-story Pontiac was designed by Holabird and Roche in 1891 and is their oldest existing building in Chicago. Booth/Hansen and Associates renovated it for office use in 1985. ✉ *542 S. Dearborn St., Downtown South.*

....

OFF THE
BEATEN PATH

PRAIRIE AVENUE HISTORIC DISTRICT – Several blocks south of Downtown South, three important historic homes and a beautiful church recall a vanished era. In the area around Prairie Avenue—Chicago's first Gold Coast—were the homes of many prominent merchants and manufacturers in the 1870s–1890s. To get to the Prairie Avenue Historic District, drive south on Michigan Avenue and take a left at 18th Street or take Bus 1, 3, or 4.

Today, two house museums show life on the urban frontier. All tours start out of the **Glessner House** (✉ 1800 S. Prairie Ave., Near South Side, ☎ 312/326–1480). Dating from 1886, the distinctive Romanesque Revival house with a pink-gray granite facade is the only surviving building in Chicago by architect H. H. Richardson, who also designed Boston's Trinity Church. The interior is filled with 19th-century decorative arts, from textiles to ceramics. Gracing the period rooms are hundreds of art objects, 85% of which belonged to John and Frances Glessner. Glessner tours: Wed.–Sun. at 1, 2, and 3.

The Greek Revival **Clarke House** (✉ 1827 S. Indiana Ave., Near South Side, ☎ 312/326–1480 or 312/745–0040) dates from 1836, making it Chicago's oldest surviving building. It is a clapboard house in a masonry city, built for Henry and Caroline Palmer Clarke to remind them of the East Coast they left behind. The Doric columns and pilasters were an attempt to civilize Chicago's frontier. Its everyday objects and furnishings reveal a typical 1830s–60s middle-class home. Clarke tours: Wed.–Sun. at noon, 1, and 2. Admission for each house is $7, or $11 for both (except on Wednesday, when both are free); call in advance for tours.

Wheeler Mansion (✉ 2020 S. Calumet Ave., Near South Side, ☎ 312/945–2020, WEB www.wheelermansion.com) was the 1870 home of an early Chicago Board of Trade president, Calvin T. Wheeler. It has been refurbished to its former splendor and is now an 11-room boutique hotel.

A block west and south of the Prairie Avenue Historic District is the handsome Gothic Revival **Second Presbyterian Church** (✉ 1936 S. Michigan Ave., Near South Side, ☎ 312/225–4951; 312/922–4533 for tours; WEB 2ndpresbyterian.org), designed in 1874 by noted New York architect James Renwick. After a fire in 1900, Howard Van Doren Shaw and Frederick Clay Bartlett renovated the church with an Arts & Crafts interior. An impressive collection of stained glass contains examples from throughout Louis Comfort Tiffany's career. Such luminaries as the Pullmans (of railroad fame) and Mary Todd Lincoln once warmed its pews. Services are held Sunday at 11.

At the **National Vietnam Veterans' Art Museum** (✉ 1801 S. Indiana Ave., Near South Side, ☎ 312/326–0270, WEB www.nvvam.org; ✏ $5; ☉ Tues.–Fri. 11–6, Sat. 10–5, Sun. noon–5) over 58,000 imprinted dog tags hang from the ceiling entranceway. Their chimelike sounds are

a haunting memorial to the soldiers that lost their lives in
war. With more than 500 pieces of art from 122 artists w
Vietnam, the museum is a journey into their experiences.

OFF THE
BEATEN PATH
RIVER CITY – If this structure's concrete curves look familiar, it's be
the complex was built in 1986 by Bertrand Goldberg, who also b
corncobs of Marina City. This curving complex of 446 apartments h
great views of beautiful boats from the expansive lobby. Interior space
are used for shops, walkways, a health club, and tenant storage closets
The marina has 62 moorings; boats can remain year-round because the
water is aerated to keep it from freezing. Tenants can walk to the Loop
or take a shuttle and also enjoy a 1-acre rooftop park off the building's
fifth floor. If you'd like to take a tour, ask the attendant at the front desk.
⊠ *800 S. Wells St., Downtown South.*

⓾ Sandmeyer's Bookstore. This intimate store, with wooden floors and
exposed brick walls, is a fine place to find books on Chicago history
and architecture, travel books, and children's literature. The unusual
iron stairway leading to the entrance is set with glass bricks. The store
is on the first floor of the Rowe Building, built in 1892 in the Romanesque
Revival style. ⊠ *714 S. Dearborn St., Loop,* ☏ *312/922–2104.* ☉ *Mon.–
Wed. and Fri. 11–6:30, Thurs. 11–8, Sat. 11–5, Sun. 11–4.*

⟲ ❹ Spertus Museum. Of special interest in this museum are many ritual objects from Jewish life and a poignant Holocaust memorial with many
photos and a tattered concentration camp uniform. The artifacts and works
of art make up the most comprehensive Judaic collection in the Midwest. A hands-on children's museum called the **Rosenbaum ARTiFACT
Center** has a simulated archaeological dig, in which junior archaeolo-
gists can search for pottery underneath the sand. ⊠ *618 S. Michigan Ave.,
Downtown South,* ☏ *312/322–1747,* WEB *www.spertus.edu.* ⊠ *$5, free
Fri.* ☉ *Sun.–Wed. 10–5, Thurs. 10–8, Fri. 10–3; children's museum: Sun.–
Thurs. 1–4:30.*

OFF THE
BEATEN PATH
ST. GABRIEL CHURCH – A tower, arched doorways, and large round window form bold masses on the exterior of this church, designed in 1887
by Daniel Burnham and John Root; the Romanesque-style interior with
vaulted arches gives a feeling of breadth and spaciousness. The parish,
in the Canaryville neighborhood, was organized to serve Irish workers
at the nearby Union Stock Yards. To the north of Canaryville, Bridgeport
has remained the Irish community it was in the late 1800s, despite ex-
pansionist pressures from Latin American Pilsen to the northwest and
Chinatown to the northeast. Bridgeport has produced many of the city's
mayors for decades, including the late Richard J. Daley and his son
Richard M., the current mayor. Take I–94 south from the Loop (43rd
Street exit), or take Bus 8 to Halsted and 45th streets and walk east on
45th Street for two blocks. ⊠ *4522 S. Wallace St., Kenwood,* ☏ *773/
268–9595.*

OFF THE
BEATEN PATH
UNIVERSITY OF ILLINOIS AT CHICAGO – One of Chicago's major universities, UIC, is a few blocks west of Downtown South's western edge. The
Jane Addams-Hull House Museum is on campus. You can either drive
here by heading west on Harrison Street, or take the El train's Blue line
to the UIC/Halsted stop.

University of Illinois at Chicago. The former Jewish flea market, Maxwell
Street, as well as much of Greektown and Little Italy were swallowed up
by the designs of architect Walter Netsch of Skidmore, Owings & Merrill. The buildings built in the mid-1960s became The Chicago Circle

rcle" and the University of Illinois Medical Center merged
ing UIC (University of Illinois at Chicago). Today student
16,000. ✉ *1200 W. Harrison St., University Village,*
00, WEB *www.uic.edu.*

House Museum. In the redbrick Victorian Hull House,
e pioneers and peace advocates Jane Addams and Ellen
Starr started the American settlement house movement in 1889
and wrought social-work miracles in their surrounding community. The
neighborhood was then a slum for new immigrants. Thirteen houses
were part of the settlement, but 11 were demolished in 1963 to make
room for the University of Illinois at Chicago. Moving displays trace the
history of Hull House and how it strived for multicultural understanding
and social service. Today, the Hull House Association has 20 social-ser-
vice centers around Chicago. ✉ *800 S. Halsted St., University Village,*
☎ *312/413–5353,* WEB *www.uic.edu/jaddams/hull.* ✱ *Free.* ☉ *Weekdays 10–4, Sun. noon–5.*

SOUTH LAKE SHORE DRIVE

A ride along South Lake Shore Drive is especially worthwhile for its
spectacular views of the downtown skyline and the lake. Those who
have followed the Loop and the Near North walks in this chapter will
get another perspective on the skyscrapers described in those tours—
from a distance and in relation to the surrounding skyline. There are
also some landmarks close to the road. In addition, the drive takes you
to the museum campus that connects three of Chicago's most popular attractions: the Field Museum, the Shedd Aquarium, and the Adler
Planetarium & Astronomy Museum.

A Good Drive

This driving tour starts from Hyde Park, but if you want to go directly
to the museum campus from downtown, take Bus 146 from Michigan
Avenue or State Street. A free museum campus trolley connects the three
museums, parking lots, and the Roosevelt Road stations for the El's
Red, Orange, and Green lines.

To ride along South Lake Shore Drive, you can drive your own car or
take the Jeffery Express Bus 6. From Hyde Park, enter Lake Shore Drive
at 57th Street northbound, with the lake to your right. At 35th Street
you will see, on your left, the **Stephen A. Douglas Tomb and Memorial,** honoring the U.S. senator who debated famously with Abraham
Lincoln. To get a close look, though the area is desolate, exit at Oak-
wood Boulevard, turn left and go a short distance to Lake Park Avenue, turn right and continue north four blocks to the memorial. To
return to Lake Shore Drive, turn left on 35th Street, turn left on Cottage Grove Avenue, and then take another left on Pershing.

As you continue north on Lake Shore Drive, you will see the Sears Tower
directly ahead in the distance. In case the perspective from here makes
it appear unfamiliar, you can recognize it by the angular setbacks that
narrow the building as it rises higher. To the left of the Sears Tower,
note the castlelike top of 311 South Wacker Drive, which is lighted at
night. Ahead, on both sides of the drive, is the **McCormick Place** complex, the largest exhibition and meeting place in North America.

In the distance, the rust-color building to the east of the Sears Tower
is the CNA Insurance Building. Farther north, the Smurfit-Stone Building is the structure with the more or less diamond-shape angled face
at the top. The tall, white, columnlike building to its right is the Aon
Center. Just to the left of the Aon Center is the shorter, severe gray Pru-

HISTORIC PULLMAN

CONCEIVED AND CONSTRUCTED by railroad entrepreneur George Mortimer Pullman, a cabinetmaker who made a fortune developing the first modern railway sleeping and dining cars, the community that bore his name was the nation's first large-scale planned industrial town. Its founder clearly understood the idea of enlightened self-interest: desirable surroundings, he believed, would attract the best workers; keeping them healthy and happy would mean higher productivity for his Pullman Palace Car Company.

Built between 1880 and 1885 on 3,000 acres surrounding the Illinois Central Railroad near Lake Calumet, Pullman thrived for 14 years as a company town. Home to about 12,000 at its peak, George Pullman's industrial utopia included shops, parks, churches, its own hospital and bank, and many cultural and recreational facilities available for the first time to working-class people, along with modern houses with indoor plumbing and gas.

Contained between 111th and 115th streets and Cottage Grove and Langley avenues, the tiny, tidy enclave was designed to include architecturally varied row houses for workers, more-spacious homes for middle managers, and individualized mansions for executives.

Nearly all the original buildings, now privately owned, remain. Many have been lovingly restored with accents in the "Pullman colors" of maroon and green. Its unique architectural continuity imbues this stately oasis with a haunting visual harmony in an undistinguished industrial desert. Present-day explorers can admire the carved wooden horse heads set into the facade of the **Pullman stables** (⊠ 11201 S. Cottage Grove Ave.) and the serpentine-stone gargoyles of the **Greenstone Church** (⊠ 11211 S. St. Lawrence Ave.) as they stroll back through time to the days when railroads ruled. Even the 120-ft-tall **central clock tower** (⊠ 11011 S. Cottage Grove Ave.) still stands despite a devastating 1998 arson fire that destroyed an empty factory building.

Pullman prospered until the depression of 1893–94, when financial pressures caused the boss to cut wages and hours but not rents in the town. The result was the Pullman Strike, one of the most famous labor clashes in Chicago's history. Pullman the man died in 1897. Soon after, the nonindustrial parts of his urban dream were sold off by court order. Pullman the town—which had been annexed to Chicago in 1889—became just another city neighborhood.

In 1960 loyal locals fought a plan to turn their Far South Side world-within-a-world into an industrial park. They succeeded instead in getting their unique hometown designated a city, state, and national historic landmark. *The Road to Perdition*, the period gangster film starring Tom Hanks and Paul Newman, was filmed in the Pullman neighborhood.

The **Historic Pullman Foundation Visitor Center** (⊠ 11141 S. Cottage Grove Ave., Pullman, ☎ 773/785–8901; 773/785–3828 tour information; 🕸 www.pullmanil.org; 🎟 $3; ⊙ weekdays noon–2, Sat. 11–2, Sun. noon–3) shows an introductory video and has exhibits on the town of Pullman. The Center also offers guided walking tours the first Sunday of the month, May through October at 12:30 and 1:30 for $4. The **Hotel Florence Restaurant and Museum** (⊠ 11111 S. Forrestville Ave., Pullman, ☎ 773/785–3828) was built in 1881 as a lodging for businessmen interested in owning their own Pullman cars. Saved from demolition in 1975, it now houses a restaurant and informational displays about George Pullman.

To get to Pullman, take I–94 south from the Loop to 111th Street and go four blocks west, or take the Illinois-Central Metra Electric train south from Randolph Street to the 111th Street stop.

dential Building, Pru Two, with its postmodern annex rising to a point behind it. The black building with the twin antennae, behind and to the right of the Aon Center, is the 100-story John Hancock Center. Off to the right, seemingly out in the lake, are the elegant black curves of the Lake Point Tower condominiums. On your right, before the museum campus, the building with the massive columns reminiscent of ancient Greece is **Soldier Field,** home of the Chicago Bears.

Follow signs from Lake Shore Drive to the 57-acre museum campus, where the Big Three—the **Field Museum,** the **John G. Shedd Aquarium,** and the **Adler Planetarium & Astronomy Museum**—are united in one pedestrian-friendly, parklike setting. Park your car in one of the lots just past the Field Museum on McFetridge Drive. A free museum campus trolley (☎ 312/409–9696) connecting the three museums and the parking lots operates daily from Memorial Day to Labor Day and on holidays; it runs only on weekends the rest of the year.

On the west side of the campus is the Field Museum, one of the country's great museums, with an emphasis on diverse cultures and environments. The Shedd Aquarium, on the lakefront just past the Field Museum, has bizarre and fantastically beautiful fish, as well as playful dolphins and beluga whales. On the east side of the campus, at the far end of a peninsula that juts out into Lake Michigan (and provides wonderful views and photo opportunities of Chicago's skyline), is the Adler Planetarium & Astronomy Museum.

After visiting the museums, retrieve your car and head north on Lake Shore Drive. Look to your right for a view of the Monroe Street harbor. Off to the left looms the handsome, massive complex of the Hilton Chicago, and soon thereafter Buckingham Fountain will appear immediately to your left. To the far right, the Navy Pier entertainment complex juts into the lake with its giant Ferris wheel and ornate towers. Having reached the north end of Grant Park, you've come to the end of this drive.

TIMING
The drive itself will take only 15 or 20 minutes, more in traffic. Try to avoid Lake Shore Drive during peak rush-hour traffic times: from 7 to 9 in the morning, from 4 to 6:30 in the afternoon. Also, traffic near the museum campus can get snarled when the Chicago Bears are playing in neighboring Soldier Field. Plan on at least a day for a visit to the three museums (you could spend a day at the mammoth Field Museum alone). Allow extra time to enjoy the spectacular skyline and lake views from the museum campus and to stroll along the harbor.

Sights to See

★ ♨ **Adler Planetarium & Astronomy Museum.** Interactive and state-of-the-art exhibits hold appeal for traditionalists as well as for technology-savvy kids and adults who can be their own navigators through the solar system. Opened in 1930 as the first public planetarium in the western hemisphere, the Adler still has a traditional in-the-round Zeiss planetarium (called the Sky Theater) that shows constellations and planets in the night sky. In this renovated 1930s building is also a Gateway to the Universe gallery where you feel like you're stepping into infinite space, as well as galleries with special exhibits and astronomical artifacts.

A $40 million upgrade has resulted in the high-tech Sky Pavilion, a glass structure that wraps around the old building and contains the interactive StarRider Theater. Through control buttons on your armrest, you can choose how you'd like to journey into space; what you see on the screen in front of you is based on the majority sentiment of the audience. (Part of the technology is based on aircraft flight simulators.) Also in this building are a telescope terrace and interactive exhibition galleries that include 3-D computer animations of the Milky Way and of the birth of the solar system. Additional charges apply for the Sky Theater planetarium shows and the StarRider interactive shows. ⊠ *1300 S. Lake Shore Dr., Museum Campus,* ☎ *312/ 922–7827,* ⓦⓔⓑ *www.adlerplanetarium.org.* 🎫 *General $5, Sky Theater planetarium additional $5, StarRider interactive theater additional $5; general admission only, free Tues.* ⊙ *Labor Day–Memorial Day, Mon.–Thurs. 9–5, Fri. 9–9, weekends 9–6; Memorial Day–Labor Day, Sat.–Wed. 9–6, Thurs.–Fri. 9–9.*

OFF THE
BEATEN PATH

BRONZEVILLE – A renaissance is under way in this historic community, originally settled by waves of African-Americans fleeing the South beginning after World War I. The most touching landmark may be the 15-ft statue at 26th Place and King Drive—the neighborhood's symbolic entrance—that depicts a new arrival from the South bearing a suitcase held together with string. The Victory monument at 35th Street and King Drive honors the all-black 8th Illinois Regiment in World War I with three life-size figures carved in relief and an African-American doughboy as a later addition on top. More than 90 sidewalk plaques lead from 25th to 35th streets, making a trail commemorating the best and brightest of the community, including Pulitzer Prize winner Gwendolyn Brooks, whose first book of poetry was called "A Street in Bronzeville." The first African-American poet to win the prize, she died in the area in December 2000. The neighborhood, which lies between Downtown South and Hyde Park, was dubbed Bronzeville after the *Chicago Bee,* a black newspaper of the time, held a contest in 1930 to elect a "Mayor of Bronzeville." The influential *Chicago Defender* newspaper, meanwhile, originally was based here and attracted talent that included literary icon Langston Hughes. Group tours are recommended for those unfamiliar with the area.

The **Chicago Office of Tourism** (☎ 312/742–1190) offers a half-day bus tour of Bronzeville. Other tours are offered by the **Black Metropolis Convention and Tourism Council** (☎ 773/548–2579), and **Tour Black Chicago** (☎ 773/684–9034). **Black CouTours** (☎ 773/233–8907) offers a 2½-hour excursion of black culture including Bronzeville and other highlights. ⊠ *Bounded roughly by 22nd and 55th Sts. and by State St. and Cottage Grove Ave.*

★ 🐾 **Field Museum.** More than 6 *acres* of exhibits fill this gigantic world-class museum, which explores cultures and environments from around the world. The interactive exhibits are stimulating, exploring the earth and its people, from the secrets of Egyptian mummies, to the peoples of Africa and the Pacific Northwest, or the living creatures in the soil. Originally funded by Chicago retailer Marshall Field, the museum was founded in 1893 to hold material gathered for the World's Columbian Exposition; its current classical-style home opened in 1921.

Shrink to the size of a bug to burrow beneath the surface of the soil in the Underground Adventure exhibit ($4 extra). You'll come face to face with a wolf spider twice your size and have other encounters with the life that teems under our feet. As part of Inside Ancient Egypt, the remarkable Mastaba complex includes a working canal, a living marsh where papyrus is grown, a shrine to the cat goddess Bastet, burial-ceremony artifacts, and 23 mummies.

Don't miss the Life over Time: DNA to Dinosaurs exhibit, which traces the evolution of life on Earth from one-celled organisms to the great reptiles. Kids especially enjoy 65-million-year-old "Sue," the largest and most complete Tyrannosaurus rex fossil ever found. More than 600 other fossils are on exhibit, including gigantic posed dinosaur skeletons. The DinoStore sells a mind-boggling assortment of dinosaur-related merchandise. In addition to hosting special exhibits, the museum also schedules music, dance, theater, and film performances. Be sure to get a map and plan your time here. ⊠ *1400 S. Lake Shore Dr., Museum Campus,* ☎ *312/922–9410,* ⓦⒺⒷ *www.fieldmuseum. org.* ⌸ *$8, free Wed.* ⊙ *Weekdays 10–5, weekends 9–5.*

OFF THE BEATEN PATH **ILLINOIS INSTITUTE OF TECHNOLOGY** – Having once headed IIT's architecture department, Mies van der Rohe, with participation by the firms of Skidmore, Owings & Merrill; Holabird and Root; as well as Alschuler and Friedman, was also the principal designer of the campus. Built between 1942 and 1958, the structures have the characteristic box shape that is Mies's trademark. Unlike most of his other work, these are low-rise buildings. S. R. Crown Hall (⊠ 3360 S. State St.), made of black steel and clear glass, is the jewel of the collection and has recently been designated a national historic landmark; the other buildings have a certain sameness and sterility. Designed by Rem Koolhaas, the new McCormick Tribune Campus Center, still under construction at press time, continues the school's tradition of architectural innovation. The one-story center with transparent glass walls will be built right under the El's Green line. A 530-ft steel and concrete acoustic tube will encase the tracks as they pass over the building. IIT's College of Architecture offers free individualized and group tours of the campus (☎ 312/512–8830). At adjoining Ed Glancy Field (⊠ 3040 S. Wabash, ☎ 312/567–3296), IIT baseball coach Jim Darrah taught Madonna and Geena Davis the finer points of the game for the movie *A League of Their Own*. The campus is about 1 mi west of Lake Shore Drive on 31st Street. Or take I–94 (Dan Ryan Expressway) south from the Loop to the 31st Street exit. If you're without a car, take the El train's Green or Red line to the 35th Street stop, and walk east two blocks to campus. ⊠ *S. State St. between 31st and 35th Sts., Douglas,* ☎ *312/567–3000,* ⓦⒺⒷ *www.iit.edu.*

★ ☾ **John G. Shedd Aquarium.** Take a plunge into an underwater world at the world's largest indoor aquarium. Interactive, walk-through environments allow you to travel from the flooded forests of the Amazon to the coral reefs of the Indo-Pacific. Built in 1930, the Shedd houses more than 8,000 aquatic animals. "Amazon Rising" takes you on a journey along the banks of the Amazon River with an up-close look at many animals including piranhas, snakes, and stingrays. You can walk through an underwater kingdom rich with marine biodiversity and coral reefs in an exhibit about the Indo-Pacific waters surrounding the Philippines, which are threatened by overfishing and rapid coastal development. In April 2003, you can get up close and personal with the "demons of the deep" on a 30-ft "diving" exhibit that explores the coral reef, one of the world's largest, as well as the mangroves and the beaches of Apo Island, Philippines.

Another attraction is the spectacular Oceanarium, with pools that seem to blend into Lake Michigan, which is visible through the huge glass wall. In the Oceanarium you can have a stare-down with one of the knobby-headed beluga whales (they love to people-watch), observe Pacific white-sided dolphins at play, and explore the simulated Pacific Northwest nature trail. An educational dolphin presentation, scheduled daily, shows natural behaviors including vocalizing, breaching, and tail-walking. Be sure to check out the underwater viewing windows for the dolphins and whales and the information-packed, hands-on activities on the lower level. In the main building, a highlight is the 90,000-gallon Caribbean Reef exhibit, where you can watch divers feed sharks, stingrays, a sea turtle, and other denizens of the deep. A special treat on Thursday evening from June through September is live jazz on the Shedd's north terrace, with a great view of the lake and skyline. ☒ *1200 S. Lake Shore Dr., Museum Campus,* ☎ *312/939–2438,* WEB *www.sheddaquarium.org.* ☒ *$15 includes the Oceanarium, $18 (includes audio pass); $7 Mon. and Tues. for Oceanarium and Aquarium.* ☉ *Memorial Day–Labor Day, Fri.–Wed. 9–6, Thurs. 9 AM–10 PM; Labor Day–Memorial Day, weekdays 9–5, weekends 9–6.*

McCormick Place Complex. Chicago's premier convention facility comprises three buildings with almost 2½ million square ft of exhibition space and a glass-enclosed pedestrian concourse with retail shops linking all three buildings. The South Building, built in 1996, is the newest of the three, made from precast concrete and glass with colorful treatments throughout the interior. Also part of the complex is the 800-room Hyatt Regency McCormick Place, accessible from Martin Luther King Drive, and the 4,000-seat Arie Crown Theater. ☒ *2301 S. Lake Shore Dr., Near South Side,* ☎ *312/791–7000.*

OFF THE BEATEN PATH

PILSEN – Formerly a neighborhood of immigrants from Bohemia, Czechoslovakia, this South Side enclave is now home to the largest Mexican community in the Midwest—making up more than 85% of the neighborhood's population—including a number of artists. Pilsen is known for its dramatic, colorful murals that show scenes from Mexican history, culture, and religion. Along the 16th Street viaduct, from Ashland Avenue to Racine Street, are murals from the 1960s that show Aztec Indian themes, though many are faded since the walls were never properly primed. The 18th Street El station is decorated with murals (though some have fallen victim to graffiti) and mosaics. The neighborhood is bordered by Halsted Street (800 W.) on the east and Western Avenue (2400 W.) on the west and extends from 16th Street to the south branch of the Chicago River. To get to Pilsen from the Loop, take I–290 west to Damen Avenue, or take the El train's Blue line south to 18th Street.

The **Mexican Fine Arts Center Museum** (☒ 1852 W. 19th St., Pilsen, ☎ 312/738–1503, WEB www.mfacmchicago.org; ☉ Tues.–Sun. 10–5) exhibits the work of contemporary Mexican artists from both sides of the border. A recent expansion tripled the size of the facility, letting the museum display more of its permanent collection that traces the development of Mexican art, culture, religion, history, and politics. The free museum also hosts performing arts festivals in the spring and fall.

The 1885 Romanesque Revival **St. Pius Church** (☒ 1901 S. Ashland Ave., Pilsen, ☎ 312/226–6161) has finely detailed arches and windows, old stained glass, stenciling, and a beautiful painting of Guadalupe in shades of blue.

The **Pilsen Together Chamber of Commerce** (☒ 1801 S. Ashland Ave., Pilsen, ☎ 312/733–7651) has a wealth of information about the area. The friendly folks here might even take you on a spontaneous neighborhood tour.

Soldier Field. Home of the Chicago Bears since 1971, Soldier Field opened in 1924 and has been the site of many events besides football games, including a heavyweight-title boxing match in 1927 between Jack Dempsey and Gene Tunney, a visit in 1944 by President Franklin D. Roosevelt, and rock concerts by the Rolling Stones and other megabands. At press time, it was the site of a major renovation, which was scheduled for completion in September 2003. ⊠ *425 E. McFetridge Dr., Museum Campus,* ☎ *312/747–1285.*

Stephen A. Douglas Tomb and Memorial. A bronze sculpture of the "Little Giant," one of the greatest orators of his day, stands high on a pedestal in a small park just west of South Lake Shore Drive. A U.S. senator and Abraham Lincoln's political rival (their 1858 debates brought Lincoln national prominence), Douglas moved to Chicago in the late 1840s and owned property in this area; he died in 1861. ⊠ *636 E. 35th St., Douglas.*

NEAR NORTH

The city's greatest tourist magnet, from the Navy Pier Ferris wheel to the 94th-floor observatory of the John Hancock Building, the Near North Side includes art museums and galleries, as well as countless shops where you could spend a few dollars or thousands. It's the part of the city most visitors imagine when they plan a trip to Chicago.

Magnificent Mile and Streeterville

The Magnificent Mile, a stretch of Michigan Avenue between the Chicago River and Oak Street, owes its name to the swanky shops that line both sides of the street—and to its once-elegant low-rise profile, which used to contrast sharply with the urban canyons of the Loop. Developer Arthur Rubloff provided the modest moniker in 1947. Unfortunately, a construction boom added a parade of high-rises with a combination of office, residential, and retail space which has made the Mag Mile more canyonlike. Another trend on the avenue is the arrival of ubiquitous chain stores. Still, you can see patches of what the entire street used to look like.

East of the Magnificent Mile is upscale Streeterville, which began as a disreputable landfill owned by the notorious Cap Streeter and his wife, Maria. The couple set out from Milwaukee in the 1880s on a small steamboat bound for Honduras. When their boat was stranded on a sandbar between Chicago Avenue and Oak Street, Streeter claimed the "land" as his own, seceding from both the city of Chicago and the state of Illinois. After Streeter invited building contractors to dump their debris on his "property," the landfill soon mushroomed into 186 acres of saloons and shanties. Today this once-infamous area is mostly high-rise apartment buildings with a smattering of older structures; these attract many of the professionals who work nearby. Where Cap Streeter's own shanty once sat is the John Hancock Center.

West of Streeterville, from Michigan Avenue to Dearborn Street, is a stretch with a few skyscrapers, lots of parking lots and garages, a sprinkling of shops and restaurants, and some isolated examples of the stone town houses that once filled the neighborhood. Despite its lack of cohesion, the area is the seat of various enclaves of power, containing two cathedrals and the headquarters of the American Medical Association, which is in a distinctive triangular high-rise at State Street and Grand Avenue. The building, by acclaimed Japanese architect Kenzo Tange, has an unusual four-story "opening" near its roof.

Numbers in the text correspond to numbers in the margin and on the Near North and River North map.

A Good Walk

Begin your walk at the **Michigan Avenue Bridge** ①, which spans the Chicago River as a gateway to North Michigan Avenue. The low-rise building on the river, west of the bridge, is the headquarters of the

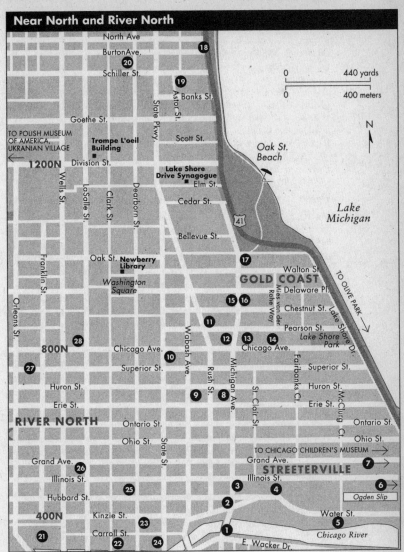

Chicago Sun-Times, one of the city's two hotly competitive dailies. Just north of the bridge on the west side of Michigan Avenue is the **Wrigley Building** ②, corporate home of the Wrigley chewing gum empire. The stark white building's wedding-cake embellishments and clock tower are a striking sight.

Across Michigan Avenue rises the crenellated **Tribune Tower** ③, home of the *Chicago Tribune.* Just south of the Tower, facing the sidewalk, is a statue of the late veteran Cubs radio announcer Jack Brickhouse. Walk across the plaza just east and north of Tribune Tower to Cityfront Plaza Drive and **NBC Tower** ④, which houses the local NBC affiliate WMAQ-TV. The riverside glass-front building near NBC Tower is the University of Chicago's Graduate School of Business Downtown Center (✉ 450 N. Cityfront Plaza Dr.). The university bookstore on the plaza has, not surprisingly, many books on business and economics.

From Cityfront Plaza Drive, walk down the stairs to the south, toward the serene concrete bank with benches and trees along the river. This private pathway, oblivious to the noisy Michigan Avenue traffic overhead, is in view of the city's most prominent buildings—a perfect lunch spot on sunny days. Turn left and head along the riverbank, past the Sheraton Chicago Hotel and Towers, just past Lizzie McNeill's Irish pub, to the **Centennial Fountain and Arc** ⑤, where you can step inside the circular part of the fountain and stand next to a wall of water—a refreshing break on a hot summer day. (It's also possible to walk west to Michigan Avenue along the river.) From the fountain, head north on McClurg Court to Illinois Street and the shopping, office, and entertainment complex called **River East Plaza** ⑥. The walkway along Ogden Slip affords a fine view in summer of some of Chicago's fanciest speedboats.

Farther east on Illinois Street, under Lake Shore Drive and across a park, is **Navy Pier** ⑦, a wonderful place to enjoy lake breezes, visit the **Chicago Children's Museum,** and sample various entertainments, including a ride on a giant Ferris wheel, a flashy addition that some condominium residents of Lake Point Tower, just east of the pier, find abominable.

Walking west from Navy Pier on either Illinois Street or Grand Avenue, you'll come back to McClurg Court. Walk north to Ontario Street; then turn left and walk west toward Michigan Avenue. If you see lots of people in white coats, don't be surprised: stretching east of Michigan Avenue from Ontario Street to Chicago Avenue are various buildings belonging to one of the city's most prominent medical centers, Northwestern Memorial Hospital. The downtown campus of Evanston's Northwestern University, including the law school, is also in this area.

Cross Michigan Avenue, turn right, and walk a block and a half to see the 19th- and 20th-century paintings and sculpture of the **Terra Museum of American Art** ⑧, a peaceful refuge on this shopping strip. A few blocks southwest at the corner of Ohio and Rush is the not-so-peaceful five-story interactive theme park **DisneyQuest.** Though tickets can be pricey and lines are especially long on weekends, it's utopia for kids, with a half dozen lurching virtual-reality rides and literally hundreds of more traditional video and pinball games. Other sanctuaries in the area are of a different nature: two blocks west of Michigan Avenue on Huron Street is **St. James Cathedral** ⑨, Chicago's oldest Episcopal church. Continue another block west to State Street and one block north to Superior Street, where **Holy Name Cathedral** ⑩, which has a grand interior, stands as a Catholic stronghold. Go east on

Chicago Avenue to Rush Street and turn left (north). At Pearson and Rush streets is **Quigley Seminary** ⑪, with its beautiful chapel.

Continue east on Pearson Street to Water Tower Park, a Chicago icon. The **Water Tower** ⑫ and the matching **Pumping Station** ⑬ across the street are among the few buildings to survive the fire of 1871.

Head east one block to the imposing quarters of the **Museum of Contemporary Art** ⑭. This museum concentrates on 20th-century art, principally works created after 1945.

Walk back to Michigan Avenue. Two blocks north on the west side is the elegant **Fourth Presbyterian Church** ⑮ and its peaceful courtyard. In contrast, across Michigan Avenue towers the tapering, 100-story **John Hancock Center** ⑯, the third-tallest building in Chicago, after the Sears Tower and the Aon Building.

At the north end of the Magnificent Mile on Walton Place, past the grand Drake Hotel, you'll find one of Chicago's nicest walks: cross Oak Street in front of the Drake and take the underground passage that leads to Oak Street Beach and the lakefront promenade (watch out for speeding bicyclists, skateboarders, and in-line skaters).

TIMING

Allow about four hours for the walk itself plus time to stop for a snack or drink. You can spend a good deal more time at a number of the attractions (or just shopping), depending on your interests. Add a couple of hours (especially if you have children) for Navy Pier, another hour if you stop at River East Plaza. At Navy Pier you could spend a few hours in the Chicago Children's Museum alone. Art lovers will want to set aside at least an hour to see the Terra Museum of American Art and one or two hours for the Museum of Contemporary Art. Note that these museums aren't open on Monday. On summer weekends, walking along the lakefront north of Oak Street is a special treat; Chicagoans throng to Oak Street Beach to soak up the sun and play beach volleyball in the shadows of skyscrapers.

Sights to See

❺ **Centennial Fountain and Arc.** Designed by Dirk Lohan, this stepped fountain was built in 1989 to commemorate the 100th anniversary of the Metropolitan Chicago Water Reclamation District of Greater Chicago. From May through September, it shoots an awesome arc of water across the river for 10 minutes daily on the hour from 10 to 2 and from 5 to midnight. On a sunny afternoon you might see the hues of a rainbow in the arc. ⊠ *300 N. McClurg Ct., Near North.*

☾ **Chicago Children's Museum.** "Hands-on" is the operative concept for this brightly colored, 57,000-square-ft Navy Pier anchor, which encourages kids to play educational video games, climb through multilevel tunnels, run their own television stations, and, if their parents allow it, get all wet. Some favorites are an early childhood exhibit with a child-size neighborhood complete with a bakery, service station, and construction site; an art studio; science exhibits on such subjects as recycling and inventing; and an activity-filled exhibit that provides children and adults with tools for addressing prejudice and discrimination. ⊠ *700 E. Grand Ave., Near North,* ☎ *312/527–1000,* WEB *www.chichildrensmuseum.org.* ☞ *$6.50, free Thurs. 5–8.* ☾ *Tues.–Sun. 10–5.*

⓯ **Fourth Presbyterian Church.** This granite church facing Michigan Avenue is a prime example of the Gothic Revival style popular at the turn of the 20th century. The courtyard of the church, a grassy spot adorned with simple statuary and bounded by a covered walkway, has provided respite for many a weary shopper. Noontime organ concerts are given occasionally in the sanctuary; call for exact dates and times. ⊠ *126 E. Chestnut St., Near North,* ☎ *312/787–4570,* WEB *www.fourthchurch.org.*

⑩ **Holy Name Cathedral.** A yellow-stone Victorian cathedral, built in 1874–75, serves as the principal church of the archdiocese of Chicago. The interior is glorious; at the back of the church is a huge, beautiful organ. The elaborate western entrance has bronze doors coming to a point under stone-carved ornamentation and a circular stained-glass window. ⊠ *735 N. State St., Near North,* ☎ *312/787–8040.*

⑯ **John Hancock Center.** The crisscross braces in this 1,107-ft-tall building help keep it from swaying in the high winds that come off the lake, although people in the apartments on the upper floors have learned not to keep anything fragile on a high shelf. Completed in 1970, Big John was the first building of such massive height on Michigan Avenue. The 94th floor has an observation deck; you can enjoy the same view while having an exorbitantly priced drink in the bar that adjoins the Signature Room at the 95th restaurant. There are restaurants, shops, and a waterfall in the lower-level public plaza. The Chicago Architecture Foundation has a shop and tour center off the plaza. ⊠ *875 N. Michigan Ave., Near North,* ☎ *312/751–3681,* WEB *www.hancock-observatory.com.* ⊠ *Observation deck $9.50.* ⊙ *Daily 9 AM–11 PM.*

NEED A BREAK?   For great fixings, try **L'Appetito** (⊠ 875 N. Michigan Ave., Near North, ☎ 312/337–0691), a take-out deli off the Hancock Center's lower-level plaza that has some of the best Italian sandwiches in Chicago.

---

❶ **Michigan Avenue Bridge.** Completed in 1920, this bridge at the south end of the Magnificent Mile has impressive sculptures on its four pylons representing major Chicago events: its exploration by Marquette and Joliet, its settlement by trader Jean Baptiste Point du Sable, the Fort Dearborn Massacre of 1812, and the rebuilding of the city after the fire of 1871. The site of the fort, at the southeast end of the bridge, is marked by a commemorative plaque erected there by the city. The bridge has two decks for traffic and can be opened to allow tall-masted boats to pass. ⊠ *400 N. Michigan Ave., Near North.*

⑭ **Museum of Contemporary Art.** Founded in 1967 by a group of art patrons who felt the great Art Institute was unresponsive to modern work, the MCA's dramatic quarters were designed by Berlin architect Josef Paul Kleihues. From the outside, the building looks like a home for modern art—it's made of square metal plates, with round bolts in each corner. Enter street level from Chicago Avenue or hike up the long flight of stairs from the adjacent street, Mies van der Rohe Way. Among the museum's highlights are four barrel-vaulted galleries on the fourth floor and a terraced sculpture garden with outdoor café tables overlooking Lake Michigan. About half the museum is dedicated to temporary exhibitions; the other half showcases objects from the MCA's growing 7,000-piece collection, which includes work by René Magritte, Alexander Calder, Bruce Nauman, Sol LeWitt, Franz Kline, and June Leaf. The museum hosts a party (⊠ $14) with live music and hors d'oeuvres from 6–10 PM on the first Friday of every month. ⊠ *220 E. Chicago Ave., Near North,* ☎ *312/280–2660,* WEB *www.mcachicago.org.* ⊠ *$8, free Tues.* ⊙ *Tues. 10–8 and Wed.–Sun. 10–5.*

★ ✋ ❼ **Navy Pier.** No matter the season, Navy Pier is a fun place to spend a few hours. Constructed in 1916 as a commercial-shipping pier, it was renamed in honor of the Navy in 1927 (the Army got Soldier Field). The once-deserted pier contains shopping promenades; an outdoor landscaped area with pretty gardens, a fountain, a carousel, a 15-story Ferris wheel, and an ice-skating rink; the lakefront **Skyline Stage** (☎ 312/

595–7437), a 1,500-seat vault-roof theater; the **Chicago Shakespeare Theatre,** in an elegant round building with a bright neon sign (☎ 312/595–5600); Crystal Gardens, one of the country's largest indoor botanical parks; an IMAX Theater; an outdoor beer garden; the **Chicago Children's Museum;** and myriad shops, restaurants, and bars. Navy Pier is also the home port for a number of tour and dinner cruises. Prices are premium for these cruises, and the food's better on land, but the voyage can be pleasant on a hot summer night. Dinner cruise operators include *Spirit of Chicago* (☎ 312/836–7899) and *Odyssey I* (☎ 630/990–0800); the *Cap Streeter* and the *Shoreline II* offer 30-minute shoreline cruises that don't require reservations (☎ 312/222–9328). **Riva** and **Joe's Be-Bop Cafe & Jazz Emporium** are good restaurant choices. ⊠ *Grand Ave. at the lakefront, Near North,* ☎ *312/595–7437,* WEB *www.navypier.com.* ☉ *Daily 6 AM–11 PM.*

❹ **NBC Tower.** This 1989 limestone-and-granite edifice by Skidmore, Owings & Merrill looks suspiciously like a building from the 1930s-vintage Rockefeller Center complex in New York, another NBC home. ⊠ *455 N. Cityfront Plaza Dr., Near North.*

OFF THE
BEATEN PATH

OLIVE PARK – Just north of Navy Pier and Lake Point Tower (⊠ 505 N. Lake Shore Dr.), the green space of Olive Park juts out into Lake Michigan. It has no roads, just paved walkways and lots of benches, trees, shrubs, and grass. The marvelous views of the city skyline, in addition to the absence of vehicular traffic, make it seem as though you're miles from the city, not just blocks from the busy Near North Side. ⊠ *Grand Ave. at the lakefront, Near North.*

⑬ **Pumping Station.** Water is still pumped to 390,000 city residents at a rate of about 250 million gallons per day from this Gothic-style structure, which, along with the very similar Water Tower across the street, survived the fire of 1871. The station is also a drop-in tourist information center, open daily 7:30 AM–7 PM, which includes a coffee stand, a gift shop, and, out front, dog biscuits. ⊠ *811 N. Michigan Ave., Near North.*

⑪ **Quigley Seminary.** The Catholic St. James Chapel in this 1918 Gothic-style building was modeled on the famous Sainte-Chapelle in Paris. It's a little jewel, with perfect acoustics and a splendid rose window. The Rev. James Edward Quigley, looking stately in statue form, overlooks the southeast corner of the intersection. ⊠ *103 E. Chestnut St., Near North,* ☎ *312/787–9343.* ☉ *Chapel tour Tues. and Thurs.–Sat. noon–2.*

 ❻ **River East Plaza.** A former shipping terminal and pier was converted to a glitzy shopping mall and office space in the late 1980s. You'll find a number of interesting retail outlets, including the City of Chicago Store, which sells unique souvenirs; a food court; several bars and restaurants; and a host of recreational games, from miniature golf to traditional arcade games to high-tech interactive games. ⊠ *435 E. Illinois St., Near North.*

❾ **St. James Cathedral.** First built in 1856, the original St. James was largely destroyed by the fire of 1871. The second incarnation, a yellow-white brick building from 1875, is Chicago's oldest Episcopal church. The cathedral has a magnificent stenciled nave in the Arts and Crafts style. If the huge red church doors are locked, ask at the church office (in the building next door, east of the cathedral) for admission. ⊠ *65 E. Huron St., Near North,* ☎ *312/787–7360.*

★ ❽ **Terra Museum of American Art.** Daniel Terra, ambassador-at-large for cultural affairs under Ronald Reagan, made his collection of American art available to Chicago in 1980; in 1987 it was moved here from Evanston. Subsequent acquisitions by the museum have further enriched these superb collections, which highlight American impressionism and folk art. Look for works by Whistler, Sargent, Winslow Homer, Cassatt, and three generations of Wyeths. ⊠ *664 N. Michigan Ave., Loop,* ☎ *312/664–3939,* WEB *www.terramuseum.org.* ⊡ *$7, free Tues. and 1st Sun. of month.* ⊙ *Tues. 10–8, Wed.–Sat. 10–6, Sun. noon–5.*

❸ Tribune Tower. In 1922 *Chicago Tribune* publisher Colonel Robert McCormick chose a Gothic design for the building that would house his paper, after rejecting a slew of functional modern designs. Embedded in the exterior wall of the tower are chunks of material taken from other famous buildings. Look for labeled blocks from Westminster Abbey, the Alamo, St. Peter's Basilica, the White House, the Berlin Wall, and the moon, among others; some of these bits and pieces were gifts to McCormick and others were "secured" by the *Trib*'s foreign correspondents. There are also inspirational quotations engraved in the building. On the ground floor, behind plate-glass windows, are the studios of WGN radio, part of the *Chicago Tribune* empire, which also includes WGN-TV, cable-television stations, and the Chicago Cubs. (Modesty was not one of Colonel McCormick's prime traits: WGN stands for the *Tribune*'s self-bestowed nickname, World's Greatest Newspaper.) At press time, *Trib*'s production facility tours at the Freedom Center (⊠ 777 W. Chicago Ave., ☎ 312/222–2116) were halted due to construction, call ahead to see if they have resumed. ⊠ *435 N. Michigan Ave., Near North,* ☎ *312/222–3232,* WEB *www.chicagotribune.com.*

⑫ Water Tower. This famous Michigan Avenue structure, completed in 1867, was originally built to house a 137-ft standpipe that equalized the pressure of the water pumped by the similar pumping station across the street. Oscar Wilde uncharitably called it "a castellated monstrosity with salt and pepper boxes stuck all over it." Nonetheless, it remains a Chicago landmark and a symbol of the city's spirit of survival following the fire of 1871. ⊠ *806 N. Michigan Ave., at Pearson St., Near North.*

❷ Wrigley Building. Brightly illuminated at night, the landmark headquarters of the chewing gum company boldly marks the south end of the Magnificent Mile. It's sheathed in terra-cotta that's remained remarkably white thanks to diligent maintenance in the face of urban pollution, and the particular shade of green used on the trim is reminiscent of Wrigley's spearmint gum wrappers. The tower was based on the Giralda Tower in Seville, Spain, and designed in the 1920s by the architectural firm Graham, Anderson, Probst & White, which also designed the Merchandise Mart and Union Station. ⊠ *400 N. Michigan Ave., Near North,* WEB *www.wrigley.com/wrigley/about/about_story_building.asp.*

NEED A BREAK?	Behind and one level down from the Wrigley Building is the (in)famous **Billy Goat Tavern** (⊠ 430 N. Michigan Ave., Near North, ☎ 312/222–1525), the inspiration for *Saturday Night Live*'s classic "cheezborger, cheezborger" skit and a longtime haunt of local journalists, most notably the late columnist Mike Royko. Grab a greasy hamburger (or cheeseburger) at this very casual grill, or just have a beer and absorb the comic undertones.

Gold Coast

This posh pocket wears Chicago's greatest treasure—the Lake Michigan shoreline—like a gilded necklace. Made fashionable after the 1871 fire by the social-climbing industrialists of the day, today's Gold Coast neighborhood is still a ritzy place to live, work, shop, and mingle.

The boundaries of this historic district are debated, thanks to gentrification that has expanded its borders; everyone wants to lay claim to a piece of Chicago's toniest turf. The generally agreed-upon limits are the lake on the east, North Avenue on the north, Oak Street on the south, and LaSalle Street on the west.

Entrepreneur and socialite Potter Palmer started the building boom in 1882 by abandoning the South Side to build a much-ballyhooed (and long since destroyed) mansion here. Following Palmer's lead, others among the already-monied and the nouveau riches settled here, making the Gold Coast a center of wealth and power. Architectural styles along E. Lake Shore Drive Historic District include Baroque, Renaissance, Georgian, and Beaux Arts—though varied, they blend together beautifully. The Roman Catholic Archdiocese of Chicago built its archbishop's residence here, where it remains.

Numbers in the text correspond to numbers in the margin and on the Near North and River North map.

A Good Walk

There's no place better to start an exploration of the Gold Coast than at the venerable **Drake Hotel** ⑰, at Oak Street and Michigan Avenue. (Near Division Street, look for the underground passageway to Oak Street Beach—a people-watching magnet in season, a pretty stroll anytime.) Cross Michigan Avenue westbound, and then walk north along Chicago's most famous thoroughfare, Lake Shore Drive.

On your left you'll see some of the city's most exclusive residences. Just north of Scott Street pause to admire two vintage beauties on your left: the 1891 Carol Constantine Heisen House (⊠ 1250 Lake Shore Dr.), designed by Frank Abbott, and its next-door neighbor, the Mason Bragman Starring House (⊠ 1254 Lake Shore Dr.), done in 1891 by Gustav Hallberg.

As you continue north across Goethe Street, make a mental note: if you're ever pressed for conversation in Chicago, just solicit opinions on how this street name should be pronounced. Then sit back and enjoy the fireworks.

The extremely eclectic mix of architecture along the Drive ranges from the ridiculous to the sublime. Some aristocratic examples can be found between Burton and North avenues: the seat of the Polish consulate (⊠ 1530 Lake Shore Dr.) and the adjoining International College of Surgeons and **International Museum of Surgical Science** ⑱.

At North Avenue turn left and proceed to the grande dame of Gold Coast promenades, Astor Street. (As you head south on Astor, don't forget to admire the archbishop's residence on the corner across the street.) On the northwest corner of Astor and Burton streets, you'll find the Georgian Patterson-McCormick Mansion (⊠ 20 E. Burton Pl.), commissioned in 1891 by *Chicago Tribune* chief Joseph Medill as a wedding gift for his daughter Cissy and her husband, Robert Patterson. Where Astor Street jogs to meet Schiller Street stands the 1892 **Charnley–Persky House** ⑲, designed in part by Frank Lloyd Wright in a style that just slightly predates his Prairie homes.

At Division Street turn west to State Parkway. Those in need of refreshment can grab a bite at P. J. Clarke's (⊠ 1204 N. State Pkwy.) or St. Germain (⊠ 1210 N. State Pkwy.). Continue north to Goethe Street, where you'll come upon the Ambassador East Hotel—home of the famous Pump Room—and its across-the-street counterpart, the Ambassador West. Walk past the former Playboy Mansion (⊠ 1340 N. State St.)—now a private residence—all the way to North Avenue for a splendid view of Lincoln Park.

Take North Avenue another block west to Dearborn Street; then head south again past the elite Latin School on the left and **St. Chrysostom's Episcopal Church** ⑳ on the right. You'll also see the Three Arts Club, a venerable residence for young women, and the Ruth Page Dance Foundation (⊠ 1016 N. Dearborn St.), on the same side of the street a block north of the church.

Where Dearborn Street meets Oak Street—the Gold Coast's famous shopping district—turn right to go east. If your feet are weary, pay homage to the Dr. William Scholl College of Podiatric Medicine on your left—the college advertises a public exhibit called "Feet First: The Scholl Story." Then cross State Street, and you'll find yourself in the heart of the Oak Street shopping district, where storefronts touting Jil Sander, Versace, Sonia Rykiel, and other designers' wares compete to lure those with time and money to spend.

Where Oak Street ends, a quick crossing of Michigan Avenue puts you back at the Drake—just in time for tea or cocktails at the Coq d'Or.

TIMING

A stroll through the Gold Coast can be done in an hour, but what's the hurry? Make an afternoon of it. Especially pleasant are Saturday and Sunday afternoons in spring or fall or just before dusk any day in summer, when the neighborhood's leafy tranquillity and big-city energy converge.

Sights to See

⑲   **Charnley–Persky House.** This outwardly simple but splendid house at the corner of Astor and Schiller streets, finished in 1891 for lumberman James Charnley, gives you the chance to see the work of two renowned architects: Louis Sullivan and Frank Lloyd Wright, who was a 25-year-old draftsman in Sullivan's office when the building was commissioned. Wright later claimed to have been the building's sole designer, although architects say the protruding covered balcony, with its stark horizontal roof and thin vertical columns, is clearly a mark of Sullivan. Admission to the house is either by a 45-minute tour on Wednesday at noon, or by an extended 90-minute tour on Saturday at 10 AM, which also takes in the 1400 block of Astor Street and the nearby **Madlener House** (⊠ 4 Burton Pl.), a Prairie-style landmark. ⊠ *1365 N. Astor St., Near North,* ☎ *312/915–0105.* ▦ *Free Wed., $9 for tour that includes Madlener House.* ☉ *Apr.–Nov., tours Wed. at noon, Sat. at 10 AM.*

⑰   **Drake Hotel.** Ever since it opened with a bang on New Year's Eve in 1920, the Drake has been a beloved Chicago landmark and gathering place. Built on landfill at the very end of North Michigan Avenue, this ornate north anchor of the Mag Mile was placed on the National Register of Historic Places in 1981. Cecil B. DeMille and Park Ridge native Hillary Rodham Clinton have been guests. ⊠ *140 E. Walton Pl., Near North,* ☎ *312/787–2200,* WEB *www.thedrakehotel.com.*

⑱   **International Museum of Surgical Science.** Filling four floors of a landmark Lake Shore Drive building patterned after a Louis XVI château, this unusual museum showcases 4,000-year-old skulls, amputation kits, an iron lung, and other intriguing (albeit slightly morbid) oddities. ⊠ *1524 N. Lake Shore Dr., Near North,* ☎ *312/642–6502,* WEB *www.imss.org.* ▦ *$6, free Tues.* ☉ *Tues.–Sat. 10–4.*

OFF THE
BEATEN PATH **LAKE SHORE DRIVE SYNAGOGUE –** Ornate stained glass decorates the interior of what is arguably the city's most magnificent synagogue, a late-1800s structure three blocks north of Oak Street, between Lake Shore Drive and State Street. ✉ *70 E. Elm St., Near North,* ☎ *312/337–6811.*

20 **St. Chrysostom's Episcopal Church.** The Gold Coast's earliest wealthy settlers worshiped in this 1895 English Gothic church, known for its 43-bell carillon imported from England. ✉ *1424 N. Dearborn St., Near North,* ☎ *312/944–1083.*

NEED A
BREAK? Make a meal out of appetizers at **Bistro 110** (✉ 110 E Pearson St., Near North, ☎ 312/266–3110). The artichoke hearts are heavenly, and the gooey French onion soup is not to be missed. There are ample choices of wine by the glass. The front bar/café area is perfect for casual dining.

OFF THE
BEATEN PATH **TROMPE L'OEIL BUILDING –** Although this building is on the northeast corner of LaSalle and Division streets, you should study its appearance from a block east, at Clark and Division streets, or approach it from the south for the full effect of its rose window, ornate arched doorway, stone steps, columns, and sculptures. As you move closer to the building, you'll discover that an ordinary high-rise has been elaborately painted to make it look like an entirely different work of architecture. ✉ *1207 W. Division St., Near North.*

RIVER NORTH

Bounded on the south and west by branches of the Chicago River, River North has eastern and northern boundaries that are harder to define than those of the Near North. As in many other neighborhoods, the limits have expanded as the area has grown more attractive; today they extend roughly to Oak Street on the north and Clark Street on the east. Richly served by waterways and by railroad tracks that run along its western edge, the neighborhood was settled by Irish immigrants in the mid-19th century. As the 20th century approached and streetcar lines came to Clark, LaSalle, and Wells streets, the area developed into a vigorous commercial, industrial, and warehouse district.

As economic conditions changed and factories moved away, the neighborhood fell into disuse and disrepair. Despite its location less than a mile from Michigan Avenue and the bustling downtown area, River North became just another deteriorated urban area. In the 1970s, craftspeople, attracted by low rents and spacious abandoned storage areas and shop floors, began to move into the neighborhood. Then developers caught the scent and began buying up properties with an eye to renovation.

Today, River North has been transformed into a vibrant neighborhood of galleries, shops, and restaurants appealing to the artsy and young urban professional crowds. Much of the massive Cabrini Green public housing, which loomed for years at the neighborhood's northern and western fringes, has been torn down, and the construction of mixed-income property development is changing the area.

The area's most charming feature is the almost complete absence of contemporary construction; the handsome buildings are virtually all renovations of properties nearly a century old. A typical River North building is a large, rectangular, solidly built structure made of Chicago

BUCKTOWN AND WICKER PARK

CREATIVE TYPES CLUSTER in the hip, somewhat grungy enclaves called Bucktown and Wicker Park, centered on Milwaukee, Damen, and North avenues. Locals flock to this area for its intriguing mix of nightclubs, cafés, theaters, coffeehouses, cutting-edge galleries, small businesses, and a bizarre bazaar of shops—plus an increasing parade of sightseers drawn by what is arguably the best people-watching in the city. Musicians, artists, and young professionals call this area home, and an abundance of Latino American–run shops and restaurants is evidence of the strong ethnic influences.

Bucktown—which is said to have taken its name from the goats kept by the area's original Polish and German immigrants—encompasses the neighborhood surrounding Milwaukee Avenue north of North Avenue. The area south of North Avenue is Wicker Park—named for Charles Wicker, who, with his brother Joel, established the community in the 1870s. The summer of 2001 brought MTV's real world cameras to a rehabbed apartment on North Avenue, right smack in the heart of the neighborhood.

If you're driving, take the Kennedy Expressway to North Avenue, then go west on North Avenue until you reach the triangular intersection where it meets Milwaukee and Damen avenues. By El train, take the northbound Blue line to the Damen/North Avenue stop. Head north on Damen Avenue to North Avenue, then briefly east to the **Flat Iron Building** (⊠ 1579 N. Milwaukee Ave., Wicker Park), an 88,000-square-ft haven for artists and galleries, many of them open to the public.

From the Flat Iron Building you can make short forays to see some of Bucktown's and Wicker Park's most colorful shops,

theaters, and clubs. Among the quirky shops on Damen Avenue is the aptly named **Eclectic Junction** (⊠ No. 1630) which sells all kinds of functional and nonfunctional art such as whimsical wine bottle stoppers, handmade necklaces, and picture frames made out of old bicycle chains. **Le Garage** (⊠ No. 1649) specializes in secondhand jeans.

On your way back toward the Flat Iron Building, look west for a great view of the remarkable triangular **Northwest Tower Building** (⊠ 1600 N. Milwaukee Ave., Wicker Park), popularly known as the Coyote Building because of the Coyote Gallery that once stood in its place.

Milwaukee Avenue is lined with some of the area's best bars, cafés, and restaurants. The funky **Soul Kitchen** (⊠ No. 1576) serves creative regional American food. There are also offbeat furniture, clothing, and antiques stores here. **U S #1** (⊠ No. 1509) sells vintage men's clothing from the '60s and '70s. **Modern Times** (⊠ No. 1538) has furniture from the 1940s, '50s, and '60s.

The most lively times to visit are late August, when Bucktown hosts its annual Arts Fest, and early September, during the Around the Coyote gallery walk. It's always fun to visit Bucktown and Wicker Park in the evening—for dinner and nightlife. The **Rainbo Club** (⊠ 1150 N. Damen Ave., Ukrainian Village) is a small bar with cheap beer and an art-school clientele. The **Double Door** (⊠ 1572 N. Milwaukee Ave., Wicker Park) is a live-music venue. Or you can have a late breakfast on the weekend, followed by a long wander among the unique local businesses. **The Bongo Room** (⊠ 1470 N. Milwaukee Ave., Wicker Park) is a crowded, eclectic café known for specialty pancakes.

redbrick, with high ceilings and hardwood floors. Even the buildings of the period that were intended to be strictly functional were often constructed with loving attention to the fine woodwork in doors and door frames, the decorative patterns set in the brickwork, the stone carvings and bas-reliefs, and the wrought-iron and handsome brass ornamentation.

Numbers in the text correspond to numbers in the margin and on the Near North and River North map.

A Good Walk

Begin your walk on the plaza of the huge **Merchandise Mart** ㉑, on the river between Orleans and Wells streets. The Mart has its own stop on the CTA Brown and Purple lines. Inside, along 7 mi of corridors, are showrooms, many of them containing home furnishings, as well as office space and retail shops. The nondescript building to the west is the **Apparel Center,** the Mart's equivalent for clothing.

From the plaza walk north on Wells Street to Kinzie Street. Turn east on Kinzie Street, cross Clark Street, and look down the block to your right to see the handsome **Quaker Oats Building** ㉒, a glass-skin box that's the company's world headquarters. At Dearborn Street notice the splendid ornamental brickwork of **33 West Kinzie Street** ㉓, the home of Harry Caray's restaurant. (The loud restaurant, filled with flags and giant drawings of the late Cubs broadcaster and his big glasses, is on "Harry Caray Drive," an honorary designation.) Walk south on Dearborn Street to the bridge to see the distinctive twin corncobs of **Marina City** ㉔. The House of Blues nightclub, a bizarre, gray-paneled building crowned with what looks like a giant bonnet, is known for its concerts of every stripe (not just blues) and Sunday gospel brunches. The club spawned a pricey look-alike hotel, found next door. Just to the east is Mies van der Rohe's austere 55-story, boxlike IBM Building, the last office building he designed (in 1971); there's a bust of the architect in the lobby.

Backtrack north on Dearborn Street two blocks to Hubbard Street, turn left, and pause at **Courthouse Place** ㉕, a splendid granite building that once housed the Cook County Criminal Courts. The restored lobby has black-and-white pictures of the original site and of Chicagoans associated with high-profile trials that took place here. Continue west on Hubbard Street, and then walk north on Clark Street, where you'll find two of Chicago's most popular Mexican restaurants, Frontera Grill and Topolobampo.

Go north on Clark Street one block to Grand Avenue. Turn left and continue one block west to LaSalle Street. The tan building with a steeple on the southwest corner is not a church but the **Anti-Cruelty Society Building** ㉖, where furry animals pray to be adopted. The adoptees can be seen through round viewing windows: cats in one corner, dogs in the other. Next door (✉ 500 LaSalle St.) is what used to be Michael Jordan's Restaurant. It's now closed for good, symbolizing the Bulls' quick, depressing fall from championship juggernaut to sub-mediocrity. (Cubs slugger Sammy Sosa's planned takeover of the restaurant never materialized, leaving an unused building with an almost-mocking mural of Jordan dunking.)

Walk north on LaSalle Street to Ontario Street and turn right. The **Rock and Roll McDonald's** (✉ 600 N. Clark St.) has a standard Micky D's menu (with slightly higher prices), 24-hour service, and a profusion of rock-and-roll artifacts and 1950s and '60s kitsch. This area has become a magnet for those enamored of the latest theme restaurants, with the **Hard Rock Cafe** (✉ 63 W. Ontario St.) vying with the **Rainforest Cafe**

(⊠ 605 N. Clark St.) for business. Another popular spot for out-of-towners is **Ed Debevic's** (⊠ 640 N. Wells St.), a '50s-style diner. For quality over kitsch, try the **Big Bowl Café** (⊠ 159 W. Erie St.).

From McDonald's head west on Ontario Street. At Wells Street turn right and walk three blocks north to Superior Street and one block west to Franklin Street, the heart of the area known as the **River North Gallery District** ㉗, the largest U.S. gallery district outside of New York's Soho. Virtually every building on Superior Street between Wells and Orleans streets houses at least one gallery. In the area bounded by Wells, Orleans, Chicago, and Erie streets are dozens of art galleries showing every kind of work imaginable. Galleries welcome visitors, so feel free to stop into any that catch your eye. On periodic Fridays throughout the year, the galleries coordinate their exhibitions and open their doors to the public for a special night to showcase new works.

For a look at a major institution in the area, go north on Franklin Street to Chicago Avenue. Two blocks east on Chicago Avenue is the large **Moody Bible Institute** ㉘. Other campus buildings spread out behind it to the north.

TIMING

You can do this walk in about two hours, but add another hour or more if you want to wander leisurely in and out of galleries on Superior Street and the nearby streets. Most galleries are closed Sunday and Monday.

Sights to See

㉖ **Anti-Cruelty Society Building.** The original building dates to 1935; architect Stanley Tigerman's whimsical wood-and-glass addition was completed in 1982. Through the curved green windows, cats and dogs in cages attempt to use their endearing cuteness to hypnotize passersby into taking them home. ⊠ *510 N. LaSalle St., River North,* ☎ *312/644–8338,* WEB *www.anticruelty.org.*

㉕ **Courthouse Place.** The former Cook County Criminal Courts building, completed in 1892, witnessed many sensational trials early in the 20th century, including the Leopold and Loeb murder trial, in which Clarence Darrow defended the two University of Chicago students who killed a 14-year-old boy. Journalists and *The Front Page* authors Ben Hecht and Charles MacArthur, as well as poet Carl Sandburg, all worked as reporters in the building's pressroom. It's now an office building; note the wonderful bas-reliefs over the arched, pillared doorway. ⊠ *54 W. Hubbard St., Near North.*

㉔ **Marina City.** Bertrand Goldberg's twin corncob buildings on the river, completed in 1967, house condominium apartments (all pie-shape, with curving balconies). Goldberg also served as architect for a redevelopment project at Marina City. In addition to the apartments and marina, the complex now has four restaurants, the House of Blues nightclub and hotel, and a huge bowling alley. ⊠ *300 N. State St., Near North.*

㉑ **Merchandise Mart.** The Mart contains 4 million square ft—more than any other building in the country except the Pentagon. Built by the architectural firm Graham Anderson Probst and White in 1930, it's now owned by the Kennedys of political fame. Inside are more than 600 permanent wholesale showrooms for all sorts of merchandise, much of it related to interior decoration. The first two floors of the Mart are a retail shopping mall, with stores from many national chains. The 13th-floor showrooms (kitchens and baths) are always open weekdays to the public, and you can view the other showrooms either accompanied by an interior designer or on one of the Mart's tours. The somewhat macabre row of heads on the plaza is the Merchandise Mart Hall of Fame, installed at Joseph P. Kennedy's behest in 1953. The titans of retail portrayed here include Marshall Field, F. W. Woolworth, and Edward A. Filene. ✉ *300 N. Wells St., River North,* ☎ *312/527–7600 or 312/644–4664,* WEB *www.merchandisemart.com.* ☑ *Tour $10.* ☉ *Weekdays 9–5, 1½-hr tour Tues. and Fri. at 1:30.*

㉘ **Moody Bible Institute.** Here, in a massive contemporary brick structure, students of various conservative Christian denominations study and prepare for religious careers. ✉ *820 N. LaSalle St., River North,* ☎ *312/ 329–4000,* WEB *www.moody.edu.* ☉ *Tour weekdays at 11 and 2.*

OFF THE
BEATEN PATH

NEWBERRY LIBRARY – This venerable research institution houses superb book and document collections in many areas and mounts exhibits in a small gallery space. ✉ *60 W. Walton St., Near North,* ☎ *312/943– 9090,* WEB *www.newberry.org.* ☑ *Free.* ☉ *Tues.–Thurs. 10–6, Fri. and Sat. 9–5.*

POLISH MUSEUM OF AMERICA – Dedicated to gathering materials on the history of the Polish people in America, the Polish Museum includes an art gallery, an exhibit on the Shakespearean actress Helena Modjeska, one on the American Revolutionary War hero Tadeusz Kosciuszko, and another on the pianist and composer Ignacy Paderewski. The stations of the cross from the first Polish church in America (which was in Texas) are on display; there's a library, too. Chicago, incidentally, has the largest Polish population of any city outside Warsaw. By car, take I–94 to the Milwaukee/Augusta exit; proceed east and turn left at North Milwaukee Avenue. The El's Blue line stop at Chicago Avenue is just a block south of the museum; during the day, the neighborhood should be safe, but be cautious as usual. ✉ *984 N. Milwaukee Ave., Wicker Park,* ☎ *773/ 384–3352.* ☑ *$3.* ☉ *Daily 11–4.*

㉒ **Quaker Oats Building.** In case the name isn't clear enough, in the lobby there are two immense replicas of the now-familiar Quaker Oats box. Designed by Skidmore, Owings & Merrill and completed in 1987, this tall glass building on the river houses the headquarters of the famous maker of breakfast cereals. ✉ *321 N. Clark St., Near North.*

NEED A
BREAK?

A riverside restaurant in the Quaker Oats Building's lower level, **Sorriso** (✉ *321 N. Clark St., Near North,* ☎ *312/644–0283*) has outdoor seating in summer with a great view of Wacker Drive's skyscrapers.

㉗ **River North Gallery District.** Don't be shy about walking in and browsing at one of the dozens of galleries in this area. Take a look at Chapter 7 (Shopping) for a list of some galleries. Although each gallery sets its own hours, most are open Tuesday through Saturday 10–5 or 11–5 and are closed Sunday and Monday. The galleries have special receptions to usher in new shows on periodic Fridays throughout the year. Patrons sip jug wine as they browse the art and chat with artists who often attend the opening festivities. For announcements of openings and other art-scene news, send a request letter for the *Chicago Gallery News* (✉ 730 N. Franklin St., 60610, ☎ 312/649–0064, www.chicagogallerynews. com), or pick up a copy at one of the visitor centers of the Chicago Office of Tourism. For general information on the area and galleries, check WEB www.rivernorthassociation.com. ✉ *Bounded by Wells, Orleans, and Erie Sts. and Chicago Ave., River North.*

UKRAINIAN VILLAGE – A number of sights are testimony to the ethnic roots of this neighborhood, currently 75% Ukrainian, which extends from Damen Avenue (2000 W.) on the east and Western Avenue (2400 W.) on the west, between Chicago Avenue (800 N.) and Division Street (1200 N.). **Holy Trinity Orthodox Cathedral** (⊠ 1121 N. Leavitt Ave., Ukrainian Village, ☎ 773/486–6064) is a Russian Orthodox church in the heart of Ukrainian Village, designed by Louis Sullivan in 1903; it is said that Czar Nicholas of Russia contributed $4,000 to the construction. The Byzantine-style **St. Nicholas Ukrainian Catholic Cathedral** (⊠ 2238 W. Rice St., Ukrainian Village, ☎ 773/276–4537), with its 13 copper-clad domes, was built in 1914 and is similar to the Basilica of St. Sophia in Kiev. At the far western edge of Ukrainian Village, the **Ukrainian Institute of Modern Art** (⊠ 2320 W. Chicago Ave., Ukrainian Village, ☎ 773/227–5522) focuses on contemporary paintings and sculpture by artists of Ukrainian descent. It's open Wednesday, Thursday, Saturday, and Sunday from noon to 4; admission is free.

Nestled under the El tracks at Superior and Franklin streets is **Brett's Kitchen** (⊠ 233 W. Superior St., River North, ☎ 312/664–6354), an excellent spot for a sandwich or an omelet Monday through Saturday.

㉓ **33 West Kinzie Street.** This Dutch Renaissance–style brick building looks as though it belongs in Amsterdam—except for the huge HOLY COW! banner that decorates it. That was the favorite expression of late Chicago Cubs announcer Harry Caray, who owned an eponymous restaurant here that's still popular. ⊠ *River North*.

LINCOLN PARK

In the early years of the 19th century, the area bounded by North Avenue (1600 N.) on the south, Diversey Parkway (2800 N.) on the north, the lake on the east, and the Chicago River on the west was a sparsely settled community of truck farms and orchards that grew produce for the city of Chicago, 3 mi to the south. The original city burial ground was on the lakefront at North Avenue. The park that today extends from North Avenue to Hollywood Avenue (5700 N.) was established in 1864, after the city transferred about 20,000 bodies to Graceland and Rosehill cemeteries, then far north of the city limits. Many of the dead were Confederate soldiers who perished at Camp Douglas, the Union's infamous prison camp on the lakefront several miles south. Called Lincoln Park after the then recently assassinated president, this swath of green became the city's first public playground. The neighborhood adjacent to the original park also became known as Lincoln Park (to the confusion of some visitors).

By the mid-1860s the area had become more populated. Germans predominated, but there were Irish and Scottish immigrants as well. The construction in 1860 of the Presbyterian Theological Seminary (later the McCormick Seminary, which moved to Hyde Park in 1977) brought modest residential construction. By the end of the century immigrants from Italy and Eastern Europe—Poles, Slovaks, Serbs, Hungarians, and Romanians—had swelled the population, and much of the housing stock in the western part of the neighborhood dates from this period.

Between the world wars expensive construction, particularly along the lakefront and the park, was undertaken in Lincoln Park. At the same time, however, the deteriorating, once elegant houses to the west were being subdivided into rooming houses—a process that was occurring at roughly the same period in Hyde Park, 10 mi to the south. Ethnic diversification and an increase in crime were also changing the face of the neighborhood, which was rocked by the St. Valentine's Day Massacre in 1929 and the FBI shooting of John Dillinger at the Biograph Theatre in 1934, both of which took place on North Lincoln Avenue (☞ Chicago's Gangster Past box, *below*).

Following World War II, the ethnic groups that had been first to arrive in Lincoln Park had achieved some affluence and began to leave for northern parts of the city and the suburbs. The subsequent wave of immigrants that moved to take their place often lacked the resources to maintain their properties. By 1960 nearly a quarter of the housing stock in Lincoln Park was classified as substandard. As housing prices fell, artists and others who appreciated the aesthetic value of the decaying buildings and were willing to work to restore them moved to the southeastern part of the area. The newcomers joined established residents in forming the Old Town Triangle Association; residents to the north, who had successfully resisted subdivision, formed the Mid-North Association. In 1954 neighborhood institutions, including DePaul University, the McCormick Seminary, four hospitals, a bank, and others, dismayed by the decline of the area, formed the Lincoln Park Conservation Association. As the University of Chicago had done in Hyde Park, this association began exploring the possibilities for rejuvenating the area.

Eventually, the original buildings along North Avenue were bulldozed and replaced with anonymous modern town-house developments, and many north–south streets were blocked off at North Avenue to create an enclosed community to the north. Since the 1960s the gentrification of Lincoln Park has moved steadily westward, spreading as far as Clybourn Avenue, formerly a light industrial strip. Today this lively neighborhood has countless thriving businesses: unique shops, hot restaurants, and clubs where lines form on weekends. It also has some of the loveliest residential streets in the city.

The walks in this section concentrate on the history and attractions of three distinct areas: the DePaul area and North Lincoln Avenue and Halsted Street; the Old Town Triangle; and the lakefront and Lincoln Park.

DePaul and North Lincoln Avenue

The serenity of DePaul University, which rules the northern part of the neighborhood, makes a pleasant contrast to the busy shops and restaurants and the raucous nightlife of two nearby upscale neighborhood arteries: North Lincoln Avenue—where the Biograph Theatre, site of John Dillinger's waterloo, still stands—and Halsted Street.

Numbers in the text correspond to numbers in the margin and on the Lincoln Park map.

A Good Walk

This walk starts at the Lincoln Park campus of DePaul University. The CTA is the best way to get here from the Loop or the Near North Side. Take the Howard (Red line) train or the Ravenswood (Brown line) train to Fullerton Avenue. Sheffield Avenue will be the nearest north–south street. If you're driving, take Lake Shore Drive to Fullerton Avenue and drive west on Fullerton Avenue to Sheffield Avenue. Parking is scarce, especially evenings and weekends, so public transit or a cab is recommended.

Begin a visit to **DePaul University** ①, one of the largest Catholic universities in the country, on its northern boundary—the southeast cor-

Lincoln Park

1600W

Greenview Ave.

Bosworth Ave.

2400N

Southport Ave.

Wayne Ave.

Lakewood Ave.

Fullerton Ave.

1200W

Altgeld St.

Racine Ave.

Clifton Ave.

TO
ST. ALPHONSUS
REDEMPTORIST
CHURCH

Lincoln Ave.

800W

Burling St.

❸ ❷ ❶

❹

❼

❺

Belden Ave.

Magnolia Ave.

Seminary Ave.

Kenmore Ave.

Sheffield Ave.

Bissell St.

Fremont St.

Webster Ave.

Dickens Ave.

Clybourn Ave.

2000N

Cortland St.

Maud St.

Poe St.

Armitage Ave.

Wisconsin St.

Dayton St.

Halsted St.

Burling St.

North Branch Chicago River

Elston Ave.

90
94

John F. Kennedy Expwy.

Clybourn Ave.

Kingsbury St.

Bissell St.

Willow St.

KEY
— Metra Lines

1600N

North Ave.

0   400 yards
0   440 meters

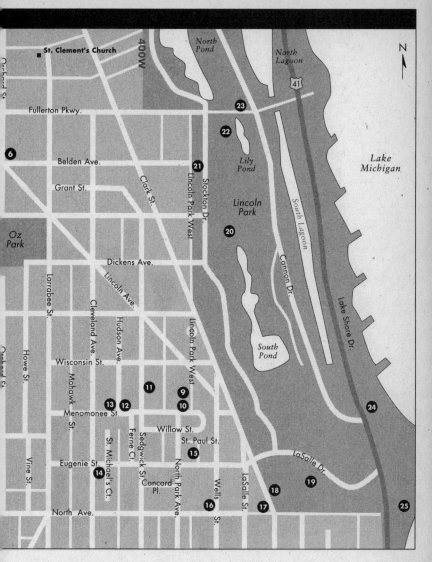

St. Clement's Church

400W

North Pond

North Lagoon

41

Lake Michigan

N

Fullerton Pkwy.

23

22

6

Belden Ave.

21

Lily Pond

Grant St.

Clark St.

Lincoln Park West

Stockton Dr.

Lincoln Park

South Lagoon

Oz Park

20

Dickens Ave.

Lincoln Ave.

Cannon Dr.

Lake Shore Dr.

Larrabee St.

Cleveland Ave.

Hudson Ave.

Lincoln Park West

South Pond

Howe St.

Wisconsin St.

Mohawk St.

11

9

10

13 12

Menomonee St.

Willow St.

St. Paul St.

24

Sedgwick St.

Ferne Ct.

15

Vine St.

Eugenie St.

14

St. Michael's Ct.

Concord Pl.

North Park Ave.

Wells St.

LaSalle St.

LaSalle Dr.

19

18

16

17

25

North Ave.

ner of Fullerton and Sheffield avenues. To the west across Sheffield Avenue, the massive brick complex extending halfway down the block is **Sanctuary Hall** ②, now a university residence hall.

For a look at the modern part of the campus, walk west on Fullerton Avenue one block to Kenmore Avenue and the **John T. Richardson Library** ③, where you should pop in to see the two-story reading room and the art gallery—the exhibits rotate regularly, and include such local and international works as: "At the Edge of Hope," new works by artists from Iraq; "Spring Remembered" and other prints by Tony Fitzpatrick, a Chicago artist; and the ceramic art of Chicagoan Ruth Duckworth. Exit through the library's courtyard, where, in a grassy, walled-in area called St. Vincent's Circle, you can sit down next to a bronze sculpture of St. Vincent de Paul, the university's namesake, engaged in discussion with two college students (you can tell they're contemporary from the sweatshirt, tennis shoes, and backpack). Continue west a short distance to what formerly was Seminary Avenue and is now a grassy quadrangle for the campus.

Walk south down the quadrangle to Belden Avenue, then east to the portion of the campus between Sheffield Avenue and Halsted Street that was the former McCormick Theological Seminary grounds, built in the 1880s. On this spot, antislavery groups met during the Civil War, and Chicagoans sought refuge from the Great Fire of 1871. The large brick building on your right as you enter the campus from Belden Avenue, just past Dayton Avenue, was built as a chapel but is now the university's Concert Hall (✉ 800 W. Belden Ave.). The small street inside the U on your left is **Chalmers Place** ④, a quiet cul-de-sac with a huge grassy area and tall trees that may make you feel you've stepped into the 19th century. The large Queen Anne building on the north side has a great turret and decorative shingles.

Head to the west end of the street to Cortelyou Commons (✉ 2324 N. Fremont Ave.), an imposing Gothic-style structure built in 1929 that is used for special events. Continue south past the Commons, east on Chalmers Place, and south again to exit the university grounds where you entered on Belden Avenue.

Continue east on Belden Avenue and turn left onto Halsted Street. Walk north to the three-way intersection of Fullerton Avenue, Halsted Street, and Lincoln Avenue. This section of Lincoln Avenue runs on a northwest–southeast diagonal. The upscale neighborhood has been an especially popular place for young professionals who are just a stone's throw from downtown Loop jobs. There are plenty of fun places to spend money and leisure time here—cafés, restaurants, bars, and boutiques. In particular, there are a number of interesting shops catering to children. You'll be hard-pressed to find a drugstore or a shoe repair shop: those conveniences have moved to Clark Street, several blocks east, or to Sheffield Avenue.

On the southeast side of the intersection, where Halsted Street and Lincoln Avenue come together at a point, is the huge **White Elephant Children's Memorial Hospital Resale Shop** (✉ 2380 N. Lincoln Ave., ☏ 773/883–6184), which carries every kind of used merchandise imaginable. Earnings benefit Children's Memorial Hospital, which is just east and south of the shop. As you head southeast down the street, note the arresting building at **2312–2310 North Lincoln Avenue** ⑤, which was designed by Adler and Sullivan. At the corner of Lincoln and Belden avenues, cross the street. The **John Barleycorn Memorial Pub** ⑥ is one of Chicago's better-known pubs—especially with dart players.

Head back up Lincoln Avenue, past the three-way intersection, to the **Biograph Theatre** ⑦, where gangster John Dillinger perished by FBI gunfire. After years as a mainstream commercial theatre, the Biograph now hosts select film festivals. Negotiations were under way at press time for a local theater company to acquire the space. Across Lincoln Avenue is the **Red Lion** (✉ 2446 N. Lincoln Ave.), an English-style pub "haunted" by a female ghost who wanders up and down the squeaky staircase, and **The Three Penny** (✉ 2424 N. Lincoln Ave.), the street's primary venue for first-run movies (usually of the arty variety).

Return now to the intersection where the White Elephant stands and head south on Halsted Street, one of the most vibrant, successful streets in Lincoln Park. Here you'll find a number of boutiques, trendy diners, and watering holes, plus such chain outposts as the Gap and Banana Republic.

Two blocks down, at Webster Avenue, walk east to **Oz Park** ⑧, a large green space named in honor of L. Frank Baum, author of the Oz storybooks, who lived and worked in Chicago. Back on Halsted Street, south of Webster Avenue, is **Cafe Ba-Ba-Reeba!** (✉ 2024 N. Halsted St.), which serves great tapas and a notorious sangria.

Continue walking south one block to Armitage Avenue, then head west a few blocks to the original location of **Old Town School of Folk Music** (✉ 909 W. Armitage Ave.) in a turn-of-the-20th-century building. The School has since opened a new location in the Ravenswood area (✉ 4544 N. Lincoln Ave.). Most classes and performances are held in this new space, though the original location still offers instruction. Pick up a schedule and check out who's performing: the School hosts concerts with folk and blues players from around the world.

To continue with an exploration of the Old Town Triangle, you'll want to either retrieve your car or jump on Bus 73, heading east on Armitage Avenue. Get off where Armitage dead-ends into Clark Street and Lincoln Park, a trip of just over ½ mi.

TIMING

You could see the sights on this walk in an hour or two. If the weather is fine, you may want to allow an extra hour or two for exploring the beautiful residential streets just south of DePaul University and for visiting the many shops along Halsted Street.

Sights to See

❼ Biograph Theatre. This theater is now on the National Register of Historic Places, since it was here that gangster John Dillinger met his end at the hands of the FBI in July 1934. The film playing was *Manhattan Melodrama*. The former multiplex theater now hosts select film festivals. ✉ *2433 N. Lincoln Ave., Lincoln Park.*

❹ Chalmers Place. This pleasant cul-de-sac in the midst of DePaul University buildings is lined with private town houses, some of which are 100 years old and served as residences for McCormick Seminary faculty members. The homes have semicircular brickwork around the windows. ✉ *½ block north of Belden Ave. between Fremont Ave. and Halsted St., Lincoln Park.*

❶ DePaul University. Founded in 1898 by the Vincentian Fathers, DePaul is the largest Catholic university in the Midwest. It serves more than 17,000 students at its Lincoln Park location and four other schools in the Loop and suburbs. DePaul has a large continuing-education program, and thousands of Chicago adults attend the many evening and weekend classes. ✉ *Bounded by Fullerton, Racine, and Belden Aves. and Halsted St., Lincoln Park,* WEB *www.depaul.edu.*

⑥ John Barleycorn. This popular pub in an 1890 building has a pleasant beer garden, a nautical theme, and plays classical music, not rock. Ship models adorn the walls, and the brass-plated door has not a window but a porthole. Some of the models date to the 1880s and were collected by a former owner during his travels to faraway places, including Sri Lanka, Hong Kong, and Cambodia. A slide show of famous works of art illuminates one wall, a great way to pass the time as the service here can be slow. The beer-battered fish-and-chips are especially tasty. ⊠ *658 W. Belden Ave., Lincoln Park,* ☎ *773/348–8899.*

❸ John T. Richardson Library. Designed by Lohan Associates of Chicago, DePaul University's library has soaring ceilings, oak woodwork, stained-glass windows made by Tiffany Studios early in the 20th century, and an impressive two-story reading room on the third floor. There's a statue of St. Vincent de Paul in the courtyard. ⊠ *2350 N. Kenmore Ave., DePaul.*

NEED A BREAK? | **Nookies, too** (⊠ 2114 N. Halsted St., Lincoln Park, ☎ 773/327–1400), one of the better-known diners in this area, is a pleasant spot for an inexpensive snack or a meal of the burger or grilled-cheese variety. It has a casual counter area in front, delicious fries, good chicken noodle soup, and more healthful items such as turkey burgers. It's open 24 hours on Friday and Saturday; note that it's cash-only, no credit cards accepted.

🖐 ❽ Oz Park. Statues of the Cowardly Lion and Tin Woodsman as well as the yellow bricks in the northeast corner of this large grassy space give away the reason for its name. L. Frank Baum, who wrote the best-selling children's book *The Wonderful Wizard of Oz* (the basis for the 1939 movie classic), once lived in this area. The park has endlessly intriguing wooden play equipment for youngsters. ⊠ *Webster and Lincoln Aves., Lincoln Park.*

❷ Sanctuary Hall. Built in 1895 as the St. Augustine Home for the Aged, this huge building is now a DePaul University dormitory with apartments for students. ⊠ *2358 N. Sheffield Ave., Lincoln Park.*

OFF THE BEATEN PATH | **ST. ALPHONSUS REDEMPTORIST CHURCH –** Built between 1889 and 1897, the Gothic St. Alphonsus originally served a German neighborhood. The beautiful interior has a vaulted ceiling and stained glass. ⊠ 1429 W. Wellington Ave., Lake View, ☎ 773/525–0709.

St. Clement's Church. Combining both Romanesque and Byzantine elements in its design, St. Clement's has beautiful mosaics and lavish stained glass. ⊠ *642 W. Deming Pl., Lincoln Park,* ☎ *773/281–0371.*

❺ 2312–2310 North Lincoln Avenue. This 1880s building with a light blue facade and bright red bricks was a bakery when druggist Ferdinand Kauffmann first had it built. (Dankmar Adler and the great Louis Sullivan were the architects.) Today it's Cella, which sells baby clothes and toys in the middle of a popular nightclub-and-restaurant area. The rickety wooden front doors are the only remaining doors in Chicago designed by Sullivan himself. ⊠ *Lincoln Park.*

Old Town Triangle

What began in the 1850s as a modest neighborhood of working-class German families now accommodates a diverse population and has some of the oldest—and most expensive—real estate in Chicago. Since the mid 1900s, many houses in the Old Town historic district have been preserved. Besides its interesting architecture, Old Town is notable for being home to the comedy club Second City.

CHICAGO'S GANGSTER PAST

TIME HAS HELPED HEAL the scars of Chicago's unsavory gangster past. Most of the gangster haunts have long since been razed, and city officials and residents have put the Prohibition-era crime and corruption well behind them. But Al Capone may still be the city's most famous citizen—a notoriety perhaps now shared by former Chicago Bulls superstar Michael Jordan.

When Prohibition ended the legal sale of alcoholic beverages in 1920, a strong demand for illegal goods and services was created. Chicago fell into the hands of Al "Scarface" Capone, George "Bugs" Moran, Earl "Hymie" Weiss, "Bloody" Angelo Genna, and "Machine Gun" Jack McGurn, among others. The '20s were punctuated by gunfire, as wars erupted between the rivals.

Capone won control of Chicago's underworld on Feb. 14, 1929, during the bloody St. Valentine's Day Massacre. His henchmen, dressed as police officers, entered the S. M. C. Cartage garage at 2122 N. Clark Street, killing six of Bugsy Moran's men and a visitor. The seven men had been lined up against a wall and riddled with bullets; to this day, no one has been convicted of the murders. Seven bushes stand at the spot, which is now a grassy area next to a senior-citizens home.

Capone ran gambling, prostitution, and bootlegging rackets, with a fortune estimated at $60 million. Under the supervision of Elliot Ness, Prohibition agents dismantled Capone's bootlegging empire, while Internal Revenue Service agents convicted him of income tax evasion in 1931. Capone was sentenced to 11 years in prison, only to be released in 1939 to retire in Florida where he died from syphilis in 1947.

Deemed "public enemy number one," Indianapolis-born John Dillinger robbed a dozen banks over 13 months. After escaping jail in Crown Point, Indiana, he moved to Chicago in 1934. He was betrayed by the "lady in red," an acquaintance who told federal agents she would wear a red dress while accompanying him to the Biograph Theatre at ⊠ 2433 North Lincoln Avenue. Federal agents fatally shot Dillinger as he left the theater, although some historians maintain Dillinger was not the man killed there.

It's unclear whether the Mafia, as defined in Capone's day, still exists in Chicago. Now and then one of the local dailies will report a story about a city contractor "with Mafia ties"—usually inspiring a what-else-is-new? reaction among the citizenry. Perhaps the most prominent modern equivalent of a Chicago mob boss is Larry Hoover, who had allegedly led the notorious Gangster Disciples from prison.

You can find pieces of gangster lore at spots sprinkled throughout the city. The **Green Mill,** for example, became mobster territory when "Machine Gun" Jack McGurn gained a 25% ownership of the club. It still has a trapdoor from speakeasy days and fabulous art deco detailing around the bar, and hosts some of the best jazz players in the city. ⊠ *Uptown.*

Untouchable Tours (☎ 773/881–1195; 🖾 $22) offers a two-hour bus tour of Prohibition-era gangster hot spots and hit spots. It's theater on wheels: the guides, dressed like wise guys and delivering wisecracks, retell gangland exploits, as well as relate other bits of Chicago history. Tours depart from in front of the Rock 'n' Roll McDonald's, at Clark and Ohio streets; advance reservations are required.

Numbers in the text correspond to numbers in the margin and on the Lincoln Park map.

A Good Walk

The Old Town Triangle begins west of the intersections of Lincoln Park West, Lincoln Avenue and Wisconsin Street. If you're driving, park at a meter on Lincoln Avenue, or if you park elsewhere, be aware that some streets are zoned—meaning you would need a special sticker to park there. Read the signs carefully to see when general parking is allowed. If you're driving around the area, know that it is filled with courts and lanes that run for only a block or so; many are one-way-only streets.

The west side of Lincoln Park West between Wisconsin and Menomonee streets is a gold mine of historic residential architecture. The two marvelous frame houses at **1838 and 1836 North Lincoln Park West** ⑨ were built in the early 1870s. The 1838 building is gray, with white trim and huge door knockers; the 1836 home is tan and dark brown. Just past these are five **Louis Sullivan row houses** ⑩. The redbrick, Queen Anne–style homes provide a unique glimpse of the architect's early work.

Before walking on, look across to the east side of the street and 1835 Lincoln Park West, a frame house built in 1874. Note the number (709) in the stained glass above the door. That was the original house number when Lincoln Park West was called Franklin Street. At 1817 Lincoln Park West is a French Renaissance–style freestanding home with unusually elaborate wooden doors, carved in the forms of curly haired children holding large fruit cornucopias.

Continue south on Lincoln Park West to Menomonee Street. The brightly painted aqua-hue home on the northwest corner, at 1802 Lincoln Park West, was originally a farmhouse, built in 1874 for Henry Meyer. Turn east on Menomonee Street and walk a short distance to Number 216, a tiny cottage that dates to 1874. It was one of the first cottages to be built as temporary quarters after the Great Fire. Backtrack west on Menomonee Street, and go two blocks to Sedgwick Street.

Turn right onto the **1800 North Sedgwick Street** ⑪ block and proceed about halfway up. Each of the houses on the right, starting with 1811, was designed for its owner at an astronomical price by a different world-renowned architect. In the small park across the street, take a look at the two unusually shiny 1975 sculptures of horses by artist John Kearney. His medium: parts of car bumpers (now a bit rusty).

Retrace your steps to Menomonee Street, turn right, and walk one block to Hudson Avenue. The Japanese-style building where the street curves is the **Midwest Buddhist Temple** ⑫. In June, Old Town Triangle hosts the popular Old Town Art Fair, and the Midwest Buddhist Temple is one of the most popular food vendors at the fair (they serve food only during the fair).

Before continuing on Menomonee Street, notice the corner building, **1800 North Hudson Avenue** ⑬, now a law firm, in a half-timber style that's unusual for Lincoln Park. Go west one block on Menomonee Street, then south on Cleveland Avenue. Walk east on Eugenie Street to St. Michaels Court. You can't miss the ornate **St. Michael's Church** ⑭, constructed for the area's German community.

Walk east on Eugenie Street six blocks and turn left onto **Crilly Court** ⑮, one of the oldest streets in Chicago. The town houses and apartments here were built in the 1880s; it's easy to picture horse-drawn carriages in front of them. When you come to St. Paul Avenue at the street's north end, turn east, proceed to Wells Street, and turn right. **Second City** ⑯, the well-known comedy club, is 1½ blocks south, between Eugenie Street and North Avenue. This area on Wells Street is the main commercial strip in Old Town, with a number of good restaurants, clubs, and stylish shops.

If you want to continue on to Lincoln Park, go south on Wells Street to North Avenue, turn left, and walk east to Clark Street.

TIMING

You can do this walk in one or two hours, or you can choose to explore Old Town's many intriguing side streets for up to a half day.

Sights to See

⑮ **Crilly Court.** This lovely tree-lined street, marked with small concrete sidewalk monuments, was created in 1884 by South Side contractor Daniel Crilly, who built the row houses on the west side and the four-story apartment buildings on the east side. They were renovated about 50 years later by Edgar Crilly, one of his sons; their restoration was one of the first steps in the renewal and gentrification of the Old Town Triangle in particular and Lincoln Park in general. Above the doors of the east-side buildings are carved the names of Daniel Crilly's children: Isabelle, Oliver, Edgar, and Erminnie. ⊠ *Bounded by Eugenie and Wells Sts. and N. Park and St. Paul Aves., Lincoln Park.*

⑬ **1800 North Hudson Avenue.** A frame house built around the turn of the 20th century has become a striking black-and-white half-timber building. In 1955 it was remodeled to look like a Bavarian dwelling after its owner, the late William Schmidt, returned from a trip to Germany, where he fell in love with this style of architecture. ⊠ *Lincoln Park.*

⑪ **1800 North Sedgwick Street.** The materials used to build the houses numbered 1811–1847 begin with handsome contemporary redbrick and move on to poured concrete, oddly colored brick, and gray wood. All were custom designed by different architects in the late 1970s. Such were the egos involved that the architects could agree on nothing—not style, not materials, not lot size, not even the height of the buildings. Although some of the structures might look good on another site, here they look like transplanted misfits, jammed in together, out of character with the neighborhood and with each other. Despite their monetary value (some have been on the market for more than a million dollars), little about them is aesthetically pleasing. ⊠ *Lincoln Park.*

⑨ **1838 and 1836 North Lincoln Park West.** Of these two frame buildings, the smaller, 1836, was built just after the fire of 1871; it has narrow clapboards, bay windows, leaded glass, and decorative iron grillwork around the miniature widow's walk above the front entrance. There are also decorative cutouts in the wood over the front door. The exterior painting has been done in contrasting brown, beige, and white to reveal the details of the woodwork. The larger house, painted gray and white, is a grand structure built to resemble a Swiss chalet. Both buildings were constructed for the Wacker family, prominent German brewers.

Frame houses are relatively uncommon in Lincoln Park, in part because of the restrictions on wood construction that went into effect following the fire of 1871. (Some areas in southwestern Lincoln Park do have extensive frame construction; the regulations were not always strictly enforced.) ⊠ *Lincoln Park.*

⑩ **Louis Sullivan row houses.** The love of geometric ornamentation that Sullivan eventually brought to such projects as the Carson Pirie Scott building is already visible in these row houses built in 1885. The terra-cotta cornices and decorative window tops are especially noteworthy. ⊠ *1826–1834 N. Lincoln Park W., Lincoln Park.*

⑫ Midwest Buddhist Temple. The temple's plain walls, landscaped gardens, and pagoda-like roof strike an unusual but harmonious note in a largely brick neighborhood. The congregation, about 80% Japanese-American, comes from all over the city and the suburbs. The temple was built in 1971 on an empty parcel of land purchased from the city in the 1960s. Call to arrange a tour. ⊠ *435 W. Menomonee St., Lincoln Park,* ☎ *312/943–7801.*

⑭ St. Michael's Church. This massive brick Romanesque-style church, which dates to 1869, partially withstood the fire of 1871. German residents of the neighborhood restored the interior of the church after the fire. Their work is a legacy of exquisite craftsmanship. Inside are beautiful stained-glass windows and a stunning altar of carved wood. Outside are classical columns of different heights, elaborate capitals, many roofs with stonework at the top, huge wooden doors, and a large clock tower beneath the cross. The building stands on land that was donated in the 1850s by Michael Diversey (the early beer baron after whom Diversey Parkway is named) for the purpose of providing a church where the area's German community could worship. ⊠ *1633 N. Cleveland Ave., Lincoln Park,* ☎ *312/642–2498.*

NEED A
BREAK?

Twin Anchors (⊠ 1655 N. Sedgwick St., Lincoln Park, ☎ 312/266–1616; no lunch weekdays), a popular Old Town restaurant and tavern for more than 60 years, is famous for its barbecued ribs.

⑯ Second City. Such talents as Elaine May, Mike Nichols, Alan Arkin, Joan Rivers, the late John Belushi, Bill Murray, Shelley Long, Rick Moranis, and *Saturday Night Live* comedienne Rachel Dratch used this improvisational comedy club as a training ground. It eventually inspired several branch theaters—Toronto's Second City, which produced Dan Aykroyd and the late John Candy and Gilda Radner, is probably the best known—as well as the hit TV show *SCTV.* After the main stage performances, actors come out for a half hour of improvisation where audience members shout out suggestions upon which the players build a skit. The improv sets are free even if you didn't attend the show and generally begin around 10:30 PM. ⊠ *1616 N. Wells St., Lincoln Park,* ☎ *312/337–3992,* WEB *www.secondcity.com.*

NEED A
BREAK?

Topo Gigio (⊠ 1516 N. Wells St., Lincoln Park, ☎ 312/266–9355; no lunch Sun.) has a wide selection of wine and Italian cuisine; you can also order appetizers and salads for a snack. The bruschetta is particularly recommended. In the summertime a lovely garden is open for dining.

Lincoln Park

The city's oldest and most popular park is one of a number of lakefront greenbelts that were wisely created as a refuge for city dwellers. Within and near Lincoln Park are a number of appealing attractions.

Numbers in the text correspond to numbers in the margin and on the Lincoln Park map.

A Good Walk

You can reach Lincoln Park by taking the Sheridan Road Bus 151 north from North Michigan Avenue. Get off at North Avenue. If you're driving, take Lake Shore Drive to the LaSalle Street–North Avenue exit. Make a right turn onto Stockton Drive and look for metered parking.

The area can be extremely congested, however, especially on weekends, so driving is not recommended.

The huge Romanesque-style structure on the west side of Clark Street is **Moody Memorial Church** ⑰, one of the largest Protestant churches in the nation. Across Clark Street is the southwest entrance to the park, but first stop in to see the exhibits at the **Chicago Historical Society** ⑱, at the northeast corner of North Avenue and Clark Street. The original Georgian structure was built in 1932; walk around to the east side (facing the lake) and see what it looked like at the time.

All of Chicago's parks, and Lincoln Park in particular, are dotted with sculptures—historical, literary, or just plain fanciful. East of the historical society is one of the most famous, the **Abraham Lincoln statue** ⑲. The figure looks down pensively—in marked contrast to the lively activities of the children who often play nearby.

Heading into the park and wandering north (an underground tunnel provides the simplest route) along the park's main north–south artery, Stockton Drive, will bring you to the **Lincoln Park Zoo** ⑳, one of the finest small urban zoos in the country. (Look west of the duck-filled pond for the red barn, home of Farm in the Zoo: the main entrance is just north of it.) The homely bronze figure just east of Stockton Drive and south of Dickens Street is Hans Christian Andersen, seated there since 1896. Beside him is the beautiful swan from his most famous story, "The Ugly Duckling."

Also near the zoo, at the western edge of the park opposite Belden Avenue, is the **Shakespeare Garden** ㉑, with a statue of the playwright. North of the zoo you can visit the **Lincoln Park Conservatory** ㉒, with its lush greenery. West of the conservatory, between Stockton Drive and Lincoln Park West, is Grandmother's Garden, a collection dating from 1893 of informal beds of perennials, including hibiscuses and chrysanthemums.

The conservatory garden, south of the building, has a joyful fountain where bronze storks, fish, and small mer-boys cavort in the spraying water. The 1887 Bates Fountain was the collaborative effort of Augustus Saint-Gaudens and his assistant, Frederick MacMonnies.

Continue north to Fullerton Parkway, turn right, and proceed to Cannon Drive, site of the Chicago Academy of Science's **Peggy Notebaert Nature Museum** ㉓. Coming out, stroll under Lake Shore Drive to the lakefront and **North Avenue Beach** ㉔. About 1 mi south of Fullerton Parkway, it is likely to be thronged on summer weekends but sparsely populated at other times. To stroll back to the Near North Side, about 2 mi from here, walk south past North Avenue Beach and follow the lakefront promenade. Notice the blue-and-white beach house, its portholes and "smokestacks" mimicking an old ocean liner. At the south end of the beach, stop by the 1950s vintage **Chess Pavilion** ㉕ to watch people of all ages engrossed in intellectual combat.

TIMING

You can visit the sights on this walk in three hours. That timing, however, does not allow for leisurely visits to Lincoln Park Zoo and the museums. You could easily spend two hours or more at each.

Sights to See

⑲ **Abraham Lincoln statue.** Known as the Standing Lincoln, this statue was completed in 1887 by the noted American sculptor Augustus Saint-Gaudens, whose portrayals of military heroes and presidents adorn almost every major city east of the Mississippi River. The sculptor used a mask of Lincoln's face and casts of his hands that were made before he became president. To Lincoln's right, below the steps, a portion of the Gettysburg address has been inscribed onto a metal ball. ⊠ *Lincoln Park, east of Chicago Historical Society, Lincoln Park.*

㉕ Chess Pavilion. The competition gets intense at this open-air structure on the lakefront. There are carved reliefs along its base, and statues of a king and queen flank it on either side. ⊠ *Lakefront at the south end of Lincoln Park, Lincoln Park.*

★ ℭ **⑱ Chicago Historical Society.** Chicago's oldest cultural institution (founded in 1856), the CHS is housed in a stately brick Georgian building dating to 1932 that was updated in 1971 with a striking addition facing Clark Street. In the south end (the curved portion) is a terra-cotta arch designed by Daniel Burnham in the late 1800s; it originally framed the doorway of the National Livestock Bank, near the now-closed Chicago stockyards. The historical society's permanent exhibits include the much-loved Diorama Room, which portrays scenes from Chicago's history and has been a part of the lives of generations of Chicago children. Other attractions are Chicago's first locomotive (which you may board), collections of costumes, and the popular Illinois Pioneer Life Gallery, where there are daily crafts demonstrations by costumed docents. ⊠ *1601 N. Clark St., Lincoln Park,* ☎ *312/642–4600,* WEB *www.chicagohistory.org.* ⌨ *$5, free Mon.* ☉ *Mon.–Sat. 9:30–4:30, Sun. noon–5.*

㉒ Lincoln Park Conservatory. Green grows on green in the lush tropical main display room of this refreshing city greenhouse built in 1892. Stroll through the permanent displays of orchids, palms and ferns. Throughout the year, there are special shows including the fragrant Easter Lily show in March or April and the festive Chrysanthemum Show in November. The peacefulness and lush greenery inside the conservatory is a refreshing respite in the heart of this bustling neighborhood. ⊠ *2400 N. Stockton Dr., Lincoln Park,* ☎ *312/742–7736.* ⌨ *Free.* ☉ *Daily 9–5.*

★ ℭ **⑳ Lincoln Park Zoo.** Begun in 1868 with a pair of swans donated by New York's Central Park, this very popular 35-acre urban zoo grew through donations of animals from wealthy Chicago residents and the purchase of a collection from the Barnum and Bailey Circus. Many of the big houses, such as the Lion House and the Elephant House, are built in the classical brick typical of 19th-century zoos. The older buildings are surrounded by newer outdoor habitats that try to re-create the animals' natural wild surroundings. Outside the Lion House there's a window that lets you stand almost face to face with the animals (if the giant cats are in the mood).

Lincoln Park Zoo is particularly noted for its Great Ape House; the 24 gorillas are considered the finest collection in the world. Because the park participates in breeding programs, there are usually several babies about. The spectacular glass-dome Regenstein Small Mammal and Reptile House has simulated jungle, river, and forest environments for animal residents, including the much-loved koalas. In addition, the zoo has a large-mammal house (elephants, giraffes, black rhinos), a primate house, a bird house complete with a lush free-flight area and a waterfall, a huge polar bear pool with two bears, plus several rare and endangered species, such as the spectacle bear (named for the eyeglasslike markings around its eyes). For youngsters, there's the children's zoo, the Farm in the Zoo (farm animals and a learning center with films and demonstrations), and the Conservation Station, with hands-on activities. ⊠ *2200 N. Cannon Dr., Lincoln Park,* ☎ *312/ 742–2000.* ⌨ *Free.* ☉ *Daily 9–5.*

Just outside the park, the venerable **R. J. Grunt's** (✉ 2056 N. Lincoln Park W, Lincoln Park, ☎ 773/929–5363) has fine burgers plus soups and a salad bar.

⑰ **Moody Memorial Church.** Dwight L. Moody, a shoe salesman who moved to Chicago to become a minister for homeless children, founded this congregation in the 1800s. Built in 1925, the nondenominational Protestant church seats 4,000; it's gigantic, with a cantilevered balcony, vaulted ceiling, and no interior columns to block worshipers' views of the main pulpit. The church is affiliated with the nearby Moody Bible Institute and broadcasts its sermons via radio and television (☞ River North). ✉ *1630 N. Clark St., Lincoln Park,* ☎ *312/943–0466,* WEB *www.moodychurch.org.*

㉔ **North Avenue Beach.** One of the city's most popular warm-weather destinations, North Avenue Beach is packed with volleyball players and sunbathers on summer weekends. ✉ *Lakefront at North Ave., Lincoln Park.*

👋 ㉓ **Peggy Notebaert Nature Museum.** You'll walk among hundreds of Midwest species of butterflies and learn about the impact of rivers and lakes on daily life at this modern, tall-window-filled museum. Like Chicago's other science museums, it's geared toward kids, with educational computer games to play and water tubes to get wet in. But even jaded adults will have trouble restraining their excitement when bright-yellow butterflies land on their shoulders. Designed by local architects Perkins and Will, the 73,000-square-ft building, which also has a Children's Gallery designed to teach three- to eight-year-olds about the environment, has extensive glass and multilevel open-air terraces. The idea is to study the nature inside without losing track of the Lincoln Park nature outside. The gift shop is chock-full of interesting hands-on gifts. ✉ *2430 N. Cannon Dr., Lincoln Park,* ☎ *773/755–5100,* WEB *www.chias.org.* ☒ *$6, free Tues.* ☉ *Weekdays 9 AM–4:30 PM, weekends 10–5.*

㉑ **Shakespeare Garden.** Flowers and plants mentioned in the Bard's works are cultivated here. The bronze statue of the great playwright was cast by William Ordway Partridge in 1894, after he had exhibited a plaster model of the work at the Columbian Exposition. ✉ *East of the intersection of Belden Ave. and Lincoln Park W, Lincoln Park.*

NORTH CLARK STREET

A car or bus ride up North Clark Street north of Lincoln Park provides an interesting view of how cities and their ethnic populations grow and change. Before the late 1960s the Clark Street area was solidly white and middle class. Andersonville, named for the Swedish community centered on Foster Avenue (5200 N.) and Clark Street, extended north a half mile and included residential buildings to the east and west as well as a vital shopping strip on Clark. In the early 1970s, immigrants from Asia began to arrive. Chicago's first Thai restaurant opened at 5000 N. Clark Street (The Thai population has since dispersed throughout the city without establishing a significant concentration here.) The Japanese community, which had shops and restaurants in the upper North 3000s of Clark Street, became more firmly entrenched, joined by a substantial Korean population. Korean settlement has since grown to the north and west, along North Lincoln Avenue in the Albany Park neighborhood. As the 1970s ended, the Asian immigrants were being joined by newcomers from the Middle East.

With the contributions of the various communities, Andersonville has become a mosaic of people and cuisines. Currently, the Andersonville

DEVON AVENUE: A BRILLIANT BAZAAR

FOR THE ULTIMATE TASTE of Chicago's vivid, vibrant ethnic scene, take a trip to Devon Avenue on the far North Side. To stroll between 2200 and 3000 west on Devon Avenue—a street that's never stopped metamorphosing since English settlers named it after Devonshire in the 1800s (although here it is pronounced deh-von)—is to inhale the heady scents of curry and smoked fish, to be dazzled by the sequined saris in store windows, and to become an eavesdropper on conversations in Hindi, Russian, and other tongues.

This area took its shape in the 1970s and '80s, when immigration laws relaxed and the number of immigrants settling in Chicago increased. The '70s saw new arrivals from the Indian subcontinent; in the '80s, Asians from Thailand, Korea, the Philippines, and Vietnam followed, as did significant numbers of Syrians, Lebanese, Turks, Palestinians, and Jewish refuseniks.

Devon Avenue—about 7 mi from downtown—has a spicy mix of these immigrants. In places its double street signs attest to its diversity: for a while it's Gandhi Marg, then Golda Meir Avenue, though it's best known locally as Little India. By any name, it's a sensory safari best undertaken on foot.

The neighborhood is reachable from downtown via the Red line Howard El (exit at the Morse Avenue station), then the 155 (Devon Avenue) bus. By car take Lake Shore Drive north to Hollywood Avenue, and then turn west to Ridge Avenue. Turn right on Ridge Avenue and head north about 1 mi to Devon Avenue; turn left, drive west to Oakley Street, and park.

As you survey the multicultural bazaar west of Oakley—including video stores specializing in Indian and Pakistani films— you will likely begin to hear the music and vernacular of those countries from car radios and shop entrances; you'll also smell incense and all kinds of foods sizzling in restaurants and local groceries, which often double as fast-food havens. When Chicagoans crave Indian food, most head to Devon Avenue for an inexpensive authentic meal. **Udupi Palace** (✉ 2543 W. Devon) is a popular choice specializing in vegetarian South Indian cuisine. Take some time to explore the neighborhood groceries such as **Kamdar Plaza** (✉ 2646 W. Devon), and pick up some spices, curries, incense, and a sample bite from the deli; there's an indoor seating area within the store. Fine handcarved items in sandalwood, white cedar, and rosewood can be found at **Kaveri** (✉ 2657 W. Devon). Among the many pieces are deity statues, such as a Ganesh, the god of prosperity and knowledge.

The splendid clothing and jewelry shops in the 2500 and 2600 blocks are guaranteed to catch your eye. Go ahead— try on a sari or slip into a Western-cut dress beautifully embroidered and embellished in the Indian fashion. If the price isn't quite right, shop owners have been known to bargain a bit.

There is a large Muslim community in the area as well. At **IQRA' Book Center** (✉ 2751 W. Devon), a Muslim bookstore, you can browse through videos, audios, gifts, and specialty books dealing Islamic topics for Muslims, children, and non-Muslims.

West of Talman Avenue you'll find kosher bakeries and butchers, and Cyrillic shop signs and windows decorated with Russian newspapers and handmade matrioshkas (nesting dolls)—all evidence of this section's concentration of Russian Jews. At **Three Sisters Delicatessen** (✉ 2854 W. Devon), you can pick up an imported teapot or a doll with your Russian rye. At **Interbook** (✉ 2754 W. Devon) you can listen to rowdy rebel Russian rock or read recent romances.

neighborhood is a rapidly gentrifying mix of young professionals—gay and straight; Asian-American, African-American, and Middle Eastern families; and a few Swedish residents who all enjoy the neighborhood's convenient shopping and its proximity to the beach and to Lake Shore Drive.

A Good Drive and Walk

You can board the northbound Clark Street Bus 22 on Dearborn Street in the Loop or on Clark Street north of Walton Street. Or you can drive to Clark Street and North Avenue, where this ride begins. The bus might be a better bet, however. Clark Street is interesting, but traffic is pretty congested. Save room for food—there's plenty of ethnic eating on the way.

North Avenue (1600 N.) is the southern boundary of the Lincoln Park neighborhood, which extends north to Diversey Parkway (2800 N.). The ride through Lincoln Park affords views of handsome renovated housing as well as housing in the process of being restored, and upscale shops. As you head north on Clark Street and pass Armitage Avenue, look closely for what is *not* there. On the left side of the street, a grassy patch at 2122 N. Clark Street looks peaceful now, but it was the site of S. M. C. Cartage garage and the 1929 St. Valentine's Day Massacre, after which Al Capone won control of gangland. For a different view of history, **Reebie Storage and Moving** (✉ 2325 N. Clark St.) dates to 1923, a year after King Tut's tomb was opened. Two colorful statues of Ramses II guard the entrance and give protection to movers' furniture.

After you pass Diversey, you've entered the funky Lake View neighborhood. At the corner of Belmont Avenue, the **Dunkin' Donuts** (✉ 3200 N. Clark St.) is sometimes called "Punkin' Donuts" by locals, because of the heavily pierced, spiky-haired kids who often hang out on this stretch of Belmont Avenue. As you cross Belmont Avenue (✉ 3200 N.), you'll notice an increasing number of ethnic restaurants and shops. Quite a few sushi restaurants serve an array of raw fish. Try highly rated **Matsuya** (✉ 3469 N. Clark St.). Several Ethiopian restaurants, including the mother of them all, **Mama Desta's Red Sea** (✉ 3216 N. Clark St.), and many reggae bars are also on the stretch of Clark Street from Belmont Avenue north to Addison Street. Red Stripe and live music are the orders of the day at **The Wild Hare** (✉ 3530 N. Clark St.) and **Exedus II** (✉ 3477 N. Clark St.).

Continuing north to Addison Street, you'll find an abundance of bars and restaurants with the word *sport* somewhere in their names, all because of nearby **Wrigley Field,** home of the Chicago Cubs and, to many, the ultimate classic baseball stadium. At Clark Street and Irving Park Road (✉ 4000 N.) starts **Graceland Cemetery,** the final resting place of many 19th-century millionaires and other local luminaries.

Foster Avenue is the old southern boundary of Andersonville. At this point, park your car, though that is not always easy. There are not a lot of garages around here, and you might have to fight for a street spot. Walk up and down a two-block area of Clark Street, where there is a lively mix of restaurants, bakeries, delicatessens, and other shops. Although later immigrants have changed the face of the neighborhood, the 5200 block still shows many signs of the earlier wave of Swedish settlers.

To start with a taste of the Swedish heritage, the **Ann Sather** restaurant (✉ 5207 N. Clark St.), on the east side of the street, carries what may be the world's most tender, delicious cinnamon rolls (you can buy some to carry out) and light lingonberry pancakes. Up the street, the

Swedish-American Museum Center has an interesting mix of exhibits—and a wonderful walk-in log cabin for the children—as well as a gift shop packed with Scandinavian items. Farther north, **Wikstrom's Gourmet Foods** (✉ 5247 N. Clark St.) stocks Swedish meatballs, lingonberries, and imported cheeses, and has a few small tables where you can sip a drink or enjoy homemade soup.

If you have a sweet tooth, cross the street and head north to the **Swedish Bakery** (✉ 5348 N. Clark St.). Among its delicious baked goods are Swedish limpa and Jutland bread, *pepparkakor* (gingerbread) cookies, and flaky strudels and turnovers. Now turn around and head south to **Erickson's Delicatessen** (✉ 5250 N. Clark St.), which has been in the same location since 1925 and stocks a full line of imported Scandinavian delicacies including crispbreads, homemade spiced herring, and imported cheese. Erickson's windows relate the history of the area with news clippings and artifacts. The cozy **Svea Restaurant** (✉ 5236 N. Clark St.) serves mouthwatering breakfasts.

Andersonville also has many women-owned businesses. An anchor of the area is the **Women & Children First** bookstore, which stocks an extensive selection of feminist and children's books. Some of the surrounding businesses, including clothing boutiques **Studio 90** (✉ 5239 N. Clark St.) and **Presence** (✉ 5216 N. Clark St.), are also owned by women.

To experience the area's Middle Eastern influences, stop by the **Middle Eastern Bakery and Grocery** (✉ 1512 W. Foster Ave.), just west of Clark Street. Here are falafel, meat pies, spinach pies, *baba ghanouj* (eggplant puree dip), oil-cured olives, grains, pita bread, and seductive Middle Eastern sweets. **Cousins** (✉ 5203 N. Clark St.) serves Turkish dishes accompanied by Middle Eastern music. **Andies** (✉ 5253 N. Clark St.), a bit farther up the street, has Lebanese, Greek, and vegetarian cuisine from curried chicken to Moroccan eggplant soup. At **Reza's** (✉ 5255 N. Clark St.), you can dine on such outstanding Persian cuisine as kebabs, *dolmeh* (stuffed grape leaves), pomegranate juice, and charbroiled ground beef with Persian rice.

TIMING

Any day would be fine for this trip, although weekends, when more people might be out shopping, are particularly interesting. Unless you choose to make the Clark Street drive at rush hour (which would not be a good idea), you can see all the sights by car in a half hour. You will have plenty of time to look around while snarled in traffic. Add another two hours to park and stroll in Graceland Cemetery and in Andersonville. You may also want to allow time for lunch before or after your walk.

Sights to See

OFF THE
BEATEN PATH

ALTA VISTA TERRACE – Lining a narrow block of Alta Vista Terrace are 40 town houses completed in 1904 as one architectural development. The facades, which mirror one another diagonally across the block, differ in detail from rooflines to windows, yet the effect is harmonious. To get here by El train, take the Red line to the Addison stop. ✉ *3800 block of N. Alta Vista Terr., between Grace and Byron Sts., 2 blocks east of Clark St., Lake View.*

ARGYLE STREET – Vietnamese, Cambodian, Laotian, Thai, and other immigrants have transformed Argyle Street (5000 N.), between Sheridan Road and Broadway (about three blocks east of Clark Street), into a bustling shopping and dining district where English is the second language. The neighborhood, which is anchored by the El Red line's Argyle Street stop, recognizable for its red pagoda, can be iffy in spots, so be alert and exercise caution. Weekends are the best time to stop by for a bit of thousand-year-old-egg cake at **Chiu Quon Bakery** (⊠ 1127 W. Argyle St., Uptown). Sample the fine Asian cuisine at **Pho Xe Lua** (⊠ 1021 W. Argyle St., Uptown).

Graceland Cemetery. Among those interred at this cemetery, which stretches east over 119 landscaped acres from Clark Street, are many famous entrepreneurs, including Marshall Field, George Pullman, and Potter Palmer. Also here are some of the late greats of architecture: Louis Sullivan, John Wellborn Root, Daniel Burnham, and Ludwig Mies van der Rohe. The Getty Tomb may be the most exquisite of the astonishingly varied monuments. You can buy a walking-tour map at the entrance Monday through Saturday and explore on your own. Don't bring your picnic hamper, though; no food, drink, camcorders, or bicycles are allowed. ⊠ 4001 N. Clark St., *Lake View and Edgewater*, ☎ 773/525–1105. ⊙ *Daily 8–4:30*.

NEED A BREAK?	Take your time over a cappuccino and a pastry while you listen to live music or peruse shelves full of travel books at **Kopi, a Traveler's Cafe** (⊠ 5317 N. Clark St., Edgewater, ☎ 773/989–5674), a travel-theme coffeehouse with a multicultural miniboutique in back.

OFF THE BEATEN PATH	**MONTROSE HARBOR –** A treeless hill near this harbor off Lincoln Park draws soccer players and kite-flying enthusiasts of all ages on sunny weekends. Windsurfers often practice at nearby Montrose Beach. ⊠ 4400 N. Montrose Ave. at the lakefront, Uptown.
	OUR LADY OF MT. CARMEL CHURCH – Two blocks east of Clark Street on Belmont Avenue is this mother church for the North Side Catholic parishes, a serene oasis in the midst of urban cacophony. Established in 1886, it was Chicago's first English-speaking parish. The current English Gothic–style building was constructed in 1913 of Indiana limestone for what was then a predominantly Irish and German neighborhood. It has two organs, one a 1920s pipe organ by E. M. Skinner. Four times a year, the William Ferris Chorale performs 20th-century choral music here, with distinguished guest artists. It's worth trying to attend. ⊠ 690 W. Belmont Ave., Lake View, ☎ 773/525–0453, WEB www.mt-carmel.org.

🕙 **Swedish-American Museum Center.** Tiny and welcoming, this museum has changing exhibits that focus on the art and culture of Sweden. On permanent display are items immigrants brought with them to Chicago, such as trunks and clothes. A gift shop sells Swedish books, greeting cards, place mats, craft items, tablecloths, and candelabra. ⊠ 5211 N. Clark St., *Edgewater*, ☎ 773/728–8111, WEB *www.samac.org*. 🎫 *$4*. ⊙ *Tues.–Fri. 10–4, weekends 10–3*.

Women & Children First. This feminist bookstore stocks an extensive selection of books by and about women and has a large children's section with a carpeted storytelling alcove. Visiting authors, such as Alice Walker, Amy Tan, and Margaret Atwood, use this area as a stage for book readings and signings. A substantial section of the store is devoted to lesbian and gay fiction and nonfiction, and there's also a wide range of magazines, music, and videos. ⊠ 5233 N. Clark St., *Edgewater*, ☎ 773/769–9299, WEB *www.womenandchildrenfirst.com*. ⊙ *Mon. and Tues. 11–7, Wed.–Fri. 11–9, Sat. 10–7, Sun. 11–6*.

Wrigley Field. The grass is real, the walls are covered with ivy, and the bleachers are always packed with the faithful at the Chicago Cubs' beloved ballpark, which looms up right next to Clark Street. The team has been playing games at Wrigley Field, also known as "the friendly confines," since 1916. Although area residents and baseball purists lost their fight in 1988 against the installation of lights for night games, many Cubs games are still played in the afternoon. Just don't expect to see the home team win—the Cubs last appeared in the World Series in 1945, and it was 1908 when they last won the Series. ✉ *1060 W. Addison St., Lake View,* ☏ *773/404–2827.*

HYDE PARK AND KENWOOD

Although farmers and other settlers lived in Hyde Park in the early 1800s and Chicago's oldest Jewish congregation was founded here in 1847, this South Side neighborhood didn't begin growing significantly until the late 19th century. Two events triggered this growth: the 1892 opening of the University of Chicago and the 1893 World's Columbian Exposition. The Exposition, whose influence on American public architecture was far-reaching, spawned the Midway Plaisance and numerous Classical Revival buildings, including the famous Museum of Science and Industry. The Midway Plaisance, which surrounded the heart of the 1893 fair, still runs along the southern edge of the University of Chicago's original campus.

Another legacy of the exposition was the civic moniker "Windy City." Contrary to popular lore, the nickname has nothing to do with the city's volatile weather but rather that in a bid to host the exhibition, city leaders couldn't stop gabbing about how Chicago was the greatest town in the world. *New York Sun* editor Charles Dana coined the phrase to belittle these efforts and suggest that Chicagoans were, in fact, a bunch of windbags.

In the 1890s the university built housing for its faculty members; the mansions that line Woodlawn Avenue are the result. Then the neighborhood began to attract well-to-do private individuals who commissioned noted architects for their homes. Many of these buildings still stand in Kenwood.

With the Depression, followed by World War II, the neighborhood entered a period of decline. Grand homes fell into disrepair, and wartime housing shortages led to the conversion of stately houses into multifamily dwellings. Alarmed by the neighborhood's decline, concerned citizens formed the Hyde Park–Kenwood Community Conference in 1949. Aided by $29 million from the University of Chicago, which worried about recruiting and retaining faculty members, this conference set about restoring the neighborhood. The activists offered prizes to those who would buy and "deconvert" rooming houses, and pressured the city to enforce zoning laws.

Beginning in the late 1950s, urban renewal started to have a lasting effect on the neighborhood. The city, with the university's backing, razed 55th Street from Lake Park Avenue to Cottage Grove Avenue and tore down most of the buildings around Lake Park Avenue. With them went the workshops of painters and artisans; the quarters of "little magazines" (some 20 chapters of James Joyce's *Ulysses* were first published at one of them); the Compass Theatre, where Mike Nichols and Elaine May got their start; the Second City comedy club (since relocated to the Old Town area); and more than 40 jazz and blues bars. In their place came town houses designed by I. M. Pei and Harry Weese and a shopping mall designed by Keck and Keck. Cynics have described the urban-renewal process, one of the first such undertakings in the country, as one of "blacks and whites together, shoulder to shoulder—against the poor."

Hyde Park and Kenwood

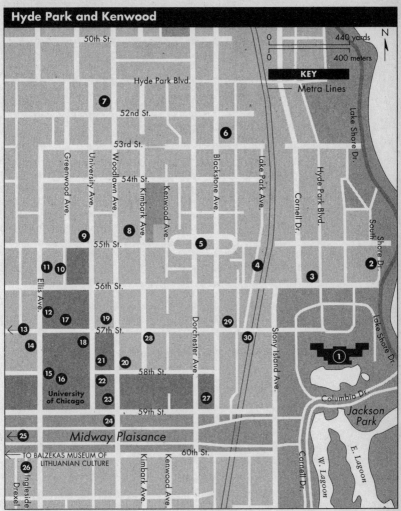

50th St.

Hyde Park Blvd.

52nd St.

53rd St.

54th St.

55th St.

56th St.

57th St.

58th St.

59th St.

60th St.

Greenwood Ave.
University Ave.
Woodlawn Ave.
Kimbark Ave.
Kenwood Ave.
Blackstone Ave.
Lake Park Ave.
Cornell Dr.
Hyde Park Blvd.
South Shore Dr.
Lake Shore Dr.
Ellis Ave.
Dorchester Ave.
Stony Island Ave.
Cornell Dr.

University of Chicago

Midway Plaisance

TO BALZEKAS MUSEUM OF LITHUANIAN CULTURE

Ingleside
Drexel

Kimbark Ave.
Kenwood Ave.

Columbia Dr.

Jackson Park

W. Lagoon
E. Lagoon

0   440 yards
0   400 meters

N

KEY
—— Metra Lines

These efforts were successful beyond the wildest imaginings of their sponsors, though it took 20 years for the neighborhood to regain its luster. Today, Hyde Park and the south part of Kenwood are surrounded by less prosperous, and at times dangerous, areas. Yet Hyde Park's wide appeal continues because of the University of Chicago, the diversity of the residential blocks, the proximity to Loop and lake, and the many tree-lined streets.

Numbers in the text correspond to numbers in the margin and on the Hyde Park and Kenwood map.

A Good Walk and Drive

This walk will take you from one of the city's greatest museums, on the lakefront, west and north into the main shopping area of Hyde Park, and then south to the heart of the University of Chicago's campus. If you're arriving by car, take Lake Shore Drive south to the 57th Street exit and turn left into the parking lot of the Museum of Science and Industry. You can also take the Metra Railroad train from Randolph Street and Michigan Avenue; get off at the 55th Street stop and walk east through the underpass two blocks, then south two blocks. Or, for a longer trip that snakes through more of the city, take the Red line El to the State Street and Lake Street stop, then pick up either the No. 6 or No. 10 bus heading southward. Either way, you are at the **Museum of Science and Industry** ①, a huge hands-on museum where adventures range from a visit to a World War II German U-505 submarine to a descent into a simulated coal mine.

Exiting the museum, cross 56th Street and head east to South Shore Drive to see some of the area's architectural history. Just north of 56th Street, on the west side of the street, are the **Promontory Apartments** ②, the first high-rise Mies van der Rohe built in Chicago. Backtrack to 56th Street and head west a few blocks to **Windermere House** ③, a huge apartment building that was originally an elegant hotel. Continuing west on 56th, go under the train viaduct and then north on Lake Park Avenue. Halfway up the block, you'll pass the **Hyde Park Historical Society** ④, headquartered in a former cable-car terminus.

Walk north on Lake Park and west on 55th Street to one of the happier results of urban renewal, **1400–1451 E. 55th Street** ⑤, twin apartment buildings designed by I. M. Pei. Head north up Blackstone Avenue, passing a variety of housing between 55th and 51st streets. These now-expensive houses were originally cottages for workers, conveniently located near the cable-car line that ran west on 55th Street. Continue north on Blackstone Avenue to 53rd Street, Hyde Park's main shopping strip. Across the street and a half block east is **Harper Court** ⑥, a small, shopping center with chain stores such as Starbucks Coffee.

Leaving the north exit of Harper Court, on 52nd Street, go west four blocks (the street dead-ends, but there's a pedestrian walkway between Kimbark and Kenwood avenues to let you through) to Woodlawn Avenue and turn right. The yellow brick **Heller House** ⑦, No. 5132, was built by Frank Lloyd Wright in 1897. Proceed south on Woodlawn Avenue to 55th Street. Walk east, then north on Kimbark Avenue to the markedly untraditional **St. Thomas the Apostle Catholic Church and School** ⑧, designed by an apprentice of Wright's.

Go back to 55th Street, the northern edge of the University of Chicago campus, and continue west to University Avenue and the **Lutheran School of Theology** ⑨, a massive structure that seems almost to float from its foundation. Across the street at 5514 South University is Pierce Hall, a student residence hall designed by Harry Weese. The dorm-room windows jut into the street in three-sided cement structures, giving the building a hivelike quality.

Head south on University Avenue and turn right onto 56th Street. Walk one block to Greenwood Avenue and the small but beautiful **David and Alfred Smart Museum of Art** ⑩, with an eclectic permanent collection ranging from classical Greek vases to contemporary paintings by Chicago imagist Roger Brown. Continue west on 56th Street to Ellis Avenue and the **Court Theatre** ⑪, home of a professional repertory company. A flag flies atop the theater when a show is on.

Walk south on Ellis Avenue about half a block beyond 56th Street; on your left, just south of the residential halls, is the Henry Moore sculpture *Nuclear Energy* ⑫, commemorating the first controlled nuclear chain reaction. Continue south on Ellis Avenue to 57th Street and walk three blocks west, crossing Cottage Grove Avenue, to the east side of Washington Park and the **DuSable Museum of African American History** ⑬, with its exhibits on history, art, and culture.

Backtrack on 57th Street to Ellis Avenue and turn right. Just across 57th Street, set into the small quadrangle on your right, is the **John Crerar Science Library** ⑭, with scientific and technical books. Farther down the block, the University of Chicago Bookstore stocks everything from scholarly books to university souvenirs. On the plaza just south of the bookstore is *Grande Disco*, a bronze sculpture by Arnaldo Pomodoro that looks like a gigantic compact disc exploding at its center.

Directly across from the bookstore, on the east side of Ellis Avenue, is the University of Chicago Administration Building. Just south of it is **Cobb Hall** ⑮, the oldest building on campus and home of the Renaissance Society, an organization that celebrates modern art. Between the Administration Building and Cobb Hall, a small passageway leads to the quadrangle of the university—a classic college campus, green and grassy, with imposing neo-Gothic buildings. Southeast of Cobb Hall, tucked between two other buildings, is **Bond Chapel** ⑯.

From the chapel cross the quadrangle, heading to the circular drive, and then follow the path that leads north from the drive. You will pass a reflecting pool (Botany Pond) before you exit through Gothic Cobb Gate, elaborately decorated with grotesque figures that appear to be chasing each other up to the pinnacle. Directly ahead is the modern **Joseph Regenstein Library** ⑰, seemingly framed in the gate. The first floor of the "Reg" is open to the public during the day.

Head east on 57th Street to University Avenue. In the massive building on the southwest corner is **Mandel Hall** ⑱, a gem of a concert hall; peek in if you can. Before leaving, have a look at Hutchinson Commons, opposite the building's main entrance. The design of this lofty space—a university cafeteria with portraits of university presidents—was based on Oxford's Christ Church Hall.

Continue east on 57th Street one block to Woodlawn Avenue. On the northwest corner is the **First Unitarian Church** ⑲, whose graceful spire is visible throughout the area. Turn right on Woodlawn Avenue and head south, noting the stately brick mansions that line both sides of the street. To the north, the building at 5605 is on the National Register of Historic Places. Many of the buildings were erected by the University of Chicago in the 1890s to provide housing for professors. Professors continue to live in several of them; others have been repurchased by the university for institutional use. Continue south on Woodlawn Avenue to Frank Lloyd Wright's **Robie House** ⑳, where sloping roofs and complex, rectangular walls and windows still give the building a futuristic look.

Cross Woodlawn Avenue and continue west one block to the **Chicago Theological Seminary** ㉑. Inside are two chapels and the broadly stocked Seminary Cooperative Bookstore. Across 58th Street, the **Oriental Institute** ㉒ has a museum focusing on the history, art, and archaeology of the ancient Near East. Go down University Avenue one block to 59th Street. To your left, set back handsomely on a grassy expanse, is **Rockefeller Memorial Chapel** ㉓, an accomplished example of the Gothic Revival style.

Continue south again, crossing 59th Street and entering the wide, grassy **Midway Plaisance** ㉔, a spacious haven for dogs and Frisbees. At its west end, just beyond Cottage Grove Avenue, you can see Lorado Taft's masterful sculpture **Fountain of Time** ㉕; be sure to walk all around it. On Cottage Grove Avenue, head south to 60th Street and turn left, heading east. At 60th Street and Ingleside Avenue is **Midway Studios** ㉖, Taft's former workplace. One block east on 60th Street at No. 969 is the School of Social Service Administration, an undistinguished example of the work of Mies van der Rohe. On 60th Street between Ellis and University avenues is the Laird Bell Law Quadrangle. This attractive building, with fountains playing in front, is the work of Finnish architect Eero Saarinen. Two blocks farther east, between Kimbark and Kenwood avenues at No. 1307, is the New Graduate Residence Hall. This poured-concrete structure, elaborately ornamented, is reminiscent of the American embassy in New Delhi, India—architect Edward Durrell Stone designed both.

At Dorchester Avenue, cross the Midway again to 59th Street. On your right, just past Dorchester Avenue, is **International House** ㉗, where many foreign students live during their tenure at the university. Turn left on 59th Street and head west to Woodlawn Avenue, then north two blocks to 57th Street, where you can visit some of the area's fine bookstores. One block east is **57th Street Books** ㉘, which carries current books of general interest. On 57th Street, spanning the block between Kimbark and Kenwood avenues, is the Ray School complex. Ray hosts the annual Hyde Park Art Fair, one of the oldest (since 1947) annual outdoor art fairs in the country.

Continue east on 57th Street to Dorchester Avenue; on your right, at 5704 South Dorchester Avenue, is an Italian-style villa constructed before the Chicago Fire of 1871. The two houses at 5642 and 5607 South Dorchester Avenue also predate the fire.

Just past Blackstone Avenue, a block farther east, is **O'Gara & Wilson Book Shop Ltd.** ㉙, with used and out-of-print books. On the next corner as you go east, **Powell's Bookstore** ㉚ also has an exceptional selection of used books, with an emphasis on scholarly titles.

To get back to the museum and your starting point, continue east on 57th Street, go under the viaduct, and cross Stony Island Avenue. The museum will be in front of you, and to the right will be the lagoons of Jackson Park.

TIMING

You'll need to break your visit into parts. Distances between some sights are quite long, particularly around the Midway Plaisance. Consider doing the early part of the route by car, parking in the heart of the campus, and retrieving your car to see sights around the Midway. Remember to exercise big-city caution here.

Especially if you have children, you may want to spend at least a half day at the Museum of Science and Industry. Go during the week to avoid weekend crowds. A visit to the University of Chicago buildings is most rewarding on weekdays, when the campus is lively with student activity. However, the university offers an architectural walking tour on Saturday morning in the spring; call ☎ 773/702–8374 to arrange an appointment.

Sights to See

OFF THE
BEATEN PATH
BALZEKAS MUSEUM OF LITHUANIAN CULTURE – The small, little-known Balzekas Museum, a half-hour drive southwest of Hyde Park, will give you a taste of 1,000 years of Lithuanian history and culture on its three floors. There are exhibits on rural Lithuania; concentration camps; rare maps, stamps, and coins; textiles; and amber. The library can be used for research. ⊠ *6500 S. Pulaski Rd., Englewood,* ☎ *773/582–6500.* ⊠ *$4.* ⊙ *Daily 10–4.*

⑯ Bond Chapel. The fanciful gargoyles adorning this Gothic-style chapel belie the simple interior of dark wood, stained glass, and delicate ornamentation. The effect is one of intimacy and warmth. The university's Divinity School gives regular services here; call ☎ 773/702–8200 for a schedule. ⊠ *1025 E. 58th St., Hyde Park.*

㉑ Chicago Theological Seminary. Of special interest for book lovers visiting this nondenominational seminary is the Seminary Cooperative Bookstore in the basement, so jam-packed with books (and, on the weekends, with people) that it's almost claustrophobic. On the second floor you can see the Reneker organ, a handcrafted replica of an 18th-century organ, in the Graham Taylor Chapel. Also worth visiting is the tiny Thorndike Hilton Memorial Chapel on the first floor. ⊠ *Seminary, 1164 E. 58th St., Hyde Park,* ☎ *773/752–5757,* WEB *www. ctschicago.edu.* ⊙ *Weekdays 8:30–4:30;* ⊠ *Bookstore, 5757 S. University Ave., Hyde Park,* ☎ *773/752–4381.* ⊙ *Weekdays 8:30 AM–9 PM, Sat. 10–6, Sun. noon–6.*

⑮ Cobb Hall. The oldest structure (completed in 1892) on the University of Chicago campus houses classrooms, offices, and the Renaissance Society, which was founded in 1915 to identify living artists whose work would be of lasting significance and influence. It was among the first hosts of works by Matisse, Picasso, Braque, Brancusi, and Miró. The Bergman Gallery on the fourth floor hosts five shows per year, all of them featuring modern art. There are no permanent installations. ⊠ *5811 S. Ellis Ave., Hyde Park,* ☎ *773/702–8670 Bergman Gallery.* ⊠ *Free.* ⊙ *Sept.–June, Tues.–Fri. 10–5, weekends noon–5.*

⑪ Court Theatre. One of the city's finest professional theater companies is based here; the building was designed by Harry Weese and Associates in 1981. It's an intimate theater with unobstructed sight lines from every seat in the house. The repertoire includes classic dramas from the likes of Moliere and Shakespeare to experimental works by Chicago playwrights. ⊠ *5535 S. Ellis Ave., Hyde Park,* ☎ *773/753–4472,* WEB *courttheatre.uchicago.edu.*

⑩ David and Alfred Smart Museum of Art. Housing the fine-arts collection of the University of Chicago, the museum was founded in 1974 with a gift from the Smart Family Foundation, whose members David and Alfred founded *Esquire* magazine. The diverse 8,000-piece permanent collection includes works by old masters; photographs by Walker Evans; furniture by Frank Lloyd Wright; sculptures by Degas, Matisse, Rodin, and Henry Moore; ancient Chinese bronzes; and modern Japanese ceramics. There's also an adjacent sculpture garden. ⊠

5550 S. Greenwood Ave., Hyde Park, ☎ *773/702–0200,* WEB *www. smartmuseum.uchicago.edu.* ⌑ *Free.* ☉ *Tues., Wed., and Fri. 10–4, Thurs. 10–9, weekends noon–6.*

⓭ **DuSable Museum of African American History.** The DuSable opened in 1961 as a collection of art and objects relating to the African-American experience. It was named for trader Jean Baptiste Pointe du Sable, a black man who was Chicago's first permanent non–Native American resident. Among intriguing permanent exhibits is one on slavery; the poignant, disturbing artifacts include rusted shackles used on slave ships. Special exhibits change frequently; a past one focused on West African textiles, displaying brightly colored blankets and cloth wall hangings. The museum also has a cinema series, jazz and blues concerts, lectures and symposiums, and children's programs. Its 1910 building, designed by Daniel Burnham and Company, is beautifully set in Washington Park. ⌑ *740 E. 56th Pl., Near South Side,* ☎ *773/947–0600,* WEB *www.dusablemuseum.org.* ⌑ *$3, free Sun.* ☉ *Mon.–Sat. 10–5, Sun. noon–5.*

🐾 ㉘ **57th Street Books.** Copies of the *New York Times Book Review* and the *New York Review of Books* are always on a table toward the front at this cooperatively owned general bookstore that is a Hyde Park institution. The staff is extremely helpful and knowledgeable, and will ship books to your home so you don't have to lug them around. An extensive children's section has its own room, where reading aloud to youngsters is encouraged. On weekends and evenings the store has programs with authors. ⌑ *1301 E. 57th St., Hyde Park,* ☎ *773/684–1300.* ☉ *Mon.–Sat. 10–10, Sun. 10–8.*

NEED A BREAK? You'll find several spots on 57th Street where you can get a quick bite and relax. **Medici Pan Pizza** (⌑ 1327 E. 57th St., Hyde Park, ☎ 773/ 667–7394) has sandwiches and snacks as well as pizza. The deep-dish pies at **Edwardo's Natural Pizza** (⌑ 1321 E. 57th St., Hyde Park, ☎ 773/241–7960) are considered by some to be the best in the city.

⓭ **First Unitarian Church.** The Gothic design of the church blends well with campus buildings. It was built in 1897 and contains the Hull Memorial Chapel. Because the church's adjacent Pennington Center offers worship classes and youth activities, the building is full of life—kids running around, parents walking in and out—during the course of the day. ⌑ *5650 S. Woodlawn Ave., Hyde Park,* ☎ *773/324–4100.*

㉕ ***Fountain of Time.*** A haunting sculpture created in 1922 by Lorado Taft (1830–1926) depicts the figure of Time observing humanity passing by. Taft was one of the most distinguished sculptors and teachers of his time; as such, he created pieces for the Columbian Exposition of 1893. One of these, the *Fountain of the Great Lakes,* is now at the Art Institute. Other works adorn Chicago's parks and public places, as well as those of other cities. ⌑ *West end of Midway Plaisance, west of Cottage Grove Ave., Hyde Park.*

⑤ **1400–1451 E. 55th Street.** I. M. Pei, architect for the Louvre's controversial glass pyramids, designed the two 10-story university apartment buildings that sit on an island in the middle of the street. Dubbed "the toasters" because the buildings look like two pieces of toast, many locals consider these Pei's least attractive works. He also designed the town houses that border them on the north, between Blackstone and Dorchester avenues. ⌑ *Hyde Park.*

⑥ **Harper Court.** A product of urban renewal, Harper Court was built to house craftspeople who were displaced from their workshops on Lake

Park Avenue. Despite subsidized rents, it never caught on with the crafts-people, who moved elsewhere, while Harper Court evolved into a shopping center with a Starbucks and chain restaurants around the corner. ⊠ *Harper Ave. between 52nd and 53rd Sts., Hyde Park,* WEB *www.harpercourt.com.*

❼ Heller House. When he designed this house in 1897, Frank Lloyd Wright was still moving toward the mature Prairie style achieved in the Robie House 12 years later. Of special interest are the sculptured nymphs cavorting at the top. The house is not open to the public. ⊠ *5132 S. Woodlawn Ave., Hyde Park.*

❹ Hyde Park Historical Society. The restored redbrick building that serves as the society's headquarters was originally a cable-car station, built at the time of the 1893 Columbian Exposition. The group focuses on area history and sponsors lectures and tours. The building is directly underneath the Metro tracks, and it gets noisy at times. ⊠ *5529 S. Lake Park Ave., Hyde Park,* ☎ *773/493–1893.* ☉ *Weekends 2–4.*

㉗ International House. Many foreign students and staff at the University of Chicago have passed through this modified Gothic-style limestone building designed in 1932 by the firm of Holabird and Root. It looks like a square castle, with small red roofs offsetting the earthy limestone color. ⊠ *1414 E. 59th St., Hyde Park.*

OFF THE BEATEN PATH | **JACKSON PARK –** Frederick Law Olmsted designed this park for the World's Columbian Exposition of 1893. Just south of the Museum of Science and Industry, Jackson Park has lagoons, a Japanese garden with authentic Japanese statuary, and the Wooded Island, a nature retreat with wildlife and 300 species of birds. ⊠ *Bounded by E. 56th and 67th Sts., S. Stony Island Ave., and the lakefront, Hyde Park.*

⓮ John Crerar Science Library. The library houses a large part of the University of Chicago's extensive biological, medical, and physical sciences collections and is open to the public. Chicago sculptor John David Mooney's work *Crystara,* made of Waterford crystal and aluminum, is suspended from the skylight in the library's three-story atrium. Fossils and findings from famed UC paleontologist John Sereno are on display here as well. ⊠ *5730 S. Ellis Ave., Hyde Park,* ☎ *773/702–7715,* WEB *www.lib.uchicago.edu/e/crerar/.*

⓱ Joseph Regenstein Library. The university's massive graduate research library has a distinctly modern look, with rough limestone instead of concrete—the more prevalent material for campus exteriors. The underground Map Collection, with 390,000 maps, atlases, aerial photos, and other directional documents, is a gold mine for navigation buffs. The Center for Children's Books, on the fourth floor, supplements the usual college-library mix (on separate floors) of film, music, geography, and the rest. And the Chicago Jazz Archive, filled with classic sheet music, reviews, and old handbills, recalls the period early in the 20th century when such jazz greats as Louis Armstrong, Joe "King" Oliver, and Benny Goodman held court at South Side clubs. Designed by Skidmore, Owings & Merrill and built in 1970, it has seven floors, two of them belowground. The library's Special Collections Exhibition Gallery is open to the public weekdays 8:30–4:45; otherwise, the library is open on a nonappointment basis only to students with valid identification. For appointments, call ☎ 773/702–8782 Monday–Thursday 8:30–6, Friday 8:30–5, or Saturday 9–1. ⊠ *1100 E. 57th St., Hyde Park,* ☎ *773/702–4085,* WEB *www.lib.uchicago.edu/e/reg/.*

⑨ Lutheran School of Theology. This striking structure, built in three sections, has transparent smoked-glass exteriors. It was constructed in 1968 by the firm of Perkins and Will. A fourth wing, to be called the McCormick Theological Seminary, is scheduled for completion in 2003. ✉ *1100 E. 55th St., Hyde Park,* ☎ *773/753–0700.*

⑱ Mandel Hall. Professional musical organizations, including ensembles from the Chicago Symphony, perform in this beautifully restored 900-seat concert hall throughout the year. Gold leaf and soft greens contrast pleasantly with the dark wood of the theater. This university building, bustling with activity and typically adorned with student banners for everything from upcoming salsa dance nights to wrestling matches, also houses the student union. ✉ *1131 E. 57th St., Hyde Park,* ☎ *773/702–8511.*

㉔ Midway Plaisance. The broad, green, hollowed-out space at the southern edge of the University of Chicago campus, created for the World's Columbian Exposition of 1893, was intended to replicate a Venetian canal. But when the "canal" was filled with water, area houses were flooded as well, and the idea had to be abandoned. It was along the Midway that the world's first Ferris wheel, 250 ft in diameter, was erected and took passengers skyward during the exposition. Today students and neighborhood residents use this green refuge. ✉ *Bounded by 59th and 60th Sts. and Jackson and Washington parks, Hyde Park.*

㉖ Midway Studios. A National Historic Landmark since 1966, the former workplace of sculptor Lorado Taft now houses the University of Chicago's studio-art program and serves as an exhibit space for student works during certain times of the year; call first to check. ✉ *6016 S. Ingleside Ave., Hyde Park,* ☎ *773/753–4821.* ✑ *Free.* ☉ *Weekdays 8–4:30.*

★ ℭ **① Museum of Science and Industry.** It's too bad the stuff here doesn't really work. Though the venerable museum is already one of Chicago's top tourist attractions, imagine the crowds who would show up to become an actual fairy (in Colleen Moore's Fairy Castle) or sail underwater into Lake Michigan (from the U-505 German submarine, captured during World War II). Constantly updating itself with new exhibits—such as "Genetics–Decoding Life" which shows how scientists can make frogs' eyes glow and explores the pros and cons of genetic engineering—the museum is a sprawling open space, with 2,000 exhibits on three floors. You can walk through the middle of a 20-ft tall model of the human heart, explore a cantilevered Boeing 727, and make noises in the acoustically perfect Whispering Gallery. The museum also has the world's first permanent exhibit on HIV and AIDS, plus Lego MindStorms and the Idea Factory. Be sure to study the museum map to decide how you want to use your time.

Of special interest for families is the Imagination Station on the lower level, with hands-on activities for children up to age 12. The Omnimax Theater shows science- and space-related films on a giant five-story screen. The museum's classical revival building was designed in 1892 by D. H. Burnham & Company as a temporary structure to house the Palace of Fine Arts of the World's Columbian Exposition. It's the fair's only surviving building. On nice days, the giant lawn out front is almost as entertaining as the museum itself with hordes of sunbathers and kite-flyers; Lake Michigan is literally across the street. ✉ *5700 S. Lake Shore Dr., Hyde Park,* ☎ *773/684–1414,* WEB *www. msichicago.org.* ✑ *$9.* ☉ *Memorial Day–Labor Day, daily 9–5:30; Labor Day–Memorial Day, weekdays 9:30–4, weekends 9:30–5:30.*

⑫ **Nuclear Energy.** Henry Moore's bulbous, 12-ft-tall bronze sculpture marks the site where Enrico Fermi and other physicists set off the first controlled nuclear chain reaction on December 2, 1942. It occurred under the bleachers of what was then Stagg Field. The sculpture is said to represent both a human skull and an atomic mushroom cloud. ⊠ *East side of Ellis Ave. between 56th and 57th Sts., Hyde Park.*

㉙ **O'Gara & Wilson Book Shop Ltd.** This bookstore, established in the mid-1930s, specializes in general used books as well as out-of-print and antiquarian titles, plus intriguing prints and maps. The store is more stately and professor-oriented than its across-the-street neighbor, Powell's. ⊠ *1448 E. 57th St., Hyde Park,* ☎ *773/363–0993.* ☉ *Mon.–Thurs. 10–9, Fri. and Sat. 10–10, Sun. noon–8.*

NEED A BREAK?

Caffé Florian (⊠ 1450 E. 57th St., Hyde Park, ☎ 773/752–4100) serves pizza and Italian entrées as well as hearty sandwiches, homemade soups and salads, decadent desserts, and lots of java. (The back cover of the matchbooks, in true U of C style, displays the molecular structure of caffeine.)

㉒ **Oriental Institute.** The institute is full of fascinating art and artifacts from the ancient Near East, including statuary, small-scale amulets, mummies, limestone reliefs, gold jewelry, ivories, pottery, and bronzes from the 2nd millennium BC through the 13th century AD. One of the most intriguing items is a 40-ton sculpture of a winged bull from an Assyrian palace. ⊠ *1155 E. 58th St., Hyde Park,* ☎ *773/702–9520.* 🎟 *Free.* ☉ *Tues., Thurs.–Sat. 10–4, Wed. 10–8:30, Sun. noon–4.*

㉚ **Powell's Bookstore.** Outside, there is usually a box of free books; inside is a tremendous selection of used and remaindered titles, including books on philosophy, ancient history, anthropology, and social sciences, as well as art books, cookbooks, and mysteries. The store clearly caters to students, with fliers announcing political events and rock bands cluttering a bulletin board outside. ⊠ *1501 E. 57th St., Hyde Park,* ☎ *773/955–7780.* ☉ *Daily 9 AM–11 PM.*

❷ **Promontory Apartments.** The tan brick building, designed by Mies van der Rohe in 1949, was named for nearby Promontory Point, which juts out into the lake. Mies's first Chicago high-rise exemplifies the postwar trend toward a clean, simple style. Even from the street level, the Lake Michigan views here are breathtaking. Note the skylines (such that they are) and belching smokestacks of Gary and Hammond, Indiana, to the southeast. ⊠ *5530 S. Shore Dr., Hyde Park.*

★ ⑳ **Robie House.** Frank Lloyd Wright's Prairie-style masterpiece, built in 1909 for inventor and businessman Frederick C. Robie, is one of the most remarkable designs in modern American architecture. Study the exterior to see the horizontal lines, from the brickwork and the limestone sills to the sweeping roofs, which Wright felt reflected the prairies of the Midwest. A cantilevered roof provides privacy while allowing in light. Like most of Wright's buildings, it seems compact from the outside, but inside it's a complex, fully thought-out maze of glass windows and 174 doors. What was once a three-car garage is now a bookstore. You can tour Robie House (headquarters of the Alumni Association) and examine the interiors, including the great hearth, leaded-glass windows, built-in cupboards, and spacious kitchen. The house is midway through a 10-year renovation; the exterior work should be completed by 2004. The house remains open to visitors. Because the exterior is hidden by scaffolding, they've opened up some new rooms on the inside, such as the kitchen and butler's pantry. ⊠ *5757 S.*

Woodlawn Ave., Hyde Park, ☏ *773/834–1847.* ⊠ *$9.* ⊙ *Tour week-days at 11, 1, and 3; weekends 11–3:30.*

★ **㉓** **Rockefeller Memorial Chapel.** An important example of the Gothic Re-vival style, this huge chapel, named for the University of Chicago's founder, was built in 1928 from plans by Bertram G. Goodhue. The imposing structure has a glorious vaulted ceiling, a beautiful hand-carved organ, and unusual stained glass in the north window above the altar. The window's five "petals" and center are composed of intensely col-ored glass; during the day the light pouring through it reflects strik-ingly on the chapel's ceiling. The chapel is elaborately decorated inside and out with carvings, sculpture, and inscriptions. Its 207-ft tower houses a carillon with 72 bells; a university carillonneur gives regular perfor-mances. ⊠ *5850 S. Woodlawn Ave., Hyde Park,* ☏ *773/702–2100; 773/702–9202 for tour;* WEB *rockefeller.uchicago.edu/.* ⊙ *Daily 9–4; tour by appointment.*

❽ **St. Thomas the Apostle Catholic Church and School.** An open, modern look inside and terra-cotta ornamentation outside mark the design of Barry Byrne, who was once an apprentice of Frank Lloyd Wright. This Roman Catholic church built in 1922 also has impressive bronze bas-reliefs of the stations of the cross. ⊠ *5472 S. Kimbark Ave., Hyde Park,* ☏ *773/324–2626.*

NEED A
BREAK?

"Jimmy's" **Woodlawn Tap** (⊠ 1172 E. 55th St., Hyde Park, ☏ 773/643–5516; ⊙ daily 11 AM–2 AM) is a favored spot where locals and university students gather. This dimly lit pub has three rooms; in the evenings, one room generally hosts a happening like a spoken word reading or jazz jam. The pub food consists of Chicago-style Polish sausages, burgers, and fries, and there are a number of beer choices on tap.

University of Chicago. The University of Chicago was built through the largesse of John D. Rockefeller. Coeducational from the beginning, it was known for progressive education. The campus covers 184 acres, dominating the physical and cultural landscape of Hyde Park and South Kenwood. Much of the original campus was designed by Henry Ives Cobb, who was also responsible for the Newberry Library, at the corner of Dearborn and Walton streets on the Near North Side. The university's stately Gothic-style quadrangles recall the residential col-leges in Cambridge and Oxford, England, and the Ivy League schools of the East Coast. But the material is Indiana limestone, and the U of C retains a uniquely midwestern quality.

The university has no less than 69 Nobel laureates as faculty, re-searchers, or former students. Its schools of economics, law, business, and medicine are world famous, and the University of Chicago Hos-pitals are leading teaching institutions. Perhaps the most world-alter-ing event to take place at U of C was the first self-sustaining nuclear chain reaction, created here in 1942 by Enrico Fermi and his team of physicists under an unused football stadium. Although the stadium is gone, there's a plaque on the spot now, near the Regenstein Library.

The University's Visitor Center, on the first floor of Ida Noyes Hall, provides maps, publications, and information on University events. Cam-pus tours for prospective students are offered by appointment by the **Office of College Admissions** (☏ 773/702–8650). Campus tours, which leave from the Visitor Center, are given to the general public daily at 10:30 AM, and again on Friday at 1:30 PM. The Office of Special Events also offers guided tours of Robie House and Rockefeller Memo-rial Chapel. A self-guided tour of campus architecture, *A Walking*

Guide to the Campus, is available for purchase in the University of Chicago Bookstore. ⊠ *Visitor Center: Ida Noyes Hall, 1212 E. 59th St., Hyde Park,* ☎ *773/702–9739,* WEB *www.uchicago.edu.* ⊙ *Weekdays 9–5.*

❸ Windermere House. Originally one of the area's grandest hotels, Windermere House was designed in 1924 by Rapp and Rapp, known for their movie palaces. Among the hotel's guests were John D. Rockefeller, Babe Ruth, and Edna Ferber. The building now houses apartments. Notice the grand gatehouse in front of the sweeping semicircular carriage path at the entrance; notice also the heroic scale of the building, with its ornate carvings. ⊠ *1642 E. 56th St., Hyde Park.*

3 DINING

Whether you want deep-dish pizza on the North Side or crunchy fried catfish on the South, Chicago's dining choices are as wide ranging as the city itself. In elegant establishments diners can scale culinary heights with exquisitely creative French or regional midwestern cuisine. Equally exciting are the superb ethnic eateries that fill neighborhoods as diverse as the food: Italian, Greek, Mexican, Swedish, Thai, and more. And although Chicago has outgrown its meat-and-potatoes image, its fine steak houses still thrive.

By Phil Vettel

Revised and
updated by
Elaine Glusac

However you judge a city's dining scene—by ethnic diversity, breadth and depth of high-quality establishments, or nationally prominent chefs—Chicago ranks as one of the nation's finest restaurant towns. Here you'll find innovative hot spots, lovingly maintained traditional establishments, and everything in between. Chicago's more than 7,000 restaurants range from those ranked among the best in the country—and priced accordingly—to simple storefront ethnic places and old-fashioned, unpretentious pubs serving good food at modest prices.

Chicago's most sophisticated cooking, once clustered neatly downtown, with the notable exceptions of Charlie Trotter's and Arun's, is increasingly busting the Loop confines. Now many of the city's most exciting meals require an outing to gentrifying Wicker Park (Spring, Fortunato), nearby West Loop (Nine, Blackbird), or the north's Lincoln Square (She She).

There's a rational price-geography correlation in Chicago: the closer you eat to downtown, the more you pay. But venture into the neighborhoods and you not only dine well but reasonably. Bistrot Margot in the Old Town section of Near North, for example, upholds downtown standards but holds the line on prices. Farther afield, you find personable places that do not rely on the expense-account crowd to survive, such as La Petite Folie to the south, Pasteur to the north, and plenty of spots in between—all well worth seeking out.

This chapter divides the restaurants of Chicago by neighborhood. Several noteworthy suburban restaurants appear at the end, with no map; other good places to eat outside the city are listed in Chapter 8, Side Trips. Within each neighborhood the restaurants are grouped first by type of cuisine and then by price range.

Reservations

Reservations are always a good idea; the reviews here note only when they're essential or when they are not accepted. In Chicago reservations can often be made a day or two in advance or even on the same afternoon, but securing a table at the more popular restaurants may take planning, especially on weekends. Some trendy restaurants don't accept reservations; at such places a wait of an hour or more on weekends is common. A popular strategy among Chicago restaurants is the limited-reservations policy, in which about half a restaurant's available space is reserved, while the rest is left open on a first-come, first-served basis. Unless mentioned otherwise, restaurants serve lunch and dinner daily.

Tipping

As a rule, you should tip 15% in restaurants in the $ and $$ price categories. You can double the 9.5% meal tax (fractionally higher in some parts of town, thanks to special taxing initiatives) when you feel generous. More expensive ($$$ and $$$$) establishments have more service personnel per table, who must divide the tip, so it's appropriate to leave 20%, depending on the service. An especially helpful wine steward should be acknowledged with $3 to $5.

What to Wear

Chicago is largely an informal dining town, and neat, casual attire is acceptable dress in most places. Jackets, however, are appropriate in many formal hotel dining rooms. In the reviews dress is mentioned only when men are required to wear a jacket or jacket and tie.

CATEGORY	COST*
$$$$	over $28
$$$	$21–$28
$$	$15–$20
$	under $15

per person for a main course at dinner.

Greater Downtown

American/Casual

$ ✕ **Lou Mitchell's.** Shelve your calorie and cholesterol concerns. Lou Mitchell's warrants it. The diner, a destination since 1923, specializes in high-fat breakfasts and comfort food lunches. Start the day with double yolk eggs and homemade hash browns by the skillet. Later break for meat loaf and mashed potatoes. Though out-the-door waits are common, tables turn rapidly and staffers dole out doughnut holes and Milk Duds to pacify pangs. ⊠ *565 W. Jackson Blvd., Loop,* ☎ *312/939-3111. AE, V. No dinner.*

Contemporary

$$–$$$$ ✕ **Nine.** Nightclub meets steak house in Nine, replete with mirrored
★ columns, futuristic plasma TV screens, and a dramatic, circular champagne-and-caviar bar set smack in the middle of the dining room. The menu favors prime steaks and chops complemented by plenty of fresh fish and shellfish. If you're in the mood for caviar you can choose anything from ounces of beluga and sevruga to a crispy cone layered with caviar and egg salad. On weekends, dress to thrill—most of the trendy patrons do. ⊠ *440 W. Randolph St., Loop,* ☎ *312/575-9900. AE, DC, MC, V. Closed Sun. No lunch Sat.*

$$–$$$$ ✕ **one sixtyblue.** Though partner Michael Jordan no longer plays ball
★ for the Bulls, interest in the fashionable one sixtyblue remains strong thanks to the French-influenced contemporary cooking of chef Martial Noguier. Noguier changes the menu seasonally but perennial MJ favorites like peekytoe crab and Delmonico steak stick around. Adam Tihany's open design includes a display kitchen, a glassed-in wine tower, and a ceiling that soars higher than Jordan on his way to a slam-dunk. The handsome zinc-topped bar makes a chic destination for drinks. ⊠ *160 N. Loomis St., Near West Side,* ☎ *312/850-0303. AE, DC, MC, V. No dinner Sun. No lunch.*

$$–$$$$ ✕ **Prairie.** The wood-trimmed interior is inspired by the architecture of Frank Lloyd Wright and the updated food by the flavors of the midwestern states. The result is a thoroughly well-conceived American regional restaurant. Specialties include horseradish-crusted sturgeon, grilled buffalo with sweet-potato risotto, and sweet corn chowder, though some regulars swear by the coho salmon and the Lake Superior whitefish. ⊠ *500 S. Dearborn St., Downtown South,* ☎ *312/663-1143. AE, D, DC, MC, V.*

$$–$$$$ ✕ **Rhapsody.** Attached to the Symphony Center, home of the Chicago
★ Symphony, Rhapsody is more than a handy spot for a pre-concert dinner. This restaurant has serious fine-dining ambitions and the presence of consulting executive chef Roland Liccioni, who also owns Les Nomades, has given the operation a decided prestige. The onion-crusted sturgeon is splendid, as are Liccioni's signature terrines. Even a prosaic rack of lamb is executed wonderfully. The handsome bar, pouring an expansive wine-by-the-glass selection, makes a popular post-performance hangout. ⊠ *65 E. Adams St., Loop,* ☎ *312/786-9911. AE, D, DC, MC, V. No lunch weekends.*

$$–$$$$ ✕ **Rivers.** On the first floor of the Chicago Mercantile Exchange, this sophisticated mahogany-and-marble dining room serves weekday

Dining

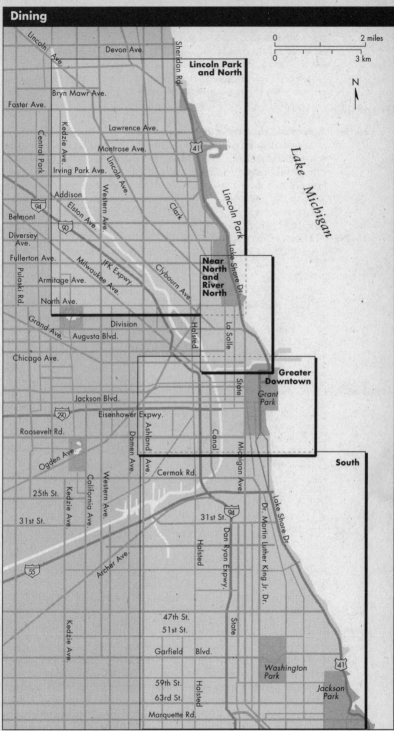

2 miles
3 km

N

Lincoln Park and North

Devon Ave.

Sheridan Rd.

Lincoln Ave.

Bryn Mawr Ave.

Foster Ave.

Lawrence Ave.

41

Montrose Ave.

Central Park

Kedzie Ave.

Lincoln Ave.

Clark

Lincoln Park

Lake Shore Dr.

Irving Park Ave.

Addison

Western Ave.

Elston Ave.

94

Belmont

90

Diversey Ave.

Fullerton Ave.

JFK Expwy.

Milwaukee Ave.

Clybourn Ave.

Lake Michigan

Pulaski Rd.

Armitage Ave.

Grand Ave.

North Ave.

Near North and River North

Division

Halsted

La Salle

Augusta Blvd.

Chicago Ave.

Jackson Blvd.

90

State

Grant Park

Greater Downtown

Eisenhower Expwy.

Ashland Ave.

Canal

Roosevelt Rd.

Damen Ave.

Michigan Ave.

Ogden Ave.

Cermak Rd.

South

25th St.

Kedzie Ave.

California Ave.

Western Ave.

31st St.

94

31st St.

Dan Ryan Expwy.

Halsted

Dr. Martin Luther King Jr. Dr.

Lake Shore Dr.

55

Archer Ave.

State

47th St.

51st St.

Kedzie Ave.

Halsted

Garfield   Blvd.

Washington Park

41

59th St.

63rd St.

Halsted

Jackson Park

Marquette Rd.

breakfasts to hungry traders, and lunch and dinner to office workers and tourists. The menu is French- and Italian-inflected American: you might find roasted-corn soup, grouper with grapefruit beurre blanc, barbecued shrimp and scallops, and crawfish ravioli. An outdoor dining area overlooks the Chicago River. Its proximity to the Civic Opera House and Loop theaters makes Rivers a handy pre-event destination; on weekends it opens before opera performances. ⊠ *30 S. Wacker Dr., Loop,* ☎ *312/559–1515. AE, D, DC, MC, V. Closed Sun. No lunch weekends.*

$$–$$$ ✕ **Atwood Cafe.** Mahogany columns, cherrywood floors, gold café curtains, and curvy light-blue banquettes fill this heart-of-the-Loop charmer with color. Floor-to-ceiling windows overlooking Michigan Avenue provide light. The mostly American menu includes reliable dishes like chicken potpie and a thick pork chop, along with contemporary dishes such as duck and manchego quesadillas and grilled salmon with charred tomato sauce. ⊠ *Hotel Burnham, 1 W. Washington St., Loop,* ☎ *312/ 368–1900. AE, D, DC, MC, V.*

$$–$$$ ✕ **Blackbird.** Cramped but convivial, this West Loop hot spot draws
★ a trendy clientele in for artfully presented renditions of contemporary American food, such as wild bass with roast fennel and baby clams and quail with parsnips, serrano ham, and braised endive. With white walls, mohair banquettes and aluminum chairs, Blackbird's minimalist design matches the black most of the customers wear. Reservations aren't required, but they might as well be; the dining room is typically booked solid on weekends. Credit cards are required to hold reservations for five or more, and a flat fee is charged for no-shows. ⊠ *619 W. Randolph St., Near West Side,* ☎ *312/715–0708. AE, D, DC, MC, V. Closed Sun. No lunch Sat.*

$$–$$$ ✕ **Printer's Row.** People thought chef Michael Foley was crazy to open a stylish restaurant in the dilapidated, if historic, Printer's Row district in the 1980s, but the gamble paid off. His is now the established institution in what has become an attractive neighborhood of renovated loft buildings and gracious older apartment houses, close enough to Loop theaters for pre-curtain dining. The American regional menu is noteworthy for its game meats and seafood: you might try seared scallops with truffle oil, grilled venison with dried cherries, or grilled peppered duck breast with almond-raisin couscous. A well-chosen, fairly priced wine list is a plus. ⊠ *550 S. Dearborn St., Downtown South,* ☎ *312/461–0780. AE, D, DC, MC, V. Closed Sun. No lunch Sat.*

$–$$$ ✕ **Encore.** By day, this Loop spot is handy for a quick lunch, offering a small list of sandwiches, half of them carved-to-order brisket, tenderloin, and the like. In the evening, the lights dim and the velvet-draped space becomes a DJ-driven lounge serving a "cocktail cuisine" menu of light appetizers (spicy chicken wings, fresh oysters, pizzas, and grilled shrimp)—perfect for a before- or after-theater nibble. ⊠ *171 W. Randolph St., Loop,* ☎ *312/338–3788. AE, D, DC, MC, V. No lunch weekends.*

French

$$$$ ✕ **Everest.** Everest's highs include its perch at 40 stories above ground
★ with sweeping views of the city's West Side. And its dinner checks are pretty lofty, too. The creative cuisine of chef Jean Joho may warrant them, however. Joho takes often-ignored, humble ingredients (particularly those from his native Alsace) and transforms them into regal, memorable dishes such as risotto with edible gold leaf or pheasant wrapped in savoy cabbage. The dining room is pleasingly neutral, focusing attention on the kitchen's exquisitely arranged plates. Service is discreet and professional. The wine list has tremendous depth, par-

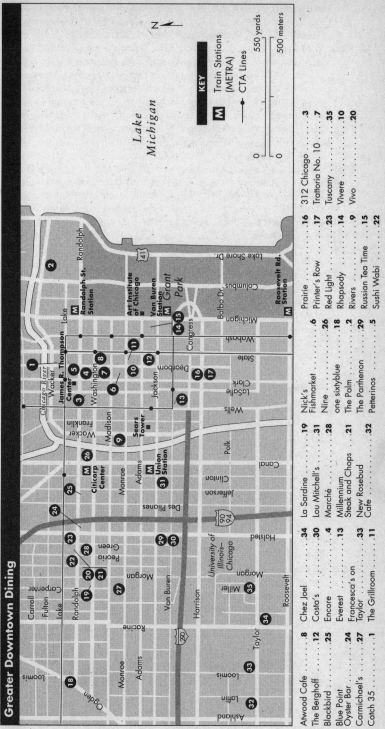

Greater Downtown Dining

KEY

M Train Stations (METRA)

◆ CTA Lines

Lake Michigan

Grant Park

Atwood Cafe	8	Chez Joel	34
The Berghoff	12	Costa's	30
Blackbird	25	Encore	4
Blue Point Oyster Bar	24	Everest	13
Carmichael's	27	Francesca's on Taylor	33
Catch 35	1	The Grillroom	11
La Sardine	19	Nick's Fishmarket	6
Lou Mitchell's	31	Nine	26
Marché	28	one sixtyblue	18
Millennium Steak and Chops	21	The Palm	2
New Rosebud Cafe	32	The Parthenon	29
		Petterinos	5
Prairie	16	312 Chicago	3
Printer's Row	17	Trattoria No. 10	7
Red Light	23	Tuscany	35
Rhapsody	14	Vivere	10
Rivers	9	Vivo	20
Russian Tea Time	15		
Sushi Wabi	22		

ticularly in its representation of Alsatian vintages. ⊠ *440 S. LaSalle St., Loop,* ☎ *312/663–8920. Reservations essential. Jacket required. AE, D, DC, MC, V. Closed Sun. and Mon. No lunch.*

$$–$$$$ ✕ **Marché.** With a display kitchen as metaphoric stage, this theatrical West Loop brasserie draws a see-and-be-seen crowd to a lively loft-like room trimmed in collage and paint and furnished with curvaceous metal chairs. Enjoy the scene but save some focus for the fine food ranging from classic French onion soup and duck confit to more updated peppercorn-crusted ostrich and an excellent steak tartare. For the finale, choose from one of the largest sweets lists in town. ⊠ *833 W. Randolph St., Near West Side,* ☎ *312/226–8399. AE, DC, MC, V. No lunch weekends.*

$–$$ ✕ **Chez Joel.** In a restaurant row populated almost exclusively with
★   Italian restaurants—the Taylor Street area is also known as Little Italy—sits one of the best French bistros in the city. The straightforward French classics such as steak frites and bouillabaisse are first rate, and the day's fresh fish is always a reliable choice. Yellow-painted walls make the room feel sunny even on dim days. ⊠ *1119 W. Taylor St., Near South Side,* ☎ *312/226–6479. AE, D, DC, MC, V. No lunch weekends.*

$–$$ ✕ **La Sardine.** True to its name, this West Side bistro across the street
★   from Harpo Studios (where Oprah tapes her talk show) packs customers in snugly. But proximity to your neighbors aside, this is a comfortable place with a simple, eye-pleasing interior of brick and wood. The menu sticks to traditional dishes such as leek-bacon tart, bouillabaisse, and mustard-crusted rack of lamb—all deftly prepared. ⊠ *111 N. Carpenter St., Near West Side,* ☎ *312/421–2800. AE, D, DC, MC, V. Closed Sun. No lunch Sat.*

German

$–$$ ✕ **The Berghoff.** This Chicago institution has been serving its signature beer since the end of Prohibition; in fact, the Berghoff holds city liquor license No. 1. The handsome oak-panel interiors evoke an authentic Old Chicago feel. You can expect to wait for a table, but once you're seated your meal will proceed rapidly—too rapidly, for some. (For even quicker service, grab a sandwich, a snort, and some elbow room among the businesspeople at the standing-only bar.) A menu of German classics (Wiener schnitzel, sauerbraten) is augmented by American favorites and, in keeping with the times, lighter dishes and even salads. ⊠ *17 W. Adams St., Loop,* ☎ *312/427–3170. AE, MC, V. Closed Sun.*

Greek

$–$$$ ✕ **Costa's.** One of the prettiest restaurants in Greektown, Costa's has a colorful, multilevel interior with terra-cotta tile work and rough-textured white walls and archways. It's inviting and somewhat noisy, best suited to gregarious diners. Start with a nice assortment of *mezes* (tapaslike Greek appetizers). Then move on to fresh fish, such as excellent whole snapper or sea bass, or a classic dish like spicy shrimp *piperates* (with vermouth, garlic, lemon, and pepper). ⊠ *340 S. Halsted St., Near West Side,* ☎ *312/263–9700. Reservations essential. AE, D, DC, MC, V.*

$–$$ ✕ **The Parthenon.** *Saganaki,* the Greek flaming cheese dish, was invented here in the late 1960s. Known for its festive atmosphere, happy customers, and hearty, inexpensive food, this old-timer claims to be the first restaurant in America to serve gyros, which are still on the menu. ⊠ *314 S. Halsted St., Near West Side,* ☎ *312/726–2407. AE, D, DC, MC, V.*

Italian

$–$$$$ ✕ **New Rosebud Cafe.** This extremely busy restaurant specializes in good old-fashioned southern Italian cuisine. One of the best red sauces in town can be found here, and the roasted peppers, homemade sausage, and exquisitely prepared pastas are not to be missed. The wait for a table can stretch to an hour or more, despite confirmed reservations, but those with patience—and tolerance for the extreme noise level—will find that the meal more than compensates. ✉ *1500 W. Taylor St., Near South Side,* ☎ *312/942–1117. AE, D, DC, MC, V. No lunch weekends.*

$–$$$$ ✕ **Petterino's.** An Italian-themed restaurant inside the Goodman Theatre complex, Petterino's meets the needs of time-pressed pre-theater diners as well as those seeking a more leisurely meal. Its retro supper club appeal features red-leather booths, soft lighting, and framed caricatures of celebrities past and present. The menu includes such classics as shrimp *de jonghe* (covered in garlicky bread crumbs then baked), Bookbinder soup, and a terrific tomato bisque, plus prime steaks, seafood, and pasta. ✉ *150 N. Dearborn St., Loop,* ☎ *312/422–0150. AE, D, DC, MC, V. Closed Sun. No lunch Sat.*

$–$$$$ ✕ **Vivo.** A pioneer of the west-of-the-Loop stretch of Randolph Street now populated with trendy eateries, this stylish Italian restaurant still provides fascinating people-watching and striking visuals—including dark walls, a black ceiling, and open wine racks. The contemporary menu is considerably less flashy, but the antipasti assortment is a fine starter, and the kitchen does a good job with grilled Portobello mushrooms and the thin-sliced veal chop. ✉ *838 W. Randolph St., Near West Side,* ☎ *312/733–3379. AE, DC, MC, V. No lunch weekends.*

$$–$$$ ✕ **Vivere.** This eye-catching dining room is worth a visit for looks alone: ★ think Italian Baroque on acid. A mesmerizing array of cones, swirls, and bright colors guarantees an interesting view from every seat. The regional-Italian menu includes excellent, beyond-the-norm dishes such as pheasant *agnolotti* (half-moon-shape ravioli) and wild boar over polenta. The restaurant also has one of the city's—make that one of the country's—great Italian wine lists. ✉ *71 W. Monroe St., Loop,* ☎ *312/ 332–7005. AE, D, DC, MC, V. Closed Sun. No lunch Sat.*

$–$$$ ✕ **Francesca's on Taylor.** Among the many Italian places on this stretch of Taylor Street, this trattoria offers some of the best cooking. You might find ravioli stuffed with a spinach and artichoke mix or blue marlin with sea scallops and roasted peppers. There's not a lot of red meat on the menu—just the occasional veal dish—but that helps keep prices down, too. Folks heading to the United Center for a Bulls game, Blackhawks game, or special event make this a popular early dining spot. ✉ *1400 W. Taylor St., Near South Side,* ☎ *312/829–2828. AE, DC, MC, V. No lunch weekends.*

$–$$$ ✕ **312 Chicago.** This Italian-accented dining room inside the hip Hotel Allegro is handy for power-breakfast, lunch, dinner, and pre-theater dining. Home-baked breads and yummy desserts may tempt you to bypass the in-between courses, but roasted sturgeon with potato-mushroom lasagna and salmon and tuna tartare will beg you to consider otherwise. Brunch is served on Sunday. ✉ *136 N. LaSalle St., Loop,* ☎ *312/696–2420. AE, D, DC, MC, V.*

$–$$$ ✕ **Trattoria No. 10.** Terra-cotta colors, arched entryways, and quarry-★ tile floors give this below-street-level dining room considerable charm and warmth. In fact, this is one of the few pre-theater locations in the Loop that is as busy after the curtain rises as before. The house specialty ravioli comes with many seasonal stuffings though the butternut squash filling is a perennial. Classic antipasti selections like prosciutto-wrapped asparagus and substantial *secondi piatti* like beef tenderloin round out the meal. For dessert try the warm chocolate truffle cake. The $10 buffet served 5:30 to 8 PM Monday through Friday is a real bargain. ✉ *10 N. Dearborn St., Loop*, ☎ *312/984–1718. AE, D, DC, MC, V. Closed Sun. No lunch Sat.*

$–$$$ ✕ **Tuscany.** As its name suggests, this restaurant focuses on the hearty, rustic flavors of the Tuscan countryside. The rotisserie-grilled chicken is especially good, as are the thin-crust pizzas and, for splurgers, the rack of lamb Vesuvio. The Taylor Street neighborhood, just southwest of the Loop, is a popular destination at lunchtime. ✉ *1014 W. Taylor St., Near South Side*, ☎ *312/829–1990. AE, D, DC, MC, V. No lunch weekends.*

Japanese

$–$$$$ ✕ **Sushi Wabi.** This funky West-Loop sushi restaurant dances to an in-
★ dustrial-pop beat—on weekend evenings, at least, when it employs a DJ (the noise level, remarkably, is tolerable). A brick and exposed-steel interior projects an urban-chic image, and the restaurant pulls in a young, hip crowd. Along with sushi and maki rolls, there are a few straight-forward entrées, such as seared tuna with gingered ponzu sauce. ✉ *842 W. Randolph St., Near West Side*, ☎ *312/563–1224. AE, D, DC, MC, V. No lunch weekends.*

Pan-Asian

$$–$$$$ ✕ **Red Light.** Chinese, Thai, Vietnamese, and Indonesian dishes com-
mingle happily on Red Light's compact yet varied menu, which is heavily weighted with appetizers, encouraging nibbling. Standout dishes include gingered pork dumplings and Taiwanese catfish. Desserts, which come from sister property Marché, are very western—and very good. ✉ *820 W. Randolph St., Near West Side*, ☎ *312/733–8880. AE, DC, MC, V. No lunch weekends.*

Russian

$$–$$$ ✕ **Russian Tea Time.** This delightful gem neighbors Symphony Center (home of the Chicago Symphony Orchestra), just steps from the Art Institute. Mahogany trim, samovars, and balalaika music set the stage for a wide-ranging menu of authentic dishes from Russia and neigh-boring republics (the owners hail from Uzbekistan). Highlights in-clude Ukrainian borscht, *blinis* (small, savory pancakes) with caviar and salmon, *shashlik* (lamb kebabs), and *golubtes* (stuffed cabbage with chicken and rice). Top-quality caviars and ice-cold vodkas and cham-pagnes entice the deep-pocketed. Afternoon tea makes a nice post-mu-seum refresher. Reservations essential for pre-event dining. ✉ *77 E. Adams St., Loop*, ☎ *312/360–0000. Reservations essential. AE, D, DC, MC, V.*

Seafood

$$$–$$$$ ✕ **Nick's Fishmarket.** A two-tiered restaurant with a moderately priced bar and grill in front and a lower-level main dining room, Nick's caters to the high-powered business set, romantic couples, and indeed any-one who appreciates overwhelmingly attentive service and is willing to pay accordingly. The menu includes a wide assortment of fresh seafood, particularly Pacific catches such as mahimahi and abalone; massive steaks are available, too. **Nick's Fishmarket** in suburban Rose-mont (✉ *10275 W. Higgins Rd.*, ☎ *847/298–8200*), near O'Hare Airport, has a virtually identical menu though a more formal look. ✉ *51 S. Clark St., Loop*, ☎ *312/621–0200. Reservations essential. AE, D, DC, MC, V. Closed Sun. No lunch Sat.*

$$–$$$$ ✕ **Catch 35.** This street-level restaurant in the Leo Burnett Building spe-cializes in Pacific fish such as ahi tuna and mahimahi, often prepared with an Asian flair; Thai curries and ginger make frequent appearances. The handsome multilevel dining room is wood paneled and designed to afford a measure of privacy. ✉ *35 W. Wacker Dr., Loop,* ☎ *312/ 346–3500. AE, D, DC, MC, V. No lunch weekends.*

$–$$$$ ✗ **Blue Point Oyster Bar.** Wooden-louvered windows and overstuffed booths impart a slick 1940s aesthetic upon this serious seafood restaurant in the West Loop. At least six varieties of oysters are featured daily, sold by the piece (making it easy to mix and match). Grab a bowl of spicy crab gazpacho when it's available, along with grilled baby octopus and chili-glazed escolar. ✉ *741 W. Randolph St., Near West Side,* ☎ *312/207–1222. AE, D, DC, MC, V. No lunch weekends.*

Steak Houses

$$$$ ✗ **The Palm.** Spacious, custom-built digs on the first floor of Swissôtel Chicago house this handsome link in the Palm steak-house chain. There's even an outdoor patio with a view of Navy Pier. Inside, walls are covered with caricatures of local celebrities and regular customers. The latter come in droves, drawn by big steaks and bigger lobsters. Even the occasional finned option, such as grilled tuna, is treated well here—and dessert is a must. ✉ *Swissôtel, 323 E. Wacker Dr., Loop,* ☎ *312/616–1000. Reservations essential. AE, D, DC, MC, V.*

$$–$$$$ ✗ **Millennium Steaks and Chops.** Despite the futuristic name (well, it was vaguely futuristic when it opened), this is a classic steak house— a handsome, two-level space with acres of oak flooring, a spacious bar, and a private cigar room. The prime steaks include a dry-aged porterhouse that's one of the best in town and a fine hickory-smoked prime rib. For dessert, choose the Chocolate Churchill, a mousse-filled "cigar" served with shaved-chocolate "ashes." The wine list includes a number of steak-friendly wines priced under $40, plus some old vintages with eye-popping prices. ✉ *832 W. Randolph St., Near West Side,* ☎ *312/455–1400. AE, D, DC, MC, V. Closed Sun.*

$–$$$$ ✗ **Carmichael's.** Though it may look like old-time Chicago—with its oak-and-brass pieces, vintage photographs, and waiters dressed in suspenders and shirtsleeve garters—this steak house opened in 1988, on a block that was once Skid Row but is now lined with $500,000 town houses. Not that you need to be a half-millionaire to eat here; certified-Angus steaks are in the upper $20s, making this one of the more reasonably priced top-tier steak houses in town. Planked salmon is a good nonbeef option, and keep your eyes peeled for the monstrous triple-thick pork chop. Desserts are huge; several—including the nine-layer Chocolate Tower—are meant to be shared. ✉ *1052 W. Monroe St., Near West Side,* ☎ *312/433–0025. AE, D, DC, MC, V. No lunch weekends.*

$$ ✗ **The Grillroom.** Across the street from the Shubert Theater, this clubby steak house is a convenient choice for pre-theater patrons. If you don't feel up to a slab of beef before the show, there are also a sizable raw bar and a large selection of seafood and pasta dishes. The wine list offers more than 40 by-the-glass options; the fleet-footed can slip over for an intermission drink if they so desire. For those with time to linger, the dining room is very comfortable, particularly if you can nab one of the soft leather booths. ✉ *33 W. Monroe St., Loop,* ☎ *312/ 960–0000. AE, D, DC, MC, V. No lunch weekends.*

Near North

American

$–$$$ ✗ **RL.** Adjacent to the Polo Ralph Lauren store on Michigan Avenue, RL looks every bit the designer den. The clubby confines have cozy leather banquettes under clustered hunt-club-style art hung on wood-trimmed walls. The upscale-leaning all-American menu spans classics like Cobb salad and lobster club sandwich at lunch, as well as herb-crusted lamb and roasted Amish chicken at dinner. Service is charm-

Near North and River North Dining

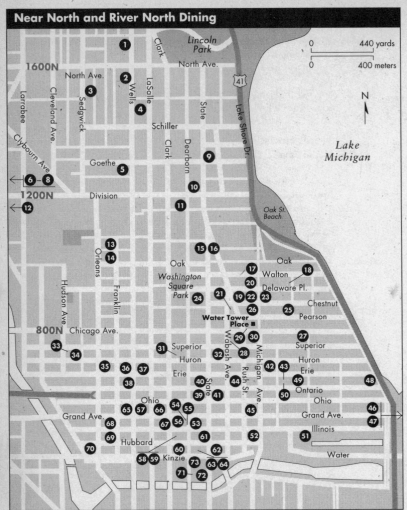

ing and extremely gracious, attentively catering to a clientele of power brokers, moneyed locals, and Michigan Avenue shoppers. ⊠ *115 E. Chicago Ave., Near North,* ☎ *312/475–1100. AE, DC, MC, V. No lunch Sun.*

American/Casual

$ ✕ **Billy Goat Tavern.** The late comedian John Belushi immortalized the Goat's short-order cooks on *Saturday Night Live* for barking, "No Coke! Pepsi!" and "No fries! Cheeps!" at customers. They still do the shtick at this subterranean hole-in-the-wall favored by reporters posted nearby at the *Tribune* and the *Sun-Times.* Griddle-fried "cheezborgers" are the featured chow, and people-watching the favored sport. ⊠ *430 N. Michigan Ave., lower level, Near North,* ☎ *312/222–1525. No credit cards.*

Barbecue

$–$$ ✕ **Joe's Be-Bop Cafe and Jazz Emporium.** Hear live jazz nightly at this casual barbecue restaurant and outdoor café, whose ribs are proving as popular as some of Chicago's finest. Or is it the delightful Navy Pier lake views? There's also a kids' menu, so bring the whole family. ⊠ *600 E. Grand Ave., Near North,* ☎ *312/595–5299. Reservations not accepted. AE, D, DC, MC, V.*

Cafés

$ ✕ **Fox & Obel Food Market Cafe.** This riverside gourmet market treats its prepared food with the same reverence for fine and organic food-stuffs as it does its grocery inventory. Service is cafeteria style but se-lections are decidedly more sophisticated, including entrée salads with duck, tortilla soup with smoked chicken, and steak-blue cheese-caramelized onion sandwiches. Only a block from Navy Pier this can be a toothsome escape from the tourist trap's funnel-cake fare. ⊠ *401 E. Illinois St., Near North,* ☎ *312/379–0112. AE, D, MC, V.*

$ ✕ **Pierrot Gourmet.** Despite the legions of shoppers on Michigan Av-
★ enue there are few casual cafés to quell their collective hunger, mak-ing this bakery/patisserie/café a most welcome neighbor. Lunches center on upscale greens like herb salad with olives and Parmesan, along with open-face *tartine* sandwiches on crusty, house-made sourdough. Break mid-afternoon for a *tarte flambée,* an Alsatian flat bread with cheese and cream, and a glass of Riesling. Dinner is a summer-only affair, but breakfast is served daily and everything can be boxed to go for pic-nicking. Solos will feel comfortable at the magazine-strewn commu-nal table. ⊠ *108 E. Superior St., Near North,* ☎ *312/573–6749. AE, D, DC, MC, V. No dinner fall, winter, spring.*

Chinese

$–$$$$ ✕ **Shanghai Terrace.** This red, lacquer-trimmed 40-seater, a Chinese
★ jewel box hidden away in the Peninsula Hotel, reveals the hotelier's Asian roots. Come for upscale dim sum, stylishly presented, though entrées are equally appealing with steamed fish, Szechuan beef, and wok-fried lobster. A summer patio seven stories above Michigan Av-enue peers at the skyline. ⊠ *108 E. Superior St., Near North,* ☎ *312/ 573–6744. AE, D, DC, MC, V. Closed Sun.–Mon.*

Contemporary

$$$$ ✕ **Seasons Restaurant.** New England and Asian influences crop up cre-atively on Seasons menu: in addition to *bento* box lunches (an assort-ment of Japanese goodies served in a box) and traditional Japanese breakfasts, you might find grilled Maine lobster, corn chowder, and pesto-crusted rack of lamb. Also notable is the fine selection of health-conscious dishes. An affordable three-course daily lunch menu is served within an hour to accommodate business folk and shoppers. The op-ulent dining room is uncommonly comfortable and roomy. Reserva-

tions are essential for Chicago's best (and most expensive) Sunday brunch. ⊠ *Four Seasons Hotel, 120 E. Delaware Pl., Near North,* ☎ *312/280–8800. AE, D, DC, MC, V.*

$$$$ ✕ **Signature Room at the 95th.** Best known for its skyline views from the John Hancock's 95th floor, the Signature Room specializes in formal dinners highlighted by superb service and classics like rack of lamb and salmon in puff pastries. But one of the best deals in town is its $13.95 lunch buffet served weekdays: choose from roasts, prepared entrées, vegetable sides, soup, and a full salad bar. Lake views and an abundance of food also characterize the appeal of the lavish and pricey Sunday brunch. Brunch reservations essential. ⊠ *John Hancock Center, 875 N. Michigan Ave., Near North,* ☎ *312/787–9596. AE, D, DC, MC, V.*

$$$$ ✕ **TRU.** Chefs Rick Tramonto and, on pastries, Gale Gand do fine din-
★ ing with a kick. The quite-serious food is leavened by humorous presentations: caviar atop a tabletop crystal staircase, between-course sorbets in cones, or dishes served over a mini fishbowl occupied by a live fish. The dining room resembles an art gallery, with white walls and carefully chosen art, including an Andy Warhol. The menu starts with a basic three-course prix-fixe, priced at $75; from there, you can expand into five, seven, or more courses. Keep in mind desserts are half the culinary appeal here, and save space. ⊠ *676 N. St. Clair St., Near North,* ☎ *312/202–0001. Reservations essential. Jacket required. AE, D, DC, MC, V. Closed Sun. No lunch.*

$$$–$$$$ ✕ **Avenues.** The super upscale Peninsula hotel sequesters the lovely Avenues, trimmed in Prairie-style glass and deluxe table appointments. But that's just the beginning of the luxuries at this fine dining room: there are tasting menus, a champagne cart, and table-side filleting. Seafood is the specialty, including the signature salt-crusted bass, but meat eaters have several options as well. Tabs quickly escalate here as some appetizers run $20 and up. ⊠ *108 E. Superior St., Near North,* ☎ *312/573–6754. Jacket required. AE, D, DC, MC, V. Closed Sun. No lunch.*

$$$–$$$$ ✕ **NoMI.** In the art-filled Park Hyatt Hotel, NoMI's seventh-floor
★ view—overlooking the historic Water Tower and Michigan Avenue beyond—is arguably the prettiest in town. The food, by chef Sandro Gamba, is special as well. There's a strong French influence on the menu, offset with Asian and Mediterranean accents; one must-try dish is Gamba's risotto, whether made with roasted beets and chanterelles, or prosciutto and mascarpone cheese. ⊠ *Park Hyatt Hotel, 800 N. Michigan Ave., Near North,* ☎ *312/239–4030. AE, D, DC, MC, V.*

$$$–$$$$ ✕ **Pump Room.** A Chicago classic since opening in 1938, the Pump Room long thrived on its celebrity, driven by radio broadcasts and a parade of celebrities passing through Chicago. They held court in the Pump Room's storied Booth One and publicity photos taken there line the entrance to the restaurant. Wealthy Gold Coasters regularly patronize the Pump Room, but new management aims to ensure its survival by luring a younger set with more contemporary and less costly meals. Meaning there's seared tuna alongside steak and potatoes here. In keeping with tradition, Booth One is off limits to all but A-list celebs. ⊠ *1301 N. State Pkwy., Near North,* ☎ *312/266–0360. AE, D, DC, MC, V.*

$$–$$$$ ✕ **Blackhawk Lodge.** Rustic vacation-lodge furnishings lend this American regional restaurant a relaxed mood. Hickory-smoked cuisine is a specialty, so the aromas coming from the kitchen are irresistible. The bacon, salmon, smoky corn chowder, and ribs are particularly good. An à la carte Sunday brunch, with live bluegrass music, is one of the city's most appealing. ⊠ *41 E. Superior St., Near North,* ☎ *312/280–4080. AE, D, DC, MC, V. No lunch Sat.*

$$–$$$$ ✕ **Molive.** The dining room of the Whitehall Hotel sports plenty of contrasting textures and colors, from faux mink trim to leopard-print fabric on the walls. The food is considerably more down to earth, featuring California-style American cuisine, with Mediterranean and Asian accents, as in oak-smoked scallops over "paella-style" risotto. The chocolate lava cake is the must-try dessert, and the sophisticated bar area is a fine place for a late-night drink. ⊠ *107 E. Delaware Pl., Near North,* ☎ *312/573–6300. AE, D, DC, MC, V.*

$$–$$$$ ✕ **Park Avenue Café.** A re-creation of Manhattan's famed Park Avenue Café, Chicago's version serves imaginative American food, artistically presented and remarkable for its complexity and quality. Salmon cured pastrami style and braised pork shank are signatures. There's also a Sunday prix fixe brunch of American appetizers served table-side, à la Chinese dim sum. ⊠ *198 E. Delaware Pl., Near North,* ☎ *312/944–4414. Reservations essential. AE, D, DC, MC, V. No dinner Sun. No lunch.*

$$–$$$$ ✕ **Twelve 12.** Duck the mayhem of round-the-corner Division Street for an elegant meal at Twelve 12. Despite raucous neighbors, the Gold Coast restaurant pulls food sophisticates from around the city for its distinguished meals in a sleek setting. Start with ceviche or duck confit crepe. Then try braised short ribs or roast rack of lamb as mains. Whatever you do leave room for the chocolate ganache cake. A budget-friendly "Street View" menu has more casual, less expensive options in the lounge bordered by street-side picture windows. ⊠ *1212 N. State Pkwy., Near North,* ☎ *312/951–1212. AE, D, DC, MC, V. Closed Sun. No lunch.*

$–$$$$ ✕ **Caliterra.** The flavors of California and Italy blend in this colorful
★   restaurant inside the Wyndham Chicago Hotel. Executive chef John Coletta creates thin pastry "cigars" stuffed with shrimp and basil, makes gnocchi out of Yukon Gold potatoes and pairs them with lobster cooked Bolognese style, and matches Sonoma lamb loin with barley risotto. Less complex dishes include well-made pizza appetizers and wok-fried calamari. The earth-tone dining room flows into a display kitchen and adjacent jazz lounge, so wherever you sit, there's something to look at. ⊠ *633 N. St. Clair St., Near North,* ☎ *312/274–4444. AE, D, DC, MC, V.*

$ ✕ **Flat Top Grill.** This crowded, narrow spot is one of the city's best do-your-own stir-fry places. You can fill your bowl from an assortment of fresh vegetables, meat, and fish; ladle on the sauce of your choice; and watch a chef stir-fry it on a hot griddle. A handy sign gives detailed advice for neophytes. Students and other budget-conscious patrons jam the place on weekends. ⊠ *319 W. North Ave., Near North,* ☎ *312/787–7676. AE, D, DC, MC, V. No lunch Mon.–Thurs.*

French

$$$$ ✕ **The Dining Room.** Gracious service and fine food in an opulent set-
★   ting make this Ritz-Carlton restaurant a classic. Walnut paneling, tapestry carpeting, and crystal chandeliers grace the room in formal French style. Chef Sarah Stegner's kitchen turns out exemplary French cuisine with nouvelle accents, such as squab breast with roasted garlic sauce and turbot in shellfish broth. Daily specials complement the seasonal menu. The cheese selection is the finest in Chicago, and few restaurants can match the breadth and depth of the wine list. The popular Sunday brunch is among the city's most elaborate and expensive. ⊠ *Ritz-Carlton, 160 E. Pearson St., Near North,* ☎ *312/266–1000. Reservations essential. Jacket required. AE, D, DC, MC, V. No lunch.*

$$$$ ✕ **Les Nomades.** If you seek elegant and formal fine dining, look to
★   Les Nomades, owned by Roland and Mary Beth Liccioni, who for 10 years ran the acclaimed Le Français. A carefully composed menu of

contemporary French food includes the usual suspects, such as duck consommé and duo of foie gras, as well as more creative pairings like sweetbreads and ostrich over an eggless béarnaise sauce. Dinner is presented as a four-course prix fixe (price $75), though there are plenty of choices in every category. ⊠ *222 E. Ontario St., Near North,* ☎ *312/649–9010. Reservations essential. Jacket required. AE, D, DC, MC, V. Closed Sun.–Mon. No lunch.*

$$–$$$$ ✕ **Bistro 110.** Like any good bistro, this place can be noisy and chaotic at times, but consider that a testimony to its popularity. Besides the lively bar scene and Water Tower views, the real draw is the food from the wood-burning oven; the kitchen consistently offers excellent renditions of French classics and vegetarians praise the roasted-vegetable platter. The Sunday jazz brunch, accompanied by a Dixieland jazz band, is a standout. ⊠ *110 E. Pearson St., Near North,* ☎ *312/266–3110. AE, D, DC, MC, V.*

$–$$ ✕ **Bistrot Margot.** From the faithfully executed menu and budget-
★ friendly prices to the Parisian Art Nouveau interior, this is a classic bistro in every sense of the word. Chef-owner Joe Doppes whips up silky chicken liver pâté, succulent *moules mariniere* (mussels in tomato sauce), and soul-satisfying coq au vin. Doppes even finds room on the menu for a bit of humor—his Taylor Street pizza, an homage to Chicago's Little Italy neighborhood, is a Frenchified pizza made with brioche dough and topped with spinach and goat cheese. ⊠ *1437 N. Wells St., Near North,* ☎ *312/587–3660. AE, D, DC, MC, V.*

Hawaiian

$$–$$$ ✕ **Roy's.** Hawaii's most exported chef, Roy Yamaguchi raids the island larder, refining the goods with Asian flourishes. The results are busy, multi-ingredient dishes that seduce with the ease of a trade wind. Roy's signatures include many seafood dishes like blackened ahi in soy mustard and butterfish in ginger wasabi sauce. But honey mustard short ribs, lamb two ways, and other carnivores' options please heartier palates. Though the cozy and warm dining room says contemporary chic, the waiters' greetings and flower-print ties spread a little aloha around the place. ⊠ *720 N. State St., Near North,* ☎ *312/787–7599. AE, D, DC, MC, V. No lunch.*

Italian

$$$–$$$$ ✕ **Spiaggia.** Refined Italian cooking dished alongside three-story pic-
★ ture window views of Lake Michigan make Spiaggia one of the city's top eateries. The tiered dining room, in shades of silver and cream, guarantees good sight lines from each table. Chef Tony Mantuano prepares elegantly simple seasonal dishes that may include pancetta-wrapped rabbit, and the lightest gnocchi on the planet. The scholarly wine list is no place for bargain hunters, but there are some remarkable bottles. You can also sample Spiaggia's wonders next door at Cafe Spiaggia, a lower-priced, casual sidekick serving lunch and dinner daily. ⊠ *980 N. Michigan Ave., Near North,* ☎ *312/280–2750. Reservations essential. Jacket required. AE, D, DC, MC, V. No lunch Sun.–Thurs.*

$–$$ ✕ **Fortunato.** This stylish Wicker Parker may be rooted in Italian coun-
★ try cooking, but its organic emphasis and contemporary flare mark it as modern. Its look, incorporating Eames dining chairs and modernist chrome chandeliers, underscores the updated theme. Expect specialty veggies like fiddlehead ferns, fine handmade pastas, and everything from baby octopus to Spanish mackerel issuing from the wood-fired oven. The glassed-in open kitchen provides a peek at the back-of-the-house proceedings. ⊠ *2005 W. Division St., Wicker Park,* ☎ *773/645–7200. AE, D, DC, MC, V. No lunch Mon.–Fri.*

Japanese

$$-$$$$ ✕ **Heat.** Fans of so-fresh-it's-breathing sushi check into this wee, chic 40-seater for chef Kee Chan's "live kill" menu. Fish tanks discretely tucked below the sushi bar hold flounder, eel, and other selections, which chefs flay alive, delivering the seconds-old sashimi on a plate. In addition to creative nigiri, sashimi, and maki, Heat also specializes in the chef's-choice 11-course *kaiseki* menu. But if it's the sushi you crave, do reserve a spot at the sushi bar for a chat with the educational Kee. ✉ *1507 N. Sedgwick, Near North,* ☎ *312/397–9818. AE, D, DC, MC, V. Closed Sun.*

$–$$$ ✕ **Tsunami.** This Gold Coast spot looks more like a nightclub than a Japanese restaurant, thanks to faux-finished walls, moody lighting, and urban-contemporary music. Still, it's a respectable option for sushi, sashimi, traditional teriyaki dishes (shrimp, steak, or salmon), hibachi-grilled seafood, and the occasional noodle dish. The location just steps from bar-filled Division Street guarantees a good-time crowd. ✉ *1160 N. Dearborn St., Near North,* ☎ *312/642–9911. AE, D, DC, MC, V. No lunch weekdays.*

Mediterranean

$$–$$$ ✕ **Wave.** The so-hip-it-hurts W Chicago Lakeshore bar spills directly into Wave. Come for the design: translucent backlit kitchen panels, pod seating in the lounge, and a row of window-side tables adjoined by settees. But—surprise—you'll come back for the food. The zesty Mediterranean fare includes homey, shareable platters of feta cheese and olives as well as more refined options like grilled baby octopus and carrot-cumin scallops. Considering the hotel's general party atmosphere, this is a good place to take a crowd. ✉ *644 N. Lake Shore Dr., Near North,* ☎ *312/255–4460. AE, D, DC, MC, V.*

Mexican

$$–$$$ ✕ **Salpicon.** The tables at this cozy, colorful restaurant are usually filled with folks eagerly devouring the authentic cooking. Chef Priscila Satkoff's upbringing in Mexico City is reflected in such boldly seasoned dishes as *pollo Yucateca* (chicken Yucatán style) with a hot-pepper salsa. Wash it down with a premium margarita made from one of a roster of 100 tequilas or a wine from the 800-vintage list. The Mexican-style Sunday brunch, with egg dishes and novelties like grilled quail, is highly recommended. ✉ *1252 N. Wells St., Near North,* ☎ *312/988–7811. AE, D, DC, MC, V. No lunch.*

$–$$ ✕ **Adobo Grill.** This lively Mexican restaurant adjacent to Second City comedy club perfects the basics and edges into more daring dishes. Guacamole is prepared table-side, a bit of culinary theater ensuring absolutely fresh dip at the spice level you prefer. Diners tend to linger over flavorful fare like grilled quail and red snapper Veracruzana. The bar prepares better-than-average margaritas and stocks an impressive number of sipping tequilas—there's even a tequila sommelier to help neophytes with selection. ✉ *1610 N. Wells St., Near North,* ☎ *312/266–7999. AE, D, DC, MC, V. No lunch.*

Seafood

$$–$$$$ ✕ **Riva.** In the middle of Navy Pier, its windows gazing southward over Lake Michigan and the lakefront skyline, this spacious, colorful restaurant gives you unparalleled views—and charges for the privilege. Grilled fish and shellfish are pricey, though the hordes that crowd the place, especially in summer, don't seem to mind (good service helps). Simpler preparations—such as grilled salmon or various pastas—are better bets than the menu's more ambitious efforts. A casual café downstairs, which spills onto the pier's promenade on warm summer days, is more budget-friendly and includes a raw bar. ⊠ *700 E. Grand Ave., Near North,* ☎ *312/644–7482. AE, D, DC, MC, V.*

$–$$$ ✕ **McCormick and Schmick's.** This large-scale fish house, part of an Oregon-based chain, has a massive menu that's updated twice daily to incorporate the freshest fish available. At least six varieties of oysters are offered, along with Louisiana crab cakes, Wisconsin rainbow trout, and other regional specialties. There's room for 350 in the dining rooms. The bar area serves low-priced appetizers during happy hours, held both early and late in the evening. ⊠ *41 E. Chestnut St., Near North,* ☎ *312/397–9500. AE, D, DC, MC, V.*

Steak Houses

$$–$$$$ ✕ **Capital Grille.** The Chicago outpost of this steak-house chain can hold its own with the city's big boys. Prime steaks are dry-aged on the premises in a glassed-in room. The decor avoids some of the steak-house clichés by mixing mounted deer heads and portraits-in-oil; the award-winning wine list includes a gratifying number of half bottles. ⊠ *633 N. St. Clair St., Near North,* ☎ *312/337–9400. AE, D, DC, MC, V. No lunch weekends.*

$$–$$$$ ✕ **Eli's the Place for Steak.** Clubby and inviting in leather and warm wood, this outstanding restaurant relies on top-quality ingredients prepared precisely to customers' tastes. Prime aged steaks are among the best in Chicago. You'll also find superb, thickly cut veal chops and excellent calf's liver. For dessert, order Eli's renowned cheesecake, now sold nationally in countless varieties. ⊠ *215 E. Chicago Ave., Near North,* ☎ *312/642–1393. AE, D, DC, MC, V. No lunch weekends.*

$$–$$$$ ✕ **Morton's of Chicago.** This is Chicago's best steak house—and that's
★ no idle statement. Excellent service and a very good wine list add to the principal attraction: beautiful, hefty steaks cooked to perfection. White tablecloths, chandeliers, and off-white walls create a classy feel despite the subterranean locale. It's no place for the budget conscious, but for steak lovers it's a 16-ounce (or more) taste of heaven. ⊠ *1050 N. State St., Near North,* ☎ *312/266–4820. AE, D, DC, MC, V. No lunch.*

$–$$$$ ✕ **Gibsons Steakhouse.** On the site once occupied by the famous Mis-
★ ter Kelly's nightclub, this is now perhaps the convention crowd's favorite steak house. The reasons? Plenty of room, attractive decor with lots of dark-wood trim, overwhelming portions, and good service. You don't see chopped liver on many appetizer lists these days, but the version here is good. ⊠ *1028 N. Rush St., Near North,* ☎ *312/266–8999. Reservations essential. AE, D, DC, MC, V. No lunch.*

$–$$$$ ✕ **Mike Ditka's Restaurant.** This sports-theme restaurant celebrates NFL Hall-of-Famer Mike Ditka, the only coach to take the Bears to the Super Bowl (sure it was in 1985, but Bears fans have long memories). The clubby, dark-wood interior, upstairs cigar lounge, and sports-memorabilia are predictable features, as is the steaks-and-chops menu. What is not predictable are the more sophisticated dishes, such as venison chops with sour-cherry sauce and the pulled-chicken, shiitake-mushroom, and black-olive fettuccine. ⊠ *Tremont Hotel, 100 E. Chestnut St., Near North,* ☎ *312/587–8989. AE, D, DC, MC, V.*

River North

American/Casual

$ ✕ **Ed Debevic's.** This tongue-in-cheek re-creation 1950s diner is busy from morning 'til midnight. Gum-snapping waitresses in garish costumes trade quips and snide remarks with customers, but it's all in good humor. The menu lists eight different hamburgers, a large sandwich selection, four chili preparations, five hot dogs, and such "deluxe plates" as meat loaf, pot roast, and chicken potpie. Unlike a real 1950s diner, Ed's has a selection of cocktails and wines, plus Ed Debevic's Beer. ⊠ *640 N. Wells St., River North,* ☎ *312/664–1707. Reservations not accepted. AE, D, DC, MC, V.*

Barbecue

$–$$ ✗ **Smoke Daddy.** A rib and blues emporium in a funky Wicker Park corner bar, Smoke Daddy serves tangy barbecued ribs with generously supplied paper towels for swabbing stray sauce. Fans pack bar stools and booths for the chow, which includes richly flavored smoked pork and homemade fries, as well as for the no-cover R&B bands that play nightly after 9:30. ⊠ *1804 W. Division St., Wicker Park,* ☎ *773/772– 6656. AE, D, MC, V. No lunch weekends.*

Chinese

$$$ ✗ **Ben Pao.** The Zen-most Chinese restaurant in town has minimalist decor in black and gray with soothing water walls. Well-prepared selections include chicken *soong* (cooked chicken presented with soft lettuce leaves for wrapping). There's also a spicy eggplant dish that's not to be missed, and featured fish entrées are always a good bet. The friendly waitstaff is helpful with explanations. ⊠ *52 W. Illinois St., River North,* ☎ *312/222–1888. AE, D, DC, MC, V. No lunch weekends.*

Contemporary

$$$–$$$$ ✗ **Kevin.** Chef/owner Kevin Shikami's namesake serves fine French-Asian fusion in an understated wood-trimmed setting. Fans come for Shikami's tuna tartare alone. Other recommended bites include pomegranate sauced duck and scallops with foie gras. Save room for fanciful desserts. ⊠ *9 W. Hubbard St., River North,* ☎ *312/595– 0055. AE, DC, MC, V. Closed Sun. No lunch Sat.*

$$$–$$$$ ✗ **Spago.** Its dining room may not be filled with the who's who of Hollywood, but the Chicago version of Wolfgang Puck's celebrated California concept is a hit in its own right. On weekends especially, the cavernous dining room is packed solid. Creations such as tangerine-glazed quail and herb-stuffed bass with basil mashed potatoes keep the crowds happy, as do offbeat Puck signatures such as the upscale meat loaf (with veal and pancetta in the mix) and the famed smoked-salmon pizza (not on the menu, but available to those who ask). ⊠ *520 N. Dearborn St., River North,* ☎ *312/527–3700. Reservations essential. AE, D, DC, MC, V. No lunch weekends.*

$$–$$$$ ✗ **Crofton on Wells.** Chef and owner Suzy Crofton breaks a few contemporary-dining rules with her eponymous restaurant. She doesn't pack
★ tables too closely together (the dining room, although small, is surprisingly comfortable), she keeps the noise level down, and there's no sponge painting on the walls. Her food is similarly short on clichés but gratifyingly long on flavor. Dig into gutsy Cajun barbecued shrimp over sweet-potato hay, or indulge in the luxury of grilled foie gras with chanterelles and red pearl onions. And save room for dessert. ⊠ *535 N. Wells St., River North,* ☎ *312/755–1790. Reservations essential. AE, DC, MC, V. Closed Sun. No lunch weekends.*

$$–$$$$ ✗ **MK.** Michael Kornick's ultrahip spot pulls in the trendy crowd with
★ its sleek look and elegant menu. An upstairs dining loft overlooks the elegant main room done in cream and charcoal hues. Little expense has been spared on fine linens, expensive flatware, and elegant wine stems. Start with tuna tartare with celery rémoulade, or, if you're feeling indulgent, the sautéed foie gras with Armagnac-laced prunes; the must-try entrée is the grilled venison with zinfandel-braised onions. An ever-changing array of imaginative desserts by acclaimed pastry chef Mindy Segal ends the meal on a high note. ⊠ *868 N. Franklin St., River North,* ☎ *312/482–9179. Reservations essential. AE, DC, MC, V. No lunch.*

\$\$–\$\$\$\$ ✕ **Naha.** Carrie Nahabedian lends her name (well, the first two syllables, anyway) and considerable culinary skills to this upscale venture. In a clean-lined space done in shades of cream and sage, Nahabedian presents eye-catching dishes such as a tower of tuna tartare, osetra caviar, and crème fraîche, or vanilla-scented roasted sea scallops with caramelized Belgian endive. Wine is treated with reverence, from the well-chosen selection to the high-quality stemware it's served in. The convivial bar also serves the main menu. ⊠ *500 N. Clark St., River North,* ☎ *312/321–6242. AE, D, DC, MC, V. Closed Sun. No lunch Sat.*

\$–\$\$\$\$ ✕ **Harvest on Huron.** One of the stars of the River North neighborhood, this contemporary American combines colorful decor, superior service, and outstanding food by Alan Sternweiler (for years the chef at renowned Printer's Row). There are always one or two vegetarian entrées, such as acorn squash filled with mushroom risotto, along with dishes like roast rabbit rolled around rabbit sausage and ancho-chili glazed pork tenderloin. Lovers of fine spirits will wax rhapsodic over the massive collection, available in half-pours for financially prudent experimentation. ⊠ *217 W. Huron St., River North,* ☎ *312/587–9600. AE, D, DC, MC, V. No lunch Sun.*

\$–\$\$\$\$ ✕ **Zealous.** Charlie Trotter protegé Michael Taus runs this haute-cuisine River North resident, serving edgy dishes that change seasonally but are typified by mango pancakes with foie gras and freshwater prawns with purple yam puree and coconut-hickory nut sauce. The menu centers around an \$85, three-course prix-fixe meal, but those in the mood to splurge may indulge in even grander multicourse degustations, each course selected by Taus and typically featuring flavors not seen on the main menu. Skylights, bamboo plants, curvy metallic half walls, and a two-story glassed-in wine room dress the upscale dining room. ⊠ *419 W. Superior St., River North,* ☎ *312/475–9112. AE, D, DC, MC, V. Closed Sun.–Mon.*

\$\$–\$\$\$ ✕ **Bin 36.** This fascinating hybrid—fine-dining establishment, lively wine
★ bar, and wine shop—pours wines by the bottle, glass, half-glass, and as "flights" of multiple 1½-ounce tastings. If you fall in love with a particular wine, chances are the on-site shop can sell you a take-home bottle. A menu of fine contemporary meals, such as striped bass with Kalamata-olive mashed potatoes and veal paillard with fingerling potatoes, lists one or two wine selections for each. The sprawling bar and dining room are dominated by 35-ft ceilings, and an all-glass west wall lets in plenty of natural light. ⊠ *339 N. Dearborn St., River North,* ☎ *312/755–9463. AE, D, DC, MC, V.*

\$\$–\$\$\$ ✕ **Napa Valley Grille.** This patch of California wine country in Chicago evokes its namesake region with creative food and an extensive wine list. The display kitchen issues vine-friendly meals to fireside tables in warm, wood-clad rooms on two levels. Though menus change seasonally, look for standouts like boar bacon–wrapped monkfish, and foie gras and duck confit grilled cheese. Graze via the "perfect pairs" menu which matches small plates with Napa wines. ⊠ *626 N. State St., River North,* ☎ *312/587–1166. AE, D, DC, MC, V.*

\$\$–\$\$\$ ✕ **Zinfandel.** Classic regional American recipes are given a contemporary twist at this ambitious restaurant. Southern "burgoo" meat-and-vegetable stews, New England clambakes, and Pacific seafood all share space on the sea-to-shining-sea menu. A supplementary menu focuses on a specific region each month; longtime customers plan visits for certain cuisines, such as Hawaiian (usually in August). The dining room's warm southwestern colors are enhanced by eclectic American folk art, which, along with aromas from the kitchen, create a homey atmosphere. Don't miss the Saturday brunch. ⊠ *59 W. Grand Ave., River North,* ☎ *312/527–1818. AE, DC, MC, V. Closed Sun. No lunch.*

$–$$$ ✕ **Hubbard Street Grill.** Slightly off the beaten path (in the western fringe of the River North neighborhood) is this comfortable, attitude-free restaurant. Chef David Schy shows a deft hand with seasonings and a fine respect for classic American food, using spicy or sweet sauces, chutneys, and relishes to enliven his grilled meats and fish; the ahi tuna burger alone justifies a visit. ✉ *351 W. Hubbard St., River North,* ☎ *312/222–0770. AE, D, DC, MC, V. Closed Sun. No lunch Sat.*

$–$$ ✕ **Wildfire.** Everything in this wide-open restaurant is cooked over an open flame; indeed, a triple hearth of roaring fires is a focal point of the room. No culinary innovations here, but you'll find exceptional aged prime rib, barbecued ribs, and roasted fish, along with wood-fired pizzas and skillet-roasted mussels. If you crave adventure, try the bacon-wrapped and horseradish-crusted filet mignon. ✉ *159 W. Erie St., River North,* ☎ *312/787–9000. AE, D, DC, MC, V. No lunch.*

French

$–$$$$ ✕ **Brasserie Jo.** Jean Joho, chef-proprietor of the acclaimed Everest, runs this fun and more affordable brasserie, authentic down to its zinc-topped bar proffering hard-boiled eggs. Come for the frites alone. But stay for the *choucroute* (a crock full of pork cuts with Alsatian sauerkraut), phyllo-wrapped shrimp, classic coq au vin, and steak tartare. Have the profiteroles for dessert and watch as a waiter decants chocolate syrup over your ice-cream-filled pastries. ✉ *59 W. Hubbard St., River North,* ☎ *312/595–0800. AE, D, DC, MC, V. No lunch.*

$$–$$$ ✕ **Cyrano's Bistrot and Wine Bar.** Chef and owner Didier Durand presents the food of his birthplace, Bergerac, in this cheerful, accomplished restaurant. Traditional dishes such as onion tart and bouillabaisse are handled deftly; the restaurant also specializes in rotisserie chicken, rabbit, and duck. The wine list includes many vintages from lesser-known producers in southern France. An express lunch option presents four courses simultaneously on a large platter—ideal for time-constrained diners. ✉ *546 N. Wells St., River North,* ☎ *312/467–0546. AE, D, DC, MC, V. Closed Sun.–Mon. No lunch weekends.*

$$–$$$ ✕ **Kiki's Bistro.** Lodged in a loft space, Kiki's looks country French, but cooks contemporary with full, aggressive flavors. Grilled rabbit sausage with garlic and rosemary is a fine starter; for an entrée try grouper with an herb-scented fish bouillon and vegetable medley. Classics, such as steak frites, are always excellent. ✉ *900 N. Franklin St., River North,* ☎ *312/335–5454. AE, D, DC, MC, V. Closed Sun. No lunch Sat.*

Greek

$–$$$ ✕ **Papagus.** Chicago's best Greek restaurant is bright, rustic, and comfortable. The menu focuses on *mezes,* literally "small plates," which are appetizers resembling Spanish tapas. There are additional appetizers on the menu, as well as substantial salads and fairly traditional entrées. Fine choices are *tirosalata* (feta-cheese spread), sensational grilled octopus, and lamb chops. Desserts, so often a throwaway on Greek menus, are remarkably good, especially the unusual dried-cherry-filled baklava. The all-Greek wine list has some wonderful inexpensive bottles; trust your waiter's recommendation. ✉ *Embassy Suites, 620 N. State St., River North,* ☎ *312/642–8450. AE, D, DC, MC, V.*

Italian

$$–$$$$ ✕ **Coco Pazzo.** This Chicago branch of a very successful Manhattan
★ restaurant shines with solid, mature, and professional service and a kitchen that focuses on Tuscan cuisine—lusty, aggressively seasoned fare, such as chicken livers with polenta. Grilled game is a particular strength, as are the risotto dishes; duck-confit risotto offers a bit of

both. ⊠ *300 W. Hubbard St., River North,* ☎ *312/836–0900. Reservations essential. AE, DC, MC, V. No lunch weekends.*

\$\$–\$\$\$\$ ✕ **Maggiano's Little Italy.** Enormous portions of red-sauce Italian food star in this homage to Little Italy. Order two entrées for every three diners in your party and you'll be as happy as the other cheerfully loud patrons in the wide-open dining room. Expect hearty, stereotypic Italian-American fare—brick-size lasagna, chicken Vesuvio, veal scallopini—as well as a doggie bag. Lunchtime sandwiches are especially good. ⊠ *516 N. Clark St., River North,* ☎ *312/644–7700. AE, D, DC, MC, V.*

\$–\$\$\$\$ ✕ **Harry Caray's.** Famed Cubs announcer Harry Caray passed away in 1998 but his legend lives on, and fans continue to pour into his namesake restaurant (where Harry frequently held court). Italian-American specialties like fine pastas and outstanding chicken Vesuvio share menu space with top-quality prime steaks and chops. The wine list has won a number of national awards. And the raucous bar serves classic bar food and televised sports. Holy cow! ⊠ *33 W. Kinzie St., River North,* ☎ *312/828–0966. AE, D, DC, MC, V. No lunch Sun.*

\$–\$\$\$ ✕ **Scoozi!** This ever-popular trattoria continues to attract a young professional crowd after work hours and plenty of wandering suburbanites on the weekend. You'll recognize it by the gigantic tomato over the front door; inside, a sprawling, two-level dining room sports loft-chic looks of exposed brick walls, open truss ceiling, and steel garage doors. The menu shines with grazeable antipasti options, wood-fired pizzas and comforting pastas, plus daily dish specials. ⊠ *410 W. Huron St., River North,* ☎ *312/943–5900. AE, D, DC, MC, V. No lunch.*

\$\$ ✕ **Pizzeria Uno/Pizzeria Due.** Chicago deep-dish pizza got its start at Uno in 1943, with Due following a few years later. Both exude old-fashioned charm, from vintage bars and paneled walls to the reproduction light fixtures. Plan on only two slices of the thick and cheesy Chicago-style pie as a full meal. Unless you're really hungry, skip the pre-pizza salad or appetizer and plan to postpone dessert. Only a block apart, the two sibling restaurants serve the same pizza; check in at both to see which has the shorter wait. Whichever you choose, you'll be experiencing a bit of Chicago history. ⊠ *29 E. Ohio St., River North,* ☎ *312/321–1000;* ⊠ *Due, 619 N. Wabash Ave., River North,* ☎ *312/943–2400. AE, D, DC, MC, V.*

Japanese

\$\$–\$\$\$ ✕ **Mirai Sushi.** This savory Japanese hipster helped turn Wicker Park's
★   Division Street west of Damen into Chicago's latest restaurant row. Make the trek for top-quality classic sushi and sashimi dishes, as well as some with lesser-known ingredients, such as monkfish pâté, horse mackerel, and rockfish. Display tanks keep a fresh supply of fish on hand. Servers are extremely knowledgeable about the menu. But for the full monty sit at the sushi bar and put yourself into the hands of the inventive sushi chefs. An upstairs lounge draws the club crowd. ⊠ *2020 W. Division St., Wicker Park,* ☎ *773/862–8500. AE, D, DC, MC, V. No lunch.*

Latin

\$\$–\$\$\$ ✕ **Mas.** Inventive nuevo Latino fare, creative pan-Latin cocktails, and
★   intimate 74-seat confines generate a significant buzz at Mas. Peruse the menu over a Chilean Pisco sour or a Cuban *mojito.* Among starters, look for the always-interesting ceviche of the day, served in an elegant martini glass, or the black-bean soup, served with a shot of Brazilian *cachaca* (sugarcane liquor). Main courses include grilled tuna with chimichurri sauce and chili-rubbed pork tenderloin. ⊠ *1670 W. Division St., Wicker Park,* ☎ *773/276–8700. AE, D, DC, MC, V. No lunch.*

$$–$$$ ✕ **Nacional 27.** The name of this sophisticated Pan-Latin hot spot refers to the 27 south-of-the-border nations whose cuisines are supposedly represented. That may be an exaggeration, but the menu does offer a lot of variety. Try the barbecued pork *arepas* (corn-bread pancakes) appetizer and follow with the pork tenderloin smeared with chili paste. The circular bar draws a following independent of the food. On weekend nights the floor in the middle of the dining room is cleared for dancing. ⊠ *325 W. Huron St., River North,* ☎ *312/664–2727. AE, D, DC, MC, V. No lunch.*

Mexican

$$–$$$ ✕ **Frontera Grill.** Chef-owner Rick Bayless and his wife, Deann, wrote
★ the book on Mexican cuisine—several books, actually, not to mention their popular TV show—and that's what you queue up for at this casual restaurant, trimmed in bright colors and Mexican folk art. The couple annually visits Mexico with the entire staff in tow to further their research. Servers, consequently, are highly knowledgeable about the food, typified by silver salmon in pumpkin-seed mole, pork in a pasilla-pepper sauce, and chiles rellenos. Since the restaurant only accepts reservations for parties of six or more, arrive early to dine or anticipate a two-margarita wait. ⊠ *445 N. Clark St., River North,* ☎ *312/661–1434. AE, D, DC, MC, V. Closed Sun.–Mon.*

$$–$$$ ✕ **Topolobampo.** Located alongside Frontera Grill, Topolobampo
★ shares Frontera's address, phone, and dedication to quality. Topolobampo is the higher-end room, with a more subdued mood and luxury menu composed of pricier ingredients. The ever-changing offerings showcase game, seasonal fruits and vegetables, and exotic preparations: tequila-cured salmon and pheasant roasted in banana leaves are two examples. Good service and an interesting wine list add to the appeal. ⊠ *445 N. Clark St., River North,* ☎ *312/661–1434. Reservations essential. AE, D, DC, MC, V. Closed Sun.–Mon. No lunch Sat.*

Seafood

$$–$$$$ ✕ **Joe's Seafood, Prime Steaks & Stone Crab.** Unlike its parent, Joe's Stone Crab in Miami Beach, this outlet doesn't close when the Florida crabs are out of season in summer. Which explains the extra emphasis on other denizens of the deep and prime steaks. One thing this restaurant does share with the Miami original is its popularity—people line up before the restaurant opens to be sure of getting a table. ⊠ *60 E. Grand Ave., River North,* ☎ *312/379–5637. AE, D, DC, MC, V. No lunch Sun.*

$$–$$$$ ✕ **Shaw's Crab House and Blue Crab Lounge.** The city's chief specialist in bivalves, Shaw's nurtures a split personality, spanning a dressy main dining room in spiffed-up loft digs and a lively exposed-brick bar where shell shuckers work harder than the barkeeps. Preparations tend toward the simple and the classic; try the fried calamari, steamed blue mussels, and Maryland crab cakes for appetizers. Crab, lobster, and shrimp are menu standards, along with a half dozen varieties of fresh oysters. ⊠ *21 E. Hubbard St., River North,* ☎ *312/527–2722. AE, D, DC, MC, V. No lunch weekends.*

Steak Houses

$$–$$$$ ✕ **Gene and Georgetti.** This classic steak house of the old school variety thrives on the buddy network of high-powered regulars who pop into the historic River North joint to carve up massive steaks, good chops, and the famed "garbage salad"—a kitchen-sink creation of greens with vegetables and meats. Service may be brusque if you're not connected, but the vibe is Chicago to the core. ⊠ *500 N. Franklin St., River North,* ☎ *312/527–3718. AE, DC, MC, V. Closed Sun.*

$$–$$$$ ✕ **Keefer's.** Few steak houses advertise their broilermen. But this un-
★   usual newcomer hired acclaimed chef John Hogan to man the stoves.
Hogan's definition of a steak-house menu breaks all conventions by
including his signature bistro fare, inventive daily specials (pray for the
seafood-rich bouillabaisse) and plenty of fish offerings as well as New
York strips and hefty porterhouses. The circular room drops the he-
man pose, too. All of which explains why Keefer's pulls the most di-
verse and gender-balanced crowd of the meat market. ⊠ *20 W. Kinzie
St., River North,* ☎ *312/467–9525. AE, D, DC, MC, V. Closed Sun.*

$$–$$$$ ✕ **Ruth's Chris Steak House.** With excellent steaks and outstanding service, the Chicago outpost of this fine-dining chain continues to demon-
strate it can hold its own in this definitive steak town. The lobster is
good, although expensive—largely because the smallest lobster in the
tank is about 3 pounds—and there are more appetizer and side-dish
options than at most other steak houses. ⊠ *431 N. Dearborn St., River
North,* ☎ *312/321–2725. AE, D, DC, MC, V. No lunch weekends.*

$$–$$$$ ✕ **Smith and Wollensky.** Aged-on-the-premises prime beef and an ex-
tensive wine cellar are hallmarks of this riverfront steak house, part
of a New York–based chain. United by remarkable river views, the din-
ing area is divided into several spaces, one of which is Wollensky's Grill,
a more casual room with a compact menu and later serving hours. Steaks
and chops are the big draw, of course, but deep-fried pork shank and
pepper-dusted "angry lobster" are customer favorites, too. ⊠ *318 N.
State St., River North,* ☎ *312/670–9900. AE, D, DC, MC, V.*

Thai

$$–$$$$ ✕ **Erawan.** Former staffers at Chicago's leading Thai fine restaurant,
★   Arun's, branched out to open Erawan. Like Arun's, the Thai food is
upscale, featuring refined versions of fiery hot and sour soup with prawns,
whole red snapper, and tea-smoked poussin. Unlike Arun's, its River
North location is convenient to visitors. Art-filled interiors evoke Thailand with carved paneling and imported tapestries. ⊠ *729 N. Clark
St., River North,* ☎ *312/642–6888. AE, D, DC, MC, V. No lunch.*

$$–$$$$ ✕ **Vong's Thai Kitchen.** A casual spin-off of chef Jean-Georges Von-
gerichten's New York Thai-French fusion Vong, Vong's Thai Kitchen
concentrates solely on Thai fare with signature upmarket accents and
pretty presentations. Look for tuna sashimi rolls, sliced New York strip
steak over noodles, and a laundry list of curries ranging from mild to
"jungle" hot. Both helpful servers and warm decor make the place invit-
ing. ⊠ *6 W. Hubbard St., River North,* ☎ *312/644–8664. AE, D, DC,
MC, V. No lunch weekends.*

Lincoln Park and North

Contemporary

$$$$ ✕ **Charlie Trotter's.** Plan at least a month in advance to dine at this tem-
★   ple of haute cuisine, namesake of top toque Charlie Trotter. The taste-
ful dining room, in a renovated Lincoln Park town house, seats only
20 tables, plus the sought-after behind-the-scenes kitchen table. Per-
haps the nation's most experimental chef, Trotter prepares his menus
daily from the best of what's available globally, never repeating a dish.
Past raves include antelope strudel with wild mushrooms and foie-gras
ravioli with mango and lemongrass sauce. Menus follow a multi-
course, $120 degustation format ($100 for the vegetarian version). For
a worthwhile splurge order the wines-to-match option. ⊠ *816 W. Ar-
mitage Ave., Lincoln Park,* ☎ *773/248–6228. Reservations essential.
Jacket required. AE, DC, MC, V. Closed Sun. No lunch.*

$$$–$$$$ ✕ **Meritage.** Like the style of wine it's named for, this Bucktown
restaurant is tricky to categorize. The chef takes his inspiration from
the flavors of the Pacific Northwest, which translates into a fair amount

Lincoln Park and North Dining

of fish (striped bass with *dauphinoise* potatoes and red-wine sauce) and a heavy Asian influence (duck spring rolls with pickled ginger and Vietnamese fish sauce). The digs are warmly lit and romantic, but in season opt for the lovely outdoor dining patio. ✉ *2118 N. Damen Ave., Bucktown,* ☎ *773/235–6434. AE, MC, V. No lunch.*

$–$$$$ ✕ **Yoshi's Cafe.** Once a pricey fine-dining restaurant of considerable renown, Yoshi's recast itself as an informal French-Asian café with much lower prices and a jeans-casual sensibility; there's even a kids' menu. Still evident is Yoshi Katsumura's exceptional cooking—such as his duck breast and leg confit with honey-sesame sauce, and grilled tofu with ginger-soy sauce that would convert many a carnivore. Sunday brunch includes egg dishes and a Japanese-inspired breakfast. ✉ *3257 N. Halsted St., Lake View,* ☎ *773/248–6160. Closed Mon.*

$$$ ✕ **North Pond.** A former Arts-and-Crafts style warming house for ice
★ skaters at Lincoln Park's North Pond, this gem-in-the-woods fittingly celebrates an uncluttered culinary style. Talented chef Bruce Sherman emphasizes organic ingredients, wild-caught fish, and artisan farm products in his flavorful preparations. Menus change seasonally but order the midwestern favorite walleye pike if available. Like the food, the wine list seeks out small American craft producers. Lunches, more casual than dinners, are popular with park walkers. ✉ *2610 N. Cannon Dr., Lincoln Park,* ☎ *773/477–5845. AE, D, DC, MC, V. Closed Mon.*

$$–$$$ ✕ **Café Absinthe.** This funky, theatrical spot in the hip Bucktown neighborhood serves the stylish set a menu that is distinctly contemporary. Dishes might included pork tenderloin with apple bread pudding and maple jus and pancetta-wrapped monkfish with basil-cream orzo. Part of the fun is finding the entrance; it's off the alley. ✉ *1954 W. North Ave., Bucktown,* ☎ *773/278–4488. AE, D, DC, MC, V. No lunch.*

$$–$$$ ✕ **Spring.** Chef Shawn McClain's artistic but unfussy fish preparations—
★ from tuna tartare with quail egg to cod in crab and sweet pea sauce—distinguish the sophisticated Spring from the seasonal restaurant crop. Occupying a former bathhouse, Spring assumes the spa's sunken quarters with its original white glazed-tile walls. Like McClain's cooking, the restaurant's interior design faces east for inspiration, beginning with a rock garden in the foyer. Expect fine dining without pretension here in the bohemian Wicker Park neighborhood. ✉ *2039 W. North Ave., Wicker Park,* ☎ *773/395–7100. AE, D, MC, V. Closed Mon. No lunch.*

$$–$$$ ✕ **Tomboy.** This funky storefront in Chicago's Andersonville neighborhood draws an eclectic crowd that makes for great people-watching. The food is visually interesting as well, from a fanciful "porcupine" shrimp coated with splayed-out spikes of phyllo dough, to crème brûlée served in a cookie cone inside a martini glass. Desserts are about all that come in martini glasses, by the way: there's no liquor license, but there is plenty of stemware for whatever you bring, and no corkage fee. ✉ *5402 N. Clark St., Uptown,* ☎ *773/907–0636. AE, DC, MC, V. No lunch.*

$–$$$ ✕ **Erwin.** This appealing spot brims with the sunny personalities of owners Erwin and Cathy Drechsler. The straightforward menu may look ordinary—roasted chicken with lemon-garlic sauce, for instance—but the skillful cooking will give you new respect for simplicity. Flavors are pure and vibrant and every dish seems perfectly put together. Polished but friendly servers know their way around the wine list, which goes beyond brand names to offer modestly priced, little-known bottles that are fun to drink. Locals jam the Sunday brunch. ✉ *2925 N. Halsted St., Lake View,* ☎ *773/528–7200. AE, D, DC, MC, V. Closed Mon. No lunch.*

$–$$$ ✕ **Green Dolphin Street.** Set in an industrial area just north of Bucktown, this sprawling complex encompasses a cool green dining room, stylish jazz club (no cover for dinner guests), cigar-friendly bar, and outdoor patio overlooking an unspoiled stretch of the Chicago River. The emphasis on good looks extends to the photogenic fare. Globally influenced American dishes include oyster-stuffed tenderloin, grilled salmon over firm polenta cake, and mushroom-asparagus risotto. ✉ *2200 N. Ashland Ave., Lake View,* ☎ *773/395–0066. AE, D, DC, MC, V. No lunch.*

$–$$$ ✕ **MOD.** You'd expect the Jetsons-like interior of bright plastic surfaces and swiveling scoop chairs to draw a trendy crowd. You don't expect this Wicker Parker to serve thoughtfully grounded cuisine. Style meets substance at MOD which emphasizes small-farmer produce and seasonal ingredients. A sense of humor is evident in a dish of "ham and eggs" that matches farm-fresh eggs and prosciutto, and a "Texas truck-stop rib eye" paired with a Stilton and Vidalia-onion fondue. ✉ *1520 N. Damen Ave., Wicker Park,* ☎ *773/252–1500. AE, D, DC, MC, V. No lunch.*

$–$$$ ✕ **She She.** In this funky Lincoln Square restaurant, the waiters wear leopard-print pants that match the dining room seat cushions, and the bar specializes in martinis named after people like Tallullah Bankhead and RuPaul. Nicole Parthemore's food can't match the decor for shock value, but she does go beyond the norm with entrées typified by coconut-crusted tilapia with lemongrass-seasoned vegetables and mustard-smeared lamb chops with a savory cranberry bread pudding. ✉ *4539 N. Lincoln Ave., Ravenswood,* ☎ *773/293–3690. AE, DC, MC, V. No lunch.*

$–$$$ ✕ **Soul Kitchen.** There's more soul music than soul food in the offing at this fun, perpetually thronged Wicker Park mainstay. Animal-print tablecloths and colorful art funk up the house. Distractions aside, there's a serious menu of creative regional American food, typically prepared with assertive amounts of spice. Sunday brunch is unconventional and lively. ✉ *1576 N. Damen Ave., Wicker Park,* ☎ *773/342–9742. Reservations not accepted. AE, DC, MC, V. No lunch.*

$–$$ ✕ **Brett's.** This storefront charmer in gentrifying Roscoe Village has soft lighting, classical music, and the kind of serious food you'd only expect downtown. Creative surprises mark the oft-changing menu: potato tacos with poblano chili sauce, Thai-style salmon, jerk pork chops. Soups are a particular strength, and desserts are heavenly. Don't miss the homemade bread. Neighborhood fans wait on the street for a seat at brunch, served both Saturday and Sunday. ✉ *2011 W. Roscoe St., Roscoe Village,* ☎ *773/248–0999. AE, D, DC, MC, V. Closed Mon.–Tues.*

$–$$ ✕ **Feast.** The gregarious communal table, cozy fireplace, and sofa-filled lounge creates a fittingly social backdrop at Feast where the world's cuisines mingle freely on the menu. Dishes from Cuba to India boldly populate the expansive menu at this casual neighborhood eatery. Past hits include a napoleon of crispy wontons layered with tuna tartare and smoked salmon, ravioli stuffed with jalapeños and black beans, or wild-mushroom Stroganoff with puff pastry. ✉ *1616 N. Damon Ave., Bucktown,* ☎ *773/772–7100. AE, DC, MC, V. No lunch.*

Ethiopian

$ ✕ **Mama Desta's Red Sea.** Dramatically different from European cooking, the stewlike dishes at Mama Desta's intriguingly combine herbs and spices with complex aromas and interesting textures. Food such as spicy chicken, lamb stew, and pureed lentils is flavorful, earthy, and simple. Instead of relying on silverware, diners use spongy, slightly sour flat bread to scoop up the chef's creations. ✉ *3216 N. Clark St., Lake View,* ☎ *773/935–7561. AE, DC, MC, V. No lunch Mon.–Thurs.*

French

$$$$ ✕ **Ambria.** In a warm Art Nouveau setting, Ambria combines classic
★ haute-cuisine style with contemporary French food—all without flash
or bombast. The modestly understated menu dazzles with blackberry-
sauced venison, lobster gazpacho, and rosemary-infused lamb loin. The
assortment of cheeses, sorbets, fruits, and pastries is upstaged by the
sensational dessert soufflé. If the à la carte offerings are too much to
contemplate, simplify your decision with one of several multicourse
dinners. The wine list is encyclopedic, but sommelier Bob Bansberg is
an unintimidating and sensitive guide. ⊠ *2300 N. Lincoln Park W, Lincoln Park,* ☎ *773/472–5959. AE, D, DC, MC, V. Closed Sun. No lunch.*

$–$$$$ ✕ **Mon Ami Gabi.** Visit Gabi for reliable bistro food just steps from
Lincoln Park. Park-front windows let in ample natural light, warming
the wood-trimmed interior with checkerboard tile floors and stuffed
game birds on the walls. Best bites include several versions of steak
frites, as well as such bistro essentials as bouillabaisse and *coquilles
St. Jacques* (scallops). The casual companion to the elegant Ambria at
the same address, Mon Ami Gabi deserves consideration on its own.
⊠ *2300 N. Lincoln Park W, Lincoln Park,* ☎ *773/348–8886. AE, D,
DC, MC, V. No lunch.*

$$–$$$ ✕ **Aubriot.** Highly regarded chef Eric Aubriot and his wife Stephanie
★ run this sunny and intimate café serving inventive French food. The
chef knows how to make meals flavorful without piling on the butter
and cream. Look for sautéed monkfish with cardamom-veal jus, and
foie gras drizzled with chocolate sauce—definitely not your standard
French fare. An upstairs wine bar, Eau, serves simplified fare to late-
night diners. ⊠ *1962 N. Halsted St., Lincoln Park,* ☎ *773/281–4211.
AE, D, DC, MC, V. Closed Mon. No lunch.*

$–$$ ✕ **Le Bouchon.** The French comfort food at this charming (if cramped)
bistro in Bucktown is in a league of its own. Onion tart has been a sig-
nature dish of owner Jean-Claude Poilevey for years; other not-to-be-
skipped delights are hunter-style rabbit and *salade Lyonnaise* (mixed
greens topped with a creamy vinaigrette and a poached egg). Don't miss
the fruit tarts. ⊠ *1958 N. Damen Ave., Bucktown,* ☎ *773/862–6600.
AE, D, DC, MC, V. Closed Sun. No lunch.*

Italian

$$–$$$$ ✕ **Via Emilia.** Everything from the complimentary breads to the lovely
desserts is made in the kitchen of this Bolognese restaurant in the toni-
est section of Lincoln Park. The earthy, rustic menu includes veal slices
with a coarse tuna puree, tagliatelle pasta with a meat-filled Bolognese
sauce, and grilled fresh fish with chopped vegetables. Simple but pretty,
the narrow dining room has an open kitchen at the far end. ⊠ *2119
N. Clark St., Lincoln Park,* ☎ *773/248–6283. Reservations essential.
AE, DC, MC, V. No lunch.*

$–$$$$ ✕ **Via Veneto.** This family-run restaurant has simple decor and so-
phisticated food. Pastas are excellent, particularly the daily specials.
Grilled veal with Chianti sauce and tuna carpaccio with bitter greens
and mustard vinaigrette show the kitchen's range. On Saturday night
the crowds are impossible; Friday is a better bet, midweek even bet-
ter. There's a small parking lot in back, but street parking is never a
problem in this extremely safe residential neighborhood. ⊠ *3449 W.
Peterson Ave., North Park,* ☎ *773/267–0888. Reservations essential.
AE, D, DC, MC, V. No lunch weekends.*

$–$$$ ✕ **La Donna.** Run by the sister of the Via Veneto owner, La Donna has
excellent pastas—try the pumpkin ravioli in creamy balsamic sauce or
the fine penne *arrabiata* (spicy tomato sauce)—and good, cracker-
crust pizzas. Like Via Veneto, it has a generally crowded dining room
that makes customers feel like part of a very large party. The wine list

is well chosen and fairly priced, and there's a bargain-price Sunday brunch. ⊠ *5146 N. Clark St., Uptown,* ☎ *773/561–9400. AE, D, DC, MC, V.*

$–$$$ ✕ **Mia Francesca.** Why is this tiny restaurant so insanely popular? Principally because of chef-owner Scott Harris's very good authentic Italian cooking. Its moderate prices and pleasant, unpretentious atmosphere don't hurt, either. Try the classic *bruschetta, quattro formaggi* (four cheese) pizza, or the full-flavored pasta and chicken dishes. While you wait for one of the small, tightly spaced tables in the single dining room— and you *will* wait—you can have a drink at the bar. ⊠ *3311 N. Clark St., Lake View,* ☎ *773/281–3310. Reservations not accepted. AE, MC, V. No lunch.*

$–$$ ✕ **Vinci.** Paul LoDuca, who also owns Adobo Grill in Old Town, created this stylishly casual restaurant dressed in faux finishes and rustic touches. The menu focuses on robust regional dishes such as grilled pork chops with fennel and garlic. Pizzas are creative; one combines fontina cheese, roasted garlic, bitter greens, and tomato. The restaurant is particularly popular for pre-theater dining and Sunday brunch. ⊠ *1732 N. Halsted St., Lincoln Park,* ☎ *312/266–1199. AE, DC, MC, V. Closed Mon. No lunch.*

Kosher

$$$–$$$$ ✕ **Shallots.** It's rare to find a glatt-kosher restaurant with fine-dining sensibilities, but chef-partner Laura Frankel tackles the constraints of Jewish dietary law as though they were no hindrance at all. Her salt-cod fritters in a spicy tomato coulis, venison au poivre, and chicken-chorizo paella are so satisfying that were it not for the certificate from the Chicago Rabbinical Council on the wall, you might imagine you were dining at any upscale, well-appointed Lincoln Park restaurant. Shallots is closed on Friday and before sundown on Saturday in observance of the Sabbath, offering only a limited sandwich menu Saturday night. ⊠ *2324 N. Clark St., Lincoln Park,* ☎ *773/755–5205. AE, D, DC, MC, V. Closed Fri. No lunch weekends.*

Mediterranean

$–$$ ✕ **Clark Street Bistro.** The comfortable surroundings and more-than-fair prices of this eclectic neighborhood charmer keep it filled with cost-cutting students, local regulars, and visiting shoppers. Dishes are pretty as a picture, whether you've ordered a complex bouillabaisse or a simple saffron couscous with cilantro and cumin. ⊠ *2600 N. Clark St., Lincoln Park,* ☎ *773/525–9992. AE, D, DC, MC, V. No lunch weekdays.*

Mexican

$$–$$$ ✕ **Ixcapuzalco.** Geno Bahena, a longtime chef at Frontera Grill, runs ★ this popular restaurant that draws diners from around the city. Hearty moles, which change daily, are his signature, paired wonderfully with grilled quail or sliced duck breast. The tight-squeeze front room provides the best viewing of cooks who, among other things, make tortillas to order. ⊠ *2919 N. Milwaukee Ave., Logan Square,* ☎ *773/486–7340. AE, D, DC, MC, V. Closed Tues.*

$–$$$ ✕ **Don Juan's on Halsted.** Patrick Concannon once worked under Charlie Trotter, so it isn't too surprising that his Halsted Street restaurant offers something beyond your typical Mexican fare. A taqueria menu accommodates light eaters and late diners, but the selection is nontraditional, including barbecued veal and grilled lamb. The main menu features tuna tartare with mango and radish, lamb shank in a chipotle barbecue sauce, and salmon drizzled with cilantro butter. If you're headed to Steppenwolf Theatre, this is your best pre-curtain bet. ⊠ *1729 N. Halsted St., Lincoln Park,* ☎ *312/981–4000. AE, DC, MC, V.*

Pizza

$–$$ ✕ **Piece.** The antithesis of Chicago-style deep-dish pizza, Piece's flat pies mimic those made famous in New Haven, Connecticut. The somewhat free-form, eat-off-the-baking-sheet pizzas come in plain (tomato sauce, Parmesan, and garlic), white (olive oil, garlic, and mozzarella) or traditional red, with numerous topping options. Stylish salads, particularly the greens with Gorgonzola and pears, make fine starters and house brewed beers pair perfectly with the chow. Local families as well as Wicker Park hipsters converge at this spot, generally crowded though it occupies a vast former garage. ✉ *1927 W. North Ave., Wicker Park,* ☎ *773/772–4422. AE, D, MC, V.*

Polish

$–$$$ ✕ **Lutnia.** The menu here is Polish-Continental, but stick to the hearty Polish creations unless you're dying for steak Diane or other similarly unremarkably prepared Continental dishes. (A bonus is that the Polish cuisine is considerably less expensive.) Start with an assortment of pierogi, and perhaps some hunter's stew; then try the terrific stuffed quail. Decor is upscale, and a pianist performs most nights. ✉ *5532 W. Belmont Ave., Portage Park,* ☎ *773/282–5335. MC, V. Closed Mon. No lunch weekends.*

Spanish

$$ ✕ **Café Ba-Ba-Reeba!** Chicago's best-known purveyor of tapas is usually crowded with fun-seeking Lincoln Parkers. Colorful interiors filled with folk art encourage the fiesta feel. Choose from among a large selection of cold and warm tapas, ranging from cannelloni stuffed with tuna, asparagus, and basil, served with tomato-basil sauce and white wine vinaigrette, to veal with mushrooms, eggplant, tomato, and sherry sauce. An entrée menu includes nearly a dozen paellas, baked salmon, and even venison. When the weather's warm, the outdoor patio is packed and the sangria flows freely. ✉ *2024 N. Halsted St., Lincoln Park,* ☎ *773/935–5000. AE, D, DC, MC, V. No lunch weekdays Sept.–Apr.*

Swedish

$ ✕ **Ann Sather.** All four branches of this light, airy Swedish restaurant, mobbed for weekend breakfast, emphasize home-style food and service. Go for the homemade cinnamon rolls alone; those without time to sit can grab a dozen to go. Dinner, available only at the Belmont Avenue location, includes specialties such as potato sausage and chicken croquettes; the Swedish sampler lets you try duck breast with lingonberry glaze, a Swedish meatball, a potato sausage, a dumpling, and sauerkraut. Lunches, also served at the other locations, include similar reasonably priced Scandinavian specialties. ✉ *5207 N. Clark St., Uptown,* ☎ *773/271–6677. No dinner;* ✉ *929 W. Belmont Ave., Lake View,* ☎ *773/348–2378;* ✉ *3416 N. Southport Ave., Lake View,* ☎ *773/404–4475. No dinner;* ✉ *2665 N. Clark St., Lincoln Park,* ☎ *773/327–9522. No dinner. AE, MC, V.*

Thai

$$$$ ✕ **Arun's.** The finest Thai restaurant in Chicago—some say in the
★   country—is also the most expensive, featuring only multicourse, custom-designed menus for a flat $85. Arun's use of fresh ingredients and beautiful presentations far exceed the efforts of other Thai kitchens. Your meal might include intricate golden pastry baskets filled with diced shrimp and shiitake mushrooms, whole tamarind snapper or veal medallions with ginger-lemongrass sauce. The quiet dining room has lots of natural wood, complemented by Thai art and a small art gallery. ✉ *4156 N. Kedzie Ave., Irving Park,* ☎ *773/539–1909. Reservations essential. AE, D, DC, MC, V. Closed Mon. No lunch.*

$ ✕ **Thai Classic.** This attractive, spotless restaurant just a few blocks south of Wrigley Field stands out with its good service and meticulously prepared dishes. Not only are prices low, but there is no liquor license (pick up a six-pack of *Singha* beer from the liquor store down the street), saving patrons additional expense. Bargain-hunters enjoy the $10.95 buffet, available Saturday afternoon and all day Sunday. It can be very difficult to park here when the Cubs are playing (though the restaurant has a few free spaces in back), so plan accordingly. ⊠ *3332 N. Clark St., Lake View,* ☎ *773/404–2000. AE, D, DC, MC, V.*

Vietnamese

$$–$$$$ ✕ **Pasteur.** Ease back into rattan-covered chairs, amid tropical plants
★ and lazily spinning ceiling fans, and prepare to be impressed by the superb food that emerges from Pasteur's kitchen. The menu sticks to staples of Vietnamese cooking, including minced shrimp with sugarcane, spicy beef salad, crisply fried whole fish, and fragrant soups. The waitstaff is knowledgeable. Be a polite guest and don't steal the adorable fu-dog chopstick rests; goodness knows the locals do that often enough. ⊠ *5525 N. Broadway, Edgewater,* ☎ *773/878–1061. Reservations essential AE, D, DC, MC, V. No lunch Mon. or Tues.*

South

American/Casual

$$–$$$$ ✕ **Chicago Firehouse Restaurant.** A historic South Side fire station makes a novel setting for this straightforward American restaurant. The menu dishes up everything from panfried rainbow trout to a superb New York strip steak. The bar area, which has two vintage fire poles, serves a pub menu of sandwiches, burgers, and pizzas. ⊠ *1401 S. Michigan Ave., Near South Side,* ☎ *312/786–1401. AE, D, DC, MC, V. No lunch Sat.*

$ ✕ **Manny's Coffee Shop and Deli.** Locals and visitors alike may bemoan the dearth of delis in Chicago, but this classic cafeteria on the Near South Side is the real deal. Favorites include thick pastrami sandwiches, soul-nurturing matzo-ball soup, and piping-hot potato pancakes, though there's plenty to choose from. Kibbitzing counter cooks provide commentary as they sling the chow, sometimes barking at dawdlers. Search for seating in two teaming rooms and pay as you leave. ⊠ *1141 S. Jefferson St., Near South Side,* ☎ *312/939–2855. Reservations not accepted. No credit cards. Closed Sun. No dinner.*

Chinese

$–$$$$ ✕ **Phoenix.** A pretty-as-a-picture restaurant with a second-floor view
★ of the Loop skyline, Phoenix has established itself as one of the area's best—thanks to lovely white-tablecloth surroundings, good cooking, and a wide-ranging menu. Rolling carts dispense dim sum daily from 8 AM to 3 PM. Weekend dim sum crowds are substantial; arrive early or be prepared to wait. ⊠ *2131 S. Archer Ave., Chinatown,* ☎ *312/ 328–0848. AE, D, DC, MC, V.*

$–$$$ ✕ **Emperor's Choice.** This sophisticated but comfortable restaurant sets out to prove that Chinese seafood specialties can go well beyond deep-fried prawns. It succeeds admirably; seafood dishes such as steamed oysters and Peking-style lobster are fresh and expertly prepared. A separate menu includes such "delicacies" as rattlesnake soup and pork bellies. Seating is a bit cramped but the food is worth it. Discounted parking (with validation) is available in the Cermak/Wentworth lot. ⊠ *2238 S. Wentworth Ave., Chinatown,* ☎ *312/225–8800. AE, D, MC, V.*

$–$$ ✕ **Hong Min.** Low prices and well-prepared food are the hallmarks of this no-frills Chinatown mainstay. The menu embraces everything from chop suey to stir-fried lobster; insiders tout the fresh oysters. And

South Dining

though decor is virtually nonexistent, the twin dining rooms, one of which is for nonsmokers, are at least comfortable. Bring your own beer and wine. ⊠ *221 W. Cermak Rd., Chinatown,* ☎ *312/842–5026. MC, V.*

$ ✕ **Lao Sze Chuan.** Come to this enticing Szechuan restaurant in the Chinatown Square Mall for the guilty pleasures of kung pao chicken and twice-cooked pork (though Lao Sze Chuan uses a lighter hand than many oil-heavy Szechuan kitchens in town). Dishes on the English-language menu are very good, but if you're feeling adventurous ask the waitperson to recommend something off the Chinese menu. ⊠ *2172 S. Archer Ave., Chinatown,* ☎ *312/326–5040. AE, MC, V.*

French

$–$$$ ✕ **La Petite Folie.** A favorite among locals and professors at the nearby
★ University of Chicago, this classic French restaurant is quiet and elegant, with white-tablecloth tables and hefty flatware. Happily, prices are modest for treats like sea scallops with artichoke and citrus reduction, or foie gras with finely sliced endive and pears. The early-bird menu is especially appealing for pre-theater patrons. ⊠ *1504 E. 55th St., Hyde Park,* ☎ *773/493–1394. AE, D, DC, MC, V. Closed Mon.*

Indonesian

$–$$ ✕ **August Moon.** Although half the menu here is indeed Chinese, the Indonesian dishes are what set this Chinatown restaurant apart. The Dutch "rice table," or *rijsttafel,* dinner is an 18-course banquet ($35 per person; minimum four people; one-day advance notice requested) that provides you with the widest possible variety of meat, fish, and vegetable dishes—and quite a full stomach. If you're not in so expansive a mood, it's quite all right to sample just a dish or two (the shrimp in spicy gravy is a good choice). The kitchen is conservative on the heat, so speak up if you like things spicy. ⊠ *225 W. 26th St., Chinatown,* ☎ *312/842–2951. Reservations essential. MC, V. BYOB. Closed Sun.– Tues.*

Italian

$$–$$$$ ✕ **Gioco.** This neighborhood Italian would seem all too typical in Lin-
★ coln Park or River North but is a refreshing addition south of Roosevelt Road. Set in a former speakeasy (the Speakeasy Room, a private dining space with its own rear-alley entrance, is an homage to the old days), Gioco has a distressed-urban decor of plaster-spattered brick walls and well-worn hardwood floors. The country-Italian menu includes rustic fare like prosciutto-wrapped scallops, pasta with veal ragout, and lobster gnocchi. And though the dish originated in Chicago, not Italy, chicken Vesuvio also makes an appearance. ⊠ *1312 S. Wabash Ave., Near South Side,* ☎ *312/939–3870. AE, DC, MC, V. No lunch weekends.*

Mexican

$–$$$ ✕ **Playa Azul.** You will find wonderful fresh oysters at both the original 18th Street location and the sister house at Broadway and Irving Park Road, along with a full selection of fish and seafood soups, salads, and entrées, including abalone, octopus, shrimp, crab, clams, and lobster. Red snapper *Veracruzaná* (deep-fried) and *al mojo de ajo* (in garlic sauce) are house specialties, both delectable. Grilled meat dishes and chiles *rellenos* (stuffed with cheese and fried) round out the menu, along with Mexican beers. ⊠ *1514 W. 18th St., Pilsen,* ☎ *312/421– 2552;* ⊠ *2005 N. Broadway, Near South Side,* ☎ *773/472–8924. Reservations not accepted. MC, V.*

$ ✕ **Nuevo Leon.** A simple storefront creates a pleasant atmosphere for this restaurant's familiar or less familiar dishes, all of which leave you satisfied. In addition to a large selection of enchiladas, tacos, tostadas, and tamales, you'll find a rich and flavorful *menudo* (tripe soup); several beef soups; chicken in mole sauce; and chopped steak simmered with tomatoes, jalapeño peppers, and onions (a house specialty). Not all servers are fluent in English, but cheerful goodwill prevails. ⊠ *1515 W. 18th St., Pilsen,* ☎ *312/421–1517. Reservations not accepted. No credit cards.*

Southern

$–$$ ✕ **Army and Lou's.** First-rate home-cooked soul food has earned a stellar reputation for this South Side institution. The fried chicken is arguably the city's best; barbecued ribs, roast turkey, turnip and mustard greens, and crunchy fried catfish are other standouts. There's even a brief wine list. The setting is surprisingly genteel for such down-home fare: waiters glide about in tuxedo shirts and bow ties, tables have starched white cloths, and African and Haitian art graces the walls. ⊠ *420 E. 75th St., Near South Side,* ☎ *773/483–3100. AE, D, DC, MC, V. Closed Tues.*

$ ✕ **Soul Queen.** Come to Soul Queen for the food, not the ambience. Plentiful quantities of southern-style entrées and down-home specials are available on a large buffet. Best bets are channel catfish steaks served with Mississippi hush puppies; ham hocks with candied yams and fresh greens or peas; and stewed chicken with homemade dumplings, greens, and deep-dish apple pie. Prices are even lower before 5 PM Monday through Thursday. ⊠ *9031 S. Stony Island Ave., South Shore,* ☎ *773/731–3366. Reservations not accepted. No credit cards.*

Worth a Special Trip

Contemporary

$$$$ ✕ **Trio.** Chef Grant Achatz worked at the acclaimed French Laundry ★ in Napa Valley before taking over the kitchen at Trio. His wildly creative cooking aims to involve all the senses, including hearing. The menu proffers three multicourse degustation options—four, eight, and a whopping 20 courses. Though the options change frequently, expect clever dishes like a savory version of Chinese bubble tea made with crème fraîche and salmon roe or the structured dishes like red mullet with six different Mediterranean accents, each lending a unique flavor when tasted with the fish. Think of dining here as theater for the palate. ⊠ *1625 Hinman Ave., Evanston (14 mi north of downtown Chicago),* ☎ *847/733–8746. Reservations essential. Jacket required. AE, D, DC, MC, V. Closed Mon. No lunch Sat.–Thurs.*

$$–$$$$ ✕ **Courtright's.** This ambitious south suburban restaurant has a dining ★ room overlooking a pretty garden and a bordering forest preserve; time your meal right and you might spot a grazing deer. Inside, the seasonally shifting menu offers such inventive American fare as Amish farm rabbit rillette and chili-dusted pork medallions with black-bean polenta and persimmon-mango sauce. Can't decide? Order the five-course degustation and let the chef choose. A marvelous wine cellar offers more than 700 selections. ⊠ *8989 Archer Ave., Willow Springs,* ☎ *708/839–8000. AE, D, DC, MC, V. No lunch weekends.*

French

$$$$ ✕ **Carlos'.** This restaurant continues to challenge Le Français for recog- ★ nition as Chicago's best French restaurant. Service is particularly good—owner Carlos Nieto (himself a Le Français graduate) gets involved in the front-room operations—but even the lowest-ranking assistant has a firm grasp of the menu. Dishes are mainly contemporary French: you might find squab ravioli with garlic sauce or rabbit tournedos with creamed leeks and truffles. Desserts are heavenly. The substantial wine list includes some magnificent vintages, although at eye-popping prices. The main dining room is dark and woody; mismatched antique china plates lend character. ⊠ *429 Temple Ave., Highland Park (26 mi north of downtown Chicago),* ☎ *847/432–0770. Reservations essential. Jacket required. AE, D, DC, MC, V. Closed Tues. No lunch.*

$$$$ ✕ **Le Français.** Where founding Le Français chef Jean Banchet, now
★ retired, left off, Don Yamauchi takes off, cooking the French fare for which the suburban restaurant is known but with a light touch and updated ideas. Luxury dishes include lobster ravioli, veal sweetbreads in truffle sauce, and foie gras in a variety of ways. A picture window in the contemporary-styled dining room allows glimpses of the chef at work. Wheeling is about 30 mi northwest of downtown Chicago. ⊠ *269 S. Milwaukee Ave., Wheeling,* ☎ *847/541–7470. Reservations essential. Jacket required. AE, D, DC, MC, V. Closed Sun. No lunch Sat.– Mon.*

4   LODGING

From the Loop to Lincoln Park, Chicago's accommodations can satisfy a yearning for old-world elegance or high-tech sophistication. Not surprisingly, the city has a number of architectural showstoppers, along with plenty of giant convention hotels and several quiet hideaways. Rates tend to be high in this business-oriented city, but if you're looking for a good value you can still find a range of options, from historic charmers to modern suite hotels.

Revised by
Elisa Kronish

CHICAGO GOES BY MANY NICKNAMES: "the city of big shoulders," "the second city," "the city that works," and, of course, the Windy City. By any name, this Midwest metropolis continues to draw both business and leisure travelers. Lodging choices range from upscale luxury hotels to basic chain fare to unique establishments in convenient areas along the lakefront, downtown, or in Lincoln Park to the north. Convention goers are the lifeblood of many hotels, with mammoth high-rises offering thousands of square feet of meeting space. Visitors desiring a more personal experience can find smaller, European-style hostelries. Many hotels have panoramic views of Lake Michigan or of the architecturally spectacular high-rises lining the Chicago River.

As one of the nation's most popular convention and trade show destinations, Chicago can sometimes be a challenging place to find a room. Advance reservations are essential, except perhaps in the dead of winter. When no major shows are in town, many hotels woo customers with special offers like corporate rates, shopping or theater packages, senior citizen savings, family discounts, honeymoon deals, or savings for clergy and military personnel. If you plan to spend a lot of time indoors at museums and shops—and you aren't averse to cold weather— visit in January or February, when hotel rates drop like the chilly winter temperatures. Weekend deals can also pack in appealing extras at a purse-satisfying price. Always be sure to ask whether you're eligible for any discounts.

Choosing a Neighborhood

Hotels are listed in this chapter by neighborhood and then by price category within each neighborhood.

Business travelers may prefer Loop hotels because they're within walking distance of the financial district and government offices. Major cultural institutions are nearby as well: the Art Institute, Orchestra Hall, the Civic Opera House, and the grand venues of the theater district. The museum campus, comprising the Field Museum, Shedd Aquarium, and Adler Planetarium, is just a short bus or cab ride away, and the skyscrapers that put Chicago on the architectural map are all around. With a few new exceptions, Loop hotels tend to be older and somewhat less expensive than those in Near North. The main drawback of staying in the Loop is how deserted the area becomes at night and on weekends. People traveling alone may prefer the brighter lights of accommodations near North Michigan Avenue.

Dining and shopping are the big draws in the Near North area, just north of the river, where upscale department stores and posh hotels line both sides of North Michigan Avenue as well as side streets. Advertising and media agencies are also here. River North bustles with art galleries and high-end antique stores, with a few lower-end, family-friendly, and boutique hotels scattered throughout. A bit north of Michigan Avenue and close to Lincoln Park and the lakefront is the Gold Coast, a stately residential neighborhood where the hotels are quiet and dignified. Farther north, less expensive properties occupy Lincoln Park and Lake View—both lively, youthful neighborhoods with an eclectic array of restaurants and shops.

A meeting or convention in Rosemont or a tight flight schedule should be the only reasons to consider an airport hotel. Even though prices are slightly lower, the area around O'Hare is drab, depressing, and far from downtown. The 15-mi trip into the city can take an hour during rush hour, bad weather, or periods of heavy construction on the Kennedy Expressway, none of which are uncommon occurrences.

Booking Your Room

When you make your reservation, be sure to get a confirmation number and keep it with you for reference. Notify the hotel if you anticipate arriving later than 5 PM; many hotels will guarantee your reservation with a credit card. Inquire about the hotel's cancellation policy at the time of booking to avoid paying for a room you didn't occupy. Should you need to cancel your reservation, notify the hotel as soon as possible—and be sure to get a cancellation number. Otherwise, you may be responsible for at least one night's charge.

One alternative to reserving a room through a hotel is to contact a booking service. These agencies book excess rooms at major hotels, often at a significant discount. A no-fee discount hotel-reservation service that specializes in Chicago is **Hot Rooms** (☎ 773/468–7666 or 800/468–3500).

Bed-and-Breakfasts

Staying in a person's home lends a personal touch to your visit and is a good way to see residential neighborhoods. You may also save some money. **Bed & Breakfast/Chicago** (✉ Box 14088, 60614, ☎ 773/394–2000 or 800/375–7084, FAX 773/394–2002, WEB www.chicago-bed-breakfast.com) is a clearinghouse for more than 70 options, from a guest room in a Victorian home to a furnished high-rise apartment. Accommodations range from $85 to $325 per night and are mostly in the Near North and Lincoln Park neighborhoods. Reservations can be made by phone (weekdays 9–5), mail, or on-line. The office will mail or fax sample listings and a reservation form.

When Not to Go

Although Chicago's frigid winters should be a consideration when planning your trip, also be aware of the more than 1,000 conventions and trade shows scheduled in the area throughout the year. During the Comdex spring show in April, the National Restaurant Association show in May, the manufacturing technology show in September, the Radiological Society of America show in late November, and the National Housewares Manufacturing show in January, not only are rooms nonexistent, but so are tables at the city's popular restaurants. To find out if a convention in Chicago will affect your travel plans, contact the **Chicago Office of Tourism** or the **Chicago Convention and Tourism Bureau** (☞ Visitor Information *in* Smart Travel Tips).

Prices

Hotel price categories in this chapter are based on the standard weekday rate for one room, double occupancy.

These are the rack rates—the highest price at which the rooms are rented. As noted above, discounts are often available. However, although standard rates are quoted *per room,* package rates are often quoted *per person, double occupancy.* Be warned that many Chicago hotels quote rates based on single occupancy, with a second person adding $10–$20 to the nightly rate.

CATEGORY	COST*
$$$$	over $260
$$$	$180–$260
$$	$100–$179
$	under $100

All prices are for a standard double room, excluding service charges and Chicago's 14.9% room tax. The tax is slightly lower at suburban hotels.

Downtown

$$$$ ⊞ **Hotel Monaco.** A French deco–inspired look contributes to this hotel's travel theme, as do the registration desk—fashioned after a classic steamer trunk—and meeting rooms named for international destinations such as Tokyo and Paris. You'll feel at home with complimentary morning coffee and a nightly wine reception. The hotel is pet friendly and will even supply your room with a pet goldfish-in-a-bowl upon request. In brightly colored guest rooms, turndown is accompanied by such surprise amenities as lottery tickets or Pixy Stix candy. ⊠ *225 N. Wabash Ave., Loop, 60601,* ☎ *312/960–8500 or 800/397–7661,* FAX *312/960–1883,* WEB *www.monaco-chicago.com. 170 rooms, 22 suites. Restaurant, room service, in-room data ports, minibars, cable TV, some in-room VCRs, gym, bar, dry cleaning, laundry service, concierge, business services, meeting rooms, parking (fee), some pets allowed, no-smoking floors. AE, D, DC, MC, V.*

$$$$ ⊞ **Swissôtel.** The Swissôtel's triangular Harry Weese design ensures panoramic vistas of either the city, lake, or river. The comfortable, contemporary-style guest rooms have two-line phones and marble bathrooms. Even those who hate to sweat may be inspired by the views from the 42nd-floor fitness center, pool, and spa. The hotel has four dining options including **The Palm** restaurant, a cousin of the New York steak house of the same name. ⊠ *323 E. Wacker Dr., Loop, 60601,* ☎ *312/565–0565 or 888/737–9477,* FAX *312/565–0540,* WEB *www. swissotel.com. 632 rooms, 36 suites. Restaurant, café, patisserie, room service, in-room data ports, in-room fax, minibars, cable TV, some in-room VCRs, indoor pool, gym, hot tub, massage, sauna, spa, steam room, 2 bars, dry cleaning, laundry service, concierge, business services, meeting rooms, parking (fee), no-smoking floor. AE, D, DC, MC, V.*

$$$–$$$$ ⊞ **Fairmont.** Just blocks from the Loop, this 45-story pink granite tower is a true standout. All rooms have marble bathrooms with oversize tubs and separate shower stalls. The suites, all of which have stunning views of Lake Michigan, are filled with plants and marble-top darkwood furniture and have living and dining rooms. Grand suites on the top floor pamper guests with fireplaces, libraries, and kitchenettes. On Friday and Saturday evenings, live entertainment in **Entre Nous,** the hotel's French-influenced restaurant, creates a festive atmosphere. ⊠ *200 N. Columbus Dr., Loop, 60601,* ☎ *312/565–8000 or 800/526–2008,* FAX *312/856–1032,* WEB *www.fairmont.com. 626 rooms, 66 suites. 2 restaurants, room service, in-room data ports, in-room fax, minibars, cable TV, some in-room VCRs, golf privileges, 3 bars, lobby lounge, cabaret, dry cleaning, laundry service, concierge, business services, meeting rooms, parking (fee), no-smoking rooms. AE, D, DC, MC, V.*

$$$–$$$$ ⊞ **Renaissance Chicago Hotel.** Behind the modern stone-and-glass exterior of this hotel on the south bank of the Chicago River is a present-day interpretation of turn-of-the-20th-century splendor. Lavish floral carpets, tapestry upholstery, crystal-bead chandeliers, and French Provincial furniture create rich-looking public areas. Rooms have sitting areas and rounded windows with spectacular river views. The in-house, 24-hour Kinko's is convenient for business travelers. ⊠ *1 W. Wacker Dr., Loop, 60601,* ☎ *312/372–7200 or 800/468–3571,* FAX *312/ 372–0093,* WEB *www.renaissancehotels.com/CHISR/. 513 rooms, 40 suites. 2 restaurants, café, room service, in-room data ports, minibars, cable TV, indoor pool, gym, hair salon, hot tub, massage, sauna, bar, lobby lounge, shops, dry cleaning, laundry service, concierge, concierge floor, business services, meeting rooms, parking (fee), some pets allowed, no-smoking floors. AE, D, DC, MC, V.*

$$$–$$$$ 🏨 **W Chicago City Center.** Elegant gilded ceilings and inlaid tile floors set a classy setting for the cushy couch-filled lobby (nicknamed the Living Room) where music plays most nights and guests gather for drinks. Stylish rooms satisfy business travelers with Internet access, cordless keyboards and phones, and CD players. Business-class rooms provide all-in-one fax/scanner/printers. Creature comforts include goose-down comforters, pillow-top mattresses, W Signature beds, and "munchie" boxes—all of which (and more) can be purchased through the hotel's catalog. Meeting spaces include a loftlike room with fireplace. The restaurant, **We**, serves French and Continental fare. ⊠ *172 W. Adams St., Loop, 60603,* ☎ *312/332–1200 or 800/621–2360,* FAX *312/332–5909,* WEB *www.whotels.com. 388 rooms, 2 suites. Restaurant, café, room service, in-room data ports, gym, health club, spa, bar, dry cleaning, laundry service, concierge, Internet, business services, meeting rooms, parking (fee), no-smoking floors. AE, D, DC, MC, V.*

$$–$$$$ 🏨 **Hilton Chicago.** On a busy day, the lobby of this Hilton might be mistaken for a terminal at O'Hare Airport; it's a bustling convention hotel, but one that retains its 1920s heritage in a Renaissance-inspired entrance hall and gold-and-gilt Grand Ballroom. The 28,000-square-ft health club includes an indoor track and swimming pool. As with many older hotels, the rooms differ in size and Renaissance-style decor. Families should ask for one of the rooms with two double beds and two baths. The hotel is convenient to McCormick Place and museums, but can feel isolated at night. ⊠ *720 S. Michigan Ave., Downtown South, 60605,* ☎ *312/922–4400 or 800/445–8667,* FAX *312/922–5240,* WEB *www.chicagohilton.com. 1,477 rooms, 67 suites. 2 restaurants, snack bar, room service, in-room data ports, minibars, indoor pool, health club, hair salon, hot tub, massage, sauna, 2 bars, pub, dry cleaning, laundry service, concierge, concierge floor, business services, meeting rooms, helipad, parking (fee), no-smoking floors. AE, D, DC, MC, V.*

$$–$$$$ 🏨 **Hotel Burnham.** This intimate hotel is housed in the famed 13-story
★ Reliance Building, which D. H. Burnham & Company built in 1895. The fully refurbished interior retains such original details as Carrara marble wainscoting and ceilings, terrazzo floors, and mahogany trim. Lavish guest rooms, which were once the building's offices, are bathed in golds and navy blues and are outfitted with deep-blue velvet headboards. Rooms average 400 square ft. On the ground floor, the intimate **Atwood Cafe** has a stylish mahogany bar and serves contemporary American fare, including its popular potpies. ⊠ *1 W. Washington St., Loop, 60602,* ☎ *312/782–1111 or 877/294–9712,* FAX *312/782–0899,* WEB *www.burnhamhotel.com. 103 rooms, 19 suites. Restaurant, room service, in-room data ports, in-room fax, minibars, cable TV, gym, bar, dry cleaning, concierge, business services, parking (fee), no-smoking floor. AE, D, DC, MC, V.*

$$–$$$$ 🏨 **Hyatt on Printers Row.** As close to a boutique hotel as Hyatt gets, this 161-room property near McCormick Place housed printing presses in its former life. The lobby and public areas show a distinctive Frank Lloyd Wright inspiration, with subdued colors, dark woods, and Tiffany-style lamps. Black lacquer furniture lends an art deco look to the rooms, which all have a soothingly muted color scheme. The restaurant, **Prairie**, serves creative cuisine of the heartland. ⊠ *500 S. Dearborn St., Downtown South, 60605,* ☎ *312/986–1234 or 800/233–1234,* FAX *312/939–2468,* WEB *www.hyatt.com. 158 rooms, 3 suites. Restaurant, room service, in-room data ports, minibars, cable TV, some in-room VCRs, exercise equipment, gym, bar, dry cleaning, laundry service, business services, meeting rooms, airport shuttle, parking (fee), no-smoking rooms. AE, D, DC, MC, V.*

$$–$$$$ 🏨 **Hyatt Regency Chicago.** Ficus trees, palms, and gushing fountains fill the two-story greenhouse lobby, but it's hardly an oasis of tranquillity.

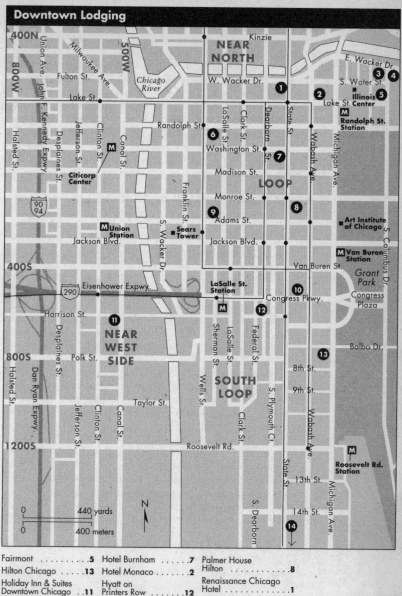

Downtown Lodging

Fairmont **5**

Hilton Chicago **13**

Holiday Inn & Suites
Downtown Chicago . .**11**

Hostelling
International–
Chicago **10**

Hotel Allegro
Chicago **6**

Hotel Burnham **7**

Hotel Monaco **2**

Hyatt on
Printers Row **12**

Hyatt Regency
Chicago **3**

Hyatt Regency
McCormick Place **14**

Palmer House
Hilton **8**

Renaissance Chicago
Hotel **1**

Swissôtel **4**

W Chicago
City Center **9**

This is one of the largest hotels in the world, with a bar called Big, and illuminated signs that guide you through the labyrinth of halls and escalators throughout the two towers. The 10,000-square-ft Crystal Ballroom has views of the Tribune Tower, the Wrigley Building, and the Chicago River through 19-ft-high windows. In the comfortably sized guest rooms, black-and-white photographs of Chicago landmarks add to the contemporary look. ⊠ *151 E. Wacker Dr., Loop, 60601,* ☎ *312/ 565–1234 or 800/233–1234,* ⅢX *312/565–2966,* Ⅷ *www.hyatt.com. 2,019 rooms, 175 suites. 4 restaurants, café, snack bar, room service, in-room data ports, some refrigerators, minibars, cable TV, some in-room VCRs, hair salon, hot tubs, massage, bar, sports bar, shops, dry cleaning, laundry service, concierge, concierge floor, business services, convention center, meeting rooms, parking (fee), no-smoking rooms, no-smoking floor. AE, D, DC, MC, V.*

$$–$$$$ 🏨 **Hyatt Regency McCormick Place.** This business-oriented hotel is connected via an enclosed walkway to the vast McCormick Place Convention Center, making it a popular choice for convention goers. Rooms have modern, but basic furnishings, with extras like fax/copier machines in the 35 Business Plan rooms. The jogging and biking path along Lake Michigan is steps away; museums, Navy Pier, Grant Park, and Soldier Field are also nearby. ⊠ *2233 S. King Dr., Near South Side, 60616,* ☎ *312/567–1234 or 800/233–1234,* ⅢX *312/567–1270,* Ⅷ *www.mccormickplace.hyatt.com. 800 rooms, 52 suites. 3 restaurants, room service, in-room data ports, cable TV with movies, indoor pool, health club, sauna, dry cleaning, laundry service, concierge, business services, convention center, meeting rooms, parking (fee), no-smoking rooms. AE, D, DC, MC, V.*

$$–$$$$ 🏨 **Palmer House Hilton.** This second-generation landmark hotel in the heart of the Loop is the essence of grand style. Ornate and elegant public areas include the opulent lobby, with its ceiling murals. Rooms are less spectacular, with reproduction antique furniture. Like many other big-meeting hotels, the Palmer House can get hectic, and service can be brusque. ⊠ *17 E. Monroe St., Loop, 60603,* ☎ *312/726–7500 or 800/445–8667,* ⅢX *312/263–2556,* Ⅷ *www.hilton.com. 1,551 rooms, 88 suites. 3 restaurants, coffee shop, room service, in-room data ports, minibars, some refrigerators, cable TV, indoor pool, gym, health club, hair salon, hot tub, massage, sauna, steam room, bar, shops, dry cleaning, laundry service, concierge, concierge floor, business services, meeting rooms, parking (fee), some pets allowed, no-smoking floor. AE, D, DC, MC, V.*

$$–$$$ 🏨 **Holiday Inn & Suites Downtown Chicago.** Though not in the heart
★   of the Loop, this Holiday Inn is still close to museums, the Sears Tower, Greek Town, the financial district, and Amtrak's Union Station. Rooms are clean and comfortable, two phone lines, and Nintendo; two-room suites add a sitting room with pull-out couch. The rooftop pool is an added attraction during the summer, and the fitness center gets you pumped up with its latest in cardiovascular equipment. The hotel's restaurant, **Harrison Street Grill,** serves everything from early breakfast to late-night snacks. ⊠ *506 W. Harrison St., Downtown South, 60607,* ☎ *312/957–9100,* ⅢX *312/583–4463,* Ⅷ *www.sixcontinentshotels.com. 455 suites. Restaurant, in-room data ports, some minibars, some microwaves, some refrigerators, cable TV, pool, health club, Internet, meeting rooms, parking (fee). AE, D, DC, MC, V.*

$$–$$$ 🏨 **Hotel Allegro Chicago.** Throughout this hip, art deco structure are
★   bold patterns and splashes of color—rooms mix coral, Tuscan yellow, and sea-foam green; window treatments resemble the entrance to a sheik's tent. Suites have whirlpool tubs, CD players, VCRs, and robes. The Palace Theater is an appropriate neighbor for this music-themed hotel: witness the clefs on the shower curtains, a music room off the lobby, and

the *High Society*–inspired watercolor mural by the lobby stairs at the entrance. A complimentary lobby wine reception is hosted every evening. ⊠ *171 W. Randolph St., Loop, 60601,* ☎ *312/236–0123 or 800/643–1500,* FAX *312/236–0197 or 312/236–3440,* WEB *www.allegrochicago.com. 451 rooms, 32 suites. Room service, in-room data ports, in-room fax, minibars, room TVs with movies, health club, hair salon, shop, laundry service, concierge, business services, meeting rooms, parking (fee), no-smoking rooms. AE, D, DC, MC, V.*

$ 🖼 **Hostelling International–Chicago.** An historic loft building in the South Loop area houses dormitory-style rooms and two private rooms that go for about $120 per night. Unlike many hostels, this one has such amenities as 24-hour security and Internet kiosks. Cafés, a members' kitchen, a student center, and a travel center are also available on-site. ⊠ *24 E. Congress Pkwy., Downtown South, 60605,* ☎ *312/360–0300,* FAX *312/360–0313,* WEB *www.hichicago.org. 500 dorm beds (summer season), 250 dorm beds (academic year), limited private rooms. Restaurant, dining room, gym, recreation room, laundry facilities, meeting rooms; no smoking. MC, V.*

Near North

$$$$ 🖼 **Chicago Marriott Downtown.** This 46-story tower of white concrete stands as a city unto itself, with its own Kinko's business center, retail stores, and coffee counter in the lobby. Rooms are basic but include amenities like two-line phones and high-speed Internet access. If you want to work out, there's a weight room and a larger cardiovascular room. ⊠ *540 N. Michigan Ave., Near North, 60611,* ☎ *312/836–0100 or 800/228–9290,* FAX *312/836–6139,* WEB *www.marriotthotels.com. 1,167 rooms, 25 suites. 2 restaurants, room service, in-room data ports, some microwaves, cable TV, some in-room VCRs, pro shop, pool (indoor), gym, hair salon, hot tub, massage, sauna, steam room, basketball, bar, lobby lounge, shops, dry cleaning, laundry service, concierge, concierge floor, business services, meeting rooms, parking (fee), some pets allowed, no-smoking floors. AE, D, DC, MC, V.*

$$$$ 🖼 **Drake Hotel.** Built in 1920, the grand dame of Chicago hotels pre-
★ sides over the northernmost end of Michigan Avenue. The lobby, inspired by an Italian Renaissance palace, envelops you in its deep-red walls and glimmering crystal. The sounds of a fountain and harpist beckon you to the Palm Court, a lovely setting for afternoon tea. There's piano music in the Coq d'Or most nights and a jazz trio in the Palm Court five nights a week. Guest rooms and suites have city or lake views and are filled with neoclassic furnishings. ⊠ *140 E. Walton Pl., Near North, 60611,* ☎ *312/787–2200 or 800/553–7253,* FAX *312/787–1431,* WEB *www.thedrakehotel.com. 482 rooms, 55 suites. Restaurant, room service, in-room data ports, some minibars, some microwaves, cable TV, some in-room VCRs, exercise equipment, gym, hair salon, bar, lobby lounge, piano bar, shops, dry cleaning, laundry service, concierge, concierge floor, business services, meeting rooms, parking (fee), no-smoking floors. AE, D, DC, MC, V.*

$$$$ 🖼 **Four Seasons.** Visiting celebrities stay here for one reason: the pam-
★ pering. The Four Seasons places a premium on service. The hotel sits atop the 900 North Michigan Shops and delivers panoramic views of the city, but it feels more like a grand English manor house than an urban skyscraper. The old-world feeling extends to the guest rooms, which include Italian marble, handcrafted woodwork, and botanical prints. ⊠ *120 E. Delaware Pl., Near North, 60611,* ☎ *312/280–8800 or 800/332–3442,* FAX *312/280–1748,* WEB *www.fourseasons.com. 174 rooms, 169 suites. 2 restaurants, room service, in-room data ports, in-room safes, minibars, cable TV, some in-room VCRs, indoor pool, gym,*

health club, hair salon, hot tub, massage, sauna, steam room, bar, lobby lounge, shops, dry cleaning, laundry service, concierge, business services, meeting rooms, parking (fee), some pets allowed, no-smoking floors. AE, D, DC, MC, V.

$$$$ ⌘ **Omni Ambassador East.** Tucked into the residential Gold Coast neighborhood, this small 1920s hotel is a 10- to 15-minute cab ride from the Loop. The secluded setting makes it popular with movie stars and literary figures, and the world-famous **Pump Room** still attracts a loyal following. The lobby has crystal chandeliers, marble floors, and curving banisters. Rooms are decorated in vibrant jewel tones and with cherrywood furniture. Special touches include crystal desk lamps and pedestal sinks in the bathrooms. Fourteen celebrity suites each have a unique look. The "author" suite has held book signings by writers including John Grisham and Maya Angelou. ⊠ *1301 N. State Pkwy., Near North, 60610,* ☎ *312/787–7200 or 800/843–6664,* ℻ *312/787–4760,* ⓦ *www.omnihotels.com. 430 rooms, 55 suites. Restaurant, room service, in-room data ports, in-room safes, minibars, some microwaves, cable TV, gym, hair salon, bar, lobby lounge, dry cleaning, laundry service, concierge, business services, parking (fee), no-smoking floors. AE, D, DC, MC, V.*

$$$$ ⌘ **Park Hyatt.** Superior service and luxurious accommodations highlight this hotel just off Chicago's Magnificent Mile. The 1968 masterpiece *Piazza del Duomo* by German painter Gerhard Richter hangs prominently in the lobby (sometimes out on national tour), and black-and-white photographs of Chicago line hallways outside guest rooms. Neutral-color rooms have contemporary, custom-designed furnishings and high-tech amenities: four two-line phones, flat-screen televisions, and DVD and CD players. Two-person tubs have sliding cherrywood doors, which open into the bedrooms. Many rooms have window seats with views of Lake Michigan or the Chicago skyline. ⊠ *800 N. Michigan Ave., Near North, 60611,* ☎ *312/239–4011 or 800/778–7477,* ℻ *312/239–4000,* ⓦ *www.parkhyatt.com. 202 rooms, 8 suites. Restaurant, room service, in-room data ports, in-room safes, minibars, indoor pool, health club, spa, bar, dry cleaning, laundry service, concierge, business services, meeting rooms, parking (fee), no-smoking rooms, no-smoking floor. AE, D, DC, MC, V. EP.*

$$$$ ⌘ **The Peninsula Chicago.** Chicago is fortunate to have one of just eight
★ Peninsula hotels in the world. High-tech amenities like 27-inch flat-screen televisions accent luxurious rooms, where gold, honey-brown, and creamy white tones create a soothing, elegant atmosphere. The lobby has a stunning 20-ft-high gilded ceiling, and floor-to-ceiling windows overlook North Michigan Avenue. Five dining options include the exquisite **Shanghai Terrace,** which serves Asian delicacies. The two-floor spa and fitness center has state-of-the-art equipment and stress-relieving body treatments. ⊠ *108 E. Superior St., Near North, 60611,* ☎ *312/337–2888,* ℻ *312/751–2888,* ⓦ *www.peninsula.com. 339 rooms and suites. 3 restaurants, café, patisserie, in-room data ports, in-room fax, in-room safes, minibars, cable TV, indoor pool, health club, hot tub, massage, sauna, spa, lobby lounge, dry cleaning, laundry service, concierge, Internet, business services, meeting rooms, parking (fee), no-smoking rooms. AE, D, DC, MC, V.*

$$$$ ⌘ **Ritz-Carlton.** The Ritz-Carlton, run by Four Seasons Hotels and Re-
★ sorts and not the Ritz-Carlton chain, is perched above Water Tower Place, Michigan Avenue's best-known shopping mall. Magnificent flower arrangements adorn the public areas. The two-story greenhouse lobby serves afternoon tea, and the **Dining Room**'s chef, Sarah Stegner, has earned a top-notch reputation. Rooms are spacious, with high ceilings, walk-in closets, and large dressing areas. All-marble bathrooms have both tubs and separate glass-enclosed showers. Pre-

miere rooms and suites on the 30th floor are larger, with more lavish fabrics and furnishings. ✉ *160 E. Pearson St., Near North, 60611,* ☎ *312/266–1000; 800/621–6906 (except IL);* FAX *312/266–1194,* WEB *www.fourseasons.com. 435 rooms, 90 suites. 3 restaurants, room service, in-room data ports, in-room safes, minibars, refrigerators, cable TV, some in-room VCRs, indoor pool, gym, health club, hot tub, massage, spa, bar, lobby lounge, dry cleaning, laundry service, concierge, business services, meeting rooms, parking (fee), some pets allowed, no-smoking floors. AE, D, DC, MC, V.*

$$$$ 🏨 **Sheraton Chicago Hotel and Towers.** This hotel has handsomely modern appointments and a distinctive location on the river, which guarantees unobstructed views. **Shula's** steak house (owned by former Miami Dolphin coach, Don Shula) serves up football-player-size meals. Rooms on the Corporate Club level are furnished with an expandable desk, replete with office supplies and a fax/printer. Although the hotel is vast, with the largest hotel ballroom in the Midwest, you won't feel in danger of getting lost. ✉ *301 E. North Water St., Near North, 60611,* ☎ *312/464–1000 or 800/233–4100,* FAX *312/464–9140,* WEB *www. sheratonchicago.com. 1,152 rooms, 52 suites. 3 restaurants, snack bar, room service, in-room data ports, minibars, cable TV, some in-room VCRs, indoor pool, exercise equipment, gym, massage, sauna, bar, lobby lounge, sports bar, dry cleaning, laundry service, concierge, concierge floor, business services, meeting rooms, parking (fee), no-smoking rooms, no-smoking floors. AE, D, DC, MC, V.*

$$$$ 🏨 **Sofitel Chicago Water Tower.** The newest luxury hotel hit Chicago
★ in June, 2002. This French gem just a block from upscale shopping, including the stores of Water Tower Place mall and the exclusive boutiques of Oak Street. Personal service and European hospitality are emphasized in the around-the-clock concierge. Spacious rooms with light African wood furnishings are sleek and sophisticated. Marble bathrooms with glass countertops have separate tubs and showers. The restaurant, **Cigale,** serves Mediterranean cuisine, and the more casual **Cafe des Architectes** has seasonal outdoor seating. ✉ *108 E. Superior St., Near North, 60611,* ☎ *312/324–4000,* FAX *312/324–4026,* WEB *www.sofitel. com. 352 rooms, 63 suites. 3 restaurants, café, patisserie, in-room data ports, in-room fax, in-room safes, minibars, cable TV, indoor pool, health club, hot tub, massage, sauna, spa, lobby lounge, dry cleaning, laundry service, concierge, Internet, business services, meeting rooms, parking (fee), no-smoking rooms. AE, D, DC, MC, V.*

$$$$ 🏨 **Sutton Place Hotel.** Modernism and tradition meet at this high-style hotel. The largest single collection of original Robert Mapplethorpe floral photographs grace the walls in rooms and common spaces. Luxurious rooms have sound-resistant walls, down duvets, plush robes, CD players, three high-speed Internet ports, three phones, and bathrooms with soaking tubs and separate glass-enclosed showers. Some rooms have terraces overlooking the bustling Rush Street nightlife. Rande Gerber (Cindy Crawford's husband) owns the **Whiskey Bar and Grill,** a sleek lounge serving seasonal selections for breakfast, lunch and dinner. ✉ *21 E. Bellevue Pl., Near North, 60611,* ☎ *312/ 266–2100 or 800/606–8188,* FAX *312/266–2141,* WEB *www.suttonplace. com. 240 rooms, 6 suites. Restaurant, outdoor café, room service, in-room data ports, some in-room safes, minibars, cable TV, in-room VCRs with movies, gym, bar, dry cleaning, laundry service, concierge, business services, Internet, meeting rooms, airport shuttle, parking (fee), some pets allowed (fee), no-smoking floors. AE, D, DC, MC, V.*

$$$$ 🏨 **Whitehall Hotel.** This small, luxury hotel provides peace and quiet, and friendly, attentive service. Video games, data ports, and voice mail bring modern touches to the intimate, old world–style rooms, many including four-poster beds. Bar and restaurant, **Molive,** serves California

cuisine with a Mediterranean flair. ⊠ *105 E. Delaware Pl., Near North, 60611,* ☎ *312/944–6300 or 800/948–4255,* FAX *312/944–8552. 213 rooms, 8 suites. Restaurant, outdoor café, room service, in-room data ports, in-room safes, minibars, cable TV, exercise equipment, gym, bar, dry cleaning, laundry service, concierge, concierge floor, business services, meeting rooms, parking (fee), no-smoking floor. AE, D, DC, MC, V.*

$$$–$$$$ 🏨 **Doubletree Guest Suites.** You'll find plenty of reasons to love this
★   place, from the homemade chocolate chip cookies at check-in to the always-fresh flowers in the lobby. The striking postmodern lobby owes its character to Prairie School architecture. The hotel's location off Michigan Avenue is well suited to families or business travelers. The 30th-floor indoor pool and fitness room have stunning views of Lake Michigan. ⊠ *198 E. Delaware Pl., Near North, 60611,* ☎ *312/664–1100 or 800/222–8733,* FAX *312/664–9881,* WEB *www.doubletreehotels. com. 345 suites. 2 restaurants, room service, in-room data ports, minibars, microwaves, refrigerators, cable TV, some in-room VCRs, indoor pool, exercise equipment, gym, hair salon, hot tub, massage, sauna, 2 bars, dry cleaning, laundry facilities, laundry service, concierge, business services, meeting rooms, parking (fee), no-smoking floors. AE, D, DC, MC, V.*

$$$–$$$$ 🏨 **Hotel Inter-Continental Chicago.** Extensive renovations that were com-
★   pleted in spring 2002 brought back many historic touches of this architecturally significant hotel, built in 1929 as the men's Medinah Athletic Club. Rooms have rich mahogany furniture, warm red and gold fabrics, and marble bathrooms. Business rooms are offices-away-from-home including copy paper, staplers, scissors, pens, and ergonomically correct chairs. The renovations also included soundproofing all rooms. The new lobby is bright and open with a custom-designed mosaic floor and a grand, spiral staircase. The international restaurant, **Zest,** is the only street-level dining option facing North Michigan Avenue. Take a swim or just admire the junior Olympic-size pool surrounded by tile walls and stained-glass windows. Self-guided audio tours of this landmark building are available. ⊠ *505 N. Michigan Ave., Near North, 60611,* ☎ *312/944–4100 or 800/628–2112,* FAX *312/944–3050,* WEB *www.chicago.interconti.com. 814 rooms, 90 suites. Restaurant, room service, in-room data ports, some in-room faxes, in-room safes, minibars, cable TV, indoor pool, gym, health club, massage, sauna, bar, lobby lounge, dry cleaning, laundry service, concierge, Internet, business services, meeting rooms, parking (fee), no-smoking floors. AE, D, DC, MC, V.*

$$$–$$$$ 🏨 **Omni Chicago Hotel.** A parade of celebrities passes through here, thanks to the Omni's tie-in with *The Oprah Winfrey Show,* but this well-situated Michigan Avenue all-suites hotel is also a favorite with business travelers. Rich colors and stocked bookshelves create a homey feel. ⊠ *676 N. Michigan Ave., Near North, 60611,* ☎ *312/944–6664 or 800/843–6664,* FAX *312/266–3015,* WEB *www.omnihotels.com. 347 suites. Restaurant, room service, in-room data ports, in-room fax, in-room safes, minibars, some microwaves, cable TV, some in-room VCRs, indoor pool, exercise equipment, gym, hot tub, sauna, bar, dry cleaning, laundry service, concierge, business services, meeting rooms, parking (fee), no-smoking floors. AE, D, DC, MC, V.*

$$$–$$$$ 🏨 **W Chicago Lakeshore.** Once a dreary Days Inn, a complete renovation has transformed this space into a hip, high-energy hotel—and the only hotel in Chicago directly overlooking Lake Michigan. The lobby is part lounge, part club scene, with velvety couches and panoramic lakeshore views. Comfortable rooms have bathrooms with Aveda bath products and shutters that open for constant views of either Lake Michigan or downtown Chicago. The hotel's "whatever/whenever" desk

is at your service 24 hours a day. ✉ *644 N. Lake Shore Dr., Near North, 60611,* ☎ *312/943–9200 or 800/541–3223,* FAX *312/255–4411. 569 rooms, 9 suites. Restaurant, room service, in-room data ports, in-room safes, cable TV, indoor pool, exercise equipment, gym, hair salon, bar, lounge, dry cleaning, laundry facilities, laundry service, business services, meeting rooms, airport shuttle, parking (fee), no-smoking floors. AE, D, DC, MC, V.*

$$$–$$$$ ⊞ **Westin Michigan Avenue.** The large Westin buzzes with activity in the lobby, where you'll find enormous icicle chandeliers. The Michigan Avenue location is perfect for shopping, especially in winter, as the major malls are steps from the door. Rooms are furnished with specially designed Simmons Heavenly Beds with quilted mattresses—which guests have raved about and even purchased—as well as foam, feather, and rolled pillows. The lobby restaurant, the **Grill on the Alley,** serves classic American favorites. ✉ *909 N. Michigan Ave., Near North, 60611,* ☎ *312/943–7200 or 800/937–8461,* FAX *312/943–9347,* WEB *www. westinmichiganave.com. 728 rooms, 23 suites. Restaurant, room service, in-room data ports, minibars, some microwaves, cable TV, exercise equipment, gym, hair salon, massage, sauna, bar, dry cleaning, laundry service, concierge, business services, meeting rooms, parking (fee), some pets allowed, no-smoking floor. AE, D, DC, MC, V.*

$$–$$$$ ⊞ **Allerton Crowne Plaza.** Named a national historic landmark in 1998, this limestone building was a residential "club hotel" for men when it opened in 1924. A major renovation in 1999 included restoring the limestone facade and completely overhauling the interior. A two-story atrium lobby on the third and fourth floors is designed with the Italian Renaissance flair of the early 1920s. Each room has a unique layout, with classic wood furnishings, dramatic floral bedspreads, and marble baths. Many also have knockout views from high above the Magnificent Mile. The view from the 25th-floor fitness center is incentive alone to exercise—or at least pretend to exercise. ✉ *701 N. Michigan Ave., Near North, 60611,* ☎ *312/440–1500 or 800/227–6963,* FAX *312/274–6437,* WEB *www.allertoncrowneplaza.com. 383 rooms, 60 suites. Restaurant, room service, in-room data ports, in-room safes, minibars, some refrigerators, cable TV, some in-room VCRs, gym, sauna, bar, laundry facilities, laundry service, concierge, business services, meeting rooms, parking (fee), no-smoking floors. AE, D, DC, MC, V.*

$$–$$$$ ⊞ **Courtyard by Marriott Chicago Downtown.** Business travelers get the necessities here: large, comfortable rooms with desks, well-lighted work areas, and voice mail. The hotel is a few blocks north of the Chicago River, making it convenient to the Loop. Shaw's Crab House and Vong's Thai Kitchen are good nearby dining options, and it's a short walk to the House of Blues restaurant and bar. If you're really beat, consider the on-site Pizza Hut. ✉ *30 E. Hubbard St., Near North, 60611,* ☎ *312/329–2500 or 800/321–2211,* FAX *312/329–0293,* WEB *www.courtyard.com/CHIWB/. 305 rooms, 32 suites. Restaurant, room service, in-room data ports, some microwaves, refrigerators, cable TV, indoor pool, exercise equipment, gym, hair salon, hot tub, bar, dry cleaning, laundry facilities, laundry service, concierge, business services, meeting rooms, parking (fee); no-smoking floor. AE, D, DC, MC, V.*

$$–$$$$ ⊞ **Homewood Suites by Hilton.** These spacious suites are ideal for families. Each has a sleeper sofa, a separate bedroom, and a fully equipped kitchen with a dishwasher. A complimentary breakfast buffet is provided seven days a week, and an evening reception with drinks and a light meal is served Monday through Thursday. You can work out for free at the adjacent Gorilla Sports. ✉ *40 E. Grand Ave., Near North, 60611,* ☎ *312/644–2222 or 800/225–5466,* FAX *312/644–7777,* WEB

132

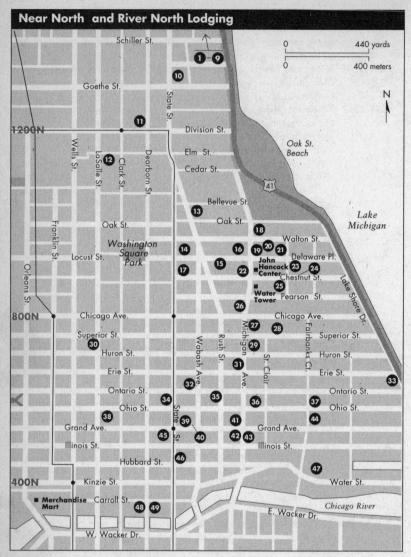

www.homewoodsuiteschicago.com. 233 suites. Restaurant, room service, kitchens, microwaves, refrigerators, in-room data ports, indoor pool, gym, laundry facilities, business services, meeting rooms, parking (fee), no-smoking rooms, no-smoking floors. AE, D, DC, MC, V. BP.

$$–$$$$ ★ ▣ **Le Meridien Chicago.** The French flair of this luxury hotel begins with a friendly "bonjour" or "bonsoir" from the staff. It continues with the Moulin Rouge–like decor of the lobby sitting area and French-inspired cuisine of **Cerise.** Rooms emphasize comfort with European duvets, oversize pillows, plush bathrobes, and slippers. The limestone facade, cut from the same quarries as the Empire State Building and Tribune Tower, depicts figures from ancient mythology and the zodiac. ⊠ *520 N. Michigan Ave., Near North, 60611,* ☏ *312/645–1500,* FAX *312/345–1550,* WEB *www.lemeridien-chicago.com. 311 rooms, 33 suites. 2 restaurants, room service, in-room data ports, in-room safes, minibars, health club, spa, lobby lounge, shops, laundry service, concierge, Internet, business services, meeting rooms, parking (fee), some pets allowed, no-smoking rooms. AE, D, DC, MC, V.*

$$–$$$$ ▣ **Lenox Suites.** Suites at this hotel resemble furnished corporate apartments and are either one or two rooms in size. The two-room suites have spacious living rooms with sleeper sofas, two televisions, and king-size beds. All suites have sofas and a dining table. Juice and a muffin greet you every morning, and the excellent shopping on Michigan Avenue is just a block away. ⊠ *616 N. Rush St., Near North, 60611,* ☏ *312/337–1000 or 800/445–3669,* FAX *312/337–7217,* WEB *www. lenoxsuites.com. 324 suites. 2 restaurants, room service, in-room data ports, kitchens, minibars, microwaves, cable TV with movies, gym, hair salon, bar, dry cleaning, laundry service, concierge, business services, Internet, meeting rooms, parking (fee), no-smoking floors. AE, D, DC, MC, V.*

$$–$$$$ ▣ **Millennium Knickerbocker Hotel.** This 1927 hotel has had a number of identities in its time—including a 1970s stint as the Playboy Hotel and Towers under owner Hugh Hefner. Rose moiré wallpaper lines the hallways, and exuberant floral bedspreads combine with gold- and cream-striped pillows for a rich, colorful decor. In keeping with its vintage heritage, bathrooms tend to be tiny, but closets are spacious. In the lobby, the Martini Bar serves 44 varieties. ⊠ *163 E. Walton St., Near North, 60611,* ☏ *312/751–8100 or 800/621–8140,* FAX *312/751–9205,* WEB *www.millennium-hotels.com/chicago. 280 rooms, 25 suites. Restaurant, outdoor café, room service, in-room data ports, minibars, some refrigerators, cable TV, exercise equipment, gym, bar, lobby lounge, dry cleaning, laundry service, concierge, concierge floor, business services, meeting rooms, parking (fee), no-smoking floors. AE, D, DC, MC, V.*

$$$ ▣ **Holiday Inn Chicago City Centre.** Many rooms have lakefront or skyline views in this standout Holiday Inn two blocks east of North Michigan Avenue. Its outdoor pool and location ½ mi from Navy Pier make it popular with families. In winter, weekend rates can drop to $150 or less. Unless you have business at the Merchandise Mart, this location is preferable to the Holiday Inn Mart Plaza. ⊠ *300 E. Ohio St., Near North, 60611,* ☏ *312/787–6100 or 800/465–4329,* FAX *312/787–6259,* WEB *www.sixcontinentshotels.com. 496 rooms, 4 suites. Restaurant, café, patisserie, room service, in-room data ports, pool, health club, hair salon, sports bar, dry cleaning, laundry facilities, laundry service, concierge, business services, meeting rooms, parking (fee); no-smoking floor. AE, D, DC, MC, V.*

$$$ ★ ▣ **Talbott.** This small, inviting hotel is just off the Magnificent Mile for easy access to shopping. The vintage structure was completely renovated in 2002, with granite and marble bathrooms and free high-speed

Internet access in every room. Rooms are spacious and bright with Victorian furnishings. You'll feel at home with coffee, tea, and chocolate turtle brownies served fireside in the lobby on winter nights and newspapers every morning. The hotel bar, Basil's at the Talbott, serves light fare and has seasonal outdoor seating. ☒ *20 E. Delaware Pl., Near North, 60611,* ☎ *312/944–4970 or 800/825–2688,* FAX *312/944–7241,* WEB *www.talbotthotel.com. 120 rooms, 30 suites. Restaurant, room service, in-room data ports, in-room safes, minibars, cable TV, bar, dry cleaning, laundry service, meeting rooms, parking (fee), no-smoking floors. AE, D, DC, MC, V.*

$$–$$$ 🏨 **Best Western Inn of Chicago.** One block east of Michigan Avenue, this heavily trafficked 1927 hotel is a great choice for visitors who want a bargain near the Magnificent Mile. Although the hotel is equipped with an exercise room, for a fee you can use the full health club across the street. ☒ *162 E. Ohio St., Near North, 60611,* ☎ *312/787–3100 or 800/557–2378,* FAX *312/573–3136,* WEB *www.bestwestern.com. 345 rooms, 25 suites. Restaurant, room service, cable TV, gym, bar, dry cleaning, laundry service, concierge, meeting rooms, parking (fee), no-smoking floors. AE, D, DC, MC, V.*

$$–$$$ 🏨 **Embassy Suites Lakefront.** Every guest in this brand-new all-suites
★   hotel has views of either Lake Michigan or the Chicago skyscrapers. Rooms have separate bedrooms and living rooms and provide frequently forgotten items like cotton balls and Q-tips. The sleek, glass atrium bustles in the morning for complimentary breakfast buffet and in the evening for complimentary happy hour. A bonus for families on vacation is the location: within walking distance of Navy Pier and North Michigan Avenue. It also has its own 21-screen movie theater. ☒ *511 N. Columbus Dr., Near North, 60611,* ☎ *888/903–8884 or 800/362–2779,* FAX *312/423–6300,* WEB *www.chicagoembassy.com. 455 suites. Restaurant, room service, kitchenettes, minibars, microwaves, refrigerators, cable TV with movies, indoor pool, health club, hot tub, sauna, bar, cinema, Internet, business services, meeting rooms, airport shuttle, parking (fee), no-smoking rooms. AE, D, DC, MC, V.*

$$–$$$ 🏨 **Gold Coast Guest House B&B.** In the heart of the Gold Coast, this 1873 brick town home–turned–bed-and-breakfast has four guest suites with private baths. The cozy living room has an 18-ft window looking out onto a lush private garden. Rooms are a mix of antiques and contemporary furnishings; bedrooms have ceiling fans. You'll feel especially welcome with extras like complimentary evening refreshments, and hospitality baskets with items such as shampoo, razors, and sunscreen. For a modest fee, you can use a health club one block away. ☒ *113 W. Elm St., Near North, 60610,* ☎ *312/337–0361,* FAX *312/337–0362,* WEB *www.bbchicago.com. 4 rooms. Cable TV, in-room VCRs, business services, parking (fee), no-smoking rooms. AE, D, MC, V. CP.*

$$–$$$ 🏨 **Hilton Garden Inn.** Basic, business-friendly rooms include work desks equipped with Internet access, desk-level outlets, and ergonomically designed chairs. Complimentary coffee is served in the lobby each morning. ☒ *10 E. Grand Ave., Near North, 60611,* ☎ *312/595–0000 or 800/445–8667,* FAX *312/595–0955,* WEB *www.hilton.com. 351 rooms, 6 suites. Restaurant, room service, microwaves, refrigerators, in-room data ports, indoor pool, gym, bar, laundry service, concierge, business services, meeting rooms, parking (fee), no-smoking rooms, no-smoking floors. AE, D, DC, MC, V.*

$$–$$$ 🏨 **Raphael Chicago.** Originally a dorm for nursing students, this charming 1920s building is on a wealthy residential street near Water Tower Place mall. The spacious, comfortable rooms have a distinctive style, with chaise longues, sitting areas, and arched entries. Obliging service, terry-cloth robes, and attractive weekend packages are among

the amenities that maintain a loyal following. ✉ *201 E. Delaware Pl., Near North, 60611,* ☎ *312/943–5000 or 800/983–7870,* FAX *312/943–9483. 100 rooms, 72 suites. Restaurant, room service, in-room data ports, in-room safes, minibars, cable TV, bar, piano bar, library, dry cleaning, laundry service, meeting rooms, parking (fee), no-smoking floors. AE, D, DC, MC, V.*

$$–$$$ ⊡ **Summerfield Suites Hotel.** A small, intimate lobby paneled in cherrywood sets the tone for this traditional-looking all-suites hotel down the block from the hub of Michigan Avenue shopping. Suites are equipped with work desks and pull-out sofa beds. A rooftop pool keeps children entertained in summer, and the **Benihana of Tokyo** restaurant provides convenient dining in the lobby. The rate includes an extensive breakfast buffet. ✉ *166 E. Superior St., Near North, 60611,* ☎ *312/787–6000 or 800/833–4353,* FAX *312/787–4331,* WEB *www.fitzpatrickhotels.com. 143 suites. Restaurant, snack bar, in-room data ports, kitchenettes, microwaves, refrigerators, cable TV, pool, exercise equipment, gym, hair salon, bar, recreation room, dry cleaning, laundry facilities, laundry service, business services, meeting rooms, parking (fee), no-smoking floor. AE, D, DC, MC, V. BP.*

$$–$$$ ⊡ **Tremont.** This small, elegant, yet understated hotel is on a side street just off North Michigan Avenue. Rooms have traditional Williamsburg-style decor and Baker furniture, with creatively mixed-and-matched florals and stripes. Standard rooms can be quite cramped, with the desk placed in the narrow entry, so ask about size. All rooms have a CD player. ✉ *100 E. Chestnut St., Near North, 60611,* ☎ *312/751–1900 or 800/621–8133,* FAX *312/751–8650. 121 rooms, 9 suites. Restaurant, room service, in-room data ports, minibars, some microwaves, cable TV, in-room VCRs, 2 bars, dry cleaning, laundry service, business services, meeting rooms, parking (fee), no-smoking floor. AE, D, DC, MC, V.*

$$ ⊡ **Seneca.** Originally solely an apartment building, the Seneca is steadily increasing the number of rooms it rents out on a nightly basis. Most are suites of varying sizes with either kitchenettes or full kitchens. High ceilings with crown moldings create a European charm. Some bathrooms include Jacuzzi tubs. The two restaurants and the popular deli in the building deliver. ✉ *200 E. Chestnut St., Near North, 60611,* ☎ *312/787–8900 or 800/800–6261,* FAX *312/988–4438,* WEB *www.senecahotel.com. 48 rooms, 82 suites. 2 restaurants, snack bar, in-room data ports, kitchenettes, refrigerators, cable TV, some in-room VCRs, exercise equipment, gym, hair salon, 2 bars, dry cleaning, laundry facilities, laundry service, business services, meeting rooms, parking (fee), no-smoking floors. AE, D, DC, MC, V.*

$–$$ ⊡ **Cass Hotel.** Built in 1927, the Cass is a favorite for those looking
★ for cheap sleeps just a short walk from North Michigan Avenue shopping and River North nightlife. Rooms are small and functional, and all bathrooms have modern vanities, fixtures, and tubs. Ask for one of the king or double rooms equipped with a refrigerator. Phones with data ports are available on request. The $1.99 breakfast in the lobby coffee shop is a steal. ✉ *640 N. Wabash Ave., Near North, 60611,* ☎ *312/787–4030 or 800/227–7850,* FAX *312/787–8544,* WEB *www.casshotel.com. 150 rooms. Restaurant, coffee shop, in-room data ports, some minibars, some refrigerators, cable TV, hair salon, bar, laundry facilities, parking (fee). AE, D, DC, MC, V.*

River North

$$$–$$$$ ⊡ **Embassy Suites.** Built primarily for business travelers, each of these fully equipped suites is arranged around an 11-story plant-filled atrium lobby, where fountains and birds add to the constant din. Bright rooms use space efficiently, with sensible separate living rooms for a pull-out sofa, four-person dining table, and extra television. You can also enjoy a complimentary full breakfast each morning and cocktails each evening. ✉ *600 N. State St., River North, 60610,* ☎ *312/943–3800 or 800/362–2779,* FAX *312/943–7629,* WEB *www.embassy-suites.com. 358 suites. Restaurant, room service, in-room data ports, kitchenettes, minibars, microwaves, refrigerators, cable TV, indoor pool, exercise equipment, gym, hair salon, hot tub, sauna, bar, dry cleaning, laundry facilities, laundry service, concierge, concierge floor, business services, meeting rooms, car rental, parking (fee), complimentary breakfast, no-smoking rooms. AE, D, DC, MC, V. BP.*

$$$–$$$$ 🏨 **House of Blues Hotel.** A gold Burmese Buddha greets you at the quirky
★   House of Blues Hotel. Other eye-catching lobby art includes the "Tela-mones"—four giant, gold statues—and ancient blue-glass panels behind the bar that come from an East Indian meditation temple. Rooms are a dizzying variety of patterns, and each include several pieces of original southern folk art. The adjacent **House of Blues** bar/restaurant serves casual fare and hosts live musical acts in a separate concert hall. ✉ *333 N. Dearborn St., River North, 60610,* ☎ *312/245–0333 or 800/235–6397,* FAX *312/923–2444,* WEB *www.loewshotels.com/houseofblueshome. html. 344 rooms, 23 suites. Restaurant, room service, in-room data ports, minibars, cable TV, in-room VCRs, health club, sauna, steam room, bar, lobby lounge, dry cleaning, laundry service, concierge, business services, meeting rooms, parking (fee), no-smoking rooms. AE, D, DC, MC, V.*

$$$–$$$$ 🏨 **Westin River North.** Rooms at this business-oriented property have stunning views of the Chicago River and nice extras, such as coffeemakers with Starbucks coffee. Skyline Rooms cost a bit more, but are more spacious. Westin Guest Offices are the ultimate business-savvy rooms with office supplies, ergonomic chairs, speaker and cordless phones, and all-in-one printer/fax/copiers by the beds. If you forget your workout gear, you can borrow from the well-equipped fitness center. ✉ *320 N. Dearborn St., River North, 60610,* ☎ *312/744–1900 or 800/ 937–8461,* FAX *312/527–2650,* WEB *www.starwood.com. 400 rooms, 22 suites. Restaurant, room service, in-room data ports, minibars, cable TV, gym, health club, massage, sauna, bar, lobby lounge, dry cleaning, laundry service, concierge, business services, meeting rooms, parking (fee), some pets allowed, no-smoking rooms, no-smoking floor. AE, D, DC, MC, V.*

$$ 🏨 **Hampton Inn & Suites.** This full-service chain hotel is a short bus or cab ride to the Loop business district and to North Michigan Avenue shopping. Local phone calls are free, as are the newspapers Monday through Friday. The indoor, skylight-lit pool provides recreation even through Chicago's cold months. ✉ *33 W. Illinois St., River North, 60611,* ☎ *312/832–0330 or 800/426–7866,* FAX *312/832–0333,* WEB *www.hamptoninn.com. 130 rooms, 100 suites. 2 restaurants, in-room data ports, some kitchenettes, cable TV with movies, indoor pool, health club, sauna, spa, laundry service, concierge, Internet, business services, meeting rooms, no-smoking rooms. AE, D, DC, MC, V.*

$$ 🏨 **HoJo Inn.** On a main thoroughfare in downtown Chicago, this classic L-shape, two-story motor lodge stands as a campy vestige of another era. The rooms are well maintained, the staff is pleasant, parking is free, and the location is just a short walk from a cluster of theme restaurants like Hard Rock Cafe. ✉ *720 N. LaSalle St., River North, 60610,* ☎ *312/664–8100,* FAX *312/664–2365,* WEB *www.hojo.com. 67 rooms, 4 suites. Coffee shop, some refrigerators, cable TV, free parking, no-smoking rooms. AE, D, DC, MC, V.*

$–$$ 🏨 **Best Western River North.** Look for this ice-warehouse–turned–Best Western in the heart of the thriving River North entertainment district. The undistinguished exterior and outdated deco-inspired lobby are more than offset by large and reasonably priced guest rooms that include black-and-white tile bathrooms. Parking is free, a cost-saving rarity downtown. The sofa sleepers in the suites and the indoor pool make it a family favorite. ✉ *125 W. Ohio St., River North, 60610,* ☎ *312/ 467–0800 or 800/727–0800,* FAX *312/467–1665,* WEB *www.bestwestern. com/rivernorthhotel. 125 rooms, 25 suites. Restaurant, pizzeria, room service, in-room data ports, in-room safes, some refrigerators, cable TV, indoor pool, exercise equipment, gym, sauna, bar, dry cleaning, business services, meeting room, free parking, no-smoking floor. AE, D, DC, MC, V.*

Lincoln Park

$$$ 🏨 **Claridge Hotel.** This vintage hotel is peaceful, quiet, and genteel. Standard rooms with one queen bed are small, but bright, with custom-designed mahogany furniture. Deluxe rooms add about twice the space and have either a king or two queen beds and a sitting area. Higher-level rooms overlook the tree-lined street. In-room amenities aren't extensive, but rates include Continental breakfast, Claridge's special roast of coffee in the lobby, and morning limousine drop-off service within a 2-mi radius are included. ✉ *1244 N. Dearborn Pkwy., Lincoln Park, 60610,* ☎ *312/787–4980 or 800/245–1258,* FAX *312/266– 0978,* WEB *www.claridgehotel.com. 161 rooms, 2 suites. Restaurant, room service, in-room data ports, minibars, cable TV, gym, bar, lobby lounge, dry cleaning, laundry service, business services, meeting rooms, parking (fee), some pets allowed, no-smoking floor. AE, D, DC, MC, V. CP.*

$–$$$ 🏨 **Comfort Inn of Lincoln Park.** This reasonably priced hotel with a half-timber Tudor exterior is wedged incongruously into a busy area of Lincoln Park, a youthful neighborhood with plenty of nightlife that's close to the lake and convenient to Wrigley Field. Unusual architectural features, such as wagon-wheel wood trim, add a quirky note to an otherwise no-frills lodging. The three suites have hot tubs, and two have saunas. A complimentary Continental breakfast is served in a room off the Victorian-style lobby. ✉ *601 W. Diversey Pkwy., Lincoln Park,* ☎ *773/348–2810 or 800/228–5150,* FAX *773/348–1912,* WEB *www. comfortinn.com. 71 rooms, 3 suites. In-room data ports, some hot tubs, cable TV, business services, meeting room, parking (fee), no-smoking rooms. AE, D, DC, MC, V. CP.*

$$ 🏨 **Belden-Stratford.** A magnificent 1920s facade beckons you to this relatively untrafficked area of Lincoln Park. The Belden-Stratford is primarily an upscale apartment building, but management keeps some attractively priced studios and suites for overnights. Hand-painted clouds grace the ceiling of the elegant lobby, which houses two popular French restaurants: **Ambria** and **Mon Ami Gabi.** ✉ *2300 N. Lincoln Park W, Lincoln Park, 60614,* ☎ *773/281–2900 or 800/800–8301,* FAX *773/880–2039. 24 rooms, 5 suites. 2 restaurants, snack bar, in-room data ports, kitchenettes, microwaves, cable TV, exercise equipment, gym, hair salon, bar, dry cleaning, laundry facilities, laundry service, business services, meeting rooms, parking (fee). AE, D, DC, MC, V.*

$$ 🏨 **Days Inn Lincoln Park North.** This well-kept Days Inn in the lively
★   Lincoln Park neighborhood is a real find. A complimentary Continental breakfast is served in a room off the lobby with a pressed-tin ceiling and brass chandeliers. Cheery floral bedspreads and light furniture brighten up the basic rooms. For about $15 extra a night, you can upgrade to a business room. All guests have free use of a nearby health club. ✉ *644 W. Diversey Pkwy., Lincoln Park, 60614,* ☎ *773/525– 7010 or 888/576–3297,* FAX *773/525–6998,* WEB *www.lpndaysinn.com. 129 rooms, 4 suites. Restaurant, some in-room data ports, in-room safes,*

microwaves, refrigerators, cable TV, bar, laundry facilities, laundry service, business services, meeting room, parking (fee), no-smoking rooms. AE, D, DC, MC, V. CP.

Lake View

$$–$$$ 🖭 **The Majestic Hotel.** In cool weather, a welcoming fire burns in the Majestic's library-style lobby. Rooms are quaint and simple with Prairie-style furnishings; suites have kitchenettes. The staff is helpful and the reasonable price includes Continental breakfast. The Lake View location puts you four blocks from Wrigley Field and close to the lakefront jogging path, restaurants, nightlife, and transportation downtown. ⊠ *528 W. Brompton Ave., Lake View, 60657,* ☏ *773/404–3499 or 800/ 727–5108,* FAX *773/404–3495,* WEB *www.cityinns.com. 31 rooms, 21 suites. Room service, in-room data ports, dry cleaning, laundry facilities, concierge, meeting room, parking (fee). AE, D, DC, MC, V. CP.*

$$–$$$ 🖭 **The Willows.** The lobby of this 1920s boutique hotel, designed in 19th-century French country style, opens onto a tree-lined street in Lake View, a lively area that's three blocks from the lake and a 10-minute walk from the Lincoln Park Zoo. Like its cousins the Majestic Hotel and City Suites Hotel, the Willows serves a complimentary Continental breakfast. ⊠ *555 W. Surf St., Lake View, 60657,* ☏ *773/528–8400 or 800/787–3108,* FAX *773/528–8483,* WEB *www.cityinns.com. 51 rooms, 4 suites. Room service, in-room data ports, cable TV, dry cleaning, laundry facilities, concierge, parking (fee), some pets allowed (fee). AE, D, DC, MC, V. CP.*

$$ 🖭 **Best Western Hawthorne Terrace.** Tucked into the heart of the Lake View community, this hotel is easy to overlook. The American Colonial lobby and street-level outdoor terrace are the best parts of the property, and the only public areas other than a small exercise room. ⊠ *3434 N. Broadway, Lake View, 60657,* ☏ *773/244–3434 or 888/ 675–2378,* FAX *773/244–3435,* WEB *www.hawthorneterrace.com. 46 rooms, 13 suites. In-room data ports, some hot tubs, some microwaves, some refrigerators, cable TV, gym, laundry facilities, business services, parking (fee). AE, D, DC, MC, V. CP.*

$$ 🖭 **City Suites Hotel.** Two-thirds of this affordable, art deco hotel consists of suites, each of which has a separate sitting room and a pull-out couch. A free Continental breakfast, afternoon cookies, and a newspaper are available daily. The hotel is on a busy street in the Lake View neighborhood, so if noise is a concern, request a room on the east side of the building. ⊠ *933 W. Belmont Ave., Lake View, 60657,* ☏ *773/404–3400 or 800/248–9108,* FAX *773/404–3405,* WEB *www. cityinns.com. 16 rooms, 29 suites. Room service, in-room data ports, some microwaves, some refrigerators, cable TV, some in-room VCRs, hair salon, dry cleaning, laundry facilities, concierge, parking (fee). AE, D, DC, MC, V. CP.*

$–$$ 🖭 **Margarita European Inn.** Just north of Chicago in the suburb of Evanston, the Margarita (two blocks from both the train and bus) is a charming alternative to the more generic hotels close to Northwestern University. Rooms range in size from monklike cells to comfortable minisuites and are furnished with cheerful prints and antiques. A complimentary Continental breakfast is served in an antique-filled parlor lined with a wall of arched windows. Downstairs, Va Pensiero serves some of the area's best regional Italian cooking at haute cuisine prices. ⊠ *1566 Oak Ave., Evanston 60201,* ☏ *847/869–2273,* FAX *847/ 869–2353,* WEB *www.margaritainn.com. 44 rooms, 20 with bath. Restaurant, in-room data ports, hair salon, library, laundry facilities, business services, meeting rooms, parking (fee); no TV in some rooms. AE, D, DC, MC, V. CP.*

$ ⊞ **Chicago International Hostel.** European students flock to these well-maintained dormitory-style accommodations near Loyola University in Rogers Park. Dorm beds go for $17 a night, linens are provided, and a kitchen is available. One drawback—there's a curfew of midnight or 2 AM, depending on the day. Also, the hostel is closed from 10 AM to 4 PM for cleaning. The El train is nearby, making it easy to zip downtown. ⊠ *6318 N. Winthrop Ave., 60660, Rogers Park,* ☎ *773/262–1011,* FAX *773/262–3673,* WEB *www.hostels.com/chicagohostel/. 120 dorm beds; 6 private rooms, 2 with bath. Laundry facilities, free parking. No credit cards.*

O'Hare Airport

$–$$$$ ⊞ **Rosemont Suites Hotel O'Hare.** The public spaces of this handsome hotel directly across the street from the Rosemont Convention Center reflect the unmistakable style of Frank Lloyd Wright. Wright's influence is also seen in the guest rooms' straight, clean lines and mission-style furnishings. Complimentary cooked-to-order breakfasts and evening cocktails are served in the garden atrium. ⊠ *5500 N. River Rd., Chicago 60018,* ☎ *847/678–4000 or 888/476–7366,* FAX *847/928–7659,* WEB *www.embassyohare.com. 296 suites. Restaurant, room service, in-room data ports, kitchenettes, minibars, microwaves, refrigerators, cable TV, indoor pool, exercise equipment, gym, hair salon, hot tub, sauna, bar, dry cleaning, laundry facilities, laundry service, concierge, business services, meeting rooms, airport shuttle, parking (fee), no-smoking floor. AE, D, DC, MC, V. BP.*

$$$ ⊞ **Hyatt Regency O'Hare.** Connected to the Rosemont Convention Center by a skyway, this Hyatt is heavily geared toward the business traveler. The atrium lobby resembles an office park, and none of the other public spaces—except the resortlike circular swimming pool—alters that impression. Rooms in the modern Executive Wing have two-line phones, in-room fax machines, and desks with built-in power strips. ⊠ *9300 W. Bryn Mawr Ave., Chicago 60018,* ☎ *847/696–1234 or 800/233–1234,* FAX *847/698–0139 or 847/696–1418,* WEB *www.hyatt.com. 1,057 rooms, 42 suites. 4 restaurants, snack bar, room service, in-room data ports, in-room fax, some minibars, cable TV, indoor pool, exercise equipment, gym, massage, sauna, bar, sports bar, shops, dry cleaning, laundry service, concierge, concierge floor, business services, meeting rooms, airport shuttle, parking (fee), no-smoking rooms, no-smoking floors. AE, D, DC, MC, V.*

$$–$$$ ⊞ **Hilton Chicago O'Hare Airport.** The only hotel actually at the air-
★ port, the Hilton is connected to the terminals and is within easy access of public transportation to the city. For a $15 daily fee, you can rent a treadmill for your room. Other recreational facilities include extensive workout equipment and an indoor pool. Day rates are available for travelers with short stopovers. ⊠ *Box 66414, O'Hare International Airport, 60666,* ☎ *773/686–8000 or 800/445–8667,* FAX *773/601–1728,* WEB *www.hilton.com. 822 rooms, 36 suites. Restaurant, coffee shop, room service, in-room data ports, minibars, indoor pool, gym, health club, hot tub, massage, sauna, steam room, bar, sports bar, dry cleaning, laundry service, concierge, business services, meeting rooms, airport shuttle, parking (fee), no-smoking floor. AE, D, DC, MC, V.*

$$–$$$ ⊞ **Hotel Sofitel Chicago O'Hare.** The murals in the lobby, the fancy restaurant and more casual café serving true French fare, and the upscale gift shop might have you wondering what continent you're on. Rooms are spacious and reflect the country French look found throughout the hotel. You'll receive a rose and a bottle of Evian at turndown. ⊠ *5550 N. River Rd., Chicago 60018,* ☎ *847/678–4488 or 800/233–5959,* FAX *847/*

678–4244, WEB *www.sofitel.com. 288 rooms, 12 suites. Restaurant, patisserie, room service, in-room data ports, minibars, some refrigerators, cable TV, indoor pool, exercise equipment, gym, massage, sauna, bar, dry cleaning, laundry service, concierge, business services, meeting rooms, airport shuttle, parking (fee), some pets allowed, no-smoking floors. AE, D, DC, MC, V.*

$ 🏨 **Travelodge Chicago O'Hare.** The rooms in this two-story cinder-block motel are basic, but they're regularly redecorated, tidy, and incomparably cheap. ✉ *3003 Mannheim Rd., Chicago 60018,* ☎ *847/296–5541 or 800/578–7878,* FAX *847/803–1984. 95 rooms. In-room data ports, pool, dry cleaning, meeting room, free parking, no-smoking rooms. AE, D, DC, MC, V.*

5 NIGHTLIFE AND THE ARTS

Chicago's nightlife scene reflects the city's verve and variety. Renowned companies such as the Lyric Opera and the Steppenwolf Theatre share the spotlight with late-night theater productions and alternative rock clubs, and the air sizzles with homegrown blues and jazz. This is the city that gave birth to the sometimes raucous "poetry slam" at the Green Mill bar. It's also the place that decades ago first unleashed comedic talent through the Second City club.

NIGHTLIFE

Updated by
Laura Baginski

CHICAGO'S ENTERTAINMENT varies from loud and loose to sophisticated and sedate. You'll find the classic Chicago corner bar in most neighborhoods, along with trendier alternatives—wine bars are hip these days. The strains of blues and jazz provide much of the backbeat to the city's groove, and an alternative country scene is flourishing. As far as dancing is concerned, the action has switched from cavernous clubs to smaller spots with DJs spinning dance tunes; there's everything from hip-hop to swing. In the past few years, Wicker Park and Bucktown have been the hottest nightlife neighborhoods, but prime spots are spread throughout the city.

The Reader and *New City* (distributed midweek in bookstores, record shops, and other city establishments) are your best guides to the entertainment scene. These free weeklies have comprehensive, timely listings and reviews. The Friday editions of the *Chicago Tribune* and *Chicago Sun-Times* are also good sources of information. On the Web, www.metromix.com gives daily updates on what's happening around town. Shows usually begin at 9 PM; cover charges generally range from $3 to $20, depending on the day of the week (Friday and Saturday nights are the most expensive). Most bars stay open until 2 AM Friday night and 3 AM Saturday, except for a few after-hours spots and some larger dance bars, which are often open until 4 AM Friday night and 5 AM Saturday. Outdoor beer gardens are the exception; these close at 11 PM on weekdays and midnight on weekends. Some bars are not open seven days a week, so call before you go.

Parking in North Side neighborhoods, particularly Lincoln Park and Lake View, is increasingly scarce, even on weeknights. If you're visiting nightspots in these areas, consider taking a cab or public transportation. If you're driving, many restaurants and clubs offer valet service at the curb for $6–$7. The list of blues and jazz clubs includes several South Side locations: be cautious about transportation here late at night because some of these neighborhoods can be unsafe. Drive your own car or ask the bartender to call you a cab.

Bars

The famous Chicago bar scene known as **Rush Street** has faded into the mists of time, although the street has found resurgent energy with the opening of a string of upscale restaurants and outdoor cafés. For the vestiges of the old Rush Street, continue north (if you dare) to Division Street between Clark and State streets. The crowd here consists mostly of suburbanites and out-of-towners on the make. The bars are crowded and noisy. Among the better-known singles bars are **Butch McGuire's** (⊠ 20 W. Division St., Near North, ☎ 312/337–9080), the **Lodge** (⊠ 21 W. Division St., Near North, ☎ 312/642–4406), and **Original Mother's** (⊠ 26 W. Division St., Near North, ☎ 312/642–7251), which was featured in the motion picture *About Last Night*.

Those who want to try some more relaxed spots have many great choices, of which these are just a few.

California Clipper (⊠ 1002 N. California St., Humboldt Park, ☎ 773/384–2547) has a 1940s vintage look, including a curving 60-ft-long Brunswick bar and tiny booths lining the long room back to back like seats on a train. Alternative country acts and soul-gospel DJs are part of the musical lineup.

Cru Café and Wine Bar (⊠ 888 N. Wabash Ave., Near North, ☎ 312/337–4001) is a swank Gold Coast wine bar that embraces the living-large ethos—from the oversize chandeliers to the extensive wine list to the international set that roosts here. In warmer months, a Euro-style sidewalk café extends the seating options.

Encore (⊠ 171 W. Randolph St., Loop, ☎ 312/338–3788) is a jazzed-up hotel lounge sandwiched between the Cadillac Palace Theater and the Hotel Allegro. Clubby seating, a live DJ, and a classic cocktail menu make it an appealing downtown destination for post-dinner or -theater drinks, a light bite, and conversation.

Fado (⊠ 100 W. Grand Ave., Near North, ☎ 312/836–0066) uses imported wood, stone, and glasswork to create its Irish look. The second floor—its bar was imported from Dublin—feels more like the real thing than the first. There's expertly drawn Guinness, a fine selection of Irish whiskeys, occasional live Irish music, and a menu of traditional Irish food.

Ghost Bar (⊠ 440 W. Randolph St., Near West Side, ☎ 312/575–9900), the latest from the owners of the popular nightclub Drink, is a sexy downtown space perched above the restaurant Nine. Cool and futuristic with cushy vinyl banquettes and designer-looking seating, the bar is white as a, well, you know what, and the muted lighting casts the fashion-conscious crowd in silhouette.

Gingerman Tavern (⊠ 3740 N. Clark St., Lake View, ☎ 773/549–2050), up the street from the Wrigley Field, deftly manages to avoid being pigeonholed as a sports bar. Folks here take their beer and billiards seriously, with three pool tables and more than 100 bottles of beer on the wall.

Harry's Velvet Room (⊠ 56 W. Illinois St., River North, ☎ 312/527–5600), one of the few downtown spots open until 4 AM, takes full advantage of its subterranean speakeasy digs with a decadent votive-lighted room styled with gilt mirrors, plush armchairs, and huge chandeliers. The dressed-up crowd sipping martinis and noshing on the eclectic desserts is as gorgeous as the surroundings. People with a low tolerance for self-consciousness may want to steer clear.

Holiday Club (⊠ 1471 N. Milwaukee Ave., Wicker Park, ☎ 773/486–0686) bills itself as "a swinger's mecca." It attracts goodfellas with its 1950s decor and well-stocked CD jukebox with selections ranging from Dean Martin and Frank Sinatra to early punk. Down a pint of good beer (or even bad beer in cans). A second location at 4000 North Sheridan Road brings the swing to Lake View.

Hopleaf (⊠ 5148 N. Clark St., Uptown, ☎ 773/334–9851), an anchor in the Andersonville corridor, continues the tradition of the classic Chicago bar hospitable to conversation (not a TV in sight). Pick one of the too-many-to-choose-from beers on the menu, with special offerings of Belgian beers and regional microbrews. You also can't go wrong with the two-for-a-quarter jukebox, stocked with old blues and country 45s.

John Barleycorn (⊠ 658 W. Belden Ave., Lincoln Park, ☎ 773/348–8899), a historic pub with a long wooden bar, can get somewhat rowdy despite the classical music and the art slides shown on video screens. It has a spacious summer beer garden, a good pub menu, a wide selection of beers, and a separate darts area.

Kitty O'Shea's (⊠ 720 S. Michigan Ave., Loop, ☎ 312/922–4400), a handsome room in the Chicago Hilton and Towers, re-creates an Irish pub with all things Irish, including the live nightly music, beer, food, and bar staff.

Lithium (✉ 1124 W. Belmont Ave., Lake View, ☎ 773/477–6513) is a casual, conversation-friendly oasis for twenty- and thirtysomethings weary of pretentious bars. Patrons chill on black leather couches or in intimate booths while sipping a "Crocodile Hunter" or "Key Lime Pie" martini. Others sit at cocktail tables playing board games like Operation and Battleship to the tunes of acid jazz, R&B, and trip-hop. It's like your living room, only hipper.

The **Map Room** (✉ 1949 N. Hoyne Ave., Bucktown, ☎ 773/252–7636) might help you find your way around Chicago, if not the world. Maps and travel books decorate the walls of this self-described "travelers' tavern," and the beers represent much of the world. Tuesday is international night, with a free buffet of cuisines from different countries.

Northside Bar & Grill (✉ 1635 N. Damen Ave., Wicker Park, ☎ 773/384–3555) was one of the first anchors of the now-teeming Wicker Park nightlife scene. Arty (and sometimes slightly yuppie) types come to drink, eat, shoot pool, and see and be seen. The enclosed indoor/outdoor patio lets you get the best out of the chancy Chicago weather.

Red Lion (✉ 2446 N. Lincoln Ave., Lincoln Park, ☎ 773/348–2695), a dark, authentic British pub, is decked out with London Metro maps and serves up fish-and-chips, Guinness, and hard cider. A bookie joint in the 1930s, it's said to be one of America's most haunted places.

Sheffield's (✉ 3258 N. Sheffield Ave., Lake View, ☎ 773/281–4989) spans the seasons with a shaded beer garden in summer and a roaring fireplace in winter. This laid-back neighborhood pub has billiards and more than 100 kinds of bottled beer that change seasonally, including regional microbrews and a "bad beer of the month," as well as 18 brands on tap.

The **Signature Room at the 95th** (✉ 875 N. Michigan Ave., Loop, ☎ 312/787–9596) has no competition when it comes to views. Perched on the 96th floor of the John Hancock Center—above even the tower's observation deck—the bar offers stunning vistas of the skyline and lake for only the cost of a pricey drink.

Sinibar (✉ 1540 N. Milwaukee Ave., Wicker Park, ☎ 773/278–7797) pairs a subterranean North African–inspired lounge with a French/Italian restaurant. In the cinnamon- and curry-color lounge, stylish urbanites sip martinis called "Fez" and "Belly Dance" while kicking back on leather benches. The house DJ spins funk and soul.

The Tasting Room (✉ 1415 W. Randolph St., Loop, ☎ 312/942–1212) makes the short list of nightspots where Chicagoans take guests they want to impress. This two-story wine bar—with a casual, loft-chic look and sweeping skyline views—has a fine selection of wine (more than 100 by the glass and twice as many by the bottle), cheese, caviar, and other light bites. If you love what you taste here, buy a bottle to take home at the adjacent wine shop, Randolph Wine Cellars.

Webster's Wine Bar (✉ 1480 W. Webster Ave., Lincoln Park, ☎ 773/868–0608), a romantic place for a date, stocks more than 250 types of wine, with at least 30 by the glass, as well as ports, sherries, single-malt scotches, a few microbrews, and a light appetizer menu at reasonable prices.

Cafés

This section has a few of the more offbeat spots, from hip, loungy coffeehouses to sophisticated cafés.

Caffe de Luca (✉ 1721 N. Damen Ave., Bucktown, ☎ 773/342–6000) is the place to go when you crave air and light with your caffeine and calories. This sophisticated Bucktown spot hints at Tuscany with richly colored walls and a fine selection of Italian sandwiches, salads, and sorbets.

Earwax (✉ 1564 N. Milwaukee Ave., Wicker Park, ☎ 773/772–4019), part comfortable café and part book and video store, tunes you in to the scene in hip Wicker Park. Choose coffee, sweets, or a light meal.

Intelligentsia (✉ 3123 N. Broadway, Lake View, ☎ 773/348–8058) was named to invoke the pre-chain days when cafés were forums for discussion, but the long, broad farmer's tables and handsome couches are usually occupied by students and other serious types who treat the café like their office. The store does all of its own coffee roasting and sells its custom blends to local restaurants.

Kopi, a Traveler's Cafe (✉ 5317 N. Clark St., Edgewater, ☎ 773/989–5674) is a study in opposites, with healthy vegetarian options as well as decadent desserts. In the Andersonville district, a 20-minute cab ride from downtown, this café has a selection of travel books (for sale), foreign artifacts, and artfully painted tables.

The **Pick Me Up Café** (✉ 3408 N. Clark St., Lake View, ☎ 773/248–6613) combines the charm of a quirky, neighborhood café with the late-night hours of those chain diners. The thrift-store treasures hanging on the walls are as eclectic as the crowd that comes at all hours of the day and night to drink bottomless cups of coffee or dine on sandwiches, appetizers, and desserts.

Third Coast Café (✉ 1260 N. Dearborn St., Near North, ☎ 312/649–0730), the oldest coffeehouse in the Gold Coast, lets you indulge your need for caffeine until the wee hours (until 2 AM on weeknights, 4 AM on weekends) with a full liquor, coffee, and food menu.

Uncommon Ground (✉ 1214 W. Grace St., Lake View, ☎ 773/929–3680), just down the block from Wrigley Field, lives up to its name with a pair of comfortable, smoke-free rooms, a fireplace when it's cold and a sidewalk café when it's not, and a steady lineup of acoustic musical acts. For sustenance, there's a full beverage menu—including bowls of coffee, hot chocolate, and a full bar—and a hearty, all-day food menu.

Improv and Comedy Clubs

Improvisation has long had a successful following in Chicago; stand-up comedy hasn't fared as well. Most comedy clubs have a cover charge ($5–$20); many have a two-drink minimum on top of that. In the stand-up circuit, keep an eye out for performances by Steve Harvey, star of his own WB television series.

Barrel of Laughs (✉ 10345 S. Central Ave., Oaklawn, ☎ 708/499–2969), in the city's southwest suburbs (a 30-minute drive from downtown), spotlights local and national comics. The dinner package includes a meal at the adjacent Senese's restaurant and reserved seats at the show.

ComedySportz (⊠ 2851 N. Halsted St., Lake View, ☎ 773/549–8080) specializes in "competitive improv," in which two teams vie for the audience's favor.

ImprovOlympic (⊠ 3541 N. Clark St., Lake View, ☎ 773/880–0199) has shows with student and professional improvisation in two intimate spaces every night but Tuesday. Team members present long-form comedic improvisations drawn on audience suggestions, including an improvised musical and a Monday-night alumni show. No drink or age minimum.

Second City (⊠ 1616 N. Wells St., Near North, ☎ 312/337–3992), an institution since 1959, has served as a launching pad for some of the hottest comedians around. Alumni include Dan Aykroyd and the late John Belushi. Funny, loony skit comedy is presented on two stages, with a free improv set after the show every night but Friday.

Zanies (⊠ 1548 N. Wells St., Near North, ☎ 312/337–4027) books outstanding national talent and is Chicago's best stand-up comedy spot. Jay Leno, Jerry Seinfeld, and Jackie Mason have all performed at this intimate venue.

Dance Clubs

Most clubs don't get crowded until 11 or 12, and they remain open into the early morning hours. Cover charges range from $5 to $15. A few dance clubs have dress codes that don't allow jeans, gym shoes, or baseball hats.

Berlin (⊠ 954 W. Belmont Ave., Lake View, ☎ 773/348–4975), a multicultural, pansexual dance club near the Belmont El station, has progressive electronic dance music and fun theme nights, such as Prince night, "women's obsession" Wednesday, and male go-go dancer nights. The crowd tends to be predominantly gay on weeknights, mixed on weekends.

Big Wig (⊠ 1551 W. Division St., Ukrainian Village, ☎ 773/235–9100) invites you to wig out with its beauty-salon-gone-bad theme. Have a drink while you sit in a barber's chair or at an old-fashioned dome hair dryer. On the second-floor dance floor, DJs spin hip-hop, house, and acid jazz on Wednesdays and weekends.

At **Circus** (⊠ 901 W. Weed St., Near North, ☎ 312/266–1200), the big dance floor feels like center ring under the big top, with flashing lights, stilt walkers, trapeze artists, and other performers, and DJ-spun tunes. There's also a raised gallery for watching the action, and other areas for mingling with the post-collegiate single crowd.

Crobar—The Nightclub (⊠ 1543 N. Kingsbury St., Near North, ☎ 312/413–7000), the reigning Chicago nightclub, is a longtime favorite for its industrial-Gothic look and top DJs spinning house and techno, plus standard mega-club amenities like dance cages over the enormous dance floor and a second-story VIP lounge.

The Dragon Room (⊠ 809 W. Evergreen Ave., Near North, ☎ 312/751–2900) has three levels of music, bars, and even a sushi bar. The claustrophobic first floor has Euro dance music as well as dance-hall and drum 'n bass; downstairs is a loungy bar lighted by red Japanese paper lanterns.

Excalibur (⊠ 632 N. Dearborn St., River North, ☎ 312/266–1944) won't win any prizes for breaking new ground, but this River North nightclub complex carved out of the Romanesque fortress that was the original home of the Chicago Historical Society has been going strong for years with its mix of dancing, dining, and posing. At the same address and phone number but with a separate entrance is the smaller, alternative dance club **Vision**.

Funky is the operative word for the **Funky Buddha Lounge** (⌧ 728 W. Grand Ave., Wicker Park, ☏ 312/666–1695), with its diverse crowd, seductive dance music, and a big metal Buddha guarding the front door. It has an intimate bar and dark dance floor, where patrons groove as DJs spin dance-hall, hip-hop, Latin, funk, and old-school house. The city's only nonsmoking VIP room is hidden in the back.

Red Dog (⌧ 1958 W. North Ave., Wicker Park, ☏ 773/278–1009) calls itself a "supreme funk parlor." The dance floor gets crowded in the wee hours of the morning with bodies moving to high-energy dance music. Monday's gay night is one of the city's best club nights. Enter from the alley off Damen Avenue behind the Border Line Tap.

Spy Bar (⌧ 646 N. Franklin St., River North, ☏ 312/587–8779) pulls some smooth moves. Image is everything at this subterranean spot with a brushed stainless-steel bar and exposed brick walls. The slick, stylish crowd hits the tight dance floor for house, R&B, and DJ remixes.

Transit (⌧ 1431 W. Lake St., Near West Side, ☏ 312/491–8600 or 312/491–9729), from the owners of the late, great club Shelter, is hidden away underneath the El tracks in a spooky stretch west of downtown. Inside, the multiroom space has a crisp design, earthy colors, and the usual young club goers.

The name **Voyeur** (⌧ 151½ W. Ohio St., River North, ☏ 312/832–1717) implies a certain see-and-be-seen attitude, but the diverse, casual crowd at this subterranean nightclub couldn't be less concerned about posing as they wantonly gyrate to hip-hop dance music on an elevated steel floor. Red-lit booths are scattered in cozy nooks, and five full bars will never leave you thirsty.

The popular **White Star Lounge** (⌧ 225 W. Ontario St., River North, ☏ 312/440–3223) attracts a partying, twentysomething crowd dressed in their best (or least, for the ladies). Dance to Euro-house beats, relax in leopard-print lounge chairs arranged in pods in the club's open-air space, or sweet-talk your way into the elevated VIP room that overlooks the dancing throng.

Gay and Lesbian Bars

Chicago's gay bars appeal to mixed crowds and tastes. Most are on North Halsted Street from Belmont Avenue to Irving Park Road, an area nicknamed Boys Town. Bars generally stay open until 2 AM weekends, but a few keep the lights on until 5 AM Sunday morning. The *Chicago Free Press, Windy City Times,* and *Gay Chicago* list nightspots, events, and gay and lesbian resources; all three are free and can be picked up at bookstores, bars, and some supermarkets, especially those in Boys Town.

Big Chicks (⌧ 5024 N. Sheridan Rd., Uptown, ☏ 773/728–5511) is a striking alternative to the Halsted strip, with a funky crowd that appreciates the owner's art collection hanging on the walls. The great jukebox and fun-loving staff are the payoffs for the hike to get here. Special attractions include weekend dancing, midnight shots, and free Sunday afternoon barbecues.

Charlie's (⌧ 3726 N. Broadway, Lake View, ☏ 773/871–8887), a country-and-western dance club, lets you dance nightly to achy-breaky tunes, though dance music is played from midnight to 4 AM Wednesday through Sunday. It's mostly a boots-and-denim crowd on weekends.

Circuit (✉ 3641 N. Halsted St., Lake View, ☎ 773/325–2233), the biggest dance club in Boys Town, is a stripped-down dance hall energized by flashing lights, booming sounds, and a partying crowd. Take a break in the up-front martini bar, Rehab.

The **Closet** (✉ 3325 N. Broadway, Lake View, ☎ 773/477–8533) is a basic Chicago tavern with a gay twist. This compact bar—one of the few that caters to lesbians, though it draws gay men, too—can be especially lively after 2 AM when most other bars close. Stop by Sunday afternoons when bartenders serve up what are hailed as the best Bloody Marys in town.

Gentry (✉ 440 N. State St., River North, ☎ 312/836–0933), one of the few gay bars downtown, is a premier piano bar/cabaret, featuring local and national talent. The staff wear tuxedos at the upscale piano bar; the video bar downstairs attracts a younger group. A smaller, Boys Town branch is at ✉ 3320 North Halsted Street.

As you might expect, **Girlbar** (✉ 2625 N. Halsted St., Lincoln Park, ☎ 773/871–4210) caters to lesbians. The downstairs has a mirrored dance floor, while the upstairs has pool tables, a dartboard, and an outdoor deck.

Roscoe's Tavern (✉ 3356 N. Halsted St., Lake View, ☎ 773/281–3355), in the heart of Boys Town, is a longtime favorite with a mix of amenities sure to please its preppy patrons, including a quaint front bar, pool tables, an outdoor garden, and lively music. The sidewalk café serves May–September.

The video bar **Sidetrack** (✉ 3349 N. Halsted St., Lake View, ☎ 773/477–9189) is tuned into a different theme every night of the week, from show tunes on Monday to comedy on Thursday—all broadcast on TV screens that never leave your sight. The sprawling stand-and-pose bar is always busy with a good-looking, professional crowd, and the vodka slushies are a house specialty.

Music

Blues

The blues traveled to Chicago during the 1930s with African-Americans who moved here from the Deep South. In the years following World War II, Chicago-style blues grew into its own musical form, flourishing during the 1950s, then fading during the 1960s with the advent of rock and roll. You can still find the South Side clubs where it all began, but since 1970 the blues has migrated to the North Side and attracted new devotees among largely white audiences. The **Chicago Blues Festival** (☎ 312/744–3370) each June testifies to the city's continuing affection for this music.

Blue Chicago (✉ 536 N. Clark St., River North, ☎ 312/661–0100; ✉ 736 N. Clark St., River North, ☎ 312/642–6261) has two bars within two blocks of each other. Both have good sound systems, regularly book female vocalists, and attract a cosmopolitan audience that's a tad more diverse than some of the baseball-capped crowds at Lincoln Park blues clubs. One cover gets you into both bars. In the basement of the **Blue Chicago Store** (✉ 534 N. Clark St., Near North, ☎ 312/661–1003), Saturday night is family night, with live blues, no alcohol, and no smoking.

B.L.U.E.S. (✉ 2519 N. Halsted St., Lincoln Park, ☎ 773/528–1012), narrow and intimate, draws the best of Chicago's musicians, including Son Seals, Otis Rush, Big Time Sarah, and Magic Slim. This Lincoln Park venue is often packed to its smoke-filled capacity.

Buddy Guy's Legends (✉ 754 S. Wabash Ave., Downtown South, ☎ 312/427–0333) serves up Louisiana-style barbecue along with the blues. This big club in the South Loop also offers good sound, good sight lines, and pool tables. Local blues legend and owner Buddy Guy performs a long home stand of sold-out shows in January.

Checkerboard Lounge (✉ 423 E. 43rd St., Kenwood, ☎ 773/624–3240) is one of the great old South Side clubs. Although the neighborhood is rough, the music by talented Chicago performers is worth the trip.

Kingston Mines (✉ 2548 N. Halsted St., Lincoln Park, ☎ 773/477–4647), the North Side's oldest blues spot, continues to attract large numbers of blues lovers and partying singles. The former group comes because of its daily top-notch, big-name, continuous live entertainment on two stages, the latter because of its late closing time (4 or 5 AM).

At **Lee's Unleaded Blues** (✉ 7401 S. South Chicago Ave., Grand Crossing, ☎ 773/493–3477), South Side locals come decked out in their showiest threads. The cramped, triangular bar may inhibit free movement, but that doesn't seem to bother the crowd that comes to see rockin' jazz and blues Thursday through Monday nights.

Rosa's (✉ 3420 W. Armitage Ave., Logan Square, ☎ 773/342–0452) could well be Chicago's friendliest blues bar. Tony, the owner, came here from Italy out of love for the blues; his mother, Mama Rosa, is a fixture behind the bar. Catch guitarist Melvin Taylor on Tuesday and harmonica player Sugar Blue on Wednesday.

Country

There are slim pickings for country music clubs in Chicago, even though country radio continues to draw wide audiences.

Carol's Pub (✉ 4659 N. Clark St., Bucktown, ☎ 773/334–2402) showcased country before it was ever cool. The house band at this urban honky tonk plays country and country-rock tunes on weekends, and the popular karaoke night on Thursday draws all walks of life, from preppie to punk.

The Hideout (✉ 1354 W. Wabansia, Bucktown, ☎ 773/227–4433), which is literally hidden away in a north-side industrial zone, has managed to make country music hip in Chicago. Players on the city's alternative country scene have adopted the friendly hole-in-the-wall, and bands ranging from the obscure to the semi-famous take the stage. The bluegrass band Devil in a Woodpile plays on Tuesday.

Eclectic

Clubs in this category don't limit themselves to a single type of music. Call ahead to find out what's playing.

At **Baton** (✉ 436 N. Clark St., River North, ☎ 312/644–5269), boys will be girls. The lip-synching revues with female impersonators have catered to curious out-of-towners and bachelorette parties since 1969. Some of the regular performers, such as Chili Pepper and Mimi Marks, have become Chicago cult figures.

Beat Kitchen (✉ 2100 W. Belmont Ave., Lake View, ☎ 773/281–4444) brings in the crowds because of its good sound system and local and touring rock, alternative rock, country, and rockabilly acts. It also serves soups, salads, sandwiches, pizzas, and desserts.

Elbo Room (✉ 2871 N. Lincoln Ave., Lincoln Park, ☎ 773/549–5549), a multilevel space in an elbow-shape corner building, has a basement rec-room feel. The bar plays host to talented live bands seven days a week, with a strong dose of acid jazz, funk, soul, pop, and rock.

CHICAGO SINGS THE BLUES

Come on baby, don't you want to go, Back to the same old place, sweet home Chicago.

–Robert Johnson

THE SEARING, SOULFUL STRAINS of the blues are deeply woven into the fabric of Chicago's history. Blues originated in the Mississippi Delta, traveled with migrating blacks through Memphis, and settled in Chicago. Here, the country blues became charged by the tougher, louder life of the city. These urban, hard-edged, electric blues are marked by a fiery style, driving rhythm, and dynamic sound.

During the migration boom of the 1920s–'60s, the first stop for many arrivals was Maxwell Street, where blues musicians played in jam sessions in the open-air flea market. That legacy is fading fast, though at the **New Maxwell Street Market** (⊠ Canal St. between Taylor and 16th Sts., University Village, ☎ 312/922–3100), relocated to a smaller space a half mile east of the original, you can sometimes find blues musicians playing on summer Sundays 7 AM–3 PM.

For a walk into history, stop by the **Blues Heaven Foundation** (⊠ 2120 S. Michigan Ave., Near South, ☎ 312/808–1286), which occupies the former home of the legendary Chess Records. Among the artists who recorded here were Muddy Waters, John Lee Hooker, and Etta James. The foundation, run by the widow and daughter of blues musician Willie Dixon, offers tours of the small facility, which displays a few artifacts including the Chess recording studio, rehearsal room, and basement echo chamber where Chuck Berry allegedly slept. Admission is $10; it's open Monday–Friday, 9:30 AM–5:30 PM and Saturday noon–2 PM.

Chicago is still active in recording the blues. Alligator Records has offices on Chicago's North Side. And Delmark Records is here, too; owner Bob Koester also runs the **Jazz Record Mart** (⊠ 444 N. Wabash Ave., Near North, ☎ 312/222–1467 or 800/684–3480), which claims to be the world's largest jazz and blues record shop.

In the 1990s blues had a resurgence, reaching new audiences and new heights of commercialization with the opening of the **House of Blues** (☎ 312/923–2000) and the House of Blues Hotel, which carries the blues theme even further with southern folk art in the rooms and leopard-print, blue-custom-dyed carpets.

Chicago is still the capital of the blues. The city's annual **Chicago Blues Festival** (☎ 312/744–3370), usually held the first weekend in June, draws some 650,000 fans to Grant Park near Chicago's lakefront for a free, four-day festival with outdoor concerts on several stages.

Year-round, the passion pours forth from blues bars seven nights a week, with such local artists as Son Seals, Lonnie Brooks, Koko Taylor, Eddy Clearwater, Otis Rush, and Pinetop Perkins.

Catch bluesman Buddy Guy at his club, **Buddy Guy's Legends** (⊠ 754 S. Wabash Ave., Downtown South, ☎ 312/427–0333). Or swing by the **Checkerboard Lounge** (⊠ 423 E. 43rd St., Kenwood, ☎ 773/624–3240), a South Side institution. Farther south, fill up at **Lee's Unleaded Blues** (⊠ 7401 S. South Chicago Ave., Grand Crossing, ☎ 773/493–3477). The two **Blue Chicago** clubs downtown often turn the spotlight on female vocalists, and even offer family night on Saturday. In Lincoln Park, **Kingston Mines** presents two bands on two stages, and the intimate **B.L.U.E.S.** pulses with rhythm. **Smoke Daddy** (⊠ 1804 W. Division St., Wicker Park, ☎ 773/772–6656) serves Southern barbecue along with a hearty side dish of blues and jazz with no cover charge, seven nights a week.

FitzGerald's (✉ 6615 W. Roosevelt Rd., Berwyn, ☎ 708/788–2118), though a bit out of the way, draws crowds from all over the city and suburbs with its mix of folk, jazz, blues, zydeco, and rock. This early 1900s roadhouse has great sound and sight lines for its roots music.

HotHouse (✉ 31 E. Balbo Ave., Downtown South, ☎ 312/362–9707) bills itself as "the center for international performance and exhibition," and delivers globe-spanning musical offerings—Spanish guitar one night, mambo the next—in a spacious venue that can be counted on to draw an interesting crowd.

House of Blues (✉ 329 N. Dearborn St., River North, ☎ 312/923–2000), though its name implies otherwise, attracts big-name performers of all genres, from jazz, roots, blues, and gospel to alternative rock, hip-hop, world, and R&B. The interior is an elaborate cross between blues bar and ornate opera house. Its restaurant has live blues every night on a "second stage," as well as a satisfying Sunday gospel brunch. Part of the Marina City complex, the entrance is on State Street.

Folk and Ethnic
Baby Doll Polka Club (✉ 6102 S. Central Ave., Southwest Side, ☎ 773/582–9706) has some of the best polka dancing in the city, with live music Saturday and Sunday. You'll see mostly regulars at the Baby Doll, a neighborhood institution since 1954 near Midway Airport on the Southwest Side.

Old Town School of Folk Music (✉ 4544 N. Lincoln Ave., Ravenswood, ☎ 773/525–7793), Chicago's first and oldest folk music school, has served as folk central in the city since 1957. This friendly spot in Lincoln Square hosts outstanding performances by national and local acts in a 425-seat concert hall.

Wild Hare (✉ 3530 N. Clark St., Lake View, ☎ 773/327–4273), with a wide-open dance floor, is the place for infectious live reggae and world-beat music seven nights a week.

Jazz
Jazz thrives all around town. For a recorded listing of upcoming live performances, call the **Jazz Institute Hot Line** (☎ 312/427–3300).

Andy's (✉ 11 E. Hubbard St., River North, ☎ 312/642–6805), a favorite after-work watering hole with a substantial bar menu, has live, local jazz daily. In addition to the evening performances, there's a jazz program at noon on weekdays—a boon for music lovers who aren't night owls.

Cotton Club (✉ 1710 S. Michigan Ave., Near South Side, ☎ 312/341–9787) draws big, diverse crowds and good bands. There's an open mike every Monday and live jazz by candlelight in the elegant Cab Calloway Room on weekends, as well as dancing to hip-hop and R&B in the Gray Room.

Green Dolphin Street (✉ 2200 N. Ashland Ave., Lake View, ☎ 773/395–0066), a stylish, upscale club/restaurant with the glamour of the 1940s (in a converted auto-body shop, no less), attracts tight ensembles and smooth-voiced jazz divas for bossa, bebop, Latin, and world jazz.

Green Mill (✉ 4802 N. Broadway, Uptown, ☎ 773/878–5552), a Chicago institution off the beaten track in untrendy Uptown, has been around since 1907. Deep leather banquettes and ornate wood paneling line the walls, and a photo of Al Capone occupies a place of honor on the piano behind the bar. The jazz entertainment is both excellent and contemporary—the club launched the careers of Kurt Elling and

Patricia Barber—and the Uptown Poetry Slam, a competitive poetry reading, takes center stage on Sunday.

Jazz Showcase (⊠ 59 W. Grand Ave., River North, ☎ 312/670–2473), the second-oldest jazz club in the country, presents national and international names in jazz, and mostly acoustic groups. This serious, no-smoking club, bedecked with photos of all the jazz greats who've played it, is one of the best places to hear jazz in Chicago. Children under 12 are admitted free for the Sunday matinee.

Pops for Champagne (⊠ 2934 N. Sheffield Ave., Lake View, ☎ 773/472–1000), despite the incongruous name, is a good spot for serious jazz fans, who come for the instrumental ensembles and jazz vocalists. A 140-strong champagne bar and a selection of tasty appetizers and desserts enhance the scene.

Velvet Lounge (⊠ 2128½ S. Indiana Ave., Near South Side, ☎ 312/791–9050) produces glorious music from a weather-beaten storefront. Owner Fred Anderson, a saxophonist, books avant-garde jazz ensembles and traditional groups at this intimate spot.

Rock

Chicago has an active rock scene with many local favorites, some of which—including Smashing Pumpkins, Wilco, and Liz Phair—have won national acclaim.

The Abbey (⊠ 3420 W. Grace St., Irving Park, ☎ 773/463–5808 or 773/478–4408) showcases rock, as well as some Irish, Celtic, and country music, in a large concert hall with a separate, busy, smoky pub. By day, the hall is used to show soccer and rugby games from the United Kingdom and Ireland.

Double Door (⊠ 1572 N. Milwaukee Ave., Wicker Park, ☎ 773/489–3160) is a hotbed for music in hip Wicker Park. The large bar books up-and-coming local and national acts from rock to acid jazz. Unannounced Rolling Stones shows have been held here. The entrance is on Damen Avenue.

Empty Bottle (⊠ 1035 N. Western Ave., Ukrainian Village, ☎ 773/276–3600) may have toys and knickknacks around the bar (including a case of macabre baby doll heads), but when it comes to booking rock, punk, and jazz bands from the indie scene, it's a serious place with no pretensions.

Fireside Bowl (⊠ 2648 W. Fullerton Ave., Bucktown, ☎ 773/486–2700) only hosts bowling after 10 PM on Tuesdays. For the rest of the week it serves as a venue for punk-rock bands—from indie superacts to brash high schoolers learning to play their guitars.

Martyrs' (⊠ 3855 N. Lincoln Ave., North Center, ☎ 773/404–9869) brings local and major-label rock bands to this small, neighborhood bar-like venue. Music fans can see the stage from just about any corner of the bar, while the more rhythmically inclined gyrate in the large standing room area. A mural opposite the stage memorializes late rock greats.

Metro (⊠ 3730 N. Clark St., Lake View, ☎ 773/549–0203) brings in progressive, nationally known artists and the cream of the local crop. A former movie palace, it's an excellent place to see live bands, whether you're moshing on the main floor or above the fray in the balcony. In the basement is **Smart Bar**, a late-night dance club that starts hopping after 12.

Schubas Tavern (⊠ 3159 N. Southport Ave., Lake View, ☎ 773/525–2508) favors local and national power pop and indie rock bands. The wood-paneled back room has good seating and a laid-back atmosphere. The bar was built in 1900 by the Schlitz Brewing Co., and it still sells Schlitz beer—a bargain at $3.50 a bottle.

Piano Bars

Coq d'Or (✉ 140 E. Walton Ave., Near North, ☎ 312/787–2200) is where Chicago legend Buddy Charles held court before retiring. The dark, wood-paneled room draws hotel guests as well as neighborhood regulars with its fine music and cocktails served in blown-glass goblets.

Davenport's (✉ 1383 N. Milwaukee Ave., Wicker Park, ☎ 773/278–1830), a sophisticated cabaret booking both local and touring acts, brings a grown-up presence to the Wicker Park club scene. The piano lounge is set up for casual listening, while the back room is a no-chat zone that requires your full attention—as well as reservations and a two-drink minimum.

Pump Room (✉ Omni Ambassador East Hotel, 1301 N. State Pkwy., Near North, ☎ 312/266–0360) shows off its storied past with photos of celebrities covering the walls. The bar at this restaurant has live piano and a small dance floor that calls out for dancing cheek to cheek, especially on weekends. Jackets are required.

Zebra Lounge (✉ 1220 N. State St., Near North, ☎ 312/642–5140), small and funky with a striped motif, attracts a good crowd of dressed-up and dressed-down regulars who come to sing along to the pianist on duty.

Sports Bars

Gamekeepers (✉ 345 W. Armitage Ave., Lincoln Park, ☎ 773/549–0400) is full of former frat boys and sports fans. With more than 40 TVs and complete satellite sports coverage, there's barely a game Gamekeepers doesn't get.

Hi-Tops Cafe (✉ 3551 N. Sheffield Ave., Lake View, ☎ 773/348–0009), within a ball's toss of Wrigley Field, may be the ultimate sports bar. Big-screen TVs, a lively crowd, and good bar food keep the Cubs fans coming. A dozen satellites and 65 TV monitors ensure that the place gets packed for a good game.

North Beach Chicago (✉ 1551 N. Sheffield Ave., DePaul, ☎ 312/266–7842) has multiple large-screen TVs plus three sand-filled indoor volleyball courts, pool tables, and four bowling lanes in this huge former warehouse.

Sluggers (✉ 3540 N. Clark St., Lake View, ☎ 773/248–0055) is packed after Cubs games in the nearby stadium, and the ballplayers make occasional appearances in summer. Check out the fast- and slow-pitch batting cages on the second floor, as well as the pool tables, air hockey tables, and indoor golf range.

THE ARTS

Chicago is a splendid city for the arts. The Shubert, Auditorium, Chicago, Oriental, and Goodman theaters—Chicago bases for Broadway-scale shows—are complemented by more than 75 small neighborhood-based theaters where young actors polish their skills. The Lyric Opera plays to houses that are always sold out; the Chicago Opera Theatre augments the Lyric's repertoire with a spring season of smaller works. The Chicago Symphony Orchestra gives world-class performances; the Ravinia Festival and the Grant Park outdoor concerts draw huge crowds in summer. Music lovers hungry for more turn to smaller performing groups: Music of the Baroque, Bella Voce, the Oriana Singers, and dozens more. Dance aficionados enjoy performances of outstanding companies, including the Joffrey Ballet of Chicago.

For complete music and theater listings, check two free weeklies, *The Reader* and *New City,* both published midweek; the Friday and Sunday editions of the *Chicago Tribune* and *Chicago Sun-Times*; and the monthly *Chicago* magazine.

Ticket prices vary wildly depending on whether you're seeing a high-profile group or venturing into more obscure territory. Chicago Symphony tickets range from $11 to $95, the Lyric Opera from $28 to $132 (if you can get them). Smaller choruses and orchestras charge from $10 to $25; watch the listings for free performances. Commercial theater ranges from $15 to $75; smaller experimental ensembles might charge $5, $10, or pay-what-you-can. Movie prices range from $9 for first-run houses to as low as $1.50 at some suburban second-run houses. Some commercial chains take credit cards.

Dance

Dance in Chicago often doesn't receive the recognition it should, but several talented companies perform regularly, with a wide range of styles.

The **Athenaeum Theatre** (✉ 2936 N. Southport Ave., Lake View, ☎ 773/935–6860) hosts innovative, small dance companies, and the fall series Dance Chicago which features all forms of dance from Chicago dance companies.

The **Dance Center of Columbia College Chicago** (✉ 1306 S. Michigan Ave., Loop, ☎ 312/344–8300), in its 272-seat theater in the South Loop, presents thought-provoking fare with leading international and national contemporary dance artists.

Gus Giordano Jazz Dance Chicago (☎ 847/866–6779), founded in 1962 and based in suburban Evanston, is an advocate for jazz dance as an indigenous American art. The repertoire varies from energetic, contemporary pieces to classic jazz dance.

Hubbard Street Dance Chicago (☎ 312/850–9744), Chicago's most notable success story in dance, exudes a jazzy vitality that has made it extremely popular. The style mixes classical ballet techniques, theatrical jazz, and contemporary dance.

The **Joffrey Ballet of Chicago** (☎ 312/739–0120) has emerged as Chicago's premier classical dance company, garnering acclaim for fine-tuned performances such as its uniquely American production of *The Nutcracker.* The Joffrey gives several performances a year here, usually at the Auditorium Theatre.

Muntu Dance Theatre of Chicago (☎ 773/602–1135) showcases dynamic interpretations of contemporary and traditional African and African-American dance. Artistic director Amaniyea Payne travels to Africa to learn traditional dances and adapts them for the stage.

River North Chicago Dance Company (☎ 312/944–2888) has attracted attention with accessible works rich in Chicago's strong jazz dance traditions.

Trinity Irish Dance Co. (☎ 773/549–6135), founded long before *Riverdance*, promotes traditional and progressive Irish dancing. In addition to the world-champion professional group, the Trinity Irish Dancers, you can also catch performances by younger dancers enrolled in the Trinity dance academy.

Film

Chicago supports an enticing variety of films, from first-run blockbusters to art and revival releases. While multiplexes have opened citywide, they've meant curtains for a few longtime Chicago favorites, such as the downtown Fine Arts and Lincoln Park's Biograph (the last movie house gangster John Dillinger attended). For recorded movie previews and show times at area theaters, call **MovieFone** (☎ 312/444–3456, WEB www.moviefone.com), a service that also allows you to purchase tickets for many cinemas in advance.

Every July through August, Grant Park hosts the **Chicago Outdoor Film Festival** (✉ 500 S. Columbus Dr., Loop, ☎ 312/742–7529) on Tuesday nights. Bring a picnic dinner and a blanket and watch classic films under the stars.

For two weeks in October, the **Chicago International Film Festival** (☎ 312/332–3456) screens more than 100 films, including premieres of Hollywood films, international releases, documentaries, short subjects, animation, videos, and student films. Movie stars usually make appearances at the opening events.

Many Near North cinemas show first-run Hollywood movies on multiple screens. The two screens of the **900 North Michigan Cinemas** (☎ 312/787–1988) are in the lower level of the Bloomingdale's/900 North Michigan Avenue shopping complex. The **600 North Michigan Cinemas** (☎ 312/255–9340), with an entrance at the corner of Rush and Ohio streets, has nine screens on three levels. **McClurg Court Cinemas** (✉ 330 E. Ohio St., Near North, ☎ 312/642–0723) has two small screens and one large theater with a great THX sound system, ideal for viewing flicks with special effects. Just off Michigan Avenue, **Esquire** (✉ 58 E. Oak St., Near North, ☎ 312/280–0101), an art deco landmark on the Gold Coast that shows first-run movies, has kept its facade but is divided into six modern theaters. For **IMAX theaters** go to **Navy Pier** (✉ Grand Ave. at the lakefront, Near North, ☎ 312/595–7437) or the **Museum of Science and Industry** (✉ 57th St. and Lake Shore Dr., Hyde Park, ☎ 773/684–1414).

Brew and View (✉ 3145 N. Sheffield Ave., Lake View, ☎ 312/618–8439) shows movies at the Vic Theatre when this hall is not in use for concerts. Expect second- and third-run films, cult films, midnight shows, and a rowdy crowd, which comes for the cheap movies and beer specials.

Facets Multimedia (✉ 1517 W. Fullerton Ave., Lincoln Park, ☎ 773/281–9075) shows rare and exotic films in its cinema and video theater; call to find out whether a particular day's fare appeals to you. Or rent an arts film from the video library, which has the largest foreign film selection in the country.

Gene Siskel Film Center (✉ 164 N. State St., Loop, ☎ 312/846–2800) specializes in unusual current films, revivals of rare classics, and film festivals. The program here changes almost daily and filmmakers sometimes give lectures to accompany the movie.

Landmark's Century Centre Cinemas (✉ 2828 N. Clark St., Lake View, ☎ 773/248–7744) brings stadium seating and seven screens devoted to art, foreign-language, and independent films to the upper floors of Lake View's Century shopping mall. (The entire building was once a grand movie palace.) Buy tickets at the ground-level or fourth-floor box offices.

Music Box Theatre (✉ 3733 N. Southport Ave., Lake View, ☎ 773/871–6604), a small and richly decorated 1920s movie palace, shows a mix of foreign flicks, classics, and outstanding recent films, emphasizing independent filmmakers. The organ is played between shows on weekends and as an accompaniment to silent films. If you love old theaters and old movies, don't miss a trip here.

Music

The Chicago Symphony Orchestra is internationally renowned, and the Lyric Opera of Chicago is one of the top two opera companies in America today. Close to 90% of all Lyric tickets go to subscribers, so the key to getting in is to call the Lyric in early August when individual tickets first go on sale. Another tack for either the Lyric or the orchestra: call a day or two before the show to see if there are any subscriber returns. If you go to Orchestra Hall or the opera house a half hour before performance time, you may find someone with an extra ticket to sell. If you can't get tickets to these draws, though, take heart: Chicago has a wealth of exciting performing groups.

Choral and Chamber Groups

Apollo Chorus of Chicago (☎ 630/960–2251), formed in 1872, is one of the country's oldest oratorio societies. Apollo performs Handel's *Messiah* every December, an annual spring concert at Symphony Center, and other choral classics throughout the year at area churches.

Bella Voce (☎ 312/461–0723), formerly known as His Majestie's Clerkes, performs mostly sacred and a cappella music, but also everything from early music to new works by Paul McCartney in churches throughout the city. The season runs October–May.

Chicago Chamber Choir (☎ 312/409–6890) is a 27-voice chorus performing everything from sacred music of the Renaissance to contemporary American pieces, with December and June performances.

Chicago Children's Choir (☎ 312/849–8300) draws its members, ages 8–18, from a broad spectrum of racial, ethnic, and economic groups. Performances are given each year during the Christmas season and in May. Other concerts are scheduled periodically, sometimes in the Chicago Cultural Center's Preston Bradley Hall.

Music of the Baroque (☎ 312/551–1414), one of the Midwest's leading music ensembles specializing in Baroque and early classical music, schedules seven programs a year from October to May. Performances are in beautiful Chicago-area churches.

Oriana Singers (☎ 773/262–4558) is an outstanding a cappella sextet with an eclectic classical and jazz repertoire.

William Ferris Chorale (✉ 690 W. Belmont Ave., Lake View, ☎ 773/325–2000), a distinguished choral ensemble based at Our Lady of Mount Carmel church, focuses on 20th-century music and gives concerts from October–June with internationally famous guest artists.

Concert Halls

The **Chicago Cultural Center**'s (✉ 78 E. Washington St., Loop, ☎ 312/346–3278 or 312/744–6630) Preston Bradley Hall hosts music and dance performances, some free and many timed for the lunch or after-work crowd. The Dame Myra Hess Memorial Concert Series presents a free concert with outstanding young musicians every Wednesday at 12:15 PM.

When you pack your MCI Calling Card, it's like packing your loved ones along too.

Your MCI Calling Card is the easy way to stay in touch when you travel. Use it to call to and from over 125 countries. Plus, every time you call, you can earn frequent flier miles. So wherever your travels take you, call home with your MCI Calling Card. It's even easy to get one. Just visit **www.mci.com/worldphone** or **www.mci.com/partners**.

EASY TO CALL WORLDWIDE

1. Just enter the WorldPhone® access number of the country you're calling from.
2. Enter or give the operator your MCI Calling Card number.
3. Enter or give the number you're calling.

Aruba ✣	800-888-8
Bahamas ✣	1-800-888-8000

Barbados ✣	1-800-888-8000
Bermuda ✣	1-800-888-8000
British Virgin Islands ✣	1-800-888-8000
Canada	1-800-888-8000
Mexico	01-800-021-8000
Puerto Rico	1-800-888-8000
United States	1-800-888-8000
U.S. Virgin Islands	1-800-888-8000

✣ Limited availability.

EARN FREQUENT FLIER MILES

Limit of one bonus program per customer. All airline program rules and conditions apply. A U.S. billing address may be required for select airline bonus programs. © 2002 WorldCom, Inc. All Rights Reserved. The names, logos, and taglines identifying MCI products and services are proprietary marks of WorldCom, Inc. or its subsidiaries. All third party marks are the proprietary marks of their respective owners.

Find America *with a Compass*

Written by local authors and illustrated throughout with spectacular color images, Compass American Guides reveal the character and culture of more than 40 of America's most fascinating destinations. Perfect for residents who want to explore their own backyards and for visitors who want an insider's perspective on the history, heritage, and all there is to see and do.

Fodor's COMPASS AMERICAN GUIDES

At bookstores everywhere.

Mandel Hall (✉ 1131 E. 57th St., Hyde Park, ☎ 773/702–8511 or 773/702–7300), on the University of Chicago campus, schedules classical music, jazz, a folk festival, and opera performances.

The neo-Georgian **Orchestra Hall** (✉ 220 S. Michigan Ave., Loop, ☎ 312/294–3000), home of the world-famous Chicago Symphony Orchestra (CSO), is part of the much larger **Symphony Center,** which also contains a restaurant and a rehearsal space. In addition to more than 100 symphonic performances between September and June, the hall's schedule includes jazz, pop, chamber, and world music concerts. If you'd like to see the inside of Orchestra Hall, call to schedule a tour, or buy a ticket to one of the recitals that are scheduled frequently, particularly on Sunday afternoon. The view from the balcony is splendid and the acoustics excellent.

Among the smaller halls in the Loop and Near North areas is **Curtiss Hall,** in the **Fine Arts Building** (✉ 410 S. Michigan Ave., Loop, ☎ 312/939–3380), a venue for recitals and chamber music. The **Newberry Library** (✉ 60 W. Walton St., Lincoln Park, ☎ 312/943–9090) hosts four concerts a year by the Newberry Consort, which performs music from the 13th to the 17th centuries, as well as a number of concerts related to events or exhibits at the library. The historic **Three Arts Club** (✉ 1300 N. Dearborn Pkwy., Near North, ☎ 312/944–6250) hosts periodic jazz performances as well as other concerts in a landmark 1914 building modeled after a Tuscan palazzo.

Opera and Light Opera

Chicago Opera Theater (☎ 312/704–8414) stages innovative versions of traditional favorites, contemporary American pieces, and important lesser-known works, emphasizing theatrical as well as musical aspects of the shows. All performances are sung in English and are held at the Athenaeum Theatre.

Light Opera Works (✉ Cahn Auditorium, Emerson St. and Sheridan Rd., 927 Noyes St., Evanston) favors Gilbert and Sullivan operettas, but takes on Viennese, French, and other light operettas and American musicals from June to early January.

Lyric Opera of Chicago (✉ 20 N. Wacker Dr., Loop, ☎ 312/332–2244) offers top-flight productions starring the big voices of the opera world, and has sold out all of its superb performances for more than a dozen years. Don't worry about understanding German or Italian; English translations are projected above the stage. The season at the Ardis Krainik Theatre in the Civic Opera House runs September–March.

Orchestras

Chicago Sinfonietta (☎ 312/236–3681) presents highly polished classical, romantic, and contemporary pieces exactly as they were written by the composer. The Sinfonietta performs about 15 times a year at various locations, including the Symphony Center and Dominican University in suburban River Forest.

Chicago Symphony Orchestra (✉ 220 S. Michigan Ave., Loop, ☎ 312/294–3000 or 800/223–7114) performs September–June at Orchestra Hall, with music director Daniel Barenboim conducting. The CSO, which dates back to 1891, is one of the world's most powerful orchestras. In addition to its regular concerts, the symphony schedules special theme series including classical, jazz, world music, chamber, and children's concerts. While tickets are sometimes scarce, they do become available, so call to check the status.

In summer you can enjoy the Chicago Symphony at the **Ravinia Festival** (☎ 847/266–5100) in Highland Park, a 25-mi train trip from

Chicago. The park is lovely, and lawn seats are always available even when those in the Pavilion are sold out. Ravinia also draws crowds with jazz, pop, and dance concerts.

Civic Orchestra of Chicago (⊠ 220 S. Michigan Ave., Loop, ☎ 312/294–3000 or 800/223–7114), the CSO's training orchestra, performs a repertoire similar to that of the parent organization and works with the same guest conductors. Performances are free, but advance tickets are required. It has the same season as the CSO, September–June.

Grant Park Music Festival (☎ 312/742–7638), a program of the Chicago Park District, gives free concerts June–August. In summer 2004, the concerts are set to move from the James C. Petrillo Music Shell to a spectacular new Frank Gehry–designed pavilion across the street in Millennium Park. Performances usually take place Wednesday–Sunday evenings.

Theater

Road-show productions of Broadway hits do come to Chicago, but the theater scene's true vigor springs from the multitude of small ensembles that have made a home here. They range from the critically acclaimed Steppenwolf and the Goodman Theatre, a pioneer of regional theater in the United States, to fringe groups that specialize in experimental work. Larger, more elaborate productions tend to be concentrated in the Loop, while theaters on the Near North Side present some offbeat productions as well as more mainstream fare.

The theater district in the Loop is enjoying a revival, and many grand old theaters have been renovated, including the Palace and the Oriental, plus the Goodman's new complex, which incorporates the facades of the old Harris and Selwyn theaters. With the completion of several of these projects, Chicago is one of the top theater markets in the country.

Many smaller companies perform in tiny or makeshift storefront theaters, where admission prices are inexpensive to moderate. You can save money on seats at **Hot Tix** (WEB www.hottix.org for listings and booth information only), where unsold tickets are available, usually at half price (plus a service charge) on the day of performance; you won't know what's available until that day. On Friday, however, you can buy tickets for Saturday and Sunday. Hot Tix booths are at 78 West Randolph Street, across from the Daley Center; the Chicago Water Works Visitor Center at the southeast corner of Michigan Avenue and Pearson Street; the North Shore Center for the Performing Arts at 9501 Skokie Boulevard, in suburban Skokie; and at Chicago-area Tower Records stores. Hot Tix also functions as a Ticketmaster outlet, selling advance, full-price, cash-only tickets. You can charge full-price tickets over the phone at **Ticketmaster** (☎ 312/559–1212 for rock concerts and general interest events; 312/902–1500 for the arts line).

Commercial Theater

Most of the houses listed here are hired by independent producers for commercial (and sometimes nonprofit) productions; they have no resident producer or company.

The **Athenaeum Theatre** (⊠ 2936 N. Southport Ave., Lake View, ☎ 773/935–6860) holds intriguing music, opera, dance, and drama performances, some brought in from around the world.

Auditorium Theatre (⊠ 50 E. Congress Pkwy., Loop, ☎ 312/922–2110), a Louis Sullivan architectural masterpiece, has excellent acoustics and sight lines. You're likely to see touring productions of hit Broadway plays and Andrew Lloyd Webber musicals here; the Joffrey Ballet of Chicago also makes the magnificent stage its home.

Briar Street Theatre (✉ 3133 N. Halsted St., Lake View, ☎ 773/348–4000 or 800/258–3626), a modest space in Lake View, transformed itself into the home of the long-running, dynamic, must-see Blue Man Group.

Cadillac Palace Theatre (✉ 151 W. Randolph St., Loop, ☎ 312/977–1700) is one of the downtown vintage theaters that was reborn after a lavish restoration. The ornate stage is home for touring musicals and other performances.

Chicago Theatre (✉ 175 N. State St., Loop, ☎ 312/443–1130), a restored former movie palace and vaudeville house with a marquee visible along State Street, hosts musicals, rock and pop concerts, and special events.

Drury Lane Theatre (✉ 100 Drury La., Oakbrook Terrace, ☎ 630/530–0111 or 630/530–8300) caters mostly to suburbanites with its dinner-theater format. Musicals and other Broadway imports are usually well produced.

The **Ford Center for the Performing Arts, Oriental Theatre** (✉ 24 W. Randolph St., Loop, ☎ 312/782–2004 or 312/902–1400), an ornate former movie palace built in 1926 with fantastic architectural hints of the Far East, has been wonderfully restored. It now stages musical theater.

Royal George Theatre Center (✉ 1641 N. Halsted St., Lincoln Park, ☎ 312/988–9000) has four theater spaces—including a large main stage with good sight lines—for musicals, plays, and improvisational comedy.

Shubert Theatre (✉ 22 W. Monroe St., Loop, ☎ 312/902–1400 or 312/977–1700), built in 1906, is a grand building in the Loop. It brings in Broadway productions and musicals such as *Chicago, Rent,* and *Stomp.*

Storefront Theater (✉ 66 E. Randolph St., Gallery 37 Center for the Arts, Loop, ☎ 312/742–8497) is a 99-seat black-box space designed to bring some of Chicago's smaller off-Loop theatrical offerings downtown.

Theatre Building (✉ 1225 W. Belmont Ave., Lake View, ☎ 773/327–5252), a rehabbed warehouse, provides three stages for small and midsize groups with varying, adventuresome fare.

Theatre on the Lake (✉ 2400 N. Lake Shore Dr., Lincoln Park, ☎ 312/742–7994) offers a two-for-one Chicago experience: watching some of the city's most innovative theater and beginning and ending the evening with an unbeatable location on Lake Michigan. Plays—held June through August—are usually reprisals of some of the season's best theatrical offerings.

Performing Groups

Chicago's reputation as a theatrical powerhouse was born from its small, not-for-profit theater companies that produce everything from Shakespeare to Sondheim. The groups listed do consistently interesting work, and a few have gained national attention. Some, such as Steppenwolf and Lookingglass, are ensemble troupes; others, notably the Goodman, the Court, and Victory Gardens, are production companies that use different casts for each show. Be open-minded when you're choosing a show; even a group you've never heard of may be harboring one or two underpaid geniuses. *The Reader* carries complete theater listings and reviews of the more avant-garde shows.

About Face Theatre (☎ 773/549–3290) is the city's best-known gay and lesbian performing group, which in its short history has garnered awards for original works, world premieres, and adaptations presented in larger theaters like the Steppenwolf and the Goodman.

Bailiwick Arts Center (✉ 1229 W. Belmont Ave., Lake View, ☎ 773/883–1090) stages new and classical material. Its Pride Performance series, held every summer, focuses on plays by gays and lesbians.

Chicago Shakespeare Theater (✉ 800 E. Grand Ave., Near North, ☎ 312/595–5600) devotes its considerable talents to keeping the Bard's flame alive in the Chicago area, with three plays a year. At this courtyard-style 525-seat theater on Navy Pier, no seat is farther than 28 ft from the thrust stage, and there are sparkling city views to appreciate during intermission.

Court Theatre (✉ 5535 S. Ellis Ave., Hyde Park, ☎ 773/753–4472), on the University of Chicago campus, revives classic plays, often presenting two plays in rotating repertory.

ETA Creative Arts Foundation (✉ 7558 S. South Chicago Ave., Grand Crossing, ☎ 773/752–3955), a South Side performing arts center, has established a strong presence for African-American theater, with six plays each year. It also hosts black cultural presentations.

Goodman Theatre (✉ 170 N. Dearborn St., Loop, ☎ 312/443–3800), one of the oldest and best theaters in Chicago, is known for its polished performances of classic and contemporary works starring well-known actors. In 2001, it christened a new complex in the heart of the Loop theater district with two stages—including a studio for new works and one-act plays—and a retail-restaurant arcade.

Lookingglass Theatre Company (✉ Ruth Page Theater, 1016 N. Dearborn St., Near North, ☎ 773/477–9257) creates a unique, acrobatic style of performance utilizing theater, dance, music, and circus arts. This ensemble, co-founded by David Schwimmer of *Friends* fame, produces physically—and artistically—daring works. Plans call for the company to move to a new theater in the Chicago Water Works building on Michigan Avenue in mid-2003.

Neo-Futurists (✉ 5153 N. Ashland Ave., Uptown, ☎ 773/275–5255) perform their long-running, late-night hit *Too Much Light Makes the Baby Go Blind* in a space above a funeral home. The piece is a series of 30 ever-changing plays performed in 60 minutes; the order of the plays is chosen by the audience. In keeping with the spirit of randomness, the admission price is set by the roll of a die, plus $5.

Performing Arts Chicago (☎ 312/663–1628), a leading presenter of new directions in theater, music, and dance, showcases daring pieces from some of the world's most innovative performing artists, such as composer Philip Glass, chanteuse Ute Lemper, and choreographer Bill T. Jones. Performances are held in various venues.

Redmoon Theater (☎ 773/388–9031) tells imaginative, seasonal stories with the magically creative use of puppets, sets, and live actors. The company's Halloween celebration and its Winter Pageant in December have become Chicago traditions for those seeking respite from the commercialism of the holidays. Performances are held everywhere, from grassroots neighborhood events to the Steppenwolf Theatre.

Roadworks Productions (☎ 312/492–7150) attracts a young crowd with its adventurous plays, often performing Midwest premieres by emerging playwrights overlooked by more traditional theatre companies.

Steppenwolf (✉ 1650 N. Halsted St., Lincoln Park, ☎ 312/335–1650), with a commitment to ensemble collaboration and artistic risk, has won national acclaim for its cutting-edge acting style and its consistently successful productions. Illustrious alumni include John Malkovich, Gary Sinise, Joan Allen, and Laurie Metcalf.

Victory Gardens Theater (✉ 2257 N. Lincoln Ave., Lincoln Park, ☎ 773/871–3000), winner of the 2001 Regional Tony Award, is known for its workshops and Chicago premieres. The theater sponsors works mainly by local playwrights on four stages.

6 OUTDOOR ACTIVITIES AND SPORTS

Many of Chicago's outdoor pleasures
are linked to the Lake Michigan shoreline,
which hugs the east side of the city. In warm
weather miles of beaches and paths beckon
joggers, bikers, swimmers, sailors, and
anyone who welcomes awesome city views
along with exercise. Spectators can join
Chicago's passionate fans for the classic
experience of cheering the Cubs at
Wrigley Field, the Sox at Comiskey,
the Bears at Soldier Field, or the Bulls
at the United Center.

Updated by
Robin Kurzer

CHICAGOANS HAVE ONE CLEAR MOTTO: It doesn't matter if you win or lose, it's how much of a fan you are. No matter what happens on the field, on the court, or on the ice, Chicago sports fans are just happy for the chance to do what they do best: make themselves heard. They'll cry, scream, laugh, argue, and celebrate, sometimes all within the same 10 seconds. It's this passion that put Chicago in the spotlight in the 1980s through a *Saturday Night Live* skit parodying super fans who lived for "da" Bulls, "da" Bears, and coach Mike Ditka, and again in the '90s through a man known simply as "Air." It's this same passion that motivated former Chicago White Sox owner Bill Veeck to invent so many of the promotions still used in modern baseball, and that helped reinvigorate the sport through the indomitable bat of Sammy Sosa. It's this same passion, this pure spirit, that makes going to any Chicago sports event memorable, no matter which team wins.

In this town sports enthusiasts are often athletes, too, particularly if they like to play at the beach. Lake Michigan creates a summer haven for joggers, volleyball enthusiasts, swimmers, windsurfers, and sailors. To enjoy the outdoors, visit from May through October, but keep in mind the summertime humidity.

BEACHES

Chicago has about 20 mi of lakefront, most of it sand or rock beach. Beaches are open to the public daily from 9 AM to 9:30 PM, Memorial Day–Labor Day, and many beaches have changing facilities. The **Chicago Park District** (☎ 312/747–2200, WEB www.chicagoparkdistrict. com) provides lifeguard protection during daylight hours throughout the swimming season. The beaches' water is too cold for swimming at other times of the year.

Along the lakefront you'll see plenty of broken-rock breakwaters with signs that warn NO SWIMMING OR DIVING. Although natives frequently ignore these signs, you should heed them. The boulders below the water are slippery with seaweed and may hide sharp, rusty scraps of metal, and the water beyond is very deep. It can be dangerous even if you know the territory.

All references to North and South in beach listings refer to how far north or south of the Loop each beach is. In other words, 1600–2400 North means the beach begins 16 blocks north of the Loop (at Madison Street, which is the 100 block) and extends for eight blocks.

North Avenue Beach (✉ 1600–2400 North, Lincoln Park) attracts many athletes. There are bathrooms, changing facilities, and showers. The south end of this beach has plenty of lively volleyball action in summer and fall.

Oak Street Beach (✉ 600–1600 North, Near North) probably rates as Chicago's most popular, particularly in the 1000 North block, where the shoreline curves. You can expect it to be mobbed with trendy singles and people-watchers on any warm day in summer. There are bathrooms, but for official changing facilities you'll have to make the walk to the North Avenue Beach bathhouse, which is at 1600 North. The concrete breakwater that makes up the southern part of Oak Street Beach is a busy promenade on hot summer nights. You can walk along the water all the way to Grand Avenue (about ¾ mi from Oak Street), where you'll find both Navy Pier and Olive Park.

South Shore Country Club Beach (✉ 7100 South, Hyde Park) stands out for being quite pretty and not overcrowded. There are bathrooms, changing facilities, and showers. Enter through the South Shore Country Club grounds at 71st Street and South Shore Drive. You may see the police training their horses in the entry area.

The best of the other Chicago beaches (all of which have changing facilities) on Lake Shore Drive include the following:

Foster Beach (✉ 5200 North, Edgewater), one of the few Chicago beaches with free parking, serves as the starting point for many beachfront races throughout the season.

Jackson Beach Central (✉ 5700–5900 South, Hyde Park) is adjacent to Jackson Park, which was built for the World's Columbian Exposition in 1893. The interactive spray fountain is a big hit today.

Leone/Loyola Beach (✉ 6700–7800 North, Rogers Park) is a popular dog park for your canine friends. A modern playground next to the beach will provide variety for your child's beach day.

Montrose Beach (✉ 4400 North, Uptown) draws anglers to its fishing pier. Sports lovers will also appreciate the abundance of tennis courts and baseball diamonds, as well as plenty of grass for frisbee.

Osterman Beach (✉ 5800 North, Edgewater) is a quiet treasure that provides solace from busier beaches. The beach concession is augmented by its popularity among ice cream vendors.

31st Street Beach (✉ 3100 South, Douglas) was recently renovated, which has reinvigorated its popularity. A newly built skate park has plenty of surface for even the most daring skaters.

12th Street Beach (✉ 1200 South at 900 East, south of Adler Planetarium, Near South Side) is a nice place to relax after a long day of museum hopping. A cup of joe from The Windy City Coffee Stand won't hurt either.

PARTICIPANT SPORTS AND FITNESS

Bicycling

There are many scenic routes along the lake, downtown, and in greater Chicago. Chicago's **lakefront bicycle path** extends about 20 mi, with fabulous views of the lake and the skyline. The panorama of the harbor, created with landfill a number of years ago when Lake Shore Drive's notorious S-curve between Monroe Street and Wacker Drive was straightened, is lovely. Note that a few blocks to the north, at Grand Avenue, is one of a few places along the route where the path crosses a city street (two others are parallel to Lake Shore Drive in the downtown area). Also keep in mind that the path can get very crowded during typical rush hours and weekends, particularly in the summer, and it's shared by in-line skaters and walkers.

The **Chicago Park District** (☎ 312/747–2200, WEB www.chicagoparkdistrict. com) is a good source for maps. For information on biking in the city, contact the **Chicagoland Bicycle Federation** (✉ 650 S. Clark St., #300, Near South Side, ☎ 312/427–3325, WEB www.chibikefed.org).

You can rent a bike for the day or by the hour from **On the Route** (✉ 3146 N. Lincoln Ave., Lake View, ☎ 773/477–5066), which stocks a large inventory of bicycles, including children's bikes. They also supply helmets and other safety equipment.

Bike Chicago (✉ 600 E. Grand Ave., Near North, ☎ 312/755–0488 or 800/915–2453, WEB www.bikechicago.com/home.asp) will deliver a bike to your hotel and pick it up after your ride. Fees start at $7.75 per hour and $30 a day. It also runs a free, two-hour, lakefront tour daily, weather permitting.

Boating

The lakefront harbors are packed with boats, but if you're not familiar with Great Lakes sailing, it's best to leave the navigating to an experienced skipper. Sailboat lessons and rentals are available from the **Chicago Sailing Club** (⊠ Belmont Harbor, Lake View, ☎ 773/871–7245, WEB www.chicagosailingclub.com). The Chicago Sailing Club focuses on sailing instruction for all levels and includes a program on keeping your boat in tip-top shape. **Sailboats Inc.** (⊠ Monroe Harbor, Loop, ☎ 312/861–1757; 800/826–7010 for reservations; WEB www.sailboats-inc.com), one of the oldest charter certification schools in the country, prepares its students to charter any type of boat.

For a more placid water outing, try the paddleboats at **Lincoln Park Lagoon** (⊠ 2021 N. Stockton Dr., Lincoln Park, ☎ 312/742–2038), just north of Farm in the Zoo.

Bowling

What's the Midwest without bowling? Rock out to live music while you roll in the 36 lanes at **Diversey River Bowl**'s Rock n' Bowl (⊠ 2211 W. Diversey Pkwy., Bucktown, ☎ 773/227–5800, WEB www.drbowl.com). Light up the eight lanes at the superhip **Lucky Strike** (⊠ 2747 N. Lincoln Ave., Lincoln Park, ☎ 773/549–2695) in fashionable Lincoln Park. Check out the newly remodeled **Waveland Bowl** (⊠ 3700 N. Western Ave., Roscoe Village, ☎ 773/472–5902, WEB www.wavelandbowl.com) for 24-hour bowling with 40 lanes.

Fishing

Plenty of folks stand ready to charter boats if you're interested in fishing for coho or chinook salmon, trout, or perch. The **Chicago Sportfishing Association** (⊠ Burnham Harbor, Loop, ☎ 312/922–1100) rents boats and supplies information on sportfishing.

If you want to skip the boat and do your fishing from the shore, **Henry's Sport and Bait,** near Burnham Harbor and McCormick Place (⊠ 3130 S. Canal, Loop, ☎ 312/225–8538) will set you up with a rod and reel and tell you where they're bitin'. At **Park Bait** (⊠ Montrose Harbor, Uptown, ☎ 312/271–2838), you can rent rods and reels as well as getting inside information on where the fish are biting.

Golf

The **Chicago Park District** (☎ 312/245–0909, WEB www.chicagoparkdistrict.com) maintains six golf courses—five with 9 holes and one (Jackson Park) with 18—as well as two driving ranges, one in Jackson Park and one at Lake Shore Drive and Diversey Avenue (which has heated stalls and an 18-hole miniature golf course). The Jackson Park facility is a couple of blocks east of Stony Island Avenue at 63rd Street. Nonresident fees are $20 for weekdays, $22 on weekends.

Chicago Family Golf Centers (⊠ 221 N. Columbus Dr., Loop, ☎ 312/616–1234), in the heart of the business and hotel district, is a 9-hole, par-3 course with lots of angled greens. The course, open year-round, costs $15 for nine holes. For 18 holes, it's $22.

Suburban Chicago has more than 125 public golf courses, with greens fees ranging from $10 to nearly $100. Most accept reservations up to a week in advance. Some require a credit card deposit. The following are a few of the more highly rated courses:

Cantigny (⊠ 27 W. 270 Mack Rd., Wheaton, ☎ 630/668–8463) has mature trees on each of the 27 holes. **Cog Hill Golf and Country Club** (⊠ 12294 Archer Ave., Lemont, ☎ 630/257–5872), with four 18-hole courses, hosts the PGA tour's Western Open in early July. **Kemper Lakes** (⊠ Old McHenry Rd., Long Grove, ☎ 847/320–3450) is one of the region's most expensive courses ($115 with mandatory cart rental included) and is the only local public course to have hosted a major PGA championship. It has one course of 18 holes. **Village Links of Glen Ellyn** (⊠ 485 Winchell Way, Glen Ellyn, ☎ 630/469–8180) has 27 holes and a driving range.

Health Clubs

Some Chicago health clubs have agreements with hotels that give guests access to their facilities. Check with your hotel. The **Chicago Fitness Center** (⊠ 3131 N. Lincoln Ave., Lincoln Park, ☎ 773/549–8181) has free and fixed weights, aerobic equipment, and classes for $10 a day. A picture ID is required. **Hoops the Gym** (⊠ 1380 Randolph St., Near West Side, ☎ 312/850–4667) has open basketball from 11:30 AM to 1:30 PM every Monday, Wednesday, and Friday for a $15 fee. One of Chicago's plushest and most well-maintained clubs is the **Lakeshore Athletic Club** (⊠ 211 N. Stetson Ave., Loop, ☎ 312/616–9000; ⊠ 441 N. Wabash Ave., Loop, ☎ 312/644–4880). At the North Stetson Avenue branch, which is close to the Fairmont Hotel, you can use an eight-lane lap pool, a full-court gym, an indoor running track, weight training, and a seven-story indoor rock-climbing wall for a $20 daily rate. At the North Wabash Avenue location, area hotel guests pay a daily rate of $18 (not including court time) to use a quarter-mile track, free and fixed weights, aerobic equipment, and a swimming pool. At the **World Gym and Fitness Center** (⊠ 100 S. Wacker Dr., Loop, ☎ 312/357–9753; ⊠ Downtown, 909 W. Montrose Ave., Uptown, ☎ 773/348–1212), you can work out to your heart's content for $12 a day.

Ice-Skating

In winter you can ice-skate at the **Daley Bicentennial Plaza** (⊠ 337 E. Randolph St., Loop, ☎ 312/742–7648), which has great views of the lake and the Loop. A small fee is charged ($2), and skate rentals for $3 are available. The rink at **Millennium Park** (⊠ 55 N. Michigan Ave., Loop, ☎ 312/742–5222) has free skating seven days a week. Skate rentals are $3 a session.

In-Line Skating

In-line skating is a popular lakefront pastime. If you're skating the lakefront path, keep to the right and watch your back for bicyclists. Skating is also allowed on Daley Bicentennial Plaza. Wrist guards, helmets, and knee pads are a good idea wherever you skate. You can rent blades from **Bike Chicago** (☞ Bicycling). **Londo Mondo** (⊠ 1100 N. Dearborn St., Near North, ☎ 312/751–2794, WEB www.londomondo.com) rents skates and sells accessories and provides services. **Windward Sports** (⊠ 3317 N. Clark St., Lake View, ☎ 773/472–6868) sells equipment for sports ranging from in-line skating to windsurfing.

Jogging

The 18-mi lakefront path accommodates joggers, bicyclists, and skaters, so you'll need to be attentive while you admire the views. You can pick up the path at Oak Street Beach (across from the Drake Hotel), at Grand Avenue underneath Lake Shore Drive, or by going through Grant Park on Monroe Street or Jackson Boulevard until you reach the lakefront.

On the lakefront path joggers should stay north of McCormick Place. Muggers sometimes lurk in the comparatively empty stretch between the convention center and Hyde Park. Loop streets are a little spooky after dark and too crowded during the day for useful running. In the Near North joggers will want to stay east of Orleans Street. And in case of unfavorable outdoor conditions, all of the health clubs listed above have indoor jogging tracks.

Various groups hold organized races. Call the **Chicago-Area Runners Association** (☎ 312/666–9836, WEB www.cararuns.org) for schedules.

Kayaking

At **Wateriders Adventure Agents** (☎ 312/953–9287, WEB www.wateriders. com) you can learn about the city while working on your kayaking skills. An architecture tour and a tour of some of the spookier Chicago spots are available for groups. The cost is $45 per person and $40 each for groups of 4 or more.

Swimming

Lake Michigan provides wonderful swimming from Memorial Day through Labor Day, particularly toward the end of the summer when the lake has warmed up. Indoor swimming facilities also are available (☞ Health Clubs).

Tennis

The **Chicago Park District** (☎ 312/747–2200, WEB www.chicagoparkdistrict. com) maintains hundreds of outdoor tennis courts, most of them free. The **Daley Bicentennial Plaza** (✉ 337 E. Randolph St., Loop, ☎ 312/742–7648) is the closest sports facility to downtown and Near North hotels. The 12 lighted tennis courts cost $5 an hour and must be reserved a day in advance, with calls taken anytime after 10 AM.

SPECTATOR SPORTS

Chicago sports fans are nothing if not loyal. Although the days of the legendary Michael Jordan–led Chicago Bulls Dream Team are long over, the beauty of the city's sports teams is always the element of surprise around the corner. After years of mediocre performances, the Chicago Bears thrilled fans in 2001 with a trip to the post-season. Fans still pack Wrigley Field and the United Center, cheering their favorites and having a great time in the process—no matter what the outcome. The rivalry between fans of the Cubs and the city's other baseball team, the White Sox, is prickly to say the least. Tickets for an individual game can be hard to get, especially when a team is doing well, so buy them as far in advance as possible.

Auto Racing

Sportsman's Park–Chicago Motor Speedway (✉ 3301 S. Laramie Ave., Cicero, ☎ 708/652–2812, WEB www.sportsmanspark.com), a dual-purpose 15,000-seat horse track and 67,000-seat auto track, hosts major races throughout the year.

Baseball

The **Chicago Cubs** (National League) play at **Wrigley Field** (✉ 1060 W. Addison St., Lake View, ☎ 773/404–2827; 312/831–2827 for tickets; WEB www.cubs.com). The baseball season begins the last week in March and ends the first weekend in October. From downtown the "friendly confines" are easily reached via the Red (Howard–Dan Ryan) subway and elevated line. Take the train toward Howard to Addison Street. Wrigley Field has had lights since 1988, when it became the last major-league ballpark in the nation to be lighted for night games. But the Cubs still play most of their home games during the day, and the bleachers are a great place to listen to Chicagoans taunt the visiting outfielders. (These "bleacher bums" are notoriously vocal.) The grandstand is more sedate but still has plenty of local flavor. Most games start at 1:20 PM, but phone for exact starting times.

The **Chicago White Sox** (American League) play from April through October at **Comiskey Park** (✉ 333 W. 35th St., Douglas, ☎ 312/674–1000, WEB www.chisox.com), a high-tech stadium with a local flavor all its own. Games usually start at 7 PM. Take the A or B Dan Ryan El to 35th Street.

The Cubs and the White Sox play two three-game series against each other in summer, one series in each ballpark. These games always sell out, so buy tickets well in advance.

Basketball

The **Chicago Bulls** play at the **United Center** (✉ 1901 W. Madison St., Near West Side, ☎ 312/455–4000, WEB www.bulls.com). Don't forget to check out the statue of Michael Jordan in front of the arena. The National Basketball Association regular season extends from November through April, and games usually start at 7:30 PM. Avoid leaving the game early or wandering around this neighborhood at night.

Football

The **Chicago Bears** play at **Soldier Field** (✉ 425 E. McFetridge Dr., Near South Side, ☎ 847/295–6600, WEB www.chicagobears.com) from August (preseason) through December. Although subscription sales generally account for all tickets, you can purchase single-game seats from local ticket brokers listed in the phone book. At press time, Soldier Field was under renovation to reorient its 67,000 seats for improved sight lines. If the project goes as planned, the Bears will resume playing there in midseason 2003. Call or check the Web site for the latest information regarding the renovation and the interim field.

The **Northwestern Wildcats** play on Saturday afternoons in the fall, under coach Randy Walker. Games are at **Ryan Field** (✉ 1501 Central St., Evanston, ☎ 847/491–2287, WEB www.nusports.com), and tickets are almost always available.

Hockey

The **Chicago Blackhawks** of the National Hockey League play games before their exuberant fans at the **United Center** (✉ 1901 W. Madison St., Near West Side, ☎ 312/455–7000, WEB www.chicagoblackhawks.com) from October through April. Games usually start at 7:30 PM. It's best not to leave the game early or to wander around the neighborhood at night.

The **Chicago Wolves** of the International Hockey League are a high-quality and more affordable alternative to the Blackhawks. The Wolves play at the **Allstate Arena** (✉ 10550 Lunt Ave., Rosemont, ☎ 847/390–0404, WEB www.chicagowolves.com), with most games starting at 7 PM. The season runs from October through April.

Horse Racing

Balmoral Park (✉ 26435 S. Dixie Hwy., Crete, ☎ 708/672–7544). **Hawthorne Race Course** (✉ 3501 S. Laramie Ave., Stickney, ☎ 708/780–3700). **Maywood Park** (✉ 8600 W. North Ave., Maywood, ☎ 708/343–4800). **Sportsman's Park** (✉ 3301 S. Laramie Ave., Cicero, ☎ 708/652–2812).

Soccer

The **Chicago Fire,** the city's professional soccer team, plays the world's most popular sport March–September at **Soldier Field** (✉ 425 E. McFetridge Dr., Near South Side, ☎ 888/657–3473, WEB www.chicago-fire.com).

7   SHOPPING

From grand old Marshall Field's on
State Street to glittering stores along the
Magnificent Mile, the Second City delivers
plenty of first-class shopping. Look for
discount jewelry and watches in the Loop,
designer boutiques on Oak Street, and
funky antiques on Lincoln Avenue. Character
still counts in Chicago, too, and all around
town are specialty shops offering personal
service and goods that convey the city's
uniqueness—whether you're looking
for Frank Lloyd Wright reproductions or
blues recordings.

A **POTENT CONCENTRATION** of famous retailers around Michigan Avenue and neighborhoods bursting with unique shops combine to make Chicago a shopper's city. The unique experience on Michigan Avenue lures thousands of avid shoppers every week. How often can you find Neiman Marcus, Marshall Field's, Nordstrom, Saks Fifth Avenue, Lord & Taylor, and Barneys New York within walking distance of each other? Those averse to paying retail, however, won't have to venture far to unearth bargains on everything from fine jewelry to business attire. The city also has singular stores renowned for various specialties, whether Prairie-style furniture, cowboy boots, or outsider art.

Updated by
Judy Sutton
Taylor

The following pages will help you plan your shopping. The first section, Blitz Tours, provides suggested itineraries for special interest shopping—from antiques to art to touring the Magnificent Mile. The rest of the chapter is organized into major shopping districts, with shops of note listed by category. If you have no concrete goals, simply choose a major shopping district and browse to your heart's content. Three maps accompany this chapter: Downtown Shopping, Near North and River North Shopping, and Lincoln Park Shopping.

Be forewarned that an 8.75% state and county sales tax is added to all purchases except groceries and prescription drugs. Neighborhood shops on the North Side (including Bucktown), especially those catering to a young crowd, tend to open late—around 11 or noon. Most stores, particularly those on North Michigan Avenue and the North Side, are open on Sunday, although this varies by type of business; where applicable, more information is provided at the beginning of each area or category.

Blitz Tours

For more detailed information and phone numbers of any of the shops included in these tours, check the individual shop listings under the relevant shopping district later in the chapter.

Antiques

Chicago tempts furniture buyers with antiques, collectibles, and architectural artifacts at prices that generally beat those on either coast. In fact, dealers from both coasts regularly troll these shops, which are clustered mostly in neighborhoods or malls, for stock to resell in their own shops. For a rundown on dealers, buy a copy of *Taylor's Guide to Antique Shops in Illinois and Southern Wisconsin* ($5.50), which is available in some bookstores and many antiques shops (to order, call ☎ 847/465–3314). Many antiques districts also publish free pamphlets that list dealers in the neighborhood; look for them in the shops. To catch the maximum number of open dealers, it's best to tackle this route after brunch on a weekend or on a Thursday or Friday.

Assuming your interest runs more toward 20th-century collectibles than Biedermeier, take the 11 Lincoln Avenue bus or a taxi to the **Chicago Antique Centre** (✉ 3036 N. Lincoln Ave., Lake View) to browse through the wares of its 35 dealers. Across the street from Chicago Antique Centre is **Red Eye Antiques** (✉ 3050 N. Lincoln Ave., Lake View), which is crammed to the gills with an eclectic selection of prime furnishings, textiles, and artifacts from different eras that you won't find elsewhere in the area. From Red Eye Antiques, it's a short walk to the **Lincoln Antique Mall** (✉ 3141 N. Lincoln Ave., Lake View), which stockpiles everything from kitchenware to furniture, mostly post-1920. There's also a huge selection of estate jewelry, sterling, oil paintings and photographs. Keep your eyes open for other antiques and vintage clothing shops along this stretch of Lincoln Avenue. Two superb sources for adventurous, mid-20th-century, modern furnishings and collectibles are **Urban Artifacts** (⊠ 2928 N. Lincoln Ave., Lake View) and **Zig Zag** (⊠ 3419 N. Lincoln Ave., Lake View). Venture north on Ashland Avenue to check out the 19th and 20th-century furnishings at **Daniels Antiques** (⊠ 3711 N. Ashland Ave., Lake View).

Next, take a taxi over to the Belmont Avenue antiques area. **Antique Resources** (⊠ 1741 W. Belmont Ave., Lake View) is worth a look for choice Georgian antiques at equally choice prices. **Danger City** (⊠ 2120 W. Belmont Ave., Lake View) is filled with great barware and other reminders of swank living from the 1950s, '60s, and '70s.

After exploring this district, there are four other compelling destinations for collectors that are short cab rides away. **Gene Douglas Decorative Arts & Antiques** (⊠ 4621½ N. Lincoln Ave., Lincoln Square) has a superb selection of late 19th- to mid-20th-century furniture. Due east of Gene Douglas is **Architectural Artifacts** (⊠ 4325 N. Ravenswood Ave., North Center), an amazing repository for statuary, garden ornaments, and the like. **Evanstonia Furniture & Restoration** (⊠ 4555 N. Ravenswood Ave., North Center) carries English and Continental furnishings. Farthest north on the antiques trail is the **Broadway Antique Market** (⊠ 6130 N. Broadway, Edgewater), where you'll find an excellent stash of mid-20th-century pieces that range from art deco and Arts and Crafts to modernism and beyond. From there, it's two blocks to the Granville El stop to get a train downtown.

Art

The contemporary art scene is thriving in Chicago, particularly in the River North area. More than 60 galleries are clustered within a one-block radius of the intersection of Superior and Franklin streets; most are open Tuesday through Saturday. A few renowned galleries are on Michigan Avenue, some above street level. Emerging artists call Wicker Park and Bucktown home; gallery hours there tend to fluctuate. For more information on exhibits and specific dealers, pick up a free copy of *Chicago Gallery News*, available at visitor information centers and galleries. Most openings are scheduled on Friday evening and don't require an invitation. The first Friday after Labor Day is the biggest night of the year, marking the opening of the season.

To get an overview of the city's vibrant art scene, start with the classics on Michigan Avenue. **R. S. Johnson Fine Art** (⊠ 645 N. Michigan Ave., Near North) carries both old masters and 20th-century works worthy of many museums. The **Richard Gray Gallery** (⊠ John Hancock Center, 875 N. Michigan Ave., Near North) displays works by modern masters. Stop at **R. H. Love Galleries** (⊠ 40 E. Erie St., Near North) for American art from the colonial period to the early 20th century.

From there, take a taxi to the intersection of Superior and Franklin streets in River North; dozens of galleries stud the neighboring blocks. **Douglas Dawson** (⊠ 222 W. Huron St., River North) always has an alluring display of art and artifacts from the Americas, Asia, and Africa. Gaze at the glass on display in **Portia Gallery** (⊠ 207 W. Superior St., River North). The **Catherine Edelman Gallery** (⊠ 300 W. Superior St., River North) is devoted to works of living photographers. For a fascinating look at extraordinary works by outsider, self-taught, folk, and visionary artists, stop by the **Carl Hammer Gallery** (⊠ 740 N. Wells St., River North) and the **Ann Nathan Gallery** (⊠ 218 W. Superior St., River North). Several galleries include Chicago artists in their exhibition programs, such as **Lyons-Wier Packer** (⊠ 300 W. Superior

St., River North) and the **Byron Roche Gallery** (✉ 750 N. Franklin St., River North). If you're a collector of art glass, European art pottery, or antique jewelry, stop by **Fly-by-Nite Gallery** (✉ 714 N. Wells St., River North) to admire early 20th-century work.

The Magnificent Mile

A visit to Chicago wouldn't be complete without a tour of the world-class stores on North Michigan Avenue; several rate as must-see attractions, either for their design, merchandise, or sheer fun. Start on the east side of the avenue at the Chicago River and continue up to Oak Street. The don't-miss stops include the four-story **Shops at North Bridge,** a mall with a 270,000-square-ft **Nordstrom** (520 N.); **Virgin Megastore** (540 N.); **Burberry** (633 N.); **NikeTown** (669 N.); **Tiffany** (730 N.); **Neiman Marcus** (737 N.); **Water Tower Place** (835 N.); **FAO Schwarz** (840 N.); **Gucci** (900 N.); and **Georg Jensen** (959 N.). Turn left on Oak Street, where you'll want to check out the shoes at **Donald J. Pliner** (106 E.), the designer clothing at **Ultimo** (114 E.), the home accoutrements and fashion accessories at **Elements** (102 E.), the handbags, shoes, and men's furnishings at **Kate Spade** (101 E.), the menswear at **Sulka** (55 E.), the minimalist styles at **Jil Sander** (48 E.), and the über-chic fashion and home accessories at **Barneys New York** (25 E.). Take a left on Rush Street to absorb street style at **Urban Outfitters** (935 N.) and **Diesel** (923 N.), and another left on Walton Street to pick up some slick French basics at **agnès b.** (46 E.). Continue down Walton Street to pop into kitchenware utopia **Sur La Table** (50–54 E.) and home furnishings stores such as **Ligne Roset** (56 E.) and **The Morson Collection** (100 E.). Just before reaching Michigan Avenue, you can duck into **Bloomingdale's** and the other stores inside the **900 N. Michigan Shops.**

The Loop

This area—named for the elevated train track that encircles it—is the heart of Chicago's business and financial district. Two of the city's major department stores, Marshall Field's and Carson Pirie Scott, anchor **State Street,** which is striving to regain the stature it had when it was immortalized as "State Street, that great street." LaSalle Street, with its proximity to the Board of Trade, has several fine men's clothiers. The blocks surrounding the intersection of Wabash Avenue and Madison Street are designated as Jewelers Row; five high-rises cater to the wholesale trade, but many showrooms sell to the public at prices 25%–50% below retail. Not all Loop stores maintain street-level visibility: several gems are tucked away on upper floors of office buildings.

Department stores and major chains are generally open on Sunday. Smaller stores are likely to be closed on Sunday and keep limited Saturday hours. Loop workers tend to start their day early, so many stores keep pace by opening by 8:30 and closing at 5 or 6.

Books

Afrocentric Bookstore (✉ Chicago Music Mart at DePaul Centre, 333 S. State St., Loop, ☎ 312/939–1956) carries a full range of books—from novels to religious titles—with an African-American orientation. The store regularly hosts prominent authors for signings.

Brent Books (✉ 309 W. Washington St., Loop, ☎ 312/364–0126) sells best-sellers at a 30% discount and provides personalized, informed service. The store is inviting for those who want to browse before buying.

Powell's Bookstore (✉ 828 S. Wabash Ave., Loop, ☎ 312/341–0748; ✉ 2850 N. Lincoln Ave., Lake View, ☎ 773/248–1444; ✉ 1501 E. 57th St., Hyde Park, ☎ 773/955–7780) focuses on used books and

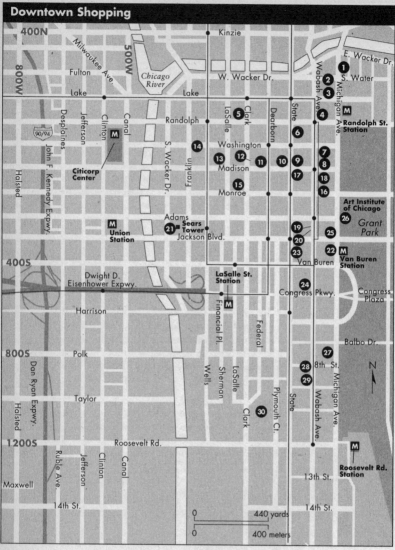

Downtown Shopping

remainders with an intellectual bent. Marxism, the occult, and philosophy all have their own sections.

Prairie Avenue Bookshop (✉ 418 S. Wabash Ave., Loop, ☎ 312/922–8311) draws architecture buffs for its nearly 7,000 new, rare, and out-of-print titles on architecture, interior design, and urban planning. Massive tables in the Prairie-style interior give browsers room to spread out.

Savvy Traveller (✉ 310 S. Michigan Ave., Loop, ☎ 312/913–9800) offers an impressive selection of travel books, maps, luggage, and videos, along with gadgets to improve the quality of life on the road.

Cameras and Electronic Equipment

Central Camera (✉ 230 S. Wabash Ave., Loop, ☎ 312/427–5580) is stacked to the rafters with cameras and darkroom equipment at competitive prices. The century-old store is a Loop institution.

Clothing

MEN'S

Syd Jerome (✉ 2 N. LaSalle St., Loop, ☎ 312/346–0333) caters to Board of Trade types who prefer European lines such as Ermenegildo Zegna and Giorgio Armani. Oxxford, an elegant local label, can be custom ordered here.

MEN'S AND WOMEN'S

Barbara Bates Design (✉ 900 S. Wabash Ave., Loop, ☎ 312/427–0284) is best known for elegant, detailed suits, occasion clothes, and leathers, not to mention bold embellishments and trims.

Department Stores

Carson Pirie Scott (✉ 1 S. State St., Loop, ☎ 312/641–7000), a long-time Chicago emporium with an emphasis on moderately priced goods, carries clothing, housewares, accessories, and cosmetics. It's also a good place to pick up Chicago souvenirs. The building, designed by famed Chicago architect Louis Sullivan, is worth visiting just to see the iron scrollwork on the northwest door, at the corner of State and Madison streets.

Filene's Basement (✉ 1 N. State St., Loop, ☎ 312/553–1055; ✉ 830 N. Michigan Ave., Near North, ☎ 312/482–8918) can pay off for patient shoppers willing to flip through racks of discounted clothing for a great find or two. The State Street branch probably has the best merchandise outside the Boston original. Women can do well at either the State Street or Michigan Avenue location, but men will find a superior selection of designer names at State Street. Watch newspaper ads midweek for special shipments and events such as the bridal gown sale.

Marshall Field's (✉ 111 N. State St., Loop, ☎ 312/781–1000; ✉ Water Tower Place, 835 N. Michigan Ave., Near North, ☎ 312/335–7700) in the Loop stands as a glorious reminder of how grand department stores used to be. Founder Marshall Field's motto was "Give the lady what she wants!" and for many years both ladies and gentlemen have been able to find everything from furs to personalized stationery on one of the store's nine levels. The basement level contains a series of small boutiques that sell kitchenware, luggage, books, gourmet food, wine, and Field's famous Frango mints, which many consider to be Chicago's greatest edible souvenirs. Make sure to see the Tiffany Dome—designed in 1907 by Louis Comfort Tiffany—visible from the fifth floor near the women's lingerie section. The glossy Water Tower branch also stocks a fine selection of merchandise but lacks the old-world atmosphere.

Sears (✉ 2 N. State St., Loop, ☎ 312/373–6000) is making a name for itself in downtown Chicago once more with a new, five-level, 250,000-square-ft store that opened in mid-2001. The store is a cornerstone in this slowly revitalizing shopping district.

T. J. Maxx (✉ 11 N. State St., Loop, ☎ 312/553–0515) is a perennially loved discount store selling apparel, shoes, accessories, underwear, gift items, and jewelry.

Discount Jewelry and Watches

Chicago Watch Center (✉ 21 N. Wabash Ave., Loop, ☎ 312/609–0003), a large street-side booth in the Wabash Jewelers Mall, has one of the city's most outstanding inventories of used luxury watches.

Harold Burland & Son (✉ 5 S. Wabash Ave., Loop, ☎ 312/332–5176), a diamond specialist, makes educating shoppers about stones part of the selling process.

M. Y. Finkelman Jewelers (✉ 5 S. Wabash Ave., Loop, ☎ 312/332–3408) carries gems of all kinds in classic settings, along with Italian gold, Breitling watches, Mont Blanc pens, and estate pieces.

Marshall Pierce and Co. (✉ 29 E. Madison St., Loop, ☎ 312/372–2415) substantially discounts top-of-the-line watches, such as Audemars Piguet, Ebel, Movado, and Rado.

New York Jewelers (✉ 11 N. Wabash Ave., Loop, ☎ 312/855–4999) is filled with quality jewelry of every ilk, from pre-owned luxury watches to designer jewelry in platinum and gold, all at great prices.

Gifts

The **Chicago Architecture Foundation** (✉ 224 S. Michigan Ave., Loop, ☎ 312/922–3432) is chock-full of architecture-related books, home accessories, and gifts. There's a smaller branch on North Michigan Avenue. Both locations are in landmark buildings (Daniel Burnham's 1904 Santa Fe Building at 224 S. and Skidmore, Owings & Merrill's 1969 John Hancock Center at 875 N.).

Gallery 37 Store (✉ 66 E. Randolph St., Loop, ☎ 312/744–7274) mounts the work of student artists in the nonprofit Gallery 37 programs, with proceeds pumped back into the organization. Selection varies greatly but may include everything from hand-painted bird baths to small ceramics, all at affordable prices.

Good Design Store (✉ 307 N. Michigan Ave., Loop, ☎ 312/372–1083), the gift shop of the Chicago Athenaeum Museum of Architecture and Design, is a spellbinding, sizable jumble of high-design goods, be they the latest black mesh Walker bags or quirky Alessi kitchenware. There's also a good selection of design books.

Illinois Artisans Shop (✉ James R. Thompson Center, 100 W. Randolph St., Loop, ☎ 312/814–5321) culls the best jewelry, ceramics, glass, and African-American dolls from craftspeople around the state and sells them at very reasonable prices. It's closed on weekends.

Music

Carl Fischer Music (✉ 333 S. State St., lower level, Loop, ☎ 312/427–6652), a venerable institution, carries the largest selection of piano and vocal sheet music in Chicago at its main store on Wabash Avenue.

Chicago Music Mart (✉ 333 S. State St., Loop, ☎ 312/362–6700) contains nearly a dozen stores devoted to all things musical—instruments, CDs, sheet music, and music-theme gifts and souvenirs. Stop by at lunchtime to rest your feet and hear a free concert.

Shoes

Altman's Men's Shoes and Boots (⌧ 120 W. Monroe St., Loop, ☎ 312/
332–0667) is usually packed with men trying on everything from Timberland and Tony Lama boots to Allen-Edmonds and Alden oxfords,
all at a decent discount. Don't be deceived by the store's minuscule size—
the stockrooms hold more than 10,000 pairs of men's shoes in sizes
from 5 to 19 and in widths from AAAA to EEE.

Souvenirs

Accent Chicago (⌧ Chicago Hilton & Towers, 720 S. Michigan Ave.,
Loop, ☎ 312/360–0115; ⌧ Sears Tower, 233 S. Wacker Dr., Loop, ☎
312/922–0242; ⌧ Water Tower Place, 835 N. Michigan Ave., Near
North, ☎ 312/944–1354) offers the requisite souvenirs and Chicago
memorabilia—miniature doodads, snow globes, and the like.

Art Institute of Chicago's Museum Shop (⌧ 111 S. Michigan Ave., Loop,
☎ 312/443–3583) sells museum reproductions in the form of jewelry,
posters, and books, along with striking tabletop accents, decorative accessories, and toys.

Special Stops

Harlan J. Berk (⌧ 31 N. Clark St., Loop, ☎ 312/609–0016) takes you
back to antiquity with its wondrous trove of classical Greek, Roman,
and Byzantine coinage and artifacts. Don't miss the gallery rooms in
the back.

Iwan Ries and Co. (⌧ 19 S. Wabash Ave., 2nd floor, Loop, ☎ 312/
372–1306) did not just jump on the cigar bandwagon; the family-owned
store has been around since 1857. Cigar smokers are welcome to light
up in the smoking area, which also displays antique pipes. Almost 100
brands of cigars are available, as are 10,000 or so pipes, deluxe Elie
Bleu humidors, and all manner of smoking accessories.

Sporting Goods

Nevada Bob's Golf (⌧ 60 E. Lake St., Loop, ☎ 312/726–4653) caters
to golfers of every level with a comprehensive inventory of equipment
and accessories. Road test the goods in the demo cage and putting area.

Michigan Avenue and Vicinity

Chicago's most glamorous shopping district, heralded as the Magnificent Mile, stretches along **Michigan Avenue** from the Chicago River
(400 N.) to Oak Street (1000 N.). Some of the most exclusive names
in retailing line the street, and even such familiar mall stores as Banana Republic (⌧ 744 N.) and the Gap (⌧ 679 N.) make an extra effort at their Mag Mile branches.

The block of **Oak Street** between North Michigan Avenue and Rush
Street is Chicago's answer to Rodeo Drive and Worth Avenue. Here
you'll find a slew of boutiques devoted to expensive clothing as well
as to fine jewelry, luxury linens, and stylish home accessories. A free
map of Chicago's Magnificent Mile area is available at hotels and tourist
information centers.

Accessories

The Coach Store (⌧ 625 N. Michigan Ave., Near North, ☎ 312/587–
3167; ⌧ 900 N. Michigan Ave., Near North, ☎ 312/440–1777; ⌧ 200
S. LaSalle St., Loop, ☎ 312/422–1772) has well-designed leather goods
in the form of purses, briefcases, and cell phone and PDA holders, plus
smart shoes and other accessories. The Loop store is closed Sundays.

Kate Spade (⌧ 101 E. Oak St., Near North, ☎ 312/604–0808), the
goddess of handbags, has filled her two-floor boutique in the heart of

Oak Street with adorable shoes, pajamas, small leather goods, men's accessories from the Jack Spade line, and, of course, her to-die-for purses and totes.

Linda Campisano Millinery (⊠ 900 N. Michigan Ave., Near North, ☎ 312/337–1004) specializes in custom hats for men, women and children, as well as exceptionally detailed bridal headpieces.

Art Galleries

Colletti Gallery (⊠ 67 E. Oak St., Near North, ☎ 312/664–6767) transports you to the late 19th century with fine antique posters, a serious collection of European ceramics and glass, and an eclectic selection of furniture.

R. H. Love Galleries (⊠ 40 E. Erie St., Near North, ☎ 312/640–1300) is installed in the historic Nickerson House, a Victorian mansion right off Michigan Avenue. The setting is perfect for the museum-quality American art that ranges from the colonial period to the early 20th century.

R. S. Johnson Fine Art (⊠ 645 N. Michigan Ave., 2nd floor, entrance on Erie St., Near North, ☎ 312/943–1661) has been on the Mag Mile for 40 years and counts more than 50 museums among its clients. The family-run gallery sells old masters along with art by Pablo Picasso, Edgar Degas, and Goya to private collectors.

Richard Gray Gallery (⊠ John Hancock Center, 875 N. Michigan Ave., Suite 2503, Near North, ☎ 312/642–8877) lures serious collectors for modern masters such as David Hockney and Roy Lichtenstein.

Books

Barnes & Noble (⊠ 1130 N. State St., Near North, ☎ 312/280–8155; ⊠ 659 W. Diversey Pkwy., Lake View, ☎ 773/871–9004; ⊠ 1441 W. Webster Ave., Clybourn Corridor, ☎ 773/871–3610) can ensnare you for a solid hour of magazine-flipping and book-browsing, especially with a Starbucks that practically begs you to linger.

Borders (⊠ 830 N. Michigan Ave., Near North, ☎ 312/573–0564; ⊠ 150 N. State St., Loop, ☎ 312/606–0750; ⊠ 2817 N. Clark St., Lincoln Park, ☎ 773/935–3909), a prominent bookstore on the Mag Mile, sells music, coffee, and snacks as well as discounted best-sellers.

SPECIALTY

Europa Books (⊠ 832 N. State St., Near North, ☎ 312/335–9677) is the place for foreign-language books, newspapers, and magazines. This well-stocked bookstore carries French, Spanish, German, and Italian titles and is known for its selection of Latin-American literature.

Rand McNally Map & Travel Store (⊠ 444 N. Michigan Ave., Near North, ☎ 312/321–1751; ⊠ 150 S. Wacker Dr., Loop, ☎ 312/332–2009) lines up a broad selection of travel books, maps, globes, and travel accessories.

Buttons

Tender Buttons (⊠ 946 Rush St., Near North, ☎ 312/337–7033) sells lots and lots of anything-but-routine buttons. These antique and vintage works of art will up the style quotient of any clothing they grace, and are priced accordingly.

Cameras and Electronic Equipment

Sony Gallery (⊠ 663 N. Michigan Ave., Near North, ☎ 312/943–3334) doesn't offer any deals but does provide plenty of high-tech diversion at this showroom, where you can sample the latest in electronics.

Near North and River North Shopping

Clothing

MEN'S

Ermenegildo Zegna (✉ 645 N. Michigan Ave., Near North, ☎ 312/587–9660) is where you can find the urbane sportswear, softly tailored business attire, and dress clothes of this Italian great, all under one roof.

Rochester Big & Tall (✉ 840 N. Michigan Ave., Near North, ☎ 312/337–8877) is a joy for larger men thanks to its broad spectrum of sizes (up to 58 extra-long) and lines—everything from designer suits to sportswear.

Saks Fifth Avenue Men's Store (✉ 717 N. Michigan Ave., Near North, ☎ 312/944–6500 or 888/643–7257) is spread over 30,000 square ft and three levels, making it the city's leading retailer for menswear. With a swanky look that emulates a 1930s luxury ocean liner and a selection that ranges from conservative to avant-garde, this is one place that has it all.

MEN'S AND WOMEN'S

Brooks Brothers (✉ 713 N. Michigan Ave., Near North, ☎ 312/915–0060), the institution that's been clothing men and women in classic, conservative dress for well over a century, also carries such fashionable items as brightly colored polo shirts.

Burberry (✉ 633 N. Michigan Ave., Near North, ☎ 312/787–2500), the label once favored by the conservatively well-dressed, is hot with young fashionistas these days, who can't get enough of the fresh takes on the label's signature plaid on everything from bikinis to baby gear.

Chasalla (✉ 70 E. Oak St., Near North, ☎ 312/640–1940) isn't for the timid, plying the bold, overtly sexy clothes and accessories of European couture houses such as Dolce & Gabbana, Gianni Versace, and Hugo Boss.

Giorgio Armani (✉ 800 N. Michigan Ave., Near North, ☎ 312/573–4220) displays his discreetly luxurious clothes and accessories in an airy, two-floor space. The store includes Armani's top-priced Black Label line, considered a cut above the department store line.

Gucci (✉ 900 N. Michigan Ave., Near North, ☎ 312/664–5504) stays a step ahead of the fashion pack with its classic clothing, shoes, and accessories. Though the prices aren't for the faint of heart, there are plenty of pieces here that will last a lifetime.

Hana K (✉ 100 E. Walton, Near North, ☎ 312/280–8188) gives new meaning to the term "luxury outerwear" with a broad collection of lightweight but warm raincoats, shearlings, and après-ski outerwear. They will also restore old furs into liners for raincoats and do custom fittings.

Jil Sander (✉ 48 E. Oak St., Near North, ☎ 312/335–0006) has captured the devotion of the fashion flock for her inventive styling, innovative fabrics, and impeccable tailoring. Prices are at the upper end of the designer range.

Paul Stuart (✉ John Hancock Center, 875 N. Michigan Ave., Near North, ☎ 312/640–2650) sells top-quality, traditional men's clothing for the boardroom and the golf course, and some equally sharp women's clothing.

Prada (✉ 30 E. Oak St., Near North, ☎ 312/951–1113) has a spare, cool look that matches its modern, minimalist inventory of clothing, shoes, and bags. In fact, unless you're a Miuccia devotee, the three-story shop can be too pared-down to hold your attention for more than a quick in-and-out.

Mark Shale (⊠ 900 N. Michigan Ave., Near North, ☎ 312/440–0720) has two floors of conservative yet stylish suits and separates geared to the corporate world.

At **Polo/Ralph Lauren** (⊠ 750 N. Michigan Ave., Near North, ☎ 312/280–1655), manor house meets mass marketing. The upper-crust chic covers men's, women's, and children's clothes and housewares. Fabrics are often enticing (suede, silk organza, cashmere), but expect to pay a pretty penny.

Urban Outfitters (⊠ 935 N. Rush St., Near North, ☎ 312/640–1919; ⊠ 2352 N. Clark St., Lincoln Park, ☎ 773/549–1711) supplies the street-hip (and often collegiate) with funky clothing, accessories, and hip home accessories—leopard-print lamp shades and the like.

WOMEN'S

agnès b. (⊠ 46 E. Walton St., Near North, ☎ 312/642–7483) is a prime source of fresh French basics like snap-front tops, crisp jackets, and skinny pants. Clean-lined backpacks and bags are especially coveted, but are often in short supply.

Chacok (⊠ 47 E. Oak St., Near North, ☎ 312/943–9391), the exuberant Parisian line, has opened its first U.S. outpost on Oak. It's known for softly structured clothes in bold colors and flowing fabrics.

Chanel Boutique (⊠ 935 N. Michigan Ave., Near North, ☎ 312/787–5500), inside the Drake Hotel, carries the complete line of Chanel products, including ready-to-wear, fragrances, cosmetics, and accessories.

Giovanni (⊠ 140 E. Walton St., Near North, ☎ 312/787–6500), a tony, old-line shop tucked away in the shopping court of the Drake Hotel, caters to socialites and party goers with its selection of gowns, suits, separates, and refined accessories for the ladies-who-lunch.

Sugar Magnolia (⊠ 34 E. Oak St., Near North, ☎ 312/787–1171), named for the Grateful Dead song, has clothes and accessories that tap into trends with a romantic, Bohemian spin.

Ultimo (⊠ 114 E. Oak St., Near North, ☎ 312/787–1171) has earned an international reputation for its well-edited selection of designer clothing from such names as John Galliano, Michael Kors, and Chloe. Oprah Winfrey is just one of the store's many high-profile customers.

Department Stores

Barneys New York (⊠ 25 E. Oak St., Near North, ☎ 312/587–1700) is a smaller, watered-down version of the Manhattan store known for austere men's and women's designer fashions. It's heavy on private-label merchandise, although Donna Karan and several European designers are represented. A full Vera Wang salon caters to brides and their wedding parties. The cosmetics department and the Chelsea Passage gift area have plenty of plum choices.

Bloomingdale's (⊠ 900 N. Michigan Ave., Near North, ☎ 312/440–4460), built in a clean, airy style that is part Prairie School, part postmodern (and quite unlike its New York City sibling), gives you plenty of elbow room to sift through its selection of designer labels and trendy housewares.

Lord & Taylor (⊠ Water Tower Place, 835 N. Michigan Ave., Near North, ☎ 312/787–7400) carries moderate to upscale clothing for men and women, plus shoes and accessories, frequently at sale prices.

Neiman Marcus (✉ 737 N. Michigan Ave., Near North, ☎ 312/642–5900) may have high prices, but they're matched by the level of taste. The selection of designer clothing and accessories for men and women is outstanding, and the gourmet food area on the top floor tempts with hard-to-find delicacies and impeccable hostess gifts.

Nordstrom (✉ 55 E. Grand Ave., Near North, ☎ 312/464–1515) has had its 270,000 square ft packed from the moment its doors opened in late 2001. Much like its other branches, this one lists a killer shoe department and extraordinary service among its strong points.

Saks Fifth Avenue (✉ 700 N. Michigan Ave., Near North; ✉ 717 N. Michigan Ave., Near North, ☎ 312/944–6500), a smaller, less-crowded cousin of the original New York flagship, doesn't scrimp on its selection of designer clothes at the main store, plus it has a men's specialty store directly across the street.

Home Decor and Gifts

Chiasso (✉ Water Tower Place, 835 N. Michigan Ave., Near North, ☎ 312/280–1249) focuses on high-style contemporary accessories for the home and office. There are plenty of sleek desk accoutrements and tricky, multitask gadgets.

Crate & Barrel (✉ 646 N. Michigan Ave., Near North, ☎ 312/787–5900; ✉ 850 W. North Ave., Lincoln Park, ☎ 312/573–9800) has its perpetually crowded flagship store on Michigan Avenue, with the exterior indeed shaped like a crate alongside a barrel. Inside are two floors of stylish and affordable cookware, glassware, and home accessories—plus two floors of well-priced furniture. A second, equally massive store is at North and Clybourn avenues.

Culture Counter at the Museum of Contemporary Art (✉ 220 E. Chicago Ave., Near North, ☎ 312/397–4000) is an outstanding museum gift shop. You'll find out-of-the-ordinary decorative accessories, tableware, and jewelry, as well as a superb collection of books on modern and contemporary art. The shop has its own street-level entrance.

Elements (✉ 102 E. Oak St., Near North, ☎ 312/642–6574) is a home-design leader in Chicago; its tempting selection includes decorative accessories, linens, and tableware from Europe and the United States. It also has a small but prime selection of European modernist and Deco furnishings and an irresistible cache of artisan-made jewelry.

Hammacher Schlemmer (✉ Tribune Tower, 445 N. Michigan Ave., Near North, ☎ 312/527–9100) beckons with upscale gadgets and unusual gifts—it even has an area where shoppers can try out some of the toys.

Material Possessions (✉ 54 E. Chestnut St., Near North, ☎ 312/280–4885) carries batteries of tabletop lines, serving pieces, and cutlery for casual and formal entertaining. It also has decorative accessories and small pieces of furniture, many from Asia or Africa.

Om for the Home (✉ 34 E. Oak St., Near North, ☎ 312/397–9181), a "spa for the spirit," offers feng shui, meditation, and yoga instruction, and a line of products to support them, including feng shui travel bags, essential oils, soaps, and meditation pillows and CDs.

Retrospect (✉ 700 N. Michigan Ave., Near North, ☎ 312/440–1270), a concept store of Room & Board, sells impeccably crafted furnishings that pay homage to historic influences, from the Ming Dynasty to the Arts and Crafts movement.

Room & Board (✉ 700 N. Michigan Ave., Near North, ☎ 312/266–0656) is a home-furnishings giant, known for its straightforward yet stylish pieces that blend quality craftsmanship and materials with affordable pricing.

Shabby Chic (⊠ 46 E. Superior St., Near North, ☎ 312/649–0080), of cushy, slip-covered furniture fame, has one of its four national outposts in a Victorian row house just off Michigan Avenue. Besides the upholstered pieces you'll find a complete stock of housewares, including an extraordinary lighting selection and a retro-inspired line of bedding.

Sur La Table (⊠ 52-54 E. Walton St., Near North, ☎ 312/337–0600) is the first Chicago retail outlet for the Seattle-based cookware and kitchen goods supplier. In addition to a great selection of gadgets and gizmos for cooks, there are culinary classes.

Malls

Aside from dozens of designer shops, Michigan Avenue has four vertical malls. **Water Tower Place** (⊠ 835 N.), with the Ritz-Carlton Hotel sitting atop the entire complex, is the most popular and contains branches of **Marshall Field's** and **Lord & Taylor,** as well as seven floors of specialty stores. Many are standard mall stores, but there are quite a few more unusual shops, including **Field of Dreams** (sports collectibles), **Alfred Dunhill, Jacadi** (children's wear), and a new **Eileen Fisher** store. The slightly ritzier **900 North Michigan Shops** houses the Chicago branch of **Bloomingdale's,** along with dozens of smaller boutiques and specialty stores, such as **Gucci, J. Crew, Coach, Club Monaco, Lalique, Williams-Sonoma,** and **Fogal.** The 900 building has a Four Seasons Hotel on top. The restaurants and movie theaters here are a good entertainment option during inclement weather. The third mall, **Chicago Place** (⊠ 700 N.), has **Saks Fifth Avenue,** the sleek furniture store **Room & Board,** and several boutiques carrying distinctive art for the table and home, including **Chiaroscuro, Design Toscano,** and **Joy of Ireland.** You get all that and an airy food court with a fabulous view on the top floor. The fourth and newest mall, the **Shops at North Bridge** (⊠ 520 N.), is anchored by **Nordstrom** and houses chains like **Sephora, Ann Taylor Loft,** and **Tommy Bahama,** plus specialty stores like **Vosges Haut-Chocolat,** a local chocolatier. The third floor is dedicated to children's fashions and toys, and includes the **LEGO Store,** and **Jordan Marie,** a baby boutique selling limited-run designs.

Music

Jazz Record Mart (⊠ 444 N. Wabash Ave., Near North, ☎ 312/222–1467) bills itself as the world's largest jazz record store, and with 8,500 square ft of inventory that includes used jazz on vinyl and a broad selection of world music, who are we to argue? A vast, in-depth selection of jazz and blues and knowledgeable sales staff make the store a must for music lovers. Sometimes you can catch a live performance here on a Saturday afternoon.

Shoes

Avventura (⊠ Water Tower Place, 835 N. Michigan Ave., Near North, ☎ 312/337–3700) rates as a favorite stop for professional basketball players in need of European-style footwear. This men's shoe shop keeps sizes up to 16 in stock.

Cole-Haan (⊠ 673 N. Michigan Ave., Near North, ☎ 312/642–8995) designs rework classic loafer, woven, and moccasin styles—all are comfortable and very well made.

Donald J. Pliner (⊠ 106 E. Oak St., Near North, ☎ 312/202–9600 or 877/654–1293), the U.S. distributor of Espace shoes, has his own line of high-fashion comfortable styles that are reasonably priced and often quite chic. The store stocks handbags, hosiery, and sunglasses, too.

Salvatore Ferragamo (✉ 645 N. Michigan Ave., Near North, ☎ 312/397–0464) makes shoes that have been the classic choice of the well-heeled for generations. But it's the designer's handbags, with a fresh, contemporary sensibility, that are generating excitement of late.

Timberland (✉ 543 N. Michigan Ave., Near North, ☎ 312/494–0171) puts its best foot forward in this showcase store, a frequent stop for Europeans seeking U.S. prices on rugged footwear for men and women.

Tod's (✉ 121 E. Oak St., Near North, ☎ 312/943–0070 or 800/457–8637) has made a name for itself among the luxury boutique lineup. Here you can choose from a wide selection of the signature-studded "8" bags and driving moccasins that made Tod's famous, as well as newer additions to the line, including high heels.

Souvenirs
Accent Chicago (✉ Water Tower Place, 835 N. Michigan Ave., Near North, ☎ 312/944–1354) offers the requisite souvenirs and Chicago memorabilia—miniature doodads, snow globes, and the like.

This branch of the **Chicago Architecture Foundation** (✉ John Hancock Center, 875 N. Michigan Ave., Near North, ☎ 312/751–1380) is smaller than the Loop's, but it has the same stylish reminders of the Windy City and its architecture in the form of books, posters, T-shirts, toys, and ties.

City of Chicago Store (✉ Chicago Waterworks Visitor Information Center, 163 E. Pearson St., Near North, ☎ 312/742–8811) is a great place to nab unusual souvenirs of the city—anything from a street sign to a brick from the old Comiskey Park. It's also a good source for guide-books, posters, and T-shirts.

Sporting Goods
NikeTown (✉ 669 N. Michigan Ave., Near North, ☎ 312/642–6363) ranks as one of Chicago's top tourist attractions. Many visitors—including professional athletes—spend more than an hour here, taking in the sports memorabilia, road testing a pair of sneakers, or watching the inspirational videos. Merchandise showcases the latest styles in athletic clothing and footwear for men, women, and children.

The **North Face** (✉ John Hancock Center, 875 N. Michigan Ave., Near North, ☎ 312/337–7200) can inspire even the most seasoned couch potato with its upscale outdoor sports equipment, clothing, and accessories.

Toys
American Girl Place (✉ 111 E. Chicago Ave., Near North, ☎ 312/255–9876) is the company's only retail store (products are sold through catalog and Internet business) and so attracts little girls from just about everywhere with their signature dolls in tow. There's easily a day's worth of activities here—shop at the boutique, take in a live musical revue, and have lunch or afternoon tea at the café where dolls can partake in the meal from their own "sassy seats." Be prepared for long lines to get in during high shopping seasons.

FAO Schwarz (✉ 840 N. Michigan Ave., Near North, ☎ 312/587–5000) is a fantasy toy emporium that's only a tad smaller than the New York flagship.

Navy Pier

Extending more than ½ mi onto Lake Michigan from 600 East Grand Avenue, Navy Pier treats you to spectacular views of the skyline, especially from a jumbo Ferris wheel set in slow motion. Stores and carts gear their wares to families and tourists and most don't merit a special trip. But if you're out there, check out **Oh Yes Chicago!** for souvenirs and **The Chicago Children's Museum Store** for educational kids' toys. Many stores are open late into the evening, especially in summer.

River North

Contained by the Chicago River on the south and west, Clark Street on the east, and Oak Street on the north, River North is home to art galleries, high-end antiques shops, home furnishings stores, and clothing boutiques. All have a distinctive style that fits in with this artsy area. It's also a wildly popular entertainment district; you'll find touristy theme restaurants such as Ed Debevic's and Rainforest Café, all of which peddle logo merchandise as aggressively as burgers.

Antiques and Collectibles

The **Antiquarians Building** (☒ 159 W. Kinzie St., River North, ☎ 312/527–0533) displays the wares of more than 20 dealers in Asian and European antiques, with some examples of modernism and art deco for good measure.

At **Christa's Ltd. Art and Antiques** (☒ 217 W. Illinois St., River North, ☎ 312/222–2520), chests, cabinets, tables, and bureaus are stacked three and four high, creating narrow aisles that are precarious to negotiate but make for adventurous exploring. Look in, over, and under each and every piece to register the gems stashed in every possible crevice.

Fly-By-Nite Gallery (☒ 714 N. Wells St., River North, ☎ 312/664–8136) chooses its exceptional decorative and functional art objects (circa 1890 to 1930) with a curatorial eye. It's particularly noted for European art glass and pottery and antique jewelry.

Jay Robert's Antique Warehouse (☒ 149 W. Kinzie St., River North, ☎ 312/222–0167) has enough antique merchandise to fill a 50,000-square-ft showroom on his own. He specializes in 19th-century European pieces, and has many large-scale armoires, dining sets, sideboards, fireplace mantels, and clocks.

Michael FitzSimmons Decorative Arts (☒ 311 W. Superior St., River North, ☎ 312/787–0496) has a homelike environment for the eponymous owner's renowned collection of furniture and artifacts from the British and American Arts and Crafts movements. On display are works by Frank Lloyd Wright, Louis Sullivan, and Gustav Stickley, along with some quality reproductions.

Rita Bucheit, Ltd. (☒ 449 N. Wells St., River North, ☎ 312/527–4080) is devoted to the streamlined Biedermeier aesthetic and carries choice furniture and accessories from the period along with art deco and modern pieces that are perfect complements to the style.

Art Galleries

Alan Koppel Gallery (☒ 210 W. Chicago Ave., River North, ☎ 312/640–0730) has an eclectic mix of works by modern masters and contemporary artists, as well as a selection of French and Italian furniture from the 1930s to 1950s.

Ann Nathan Gallery (☒ 218 W. Superior St., River North, ☎ 312/664–6622) specializes in contemporary paintings, but also showcases sculpture and singular artist-made furniture.

Bryon Roche (⊠ 750 N. Franklin St., River North, ☎ 312/654–0144) shows contemporary paintings and drawings, many by Chicago artists.

Carl Hammer Gallery (⊠ 740 N. Wells St., River North, ☎ 312/266–8512) focuses on outsider and self-taught artists, such as Lee Godie and Mr. Imagination.

Catherine Edelman Gallery (⊠ 300 W. Superior St., River North, ☎ 312/266–2350) specializes in contemporary photography with an emphasis on emerging, mixed-media, photo-based artists such as Maria Martinez-Canes and Jack Spencer.

Douglas Dawson (⊠ 222 W. Huron St., River North, ☎ 312/751–1961) brings the spirit of ancient peoples to life with art, textiles, furniture, and urns from Africa, China, and Tibet.

G.R. N'Namdi Gallery (⊠ 230 W. Huron St., River North, ☎ 312/587–8262) represents contemporary painters and sculptors, with an emphasis on black and Latin American artists.

Habitat (⊠ 222 W. Superior St., River North, ☎ 312/440–0288) draws collectors of fine studio art glass by luminaries such as Dale Chihuly.

Lyons-Wier Packer Gallery (⊠ 300 W. Superior St., River North, ☎ 312/654–0600) sells contemporary art in all media, with an emphasis on realism, Chicago artists, and the unusual.

Portia Gallery (⊠ 207 W. Superior St., River North, ☎ 312/932–9500) showcases glowing examples of contemporary glass.

Auctions

Susanin's Auctioneers and Appraisers (⊠ River North, ☎ 312/832–9800) holds live, usually themed sales every Sunday morning. Preview items are also displayed on the floor for immediate sale at a set price.

Books

Abraham Lincoln Book Shop (⊠ 357 W. Chicago Ave., River North, ☎ 312/944–3085) has been around since 1938 and specializes in buying, selling, and appraising books, paintings, documents, and other paraphernalia associated with American military and political history.

Clothing

MEN'S

Irv's (⊠ 431 N. Orleans St., River North, ☎ 312/832–9900) is where sharp-dressed men in the know head for in-season designer clothes at 30%–50% off retail prices. The array of suits is stellar, with more than 4,000 to choose from, among them creations by Calvin Klein, Perry Ellis, and Chaps by Ralph Lauren. There's a good selection of sportswear, tuxes, shoes, and outerwear, too. It's closed Sundays.

MEN'S AND WOMEN'S

June Blaker (⊠ 200 W. Superior St., River North, ☎ 312/751–9220) has developed a loyal following, especially among gallery district types, for carrying avant-garde Japanese labels such as Comme des Garçons and Yohji Yamamoto.

WOMEN'S

Biba Bis (⊠ 732 N. Wells St., River North, ☎ 312/988–9560) offers a good price-to-quality ratio for its private-label line of classy, high-quality (but slightly subdued) reinterpretations of the day's latest trends.

Home Decor and Gifts

Cambium (⊠ 119 W. Hubbard St., River North, ☎ 312/832–9920) is loaded with tempting home furnishings, including a particularly expansive line of kitchen fittings and accoutrements.

Galleria M (✉ 313 W. Superior St., River North, ☏ 312/988–7790) offers romantic decorating with Dialogica, a dreamy home furnishings line, as well as tailored counterpoints with Mike furniture from San Francisco. There's also a healthy stash of accessories, especially lighting.

Golden Triangle (✉ 72 W. Hubbard St., River North, ☏ 312/755–1266) falls at the outskirts of River North, and is a must for anyone enamored with the East-meets-West aesthetic. Achieve it with the antique Chinese and British colonial Raj furniture from Burma, the Asian accessories, and the smattering of idiosyncratic pieces from Thailand.

Luminaire (✉ 301 W. Superior St., River North, ☏ 312/664–9582) is the city's largest and most interestingly arrayed showroom of international contemporary furniture. Represented designers include Philippe Starck, Antonio Citterio, Alberta Meda, and Shiro Kuromata. You'll also find sleek kitchen designs from Italian manufacturer Bofi and a large home accessories section with equally edgy offerings from Alessi, Zani & Zani, Rosenthal, and Mono.

Manifesto (✉ 755 N. Wells St., River North, ☏ 312/664–0733) is housed in an expansive, street-level space, making it one of the largest design ateliers in the city. It showcases work by furniture designer (and owner) Richard Gorman, plus contemporary furniture from Italy, Austria, Spain, and Mexico and streamlined Finnish accessories.

No Place Like (✉ 300 W. Grand St., River North, ☏ 312/822–0550) carries ultra-contemporary lines of furniture, ceramics, glass, pottery, and accessories that are clean-lined, colorful, and hip.

Sawbridge Studios (✉ 153 W. Ohio St., River North, ☏ 312/828–0055) displays custom handcrafted furniture by about 40 American artisans. The specialties include Frank Lloyd Wright reproductions, newly designed pieces with an Arts and Crafts or Shaker aesthetic, and contemporary pottery.

Merchandise Mart

This massive marketplace between Wells and North Orleans streets just north of the Chicago River is notable for its art deco design but not for its shopping. Although much of the building is reserved for the design trade, the first two floors have been turned into retail. Stores are predominantly run-of-the-mill mall fare. Unlike the Michigan Avenue malls, it is usually closed on Sunday, and stores keep relatively short Saturday hours.

Paper

Paper Source (✉ 232 W. Chicago Ave., River North, ☏ 312/337–0798) sells reams and reams of different types of paper, a lot of it eclectic and, therefore, expensive. There are a custom invitation department and a good selection of rubber stamps and bookbinding supplies. Ask about the classes offered.

Sporting Goods

Sportmart (✉ 620 N. LaSalle St., River North, ☏ 312/337–6151; ✉ 3134 N. Clark St., Lake View, ☏ 773/871–8500; ✉ 6420 W. Fullerton Pkwy., Brickyard Mall, ☏ 773/804–0044) carries more than 60,000 items for athletes and spectators at competitive prices, including plenty of team merchandise. Take a minute to compare handprints with famous athletes (all with a local connection) on the exterior and first floor of the LaSalle Street flagship.

Bucktown and Wicker Park

Once artists and musicians claimed this run-down area near the intersection of North, Damen, and Milwaukee avenues, the trendy coffeehouses, nightclubs, and restaurants followed. Shopping here has since snowballed, thanks to the area's reasonable rents. Now scads of edgy clothing boutiques, art galleries, home design ateliers, alternative music stores, and antiques shops dot the area, making it a shopping destination that deserves a solid chunk of time. The neighborhood is very youth-oriented and still a bit gritty, so it's not for everyone. Many stores don't open until at least 11 AM, some shops are closed on Monday and Tuesday, and hours can be erratic. Spend a late afternoon shopping before settling in for dinner at one of the neighborhood's popular restaurants. To get here from downtown on the El, take the Blue Line toward O'Hare and exit at Damen Avenue.

Accessories

Miss B Haven (⊠ 1802 N. Damen Ave., Bucktown, ☎ 773/862–3185) is a welcome addition to the neighborhood mix, with a sassy mix of lingerie (in-house designs, plus pieces from Bedhead and Lola & Co.), lotions, fragrances, and hand-tailored handbags by local designer Janelle Davis.

Sassabee (⊠ 1849 W. North Ave., Bucktown, ☎ 773/862–7740) has everything to keep man, woman and even pet looking and smelling good. Try the extensive line of fresh-smelling items from Athens-based Korres for yourself, and the smartly packaged pet grooming goods from Mes Bon Amis for your furry friends.

Antiques and Collectibles

Bleeker Street (⊠ 1946 N. Leavitt St., Bucktown, ☎ 773/862–3185) is rich in British, Irish, and French provincial home and garden wares. Its strong suits are home accessories that were proper in their day but look fanciful now, such as painted Victorian mirrors and sets of cigarette cards. In summer, garden items are displayed in an inviting backyard.

Modern Times (⊠ 1538 N. Milwaukee Ave., Wicker Park, ☎ 773/772–8871) celebrates the home furnishings of the 1900s, particularly the '40s, '50s, and '60s. There's also a good selection of vintage clothing and jewelry.

Pagoda Red (⊠ 1714 N. Damen Ave., Bucktown, ☎ 773/235–1188) is packed with prime, exceptionally well-priced Asian furnishings. Most are true antiques as opposed to vintage; one notable exception is a rare collection of 20th-century Chinese advertising posters.

Pavilion (⊠ 2055 N. Damen Ave., Bucktown, ☎ 773/645–0924) has an uncommon mix of industrial and decorative furnishings, accessories, and fixtures. The finds reflect the collecting acumen of its two idiosyncratic owners, who scour Europe and the Midwest for items in the perfect state of intriguing decay.

Clothing

WOMEN'S

p. 45 (⊠ 1643 N. Damen Ave., Wicker Park, ☎ 773/862–4523) shows the most forward styles of a cadre of up-and-coming designers. Styles range from adventurous to elegant, and prices don't get out of hand. Unfortunately, the size range is limited.

Robin Richman (⊠ 2108 N. Damen Ave., Bucktown, ☎ 773/278–6150) displays her nationally known knitwear in this art gallery/retail store, along with antique goods and wood furniture made by sculptor Floyd Gompf.

Saffron (✉ 2064 N. Damen Ave., Bucktown, ☎ 773/486–7753) lures you in with merchandise as indulgent and decadent as the namesake spice, including fluid, finely finished clothes made of natural fabrics, organically inspired jewelry, and lavish bath products.

Tangerine (✉ 1719 N. Damen Ave., Bucktown, ☎ 773/772–0505) carries fun, feminine clothes and accessories by such popular designers as Three Dots and Ashley, as well as labels that are hard to find elsewhere in town, like Built by Wendy.

Home Decor and Gifts

Casa Loca (✉ 1130 N. Milwaukee Ave., Wicker Park, ☎ 773/278–2972) is rife with handsome, new, rustic pine furniture from Mexico that is carved, painted, or fashionably primitive. The furniture is complemented by superb vintage and antique Mexican folk art and *tolevara* (tinware) from Guanajuato.

Eclectic Junction for Art (✉ 1630 N. Damen Ave., Bucktown, ☎ 773/342–7865) showcases functional art—from drawer pulls and toilet seats to tableware and furniture—that expresses an irrepressible joie de vivre.

Embelezar (✉ 1639 N. Damen Ave., Bucktown, ☎ 773/645–9705) is Portuguese for "embellish," and after a visit to this airy shop you'll be able to do just that. Everything's geared for gracious living, from the hand-painted, silk-covered, Venetian fixtures to the sumptuous sofas.

For Dog's Sake (✉ 2257 W. North Ave., Bucktown, ☎ 773/278–4355) carries only the finest foods and accessories for pampered pets and their owners, from brightly colored toys and bowls by Otis and Claude to the smartly designed beds, baseball hats, and collars by San Francisco's George.

Jean Alan Upholstered Furniture and Furnishings (✉ 2134 N. Damen Ave., Bucktown, ☎ 773/278–2345) is a design atelier owned by a former feature film set decorator; the offerings range from Victorian to mid-20th-century modern. There's always a healthy assortment of sofas and chairs recovered in eclectic fabrics, plus pillows made of unusual textiles and refurbished vintage lamps with marvelous shades.

Lille (✉ 1923 W. North Ave., Bucktown, ☎ 773/342–0563) hides behind a low-profile storefront in the middle of a hectic street, but unassuming gives way to beautiful treasures once inside. There's a carefully selected mix of home furnishings and personal accessories by well-known artists (vases from Parisian designer Christian Tortuby) and lesser-known ones (jewelry by local Spago manager Amanda Puck Larsen).

Stitch (✉ 1723 N. Damen Ave., Bucktown, ☎ 773/782–1570) carries home furnishings and personal accessories in a seemingly minimalist, airy space. You'll find spare pottery, jewelry, leather goods, backpacks, briefcases, and bags of every ilk, plus contemporary furniture with a modernist bent.

Techstyles Custom Rugs (✉ 1738 W. Division Ave., Wicker Park, ☎ 773/276–8150) is actually a studio, where School of the Art Institute grad Lisa Capaul designs and produces one-of-a-kind area rugs that are exuberantly bold, often with a modernist bent. Prices are surprisingly reasonable. Call first for a consultation.

Music

Beat Parlor (✉ 1653 N. Damen Ave., Bucktown, ☎ 773/395–2887) is where DJs and young urban music aficionados head for rare dance and hip-hop scores. There are turntables for testing out old, poorly labeled LPs, and a great selection of Japanese cartoons and Hong Kong martial arts flicks, too.

Shoes

John Fluevog (✉ 1539–41 N. Milwaukee Ave., Wicker Park, ☎ 773/772–1983) designs alternative shoes with chunky platforms and bold designs that grace the famous feet of Madonna and throngs of other loyal devotees.

Sporting Goods

Shred Shop (✉ 2121 W. Division St., Wicker Park, ☎ 773/384–2100) houses everything a skate- and snowboarder's heart desires. They do rentals and servicing, too.

Ethnic Enclaves

Chicago is famed for its ethnic neighborhoods, that give you the chance to shop the globe without actually leaving the city. **Chinatown** has a dozen or so shops along four blocks of Wentworth Avenue south of Cermak Road. The Far Eastern imports range from jade to ginseng root to junk. In the **North Side Lincoln Square neighborhood,** a stretch of Lincoln Avenue between Leland and Lawrence avenues, are German delis and stores that sell imported toys and European-made health and beauty products. Many non–U.S. visitors make the trek to a cluster of dingy but well-stocked electronics stores in an **Indian neighborhood** on the city's far North Side (✉ Devon Ave. between Western and Washtenaw Aves.) to buy electronic appliances that run on 220-volt currency. Because the United States has no value-added tax—as of yet—it's often cheaper for international visitors to buy here than at home. The same stretch of Devon Avenue is a great source for spectacularly rich sari fabrics.

Lincoln Park

The upscale residential neighborhood of Lincoln Park entices with its mix of distinctive boutiques. **Armitage Avenue** between Orchard Street (700 W.) and Kenmore Avenue (1050 W.) is one of the city's best areas for browsing through stores filled with clothing, tableware, jewelry, and gifts. There are also worthwhile stops on Halsted Street and Webster Avenue. The area is easily reached by taking the Ravenswood (Brown Line) El to the Armitage stop.

Accessories

Fabrice (✉ 1714 N. Wells St., Lincoln Park, ☎ 773/280–0011) is where you'll find an abundance of French accessories: Herve Chapelier and Longchamp handbags, Catherine Masson sachets, wonderful floral pins and other jewelry. This is the only Fabrice boutique outside of Paris.

1154 Lill Studio (✉ 2523 N. Halsted St., Lincoln Park, ☎ 773/477–5455) is where creative types come to design their own handbags and makeup cases from tons of fabric and shape options. The helpful staff assembles the pieces. Some limited-edition, ready-made bags are available, too.

Isabella Fine Lingerie (✉ 1101 W. Webster Ave., Lincoln Park, ☎ 773/281–2352) is run by Jennifer Amerine, a self-confessed lingerie addict who herself has inspired many obsessions among her loyal clientele. Look for Cosa Bella, Parah, and Eberjey, plus bridal pieces and swimwear, at this little jewel of a shop.

Books

Act I Bookstore (✉ 2540 N. Lincoln Ave., Lincoln Park, ☎ 773/348–6757) is dedicated to theater, film, and television materials. It also sells

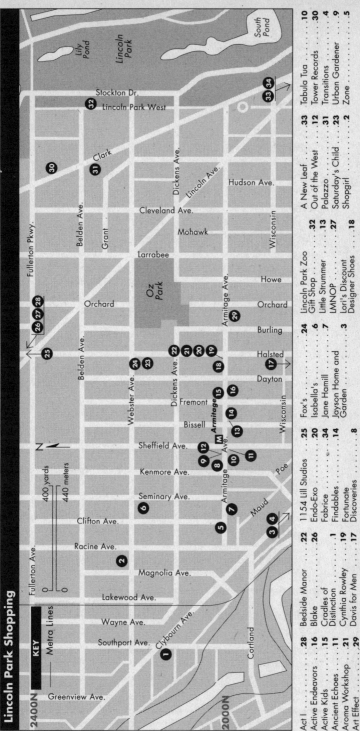

Lincoln Park Shopping

KEY

— Metra Lines

stage makeup and offers a résumé service for performers, directors, designers, and others in the profession.

Transitions Bookplace (⊠ 100 W. North Ave., Lincoln Park, ☎ 312/951–7323) is one of the country's top New Age bookstores, stocking books on such subjects as alternative healing, religion, mythology, and folklore. There's a lively program of author appearances and workshops, and a nice café.

Clothing

CHILDREN'S

Cradles of Distinction (⊠ 2100 N. Southport Ave., Lincoln Park, ☎ 773/472–1001) has virtually everything a stylish baby will need, including high-quality bedroom furniture, luxury bedding, and a major-league assortment of toys.

LMNOP (⊠ 2574 N. Lincoln Ave., Lincoln Park, ☎ 773/975–4055) sells fun clothes for newborns and kids up to size 8 from designers such as Flora & Henri and Cotton Caboodle.

MEN'S

Davis for Men (⊠ 824 W. North Ave., Lincoln Park, ☎ 312/266–9599; ⊠ 900 N. Michigan Ave., Near North, ☎ 312/440–0016) ranks as one of Chicago's hippest haberdashers. The all-European labels run the gamut from business to casual wear, understated to avant-garde.

MEN'S AND WOMEN'S

Active Endeavors (⊠ 935 W. Armitage Ave., Lincoln Park, ☎ 773/281–8100) strives to outfit the active set from sunup to sundown with the latest brands of high performance threads. For wee athletes, check out **Active Kids** (⊠ 838 W. Armitage Ave., Lincoln Park, ☎ 773/281–2002), just down the block.

WOMEN'S

Art Effect (⊠ 934 W. Armitage Ave., Lincoln Park, ☎ 773/929–3600) is in new digs down the block from the old location. This bright, well-stocked boutique can be counted on for relaxed clothing with a creative spin and well-designed accessories and tabletop accents. Several local designers are represented.

Blake (⊠ 2448 N. Lincoln Ave., Lincoln Park, ☎ 773/477–3364) has a spare aesthetic that matches its edgy European fashions. This is the place to score hard-to-find, ultra-hip designers such as Martin Margiela, Helmut Lang, Ann Demeulemeester, and Dries Van Noten—and it has an exceptional staff to help you put ensembles together. A small but choice men's section is definitely worth sifting through.

Cynthia Rowley (⊠ 808 W. Armitage Ave., Lincoln Park, ☎ 773/528–6160), a Chicago-area native, fills her Lincoln Park store with the exuberant, well-priced dresses, separates, and accessories that have made her so popular.

Fox's (⊠ 2150 N. Halsted, Lincoln Park, ☎ 773/281–0700) carries cancelled and overstocked designer clothes at 40%–70% discounts. New shipments come in several times a week, so there's always something new to try on.

Jane Hamill (⊠ 1117 W. Armitage Ave., Lincoln Park, ☎ 773/665–1102) sells her own interpretations of the season's top silhouettes at reasonable prices.

Palazzo (⊠ 2262 N. Clark St., Lincoln Park, ☎ 773/665–4044) designers Jane and Saeed Hamidi have a clean-lined bridal collection that draws chic urban brides who want gowns with beautiful, subtle details, not reams of ruffles.

Shopgirl (✉ 1206 N. Southport Ave., Lincoln Park, ☎ 773/284–7467) has a loyal following of devoted customers, who love the pieces by Trina Turk, Shoshana, and Katayone Adeli, as much as the fun fashion events the store hosts.

Zone (✉ 1154 W. Armitage Ave., Lincoln Park, ☎ 773/472–4007), the tiniest of shops tucked just off Webster Street, has original designs by local Pamela Vanderelinde. She favors simple silhouettes that make use of unusual fabrics, contrast linings, and vintage buttons. Expect to spend $500 on a suit. It's closed Monday and Tuesday.

Home Decor and Gifts

A New Leaf (✉ 1818 N. Wells St., Lincoln Park, ☎ 312/642–8553; ✉ 1645 N. Wells St., Lincoln Park, ☎ 312/642–1576; ✉ 700 N. Michigan Ave., Near North, ☎ 773/871–3610) is the grand dame of Chicago home and garden shops. Along with one of the best selections of fresh flowers in town, the Wells Street stores stock singular antique and vintage furnishings and accessories as well as a mind-boggling selection of candles, vases, tiles, and pots.

Ancient Echoes (✉ 1003 W. Armitage St., Lincoln Park, ☎ 773/880–1003) is laden with ornamented home items, from decorative boxes and vases to chests. Pieces often incorporate references to allegorical symbols from cultures all over the world.

Aroma Workshop (✉ 2050 N. Halsted St., Lincoln Park, ☎ 773/871–1985) has more than 100 fragrances to custom scent lotions, massage oils, and bath salts. They make their own line of facial care products, too.

Bedside Manor (✉ 2056 N. Halsted St., Lincoln Park, ☎ 773/404–2020) makes dreamland even more inviting with handcrafted beds and lush designer linens, many of which come in interesting jacquard weaves or are nicely trimmed and finished.

At **Endo-Exo Apothecary** (✉ 2034 N. Halsted St., Lincoln Park, ☎ 773/525–0500), a DJ sometimes spins for shoppers, and vintage pharmacy cabinets mingle with mod furnishings. You can sample from a well-chosen stock of hard-to-find beauty lines like Peter Thomas Roth, Uvavita, and Mythic Tribe.

At **Findables** (✉ 907 W. Armitage Ave., Lincoln Park, ☎ 773/348–0674), sort through a sizable collection of bed, bath, and table linens and a tableware selection that ranges from rustic Italian sets to ornate, painted china and glassware. An extraordinary array of Christmas ornaments turns up for the holiday season.

Fortunate Discoveries (✉ 1022 W. Armitage Ave., Lincoln Park, ☎ 773/404–0212) is the place for ethnic rugs, furnishings, and accessories. Kilims and knotted rugs are stacked in enticing piles, interspersed with groups of vintage and contemporary furniture from Indonesia, India, Africa, and New Guinea.

Jayson Home & Garden (✉ 1885 and 1911 N. Clybourn Ave., Lincoln Park, ☎ 773/525–3100) is loaded with vintage European and American furnishings. Look for oversize cupboards and armoires, decorative accessories, and stylish garden furniture and fixings.

Out of the West (✉ 1000 W. Armitage Ave., Lincoln Park, ☎ 773/404–9378) carries blue jeans, other clothing and home furnishings that reflect all manner of Western styles, whether Native American, farmhouse, or log cabin.

Tabula Tua (⊠ 1015 W. Armitage Ave., Lincoln Park, ☎ 773/525–3500) stays away from standard formal china. Instead, the emphasis is on colorful, contemporary, mix-and-match dishes and tabletop accessories. Offerings include breathtaking mosaic tables handmade to order, rustic furniture crafted from old barn wood, and the sleek, polished pewter pieces of renowned British designer Nick Munro.

Urban Gardener (⊠ 1006 W. Armitage Ave., Lincoln Park, ☎ 773/477–2070 or 800/998–7330), housed in a charming old brownstone, has a tempting inventory of hand-thrown pots, exquisite, hand-painted tole (painted tinware), and curvy topiaries. And you can glean decorating ideas from the creative displays.

Music and Instruments

Little Strummer Music Store (⊠ 909 W. Armitage Ave., Lincoln Park, ☎ 773/728–6000) specializes in children's music and instruments. They have a good selection of new and used instruments, plus violins and guitars for rent. The affiliated **Different Strummer Store** in Lincoln Square (⊠ 4544 N. Lincoln Ave., North Central, ☎ 773/728–6000) is for grownup musicians and devoted to musical products of every type—from acoustic and electric instruments to sheet music, books and CDs.

Tower Records/Videos/Books (⊠ 2301 N. Clark St., Lincoln Park, ☎ 773/477–5994), open until midnight, stocks more than 150,000 music titles, covering all musical tastes, plus good selections of videos and books—mainly best-sellers, pop culture, music, and art titles. The store's selection of Latin and world music is particularly good.

Shoes

Lori's Designer Shoes (⊠ 824 W. Armitage Ave., Lincoln Park, ☎ 773/281–5655) is considered by many fine-footed women to be the best shoe shop in Chicago. Here you can find shoes by designers like Franco Sarto, Joan & David, Gastone Luciole, janet & janet, and Steve Madden at competitive prices. Terrific handbags, jewelry, bridal shoes, and other accessories are also available.

Toys

Lincoln Park Zoo Gift Shop (⊠ 2200 N. Cannon Dr., Lincoln Park, ☎ 312/742–2000) has puppets, coloring books, and games, as well as stuffed creatures that match the live ones ones you can visit at this free zoo.

Saturday's Child (⊠ 2146 N. Halsted St., Lincoln Park, ☎ 773/525–8697) feels like an old-fashioned toy store, but one that emphasizes educational and creative toys. Their doll selection is unusually good.

Lake View

Lake View, a diverse neighborhood just north of Lincoln Park, has spawned a number of worthwhile shopping strips. **Clark Street** between Diversey Avenue (2800 N.) and Addison Street (3600 N.) has myriad clothing boutiques and specialty stores. Farther north on **Halsted Street** between Belmont Avenue (3200 N.) and Addison Street (3600 N.) are more gift shops and boutiques—several with a gay orientation—as well as a smattering of vintage-clothing and antiques stores. In West Lake View, distinctive boutiques have sprung up on **Southport Avenue** between Belmont Avenue (3200 N.) and Grace St. (3800 N.). **Broadway** between Diversey Avenue and Addison Street also claims its share of intriguing shops. The **Century Mall,** in a former movie palace at Clark Street, Broadway, and Diversey Parkway, houses stores catering to a young and trendy crowd. To reach this neighborhood from downtown, take the 22 Clark Street bus at Dearborn Street or the 36 Broadway bus at State Street heading north. Or, take the Howard (Red Line) or Ravenswood (Brown Line) El north to the Belmont stop from downtown, which will drop you into the heart of Lake View.

Antiques and Collectibles

BELMONT AVENUE

Fans of art deco, kitchen collectibles, and bar memorabilia can poke into the shops and malls lining Belmont Avenue, starting a bit west of Ashland Avenue (1600 W.) and running to Western Avenue (2400 W.). You may have to scrounge around to unearth treasures in these stores, but you'll be rewarded with some of the lowest prices in the city. The shops are usually open weekends but may be closed on one or more weekdays. Call before making a special trip.

Antique Resources (⊠ 1741 W. Belmont Ave., Lake View, ☎ 773/871–4242) is full of choice Georgian antiques at fair prices. This is an excellent source for stately desks and dignified dining sets, but the true find is a huge trove—numbering in the hundreds—of antique crystal and gilt chandeliers from France.

Danger City (⊠ 2120 W. Belmont Ave., Lake View, ☎ 773/871–1420) can be counted on for fun and funky remnants of the mid-20th century. Among the furniture, lighting, and accessories, the bar- and kitchenware from the 1940s, '50s, and '60s stand out.

Father Time Antiques (⊠ 2108 W. Belmont Ave., Lincoln Park, ☎ 773/880–5599) bills itself as the Midwest's largest restorer of vintage timepieces; it also stocks vintage Victorian and art deco European furniture.

The **Good Old Days** (⊠ 2138 W. Belmont Ave., Lake View, ☎ 773/472–8837) carries a wide selection of vintage radios along with bar and sports memorabilia among its three floors of furniture.

LINCOLN AVENUE

A 1½-mi stretch of Lincoln Avenue is noted for its funky antiques, collectibles, and vintage clothing. The shops start around the intersection of Lincoln Avenue and Diversey Parkway (2800 N.) and continue until Irving Park Road (4000 N.). A car or the 11 Lincoln Avenue bus is the best way to navigate this area. To get the bus from downtown, take the Howard (Red Line) or Ravenswood (Brown Line) El to the Fullerton stop; after exiting the El station, walk ½ block east to the intersection of Fullerton and Lincoln. Then catch the 11 Lincoln Avenue bus to your stop. Most of these shops are open weekends but may be closed early in the week.

The **Chicago Antique Centre** (⊠ 3036 N. Lincoln Ave., Lake View, ☎ 773/929–0200) houses 35 dealers, some with especially good selections of vintage dishes and jewelry.

Daniels Antiques (⊠ 3711 N. Ashland Ave., Lake View, ☎ 773/868–9355), five blocks north of the six-way Lincoln, Belmont, and Ashland intersection, is a cavernous shop with a huge stash of Victorian and 20th-century furnishings, especially larger pieces and complete sets.

Lincoln Antique Mall (⊠ 3141 N. Lincoln Ave., Lake View, ☎ 773/244–1440) has 11,000 square ft filled with dozens of dealers carrying antiques and collectibles. There's a good selection of French and mid-century modern furniture, plus estate jewelry, oil paintings, and photographs.

Red Eye Antiques (⊠ 3050 N. Lincoln Ave., Lake View, ☎ 773/975–2020) begs to be browsed; it's so overloaded with prime furnishings, accessories, and paintings that something catches your eye with every scan of the shop. Items span a wide range in age and price; some date back to the 1500s, others are just a few decades old.

Steve Starr Studios (✉ 2779 N. Lincoln Ave., Lake View, ☎ 773/525–6530) seduces with its art deco frames, glass, jewelry, lamps, and furnishings. It also publishes and distributes a helpful pamphlet listing all the Lincoln Avenue shops.

Turtle Creek Antiques (✉ 3817 N. Lincoln Ave., Lake View, ☎ 773/327–2630) is a key source for antique and vintage quilts, tabletop pieces, linens, furniture (mostly Victorian), and estate jewelry. Just about every piece is in mint condition.

Urban Artifacts (✉ 2928 N. Lincoln Ave., Lake View, ☎ 773/404–1008) plays on the industrial nature of modern furnishings with a superb selection of furniture, lighting, and decorative accessories from the 1940s to the '70s.

Zig Zag (✉ 3419 N. Lincoln Ave., Lake View, ☎ 773/525–1060) displays a well-edited collection of pristine art deco and modern furnishings and jewelry.

Books

The Bookworks (✉ 3444 N. Clark St., Lake View, ☎ 773/871–5318) stocks more than 40,000 titles, most of them used and/or rare. There's an emphasis on sports (for Cubs' fans strolling by from nearby Wrigley Field) and contemporary fiction. Check out the neat vintage vinyl record section.

Unabridged Bookstore (✉ 3521 N. Broadway, Lake View, ☎ 773/883–9119) has maintained a loyal clientele for more than 20 years with its vast selection of general, children's, and gay and lesbian books. There's an impressive magazine section, too.

Clothing

Flashy Trash (✉ 3524 N. Halsted St., Lake View, ☎ 773/327–6900) fills its store with men's and women's vintage clothing, including some couture pieces, and accessories in beautiful condition. The prices attract prom goers as well as more mature buyers looking for classics. Goods on the super-trendy side are up front, and there's often an excellent spread of vintage jewelry, too.

Hubba-Hubba (✉ 3309 N. Clark St., Lake View, ☎ 773/477–1414) mixes well-chosen vintage clothing and new clothing with a retro flavor. Jewelry and accessories convey the same period mood.

She One (✉ 3402 N. Southport Ave., Lake View, ☎ 773/549–9698) has a plentiful assortment to dress the stylish young urban woman, from bright T-shirts to trendy jewelry.

Silver Moon (✉ 3337 N. Halsted St., Lake View, ☎ 773/883–0222) showcases fine vintage clothing and accessories for men and women. Vintage wedding gowns and tuxedos are a specialty.

Gifts

Barker & Meowsky (✉ 3319 N. Broadway, Lake View, ☎ 773/880–0200), a "paw firm," carries great gifts for dogs, cats, and humans. There are beautiful bowls, plush beds, picture frames, treats, and more. The friendly service will make any tail wag.

Glam to Go (✉ 2002 W. Roscoe St., Lake View, ☎ 773/525–7004) carries lotions and potions that will help you stay soft and smell good, plus candles, makeup, and kids' toys.

Uncle Fun (✉ 1338 W. Belmont Ave., Lake View, ☎ 773/477–8223) delights all ages with its astonishing and goofy inventory of new (trendy bobbing head dolls) and vintage (The Official John Travolta Picture/Postcard book) tricks, gags, party favors, and more, all at reasonable prices. It's closed Mondays and Tuesdays.

Waxman Candles (✉ 3044 N. Lincoln Ave., Lake View, ☎ 773/929–3000) makes its goods on the premises in countless shapes, colors, and scents. There's an incredible selection of holders for votives and pillars, and incense, too.

Home Decor

CB2 (✉ 3757 N. Lincoln Ave., Lake View, ☎ 773/755–3900) is the first neighborhood concept store by furniture giant Crate & Barrel. Its emphasis is on stylish, bold basics for trendy urban abodes—all sans big-ticket price tags.

Equinox (✉ 3401 N. Broadway Ave., Lake View, ☎ 773/281–9151) literally glows from within, thanks to its Tiffany-style lamps, but the true strength here is the selection of Arts and Crafts–style art tiles and reproduction pottery.

Gallimaufry (✉ 3345 N. Halsted St., Lake View, ☎ 773/348–8090) stocks affordable, American-made objects, from art glass vases and perfume bottles to kaleidoscopes.

Warehouse-style **J. Toguri Mercantile Company** (✉ 851 W. Belmont Ave., Lake View, ☎ 773/929–3500) carries all things Asian, including tea sets, lacquerware, kimonos, hard-to-find pots, and Japanese music.

Pass the Salt and Pepper (✉ 3310 N. Broadway, Lake View, ☎ 773/975–9789) specializes in all types of custom linens, from tablecloths to duvets. They do laminate work that can turn beloved fabrics into place mats, too.

P.O.S.H. (✉ 3729 N. Southport Ave., Lake View, ☎ 773/529–7674) piles never-used, vintage hotel and restaurant china in such charming displays that you'll find it all hard to resist. There's also an impressive selection of silver gravy boats, creamers, and flatware that bear the marks of ocean liners and private clubs.

Music

Reckless Records (✉ 3157 N. Broadway, Lake View, ☎ 773/404–5080) ranks as one of the city's leading alternative and secondhand record stores. Besides the indie offerings, you can flip through jazz, classical, and soul recordings, or catch a live appearance by an up-and-comer passing through town.

Paper

Aiko's Art Materials (✉ 3347 N. Clark St., Lake View, ☎ 773/404–5600) attracts the creatively inclined with its hundreds of stenciled, marbled, textured, and tie-dyed papers—most from Japan. You can find bookbinding materials here, too.

Paper Boy (✉ 1351 W. Belmont Ave., Lake View, ☎ 773/388–8811) is a great source for cards, gift wrap, and invitations with a hip sensibility.

Worth a Special Trip

Antiques and Collectibles

Architectural Artifacts (✉ 4325 N. Ravenswood Ave., Lake View, ☎ 773/348–0622) has warehouse proportions and a selection to match. The mammoth two-story space houses oversize garden ornaments (arbors, benches), statuary, iron grills, fixtures, and decorative tiles. Architectural fragments—marble, metal, wood, terra-cotta—hail from American and European historic buildings. The store is a few blocks from the Montrose stop on the Brown Line.

Broadway Antique Market (✉ 6130 N. Broadway, Edgewater, ☎ 773/743–5444) is well worth the trek since the 85 dealers are hand-picked and quality is more carefully monitored here than at most malls. Mid-20th-century is the primary emphasis, but items range from Arts and Crafts and art deco to Heywood-Wakefield. Display is the market's strong suit—the furniture, jewelry, and bibelots are wonderfully presented. The building itself is a prime example of deco architecture; it's near the Thorndale stop on the Red Line.

Evanstonia Furniture & Restoration (✉ 4555 N. Ravenswood Ave., North Center, ☎ 773/907–0101) has a rich collection of fine English and Continental antiques.

Gene Douglas Decorative Arts & Antiques (✉ 4621½ N. Lincoln Ave., Lincoln Square, ☎ 773/561–4414) is the dealer's dealer in Chicago. Noted for his keen eye, Douglas concentrates on clean-lined furniture and decorative accessories from the late 19th to mid-20th century. He's also got one of the best collections of modernist and mid-20th-century jewelry in town. The store is one block away from the Western Avenue El stop on the Brown Line.

Salvage One (✉ 1840 W. Hubbard St., Ukranian Village, ☎ 312/733–0098) draws creative home remodelers and restaurant designers from around the country to its enormous warehouse chock-full of stained lead glass, garden ornaments, fireplace mantels, bathtubs, bars, and other architectural artifacts. This is the place to hunt for all kinds of treasures, from vintage dental chairs to Paris street lamps. This area is best reached by car or taxi.

Apothecary

Merz Apothecary (✉ 4716 N. Lincoln Ave., Lincoln Square, ☎ 773/989–0900) carries homeopathic and herbal remedies. This store, about 6½ mi northwest of the Loop, also carries hard-to-find European toiletries. From downtown, take the Ravenswood El (Brown Line) north to the Western Avenue stop and walk one block east to Lincoln. The shop is closed Sunday.

Books

Women & Children First (✉ 5233 N. Clark St., Andersonville, ☎ 773/769–9299) specializes in books for and about women. This feminist bookstore 6½ mi north of the Loop stocks fiction and nonfiction, periodicals, journals, and small-press publications. The children's section has a great selection of books, all politically correct. From downtown, take the Howard El (Red Line) north to Berwyn, walk west to Clark Street, then go ½ block south.

Cameras and Electronic Equipment

Helix Camera & Video (✉ 310 S. Racine Ave., Near West Side, ☎ 312/421–6000; ✉ 70 W. Madison St., Loop, ☎ 312/444–9373; ✉ 233 N. Michigan Ave., Loop, ☎ 312/565–5901) draws professional photographers to its eight-story warehouse on Racine Avenue just west of Greektown (1½ mi west of the Loop) to buy or rent camera and darkroom paraphernalia. A good selection of used equipment is available, and underwater photography is a specialty. Take a taxi or drive to the Racine Avenue location; the others are in the Loop.

Factory Outlets and Off-Price Stores

Crate & Barrel Outlet (✉ 800 W. North Ave., Lincoln Park, ☎ 312/787–4775) is just across the street from a massive outpost of the retail store and carries odds and ends from the company's housewares and kitchen lines. Look for discounts of up to 75% on out-of-season items.

Fitigues Surplus (⊠ 1535 N. Dayton Ave., Clybourn Corridor, ☎ 312/ 255–0095) is where devotees of the comfy, loose-fitting separates go for discounts of 30%–70% off retail prices.

Gap Factory Outlet (⊠ 2778 N. Milwaukee Ave., Logan Square, ☎ 773/252–0594) is worth a detour to net substantial savings on over-runs and seconds on Gap men's, women's, and children's clothing. From downtown, it's a 3-mi ride northwest on the O'Hare El (Blue Line) to the Logan Square stop.

Mark Shale Outlet (⊠ 2593 N. Elston Ave., Logan Square, ☎ 773/772– 9600) lowers the prices on unsold men's and women's clothing from Mark Shale stores by 30%–70%. In a strip shopping center about 2¼ mi northwest of the Loop, this outlet stocks corporate and weekend clothing from the likes of Polo and Joseph Abboud. A car is necessary to navigate this area, which is just west of the Clybourn Corridor and full of strip shopping centers.

Western Wear

Alcala's Western Wear (⊠ 1733 W. Chicago Ave., Ukrainian Village, ☎ 312/226–0152) stocks more than 10,000 pairs of cowboy boots— many in exotic skins—for men, women, and children. About 2½ mi west of Michigan Avenue, it's a bit out of the way, but the amazing array of Stetson hats and rodeo gear makes this a must-see for cow-boys, caballeros, and country-and-western dancers. It's best to drive or take a taxi to this area.

8 SIDE TRIPS

Chicago's architectural tradition stretched its elbows in Oak Park, where you can walk a time line of Frank Lloyd Wright's architectural evolution. Farther west and further back in time, the first white settlers to the area created prairie farming communities now dotted with historical sites. This heritage is kept alive in Old Naper Settlement, in Naperville, and Cantigny, in Wheaton. Meanwhile, lush suburbs stretched north along the Lake Michigan shoreline offer rarified shopping and pleasant vistas for lakeside strolling.

THE CHICAGO SUBURBS showcase some outstanding examples of American architecture as well as appealing natural, historic, and human-made attractions. Frank Lloyd Wright lived in Oak Park, just west of the city, and had a great influence not only in that town but in many villages that hug Chicago's border. The homes, parks, and gardens north of the city—built by wealthy midwestern industrialists— are beautiful and can be a pleasant escape whether on a hot summer day or in the fall.

Updated by
Joanne Cleaver

Many of the varied sights on these side trips, which are all less than two hours from downtown, are popular destinations for area residents. Each trip has its pleasures, but visitors to a city such as Chicago, which already has so much to do within its borders, will most likely decide to go on a day trip only because of a special interest. Architecture and literary buffs may choose the North Shore or Oak Park, while fans of botanical gardens may head to the Chicago Botanic Garden in Glencoe. If you enjoy zoos, the Brookfield Zoo is a must-see; music lovers may plan an evening at the Ravinia Festival. Families will want to visit Blackberry Historical Farm or the Kohl Children's Museum. Most of the trips require a car, but there is train or bus service to individual sights that are worthwhile by themselves.

The eateries listed are either some of the best in the area or the most convenient for the destinations. For approximate costs, *see* the dining price chart *in* Chapter 3. Because side trips to the Chicago suburbs are only an hour or two from downtown, no hotels are suggested.

THE WESTERN SUBURBS

In Chicago's western suburbs, gracious villages that date from the 1800s mingle with more modest developments from the postwar housing boom. An essential stop is Oak Park, one of the most interesting neighborhoods of residential architecture in the United States. Brookfield has one of the country's foremost zoos. And farther west in Du-Page County is a string of pleasant destinations, including Old Naper Settlement, the best living-history museum in the Chicago area, and Cantigny, the lavish estate of *Chicago Tribune* publisher Robert Mc-Cormick (a turn-of-the-20th-century Chicago mogul), now a complex of public museums and gardens.

Numbers in the margin correspond to numbers on the Northeastern Illinois and Oak Park maps.

Oak Park

★ *10 mi west of downtown Chicago.*

Founded in the 1850s just west of the city's border, Oak Park is not only one of Chicago's oldest suburbs but also a living museum of American architectural trends and philosophies. It has the world's largest collection of buildings from the Prairie School, an architectural style created by resident Frank Lloyd Wright to reflect the expanses of the Great Plains. Here, among familiar clapboard and Colonial-style homes, are 25 houses designed or renovated by Wright and many others designed by architects who followed his teachings. Constructed from materials indigenous to the region, Prairie School houses hug the earth with their uncompromising horizontal lines; inside, open spaces flow into each other rather than being divided into individual rooms (☞ "The Builders of Chicago" *in* Chapter 9).

Ernest Hemingway once called Oak Park—his birthplace and childhood home from 1899 to 1917—a town of "broad lawns and narrow minds." The ethnic and political leanings of this village have diversified quite a bit since Hemingway played on its streets, due in part to an influx of young professionals fleeing the city with their children in search of safer streets, better public schools, and easy access to the Loop.

Numbers in the text correspond to numbers in the margin and on the Oak Park map.

A Good Drive and Walk

To get to the heart of Oak Park by car, take the Eisenhower Expressway (I–290) west to Harlem Avenue and exit to the left. Turn right at the top of the ramp, head north on Harlem Avenue to Chicago Avenue, turn right, and proceed to Forest Avenue, where a right turn leads to the Oak Park Visitors Center; there's ample free parking nearby. You can also take the Green line of the El to the last stop, the Harlem Avenue exit, or the Chicago & North Western train to the Oak Park stop at Marion Street. To get to the Oak Park Visitors Center from either the El or the train station, walk north on Harlem Avenue, make a right onto Lake Street, and a left onto Forest Avenue. It's a 10-minute walk.

Start by getting oriented at the **Oak Park Visitors Center** (⌧ 158 N. Forest Ave., ☎ 708/848–1500 or 888/625–7275, Ⓦᴇʙ www.visitoakpark. com), where you can purchase tickets for area attractions, get maps and guidance, and browse the books and collectibles inside the gift shop. Then head north on Forest Avenue, making a right turn onto Chicago Avenue to reach the **Frank Lloyd Wright Home and Studio** ①, an important bridge between the Victorian tradition in which Wright was trained and the budding of his own notions of space, light, and exterior elevation. Wright designed and built his house when he was only 22, in 1889, on the strength of a $5,000 loan from his then-employer and mentor, seminal Chicago architect Louis Sullivan.

Armed with a new perspective on the design philosophies of Frank Lloyd Wright, take some time to stroll around the neighborhood to admire a number of **Frank Lloyd Wright houses** and other spectacular examples of early 20th-century architecture. All are privately owned, so you'll have to be content with what you can view from the outside.

Take a look at 1019, 1027, and 1031 Chicago Avenue—these typical Victorians, which Wright designed while working for Sullivan, show few indications of the ideas developed a few years later in his home. In Oak Park, Wright both reacted against Victorian preferences and began to define his own style. Here you can see the roots of his sweeping horizontal lines that were later epitomized by Falling Water.

Turn left on Marion Street and then left again on Superior Street to reach 1030 Superior Street, a very early (1893) Wright building that, like those on Chicago Avenue, reflects his traditional origins. Continue down Superior Street and turn right back onto Forest Avenue, which is lined with textbook examples of late 19th- and early 20th-century architecture—in particular, note the horizontal lines of Wright's 1902 house at 318 Forest Avenue and his 1906 house at 238 Forest Avenue.

Don't miss the **Moore–Dugal Home** (⌧ 333 Forest Ave.), built in 1895, which reflects Wright's evolving architectural philosophy with its huge chimney and overhanging second story. Around the corner at 6 Elizabeth Court is another Wright house that reveals his early experimentation with cantilevering. Along this walk, you can compare and contrast then-revolutionary Wright homes cheek by jowl with overdecorated Victorians, blowsy Queen Annes, and upright Tudors.

Wright's work was considered revolutionary because he eschewed the frowsy ornamentation so beloved by the Victorians and instead aimed for clean, geometric lines and organic, flowing interior spaces. One of his early hallmarks was the ribbon window, a strip of panes forming a horizontal band. Wright also loved to incorporate art glass—stained and colored glass arranged in intricate geometric designs—in windows, doors, and light fixtures. Shifting light through the glass subtly changes the interior atmosphere of Wright houses as the day progresses.

Head back along Forest Avenue to the Frank Lloyd Wright Home and Studio, then walk east along Chicago Avenue to see a few sights that illuminate the charged life of Ernest Hemingway, one of America's greatest—and most distinctive—literary voices. A left turn onto North Kenilworth Avenue takes you by **Ernest Hemingway's boyhood home** (⊠ No. 600). This unassuming gray stucco house is privately owned and not open to the public. Return to Chicago Avenue, continue east, and make a right turn onto Oak Park Avenue, where you'll soon come to the **Ernest Hemingway Birthplace** ②, and a block south of that the **Ernest Hemingway Museum** ③, which focuses primarily on the author's early years.

A block south of the museum, make a right turn onto Lake Street. After passing the Oak Park Public Library at 834 Lake Street, stop before one of Frank Lloyd Wright's most important accomplishments, **Unity Temple** ④, which was commissioned by a Unitarian congregation in 1906 and is still in use as a house of worship. From the temple, you can continue heading west on Lake Street, either to return to the visitor center or the train stations. If you are headed down toward the train station and need a quick pick-me-up, try **Prairie Bread Kitchen** (⊠ 103 N. Marion St., ☎ 708/445–1234), where you can pick up a cup of fresh-ground coffee and a crumble-top chocolate muffin.

TIMING

From downtown Chicago, it's about an hour trip to Oak Park either by the El or the train. By car, the trip takes about 40 minutes. Allow yourself about three hours to walk Oak Park's sights and tour the Wright Home and Studio. Allow an additional two hours if you plan to go inside Hemingway's birthplace and museum, and tour Unity Temple.

Sights to See

❷ **Ernest Hemingway Birthplace.** Part of the literary legacy of Oak Park, this three-story turreted Queen Anne Victorian, which stands in frilly contrast to the many streamlined Prairie-style homes elsewhere in the neighborhood, contains period-furnished rooms and many photos and artifacts pertaining to the writer's early life. Using original family photos of the home's interior, museum curators have redecorated rooms and in some cases moved entire walls to faithfully depict the house as it looked at the turn of the 20th century; you can even poke your head inside the room in which the author was born on July 21, 1899. ⊠ *339 N. Oak Park Ave.,* ☎ *708/848–2222,* WEB *www.hemingway.org.* 🎫 *$6; joint ticket with Hemingway Museum $6.* ☉ *Thurs., Fri., and Sun. 1–5; Sat. 10–5.*

❸ **Ernest Hemingway Museum.** Fashioned out of a former Christian Science church, this museum contains exhibits and videos focusing on the author's first 20 years in Oak Park and their impact on his later work. The subjects of special exhibits range from movies made from Hemingway's books to his war experiences. Highlights include his first "book," a set of drawings with captions written by his mother, Grace. You'll also find many examples of reproduced manuscripts and letters. ⊠ *200 N. Oak Park Ave.,* ☎ *708/848–2222.* 🎫 *$6; students and se-*

204

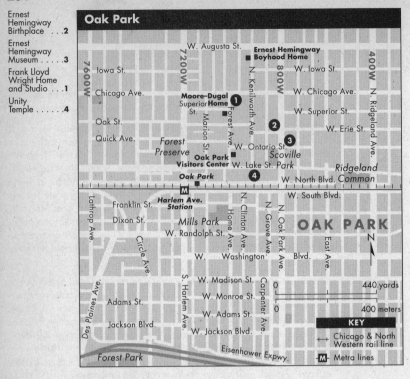

niors $4.50; joint ticket with Hemingway Birthplace $6. ⊗ Thurs., Fri., and Sun. 1–5; Sat. 10–5.

❶ Frank Lloyd Wright Home and Studio. A visit here provides a unique look into the architect's developing ideas over time as he continually remodeled the house. This is where Wright's nascent architectural philosophy first bloomed; he designed the house not only to hold his rapidly growing family but also to showcase his then-revolutionary notions. The home combines elements of the 19th-century Shingle style with subtle innovations that stamp its originality. Over the next 20 years Wright expanded his business as well as his modest cottage, establishing his own practice in 1894 and adding a studio to the house in 1898.

In 1909 Wright spread his innovative designs across the United States and abroad (at this time he also left his wife and six children for the wife of a client). He sold his home and studio in 1925; they were subsequently turned into apartments that eventually fell into disrepair. In 1974 a group of local citizens calling itself the Frank Lloyd Wright Home and Studio Foundation, together with the National Trust for Historic Preservation, embarked on a 13-year restoration that returned the building to its 1909 appearance.

Wright's home, made of brick and dark shingles, is filled with natural wood furnishings and earth-tone spaces. The architect's determination to create an integrated environment prompted him to design the furniture as well—though his apparent lack of regard for comfort is often the subject of commentary by visitors. In the lead windows are colored-glass art designs, and several rooms have skylights or other indirect lighting. A spacious barrel-vault playroom on the second floor includes a hidden piano for the children's theatrical productions. The adjacent studio is made up of four spaces—an office, a large reception room, an octagonal library, and an octagonal drafting room that uses a chain harness system rather than traditional beams to support its balcony, roof, and walls. Well-informed guides take small groups on tours throughout the day, discussing the architecture, pointing out various artifacts from the family's life, and telling amusing stories of the rambunctious Wright clan.

The **Ginkgo Tree Bookshop** at the home and studio carries architecture-related books and gifts and has tour information. Pick up a map to guide you to other examples of Wright's work that are within easy walking or driving distance. Try to join a guided tour of the neighborhood led by volunteers.

Reservations are required for groups of 10 or more for the home and studio tours. Note that you need to arrive as early as possible to be assured a spot on one of these tours—not later than early afternoon to make the last tour on any given day. ⊠ *951 Chicago Ave.*, ☎ *708/848–1976,* WEB *www.wrightplus.org.* ☞ *Museum admission or walking tour, separately, are $9 for adults, $7 for children and seniors; walking tour $8; combination ticket $16.* ☉ *Weekday tours at 11, 1, and 3; weekend tours leave 11–3:30 every 20 mins.*

❹ **Unity Temple.** One of Wright's early public works and one of the great religious buildings of the 20th century, this stark concrete structure consists of two spaces, a sanctuary and a parish house, connected by the low-ceiling main entrance. The cubical sanctuary, stucco with wood trim, is crowned by art-glass skylights that capture natural light while cloistering worshipers from the bustle of street life. Renovations are ongoing at the temple, but rarely interrupt scheduled tours. ⊠ *875 W. Lake St.*, ☎ *708/383–8873.* ☞ *Guided tours in English $6, students and seniors $4. Self-guided tours in English, German, Japanese, Spanish, French, and Italian $4; students and seniors $3.* ☉ *Weekdays 1–4 (Memorial Day–Labor Day 10–5); guided tours weekends only at 1, 2, and 3 PM.*

Dining

$$–$$$$ ✕ **Philander's.** This hotel dining room feels like a classy tavern and serves a wide selection of both traditional and contemporary seafood, pastas, and vegetarian dishes. One of Oak Park's few fine-dining spots, Philander's usually has a crowd. ⊠ *Carleton Hotel, 1120 Pleasant St.*, ☎ *708/848–4250. AE, D, DC, MC, V. Closed Sun. No lunch.*

$–$$ ✕ **Khyber Pass.** The clubby interior of this Indian and Afghan restaurant in downtown Oak Park belies a reasonably priced menu of imaginative curries and stews, not to mention a fragrant *nan* (Indian flat bread). Be sure to try the chicken *mukhni*, tender chunks of chicken in a spiced tomato sauce, or the chicken or lamb vindaloo. ⊠ *1031 Lake St.*, ☎ *708/445–9032. Reservations not accepted. AE, MC, V.*

$ ✕ **Original Pancake House.** Indulge in a Chicago tradition by ordering a German pancake served with powdered sugar and a wedge of lemon (the smaller version is amusingly called a Dutch Baby) along with a cup of excellent coffee. ⊠ *954 Lake St.*, ☎ *708/524–0955. AE, MC, V. No dinner.*

$ ✕ **Peterson's Old-Fashioned Ice Cream Parlor.** As its name implies, this place has ice-cream sodas, malts, and sundaes that'll make you nostalgic for the good old soda-fountain days. Light meals are also available. ⊠ *1100 Chicago Ave.*, ☎ *708/386–6131. No credit cards.*

Shopping

Though retail offerings in downtown Oak Park are spotty, a couple of intriguing shops—both of them near the El and train stations—bear exploring. The funky-retro shop **Pumpkin Moon** (⊠ 1028 North Blvd., ☎ 708/524–8144) carries such silly curiosities as replica '50s sitcom

Northeastern Illinois

WISCONSIN ↑ TO MILWAUKEE

10 miles

15 km

Channel Lake
Loon Lake
Grass Lake
12
Pistakee Lake
McHenry
Fox R.
Volo
60
Wauconda
Ivanhoe
Lake Zurich
Barrington Hills
59
Carpentersville
14
Dundee
Elgin
20
Hanover Park
Roselle
West Chicago
64
Cantigny
7
Warrenville
Fermi National Accelerator Laboratory
88
9
Aurora
8
Naperville
Plainfield
Joliet
52
55

Old Mill Creek
Fox Lake
Lake Villa
Grayslake
120
45
Libertyville
Mundelein
21
Long Grove
Buffalo Grove
12
Schaumburg
90
72
Mt. Prospect
290
Des Plaines
Elgin-O'Hare Expwy
Chicago-O'Hare International Airport
190
Eisenhower Expwy
355
Villa Park
Lombard
Glen Ellyn
Wheaton
53
Oak Brook
34
Morton Arboretum
6
Lisle
Downers Grove
355
Darien
53
55
83
59
Des Plaines R.
171
Lockport
Marley
30

Zion
137
Illinois Beach State Park
Wadsworth
Gurnee
North Chicago
Waukegan
Lake Bluff
Lake Forest 14
Highwood 13
Highland Park 12
94
43
Deerfield
Northbrook
94
Chicago Botanic Garden
Glenview
15
Glencoe
Winnetka
Kenilworth
Wilmette 11
Baha'i House of Worship
10 Evanston
Skokie
41
14
Morton Grove
Park Ridge
Franklin Park
294
River Forest
Elmhurst
Hillside
290
Berwyn
Cicero
55
5
Riverside
Brookfield Zoo
Chicago Midway Airport
Bedford Park
Burbank
12
294
Riverdale
45
43
Orland Park
Homewood
80
Chicago Heights
57
Park Forest

Grayslake
Sheridan Rd.

Lake Michigan

N

CHICAGO

UPTOWN

See Oak Park Map
1 - 4

LOOP

Hyde Park
94
Chicago Skyway
Evergreen Park
90
57
Calumet City
94
Lansing
394

INDIANA

lunch boxes. **Antiques Etc. Mall** (✉ 125. N. Marion St., ☎ 708/386–9194) sells Tiffany table lamps and Arts and Crafts decorative arts.

Brookfield

15 mi southwest of downtown Chicago. To get here from Oak Park, take I–290 west to 1st Ave.; go south and turn right on 31st St.

Brookfield itself is simply a quiet bedroom community. Most people come here to see its highly acclaimed zoo. The zoo is 3½ mi southwest of Oak Park (from Oak Park, take Harlem Ave. south 2 mi, turn west on Cermak Rd. 1 mi, then south on 1st Ave. to the zoo entrance).

★ ℃ ❺ The naturalistic settings of the 200-acre **Brookfield Zoo** aim to give you the sense of being in the wild (though you'll have to pretend not to see the hordes of schoolchildren and strollers that regularly migrate through the zoo). It's easy to spend most of a day here studying the more than 2,000 animals. The popular **Tropic World** exhibit, which simulates a tropical rain forest, comprises the world's largest indoor zoo of mixed species: monkeys, otters, birds, and other rain-forest fauna cavort in a carefully constructed setting of rocks, trees, shrubs, pools, and waterfalls. Thunderstorms occur at random intervals, although the raised walkway is sheltered from the rain.

In the **Be a Bird House** you can test your "flying strength" by flapping your "wings" on a machine that simultaneously measures wing action and speed and decides what kind of bird you would be, based on how you flap. A 5-acre **Habitat Africa** has a water hole, rock formations characteristic of the African savannah, and a new forest exhibit featuring termite mounds, okapi, and a re-creation of a native Bila village. Here you can see such tiny animals as klipspringer antelope, which are only 22 inches tall, and rock hyraxes, which resemble prairie dogs. The **Swamp** is about as realistic as you would want an exhibit on swamps to be, with a springy floor, push-button alligator bellows, and open habitats with low-flying birds vividly demonstrating the complex ecosystems of both southern and Illinois wetlands. Like many of the zoo's other exhibits, it has a touch table where you can handle artifacts such as turtle shells and animal skins. At the **Living Coast**, venture into a totally dry underwater environment with sharks, rays, jellyfish, and turtles swimming through huge glassed-in passageways. Numerous interactive exhibits explain the daily lives of penguins, turtles, shore critters, and even anchovies. Back at ground level, the daily dolphin shows, a highlight of the zoo, are a favorite even among jaded adults—the show area accommodates 2,000 spectators. Seals and sea lions inhabit a rocky seascape exhibit that simulates a Pacific Northwest environment, and there's a splendid underwater viewing gallery.

From late spring through early fall the "motorized safari" tram will carry you around the grounds for $2.50; in winter the free, heated *Snowball Express* tram does the job. You can also rent strollers and wheelchairs. The **Children's Zoo** (✉ $1, children and seniors 50¢) includes a petting farm, excellent animal shows, and the Big Barn with its daily milking demonstrations. ✉ *8400 W. 31st St.,* ☎ *708/485–0263,* WEB *www.brookfieldzoo.org.* ✉ *Zoo $7 (free on Tues. and Thurs. Oct.–Mar.); twice-daily dolphin show $2.50; parking $6.75.* ☉ *Daily; exhibits 10–5; grounds 10–5:30; open later in summer.*

Lisle

10 mi west of Brookfield, 25 mi southwest of downtown Chicago.

The old farm town of Lisle has been overtaken by subdivisions and sprawling corporate campuses. Its main public attraction, the Morton

Arboretum, was once in the countryside; now major roads surround it. To get to Lisle from Brookfield or downtown Chicago, take I–290 west to I–88 (the East–West Tollway) going west. Exit at Route 53 and go north a half mile.

★ ❻ Established by salt magnate Joy Morton in 1922, the **Morton Arboretum** is a wonderful place for a quiet tramp among 1,700 acres of plants, woodlands, and outdoor gardens. Trees, shrubs, and vines flower year-round, but in spring the flowering trees are particularly spectacular. A love of trees ran in the Morton family: Joy's father, J. Sterling Morton, originated Arbor Day.

Unlike other arboretums, this one allows cars to drive through some of its grounds. Still, you'll see more by walking along the 12 mi of trails. Most take only 15–30 minutes to complete; some are designed around themes, such as conifers or plants from around the world.

Plan your tour with the assistance of the free map, which will help you decide among such options as "Northeast Asia" and "Azaleas and Rhododendrons." Ten interactive visitor stations (with more planned) help you understand the unique characteristics of the surrounding flora. The arboretum is also a great place for bird-watchers. Inside the visitor center, you'll find a restaurant, coffee shop, library, and gift shop. Tours and special programs are scheduled most Sunday afternoons. ⊠ *Rte. 53,* ☎ *630/719–2400,* WEB *www.mortonarb.org.* ✉ *$7 per car, Wed. $3; walk-ins free.* ◷ *Daily 7–7; until 5 in winter; visitor center 9–5 year-round.*

Wheaton

5 mi northwest of Lisle, 30 mi west of downtown Chicago.

Several dozen religious publishers and organizations are based in Wheaton, the county seat of suburban DuPage County; evangelical Wheaton College is here, too. Many visitors, however, come to see the magnificent grounds and museum of Cantigny. You can take I–90 west to I–88; exit at Winfield Road and head north 3 mi.

❼ Colonel Robert McCormick, legendary editor and publisher of the *Chicago Tribune* from 1925 to 1955, willed his 500-acre estate, **Cantigny,** to Wheaton as a public park. Beautiful formal gardens, a restored 1870s mansion, and a tank park make it one of the key attractions in this old town. The estate is named after the village of Cantigny, France, which McCormick helped capture in World War I as a member of the U.S. Army's First Division. The **First Division Museum** is devoted to the history of this infantry division from 1917 to Desert Storm. In the **tank park** you'll see tanks from World War II, the Korean War, and the Vietnam War. Children are encouraged to play on the tanks, which are surrounded by soft wood chips. The first and second floors of the 35-room plantation-style mansion are open to the public and are furnished with antiques and artwork collected by Colonel McCormick's two wives. An entertaining introductory video is shown periodically in the home's own art-deco theater. Well-informed guides help provide a glimpse into the "Upstairs, Downstairs" lifestyle of mid-20th-century gentry: they'll even show you the dumbwaiters that delivered course after course from the basement kitchen to the formal dining room. On the grounds is a beautiful wooded picnic area. Cantigny hosts a parade of special events throughout the year, including regionally known art shows and family festivals. Call ahead for details. ⊠ *1 S. 151 Winfield Rd.,* ☎ *630/668–5161.* ✉ *Free, parking $7.* ◷ *Feb.–Mar., Fri.–Sun. 10–4; Apr.–May and Sept.–Dec., Tues.–Sun 10–4; Memorial Day– Labor Day, Tues.–Sun. 10–5. Free concerts.*

Just 4 mi northeast of Cantigny, the **Wheaton Park District Community Center** makes a fun summertime stop. At the excellent **DuPage Children's Museum** (⊠ 301 N. Washington St., Naperville, ☎ 630/637–8000, WEB www.dupagechildrensmuseum.org), a carpentry shop with real hand drills, hammers, and saws is perpetually popular with children who have edifice complexes. Kids can stand at waist-high water tables, splashing simulated dams and channels, and arrange their own multistory marble raceways from wooden tubes and chutes. Admission is $6.50, and it's open Tuesday–Wednesday and Friday–Saturday 9–5, Thursday 9–8, and Sunday noon to 5. Outside is the municipally owned **Rice Water Park** (☎ 630/690–4880), a huge complex with several multistory water slides, children's play areas, and a sand volleyball pit. Admission is $14 ($8 for children), and the park is open from mid-June to late August, Monday–Saturday 11:30–8:30 and Sunday noon–8:30. From Cantigny, take Winfield Road (Rte. 13) south, turn left onto Butterfield Road (Rte. 56), and follow this a little more than 3 mi. Turn left onto South Naperville Road, and fork right onto South Blanchard about ⅓ mi later. ⊠ 1777 S. Blanchard Rd.

Naperville

8 *4 mi south of Cantigny, 25 mi southwest of downtown Chicago.*

Though the far-western suburb of Naperville is often cited as a prime example of suburban sprawl (with good reason), its prairie-village heritage is still happily intact. Winding its way through Naperville is the sluggish, shallow DuPage River. Two miles of landscaped, park-studded river walks line its banks, with the most scenic stretch at the city's downtown. You can string together an agreeable outing from **Naper Settlement** (the Chicago area's only living-history museum worth mentioning), lunch or afternoon tea in downtown Naperville, and a leisurely stroll along the river walk. From I–88 exit south on Naperville Road. Proceed south, passing through the city's lovely historic residential district and downtown Naperville, and follow signs to Naper Settlement.

When Chicago was incorporated in 1837, Naperville was already six years old. One of its original families prospered, built a huge Italianate mansion (the Martin-Mitchell House), and early in the century willed the house and several hundred acres to the city. The local historic society began buying historically significant houses in the area, moving them to the grounds of Naper Settlement, and restoring and furnishing them. The impressive result is a bricks-and-sticks time line of the evolution of a 19th-century prairie town. Unlike many other living-history museums, Naper Settlement is relatively compact and can be visited in a single afternoon. Many of its buildings have hands-on activities and demonstrations.

Start at the **Pre-Emption House Visitor Center,** modeled after an inn and tavern that was at the epicenter of the town's growth in the 1830s and 1840s. Exhibits here include "Settling Down Roots," which explores Naperville's pioneer settlements and how they grew. Must-sees on the grounds include the 1864 **Century Memorial Chapel,** with its board-and-battens exterior and Pre-Raphaelite–style stained glass. The **Martin-Mitchell Mansion** is a rare, nearly untouched celebration of Victorian excess, right down to the original light fixtures, mourning wreaths of braided human hair, and massive mahogany furniture. The Greek Revival **Murray House** represents the typical (read: cramped) life of a first-generation prairie lawyer. Children particularly enjoy the re-created log-picket **Fort Payne** and the rough-hewn, one-room **Howard House,** where they can climb a ladder and peek into the sleeping loft. Naper Settlement regularly stages special events and weekend-long historical reenactments. Call ahead for details. ✉ *523 S. Webster St.,* ☎ *630/420–6010,* WEB *www.napersettlement.org.* 🎟 *Apr.–Oct. $6.50; Nov.–Mar. $4.25.* ⏲ *Apr.–Oct., Tues.–Sat. 10–4, Sun. 1–4; July–Aug., also Thurs. 10–8; Nov.–Mar., Tues.–Fri. 10–4.*

Just a mile north of Naper Settlement, **downtown Naperville** is a charming two- by four-block area bordered to the west by the DuPage River. Stroll along the river walk, stopping to enjoy its many shrubbery-shaded nooks, playgrounds, and even a covered bridge. Shoppers will enjoy the specialty clothing stores, home accessories shops, and reasonably priced antiques stores.

Dining

$$$–$$$$ ✕ **Elaine.** Nationally renowned chef Ted Cizma offers a slightly simplified version of the hearty Continental fare he serves up at Grace, his Chicago restaurant. The menu changes monthly; typical is a veal chop decorated with apple, ham, and foie gras. Desserts made on premises are a highlight. Reservations are recommended. ✉ *10 W. Jackson Ave.,* ☎ *630/548–3100. AE, MC, V.*

$$–$$$ ✕ **La Sorella di Francesca.** Innovative twists on pasta and contemporary sauces earn this trattoria a loyal following. Light eaters and vegetarians will find plenty to please, with imaginative salads and pizzas. Try the *quattro formaggi* pizza, topped with mozzarella, mascarpone, blue cheese, and swiss cheese. ✉ *18 W. Jefferson St.,* ☎ *630/961–2706. MC, V.*

$ ✕ **Jefferson Hill Tea Room.** Walking into this Victorian mansion–cum–shopping arcade is like stepping into the pastel-sweet interior of a wedding cake. All manner of feminine accoutrements, from stationery to decorative dolls, are arranged in little alcoves. The tearoom is regionally famous for its delicate salads, particularly the rich, tangy hot chicken salad, and commensurately rich desserts. Serves lunch only. ✉ *43 E. Jefferson Ave.,* ☎ *630/420–8521. MC, V.*

Aurora

❾ *8 mi west of Naperville via I–88, 33 mi southwest of downtown Chicago.*

Aurora's an old factory town, with some rough edges but also some lovely old buildings. Downtown has little to offer in the way of charm, but a few nearby sights make a trip worthwhile, especially if you're coming from Naperville. Within the downtown area is the **Paramount Arts Center** (✉ 23 E. Galena Blvd., ☎ 630/896–6666, WEB www.paramountarts.com), which hosts large-scale concerts and plays in its meticulously restored 1920s theater. From Naperville, take I–88 west for about 6 mi. Exit south on Farnsworth Avenue and turn west (right) at New York Street.

Three blocks north of downtown Aurora is the **Roundhouse,** a pet project of the late football great Walter Payton, which alone merits a trip. Payton and his partners transformed a decaying railroad repair station into a huge steak house ($$–$$$) and on-site microbrewery. Inside the complex, the one-room **Payton Museum** displays a 5-ft-high replica of Payton on a Wheaties box, among other Super Bowl memorabilia. The doughnut-shape building has an entirely enclosed plaza with a golf-putting green, gardens, and outdoor dining. From Chicago you can take the train from the North Western station straight to the Roundhouse and back again to the Loop without setting foot outside—an appealing option in winter. ✉ *205 N. Broadway,* ☎ *630/264–2739.* 🎟 *Free.* ⏲ *Daily noon–midnight.*

☺ Three miles west of the Roundhouse on Galena Boulevard is **Blackberry Historical Farm-Village,** where pioneer life is re-created in a prairie-town streetscape with a replica log cabin and an 1840s farmhouse. At the center of the complex is a small lake; a miniature train circles its gentle shoreline. There are also pony rides, a carousel, and a water park with a large safe area where small children can splash. Sheep-shearing days, quilting bees, and other special events are held throughout the summer. ⊠ *Galena Blvd. and Barnes Rd.,* ☎ *630/892–1550; 630/906–7981 water park.* ⊡ *$7.50; water park $11; combination ticket $14–$15.* ⊙ *Late Apr.–Labor Day, daily 10–4:30; Sept.–Oct., Fri.–Sun. 10–4:30.*

Western Suburbs A to Z

To research prices, get advice from other travelers, and book travel arrangements, visit www.fodors.com.

CAR TRAVEL

This side trip is best done by car, and all towns are within 5–15 mi of one another. The main arteries serving the western suburbs are the Eisenhower Expressway (I–290), which goes west from the Loop and turns into I–88 at the border of DuPage County; the Tri-State Tollway (I–94/294), which semicircles the region from north to south; and I–355, which connects I–290 with I–55, the road from Chicago to St. Louis.

TOURS

The Chicago Architecture Foundation has tours of Oak Park and occasional tours of other suburbs. The Oak Park Visitors Center (☞ Visitor Information) has self-guided tours of Oak Park and adjacent River Forest, as well as information on guided tours.

➤ ARCHITECTURE TOURS: **Chicago Architecture Foundation** (☎ 312/922–3432, WEB www.architecture.org).

TRAIN TRAVEL

You can take Metra commuter trains to individual attractions mentioned in this tour. The Metra Union Pacific West Line departs from the station at Citicorp Center (⊠ 165 N. Canal St.) and stops in Oak Park and Wheaton. The Metra Burlington Northern Line departs from Union Station (⊠ 210 S. Canal St.) and stops at Brookfield, Lisle, Naperville, and Aurora.

➤ TRAIN LINES: **Metra** (☎ 312/322–6777, WEB www.metrarail.com).

VISITOR INFORMATION

➤ TOURIST INFORMATION: **Chicago Office of Tourism** (⊠ 78 E. Washington St., ☎ 312/744–2400 or 800/226–6632). **Illinois Bureau of Tourism** (⊠ 100 W. Randolph St., Suite 3-400, ☎ 312/814–4732 or 800/226–6632, WEB www.enjoyillinois.com). **Oak Park Visitors Center** (⊠ 158 N. Forest Ave., ☎ 708/848–1500 or 888/625–7275, WEB www.visitoakpark.com).

SHERIDAN ROAD AND THE NORTH SHORE

All along the shore of Lake Michigan north of Chicago you'll find well-to-do old towns with gracious houses on lots ever larger and more heavily wooded the farther you travel north. The most southern of these towns is Evanston, which sits on the northern border of Chicago and is home to the lakefront campus of Northwestern University.

The drive up Sheridan Road, in most spots a stone's throw from the lakefront, is pleasant in itself, even if you don't stop. It's particularly scenic in spring, when the trees flower profusely, and in the fall, when their foliage is downright gaudy. Although Sheridan Road goes all the way to the Wisconsin border, it twists and turns and occasionally disappears. Don't lose hope; just look for small signs indicating where it went. When in doubt, keep heading north and stay near the lake. You can make a pleasant loop by heading north on Sheridan Road from Evanston to Lake Forest, then returning via Green Bay Road. You'll pass through the self-consciously tasteful downtowns of Highland Park, Winnetka, Kenilworth, and Wilmette on your way back to Evanston.

This side trip is designed as a drive, although you can take a commuter train to individual attractions.

Evanston

⑩ *14 mi north of downtown Chicago.*

First settled in 1826, Evanston is the home of five institutions of higher learning, among them Northwestern University. The student population and the diversity of its residents have given the town a distinct identity: here Birkenstocks never went out of style. Well-preserved or meticulously restored Victorians, Prairie houses, hip-roof bungalows, and turreted Queen Anne–style houses create a kaleidoscope of architectural styles on elm-arched streets, making the area delightful for walking any time of year. Throughout the warm months Evanston's lakefront parks are the stage for diverse special events, from highbrow art fairs to nearly rowdy ethnic music festivals. Even when things are quiet, the sandy beaches, sailboat launches, and playgrounds that dot the city's Lake Michigan shore give this area lasting appeal. Frances Willard, who started the Women's Christian Temperance Union, lived in Evanston, and the town is still the WCTU headquarters—though these days the town is by no means dry.

The **Evanston Historical Society** occupies the châteaulike former home of Nobel Peace Prize winner Charles Gates Dawes, U.S. vice president under Calvin Coolidge. The 28-room mansion, built in 1894, has been restored to its 1920s appearance and has spectacular 20-ft vaulted ceilings, stained-glass windows, Renaissance-style paneling, and period furniture, much of it original to the Dawes family and evocative of Dawes's diplomatic travels. The historical society also maintains a small but well-preserved costume collection and research facilities. ⊠ *225 Greenwood St.,* ☎ *847/475–3410,* WEB *www.evanstonhistorical.org.* 🖼 *$5.* ⊙ *Thurs.–Sun. 1–5.*

Founded in 1855, **Northwestern University** has an attractive campus that stretches along the lakefront for 1 mi starting two blocks north of the Dawes House. Some 7,500 undergraduates and 5,500 graduate students attend Northwestern, which also has professional schools in Chicago. The university's schools of business, journalism, law, and medicine are nationally known, and its school of speech has trained many actors, including Charlton Heston, Ann-Margret, Marg Helgenberger, and Kimberly Williams. Its football team is a perennial underdog in the Big Ten Midwestern Conference, but fans are diehards, which accounts for the many purple "N" flags that adorn houses and cars in the area.

There is no public access road running north–south through the school. You can park on either end of the campus and walk to the interior or to the peninsula, where winding paths loop around the lagoon (a panoramic view of the Loop skyline will tempt you to linger). To the west is the heart of the old campus, with shady groves of mature trees and the idyllic Deering Meadow.

The Office of Undergraduate Admissions at Clark and Hinman streets gives complete campus tours (☞ Tours *in* Sheridan Road and the North Shore A to Z, *below*).

The **Mary and Leigh Block Gallery,** a Northwestern-owned fine-arts museum, hosts traveling exhibits: European Impressionist and American Realist paintings, photography, decorative arts, and modern sculpture. The adjacent sculpture garden has large-scale sculptures by Henry Moore, Joan Miró, and Arnoldo Pomodoro. ⊠ *1967 S. Campus Dr.,* ☎ *847/491–4000,* WEB *www.blockmuseum.northwestern.edu.* ⊠ *Free.* ☉ *Sept.–May, Tues.–Wed. noon–5, Thurs.–Sun. noon–8; shortened hrs in summer.*

The irregularly shaped white building on campus is the **Pick-Staiger Concert Hall** (⊠ 1977 S. Campus Dr., ☎ 847/491–5441; 847/467–7400 for performance schedules), with a 1,003-seat auditorium that presents performances by internationally known artists as well as Northwestern faculty and students. The hall is acclaimed for its acoustics.

The **Shakespeare Garden** (⊠ Sheridan Rd. between Garrett Pl. and Haven St.) provides a tranquil campus refuge. Set back from the street and enclosed by 6-ft hedges, it is planted with 70 flowers, herbs, and trees mentioned in Shakespeare's plays. Park on the side streets west of Sheridan Road.

Grosse Point Lighthouse was built in 1873 to help guide ships into the port of Chicago. Although Lake Michigan looks placid most of the time, it has enough fog, violent storms, and sandbars to make navigation treacherous. The lighthouse was decommissioned in 1935, but the Evanston Historical Society (☞ *above*) has restored it and leads guided tours of the interior several months of the year. The surrounding park is open year-round and has a nature center and a community arts center. Note that for safety reasons, no children under 8 or groups of more than 12 people are allowed in the lighthouse. ⊠ *2601 Sheridan Rd.,* ☎ *847/328–6961.* ⊠ *$5.* ☉ *Lighthouse tours June–Sept., weekends 2, 3, and 4 PM.*

Dining

Evanston has many ethnic restaurants and a handful of elegant establishments such as Trio (☞ Worth a Special Trip *in* Chapter 3).

$–$$$ ✕ **Davis Street Fishmarket.** In this casual storefront you can sample the closest approximation of New England clam chowder that the Midwest can muster, plus daily specials of succulent grilled fillets and imaginative sandwiches and seafood salads. It's two blocks west of Sheridan Road on the eastern edge of downtown Evanston. ⊠ *501 Davis St.,* ☎ *847/869–3474. AE, MC, V.*

$–$$$ ✕ **The Roxy Café.** Academics come here for imaginative salads and pasta dishes. For dessert try the caramel apple pizza, made with a sweet-roll crust. ⊠ *626 Church St.,* ☎ *847/864–6540. AE, MC, V.*

$–$$ ✕ **Tommy Nevin's Pub.** This cozy Irish-style pub at the southern end of Evanston's downtown has delectable main dish pies for lunch; don't skip the toffee pudding, a perfect coffee accompaniment. ⊠ *1450 Sherman Ave.,* ☎ *847/869–0450. MC, V.*

Wilmette

⓫ *4 mi north of Evanston (from Sheridan Rd., turn west on Central St. in Evanston and continue to Green Bay Rd.; turn north and continue 1 mi to Green Bay/Lake intersection), 18 mi north of downtown Chicago.*

In this affluent village along the North Shore you'll find one of the area's most popular destinations, the Baha'i House of Worship, as well as many delightful, verdant streets.

Consider dropping in at the **Kohl Children's Museum.** The big draw for preschoolers and young elementary students is the construction zone, where they can use a kid-size crane to move big foam blocks. On the first floor there's a child-size grocery store, a re-created ancient sailing ship, and an excellent educational toy store. ⊠ *165 Green Bay Rd.,* ☎ *847/256–6056 or 888/564–5543,* WEB *www.kohlchildrensmuseum. org.* ⊠ *$6.* ☺ *Mon. 9–noon, Tues.–Sat. 9:30–5, Sun. noon–5.*

Rising near the lake, the **Baha'i House of Worship** is an intriguing nine-sided building that incorporates architectural styles and symbols from many of the world's religions. The temple is the U.S. center of the Baha'i faith, which celebrates the unity of all religions. With its delicate lacelike details and massive dome, the Louis Bourgeois design emphasizes the 19th-century Persian origins of the Baha'i religion. As symmetrical and harmonious as the 191-ft-tall building are the formal gardens that surround it. The visitor center has exhibits explaining the Baha'i faith; here you can also ask for a guide to show you around. ⊠ *100 Linden Ave.,* ☎ *847/853–2300.* ⊠ *Free.* ☺ *May–Sept., daily 10–10; Oct.–Apr., daily 10–5.*

Gilson Park, the jewel of Wilmette's lakefront, is ⅛ mi north of the Baha'i House of Worship along Sheridan Road. Its public beach is good for swimming and is rarely crowded. Bordering the east side of the park is a row of impressive houses that gives you a glimpse of the area's wealth.

Dining

$$–$$$ ✕ **Betise.** Though it's in a shopping center (the Plaza del Lago, just west of Sheridan Road in northern Wilmette), Betise serves surprisingly tasty Italian dishes, most of them based on tomatoes, potatoes, fish, and roasted chicken. ⊠ *1515 Sheridan Rd.,* ☎ *847/853–1711. AE, D, DC, MC, V.*

$ ✕ **Walker Bros. Original Pancake House.** This popular, traditional, breakfast-all-day spot has fluffy omelets, several varieties of pancakes (try the apple), and fresh-ground coffee served with whipped cream. The potato pancakes are divine. ⊠ *153 Green Bay Rd.,* ☎ *847/251–6000. D, MC, V.*

Highland Park

⓬ *7 mi north of Wilmette, 26 mi north of downtown Chicago.*

The attractive homes of Highland Park are a year-round pleasure, but in warm weather come here to see one of Chicago's top musical events. If you enjoy music under the stars, the outdoor concerts at **Ravinia Park** are a stellar treat. The Ravinia Festival (☞ The Arts *in* Chapter 5) is the summer home of the Chicago Symphony Orchestra, and the festival also showcases superb jazz, chamber music, pop, and dance performances. You can pack a picnic and blanket and sit on the lawn for about the cost of a movie ($10). Seats are also available in the pavilion for a significantly higher price ($15–$60). There are restaurants and snack bars on the park grounds. Concerts usually start at 8; plan to arrive at the park no later than 6:30 to allow time for parking, hiking from the parking lot to the lawn, and getting settled. ⊠ *Green Bay and Lake Cook Rds.,* ☎ *847/266–5100,* WEB *www.ravinia.org.*

A successful early example of the Prairie style, the **Willits House,** at 1445 Sheridan Road, was built by Frank Lloyd Wright in 1902. Outside, the house shows the influence of Japanese architecture in its overhanging eaves. The cruciform plan of the interior is built around a large central fireplace—a technique that Wright and other Prairie School architects used frequently. The house is now privately owned.

Highwood

🔞 *2 mi north of Highland Park, 28 mi north of downtown Chicago.*

A working-class Italian-American community, Highwood is an anomaly on the North Shore. The village was incorporated in 1887, and its fortunes have been entwined with those of the adjacent army post, Fort Sheridan, which was opened in the same year to maintain an army presence near Chicago in the wake of labor unrest surrounding the Haymarket Riot. During its early days Highwood was the only place nearby where soldiers could get a drink because most of the North Shore suburbs were dry. A large Italian population has given rise to a number of excellent dining spots, including generations-old Italian restaurants.

NEED A BREAK?
Many of Highwood's restaurants are open only for dinner, but you can grab a bite throughout the day at **Virginia's Restaurant** (⊠ 415 Sheridan Rd., ☎ 847/433–1555). For Italian-style picnic fare, try **Bacio Foods** (⊠ 424 Sheridan Rd., ☎ 847/432–1090).

Dining

$$–$$$ ✕ **Froggy's French Cafe.** This comfortable bistro is known for lavish six-course prix-fixe dinners and lunches, excellent cassoulet and other hearty dishes, and a huge wine list. Expect a wait at peak hours, and always take the chef's recommendations seriously. ⊠ *306 N. Green Bay Rd.,* ☎ *847/433–7080. D, DC, MC, V. Closed Sun.*

Lake Forest

🔞 *4 mi north of Highwood, 32 mi north of downtown Chicago.*

By the 1870s this village was acknowledged as the toniest and most exclusive of the city's suburbs. The town plan created winding roads that follow the course of the ravines near the lake, taking you past the beautifully landscaped campuses of Lake Forest and Barat colleges, as well as many sumptuous mansions set far back on heavily wooded lots. One of the nation's oldest planned shopping centers, **Market Square,** built in 1916, still thrives, with intriguing shops and boutiques selling high-price, one-of-a-kind clothes, home accessories, and knickknacks. To reach Market Square and the quaint Lake Forest business district, veer west off Sheridan Road onto Deerpath Road.

NEED A BREAK?
Within Market Square, **Lake Forest Food & Wine Specialties** (⊠ 672 Western Ave., ☎ 847/234–0620) is the perfect place to buy picnic supplies or to stop for a quick midday snack.

Glencoe

7 mi south of Lake Forest (take Deerpath Rd. west to Green Bay Rd., turn right to go south), 24 mi from downtown Chicago.

★ ⑮ Glencoe is a gracious, quiet village studded with oversized homes. Among the sprawling estates is the **Chicago Botanic Garden.** Fifteen gardens, each with its own specialty and approach, cover 300 acres. Among the different environments are a rose garden, a three-island Japanese garden, an Illinois prairie, a waterfall garden, a sensory garden for people with visual impairments, an aquatic garden, and a 4-acre fruit-and-vegetable garden whose yields are donated to area soup kitchens. The garden's three big biodomes showcase a desert, a rain forest, and a formal topiary garden year-round, and 10 greenhouses are full of flowers all winter long. Special events and shows are scheduled most weekends, many sponsored by local plant societies; standouts are the spring daffodil show, the Japan Festival in June, an August bonsai show, and a winter orchid show. Other popular times to visit are the spring blooming season and the burst of roses in mid-June. To get here from Lake Forest, turn right off Green Bay Road onto Lake Cook Road and follow it to Glencoe's northwest corner. To reach the Botanic Garden from elsewhere, exit I–94 at Lake Cook Road heading east and proceed ¼ mi to the entrance. ⊠ *Lake Cook Rd. and U.S. 41,* ☎ *847/835–5440,* WEB *www.chicago-botanic.org.* ⊠ *$7.75 per car, tram tour $4.* ☉ *Daily 8 AM–sunset; 45-min tours through Oct. 10–3.*

Sheridan Road and the North Shore A to Z

To research prices, get advice from other travelers, and book travel arrangements, visit www.fodors.com.

CAR TRAVEL

The route outlined in this trip follows Sheridan Road along the lakeshore, then turns west at Lake Forest to connect with Green Bay Road heading south. The other major artery serving the North Shore is the Edens Expressway (I–94).

TOURS

The Chicago Architecture Foundation has occasional walking, bicycle, and bus tours of parts of the North Shore. The Office of Undergraduate Admissions at Northwestern University organizes tours of the campus October–April, daily at 1:15, with additional tours Saturday at 11:45.

➤ TOUR OPERATORS: **Chicago Architecture Foundation** (☎ 312/922–3432, WEB www.architecture.org). **Office of Undergraduate Admissions, Northwestern University** (⊠ 1801 Hinman Ave., ☎ 847/491–7271, WEB www.nwu.edu).

TRAIN TRAVEL

The Metra Union Pacific North line departs from the station at Citicorp Center (⊠ 165 N. Canal St.) and stops in Evanston (Davis Street), Wilmette, Glencoe, Ravinia Park (on concert nights), Highland Park, Highwood, Fort Sheridan, Lake Forest, Waukegan, and Zion.

The Chicago Transit Authority's Howard (Red) line and an extension will take you as far as Wilmette, with multiple stops in Evanston. Board it northbound along State Street in the Loop or at Chicago Avenue and State Street in the Near North area. Change at Howard for the Evanston (Purple line) shuttle. To reach the Northwestern campus, get off at Foster Avenue and walk east to Sheridan Road. The Howard line is not recommended after dark.

➤ TRAIN LINES: **Chicago Transit Authority** (☎ 312/836–7000, WEB www.transit-chicago.com). **Metra** (☎ 312/322–6777 or 312/836–7000, WEB www.metrarail.com).

VISITOR INFORMATION

➤ TOURIST INFORMATION: **Evanston Convention & Visitors Bureau** (⊠ 1560 Sherman Ave., Suite 860, Evanston 60201, ☎ 847/328–1500, WEB www.evanston-illinois.org). **Illinois Bureau of Tourism** (⊠ 100 W. Randolph St., Suite 3-400, ☎ 312/814–4732 or 800/226–6632, WEB www.enjoyillinois.com). **Lake County Illinois Convention & Visitors Bureau** (⊠ 5455 W. Grand Ave., Suite 302, Gurnee 60031, ☎ 847/662–2700, WEB www.lakecounty.org).

9 BACKGROUND AND ESSENTIALS

Portrait of Chicago

Books and Movies

THE BUILDERS OF CHICAGO

City dwellers devastated by the aftermath of the Great Chicago Fire of 1871 couldn't have known that the leveled landscape before them would soon set the stage for the birth of a modern architecture that would influence the entire world.

Because Chicago had been built mainly of wood, it was wiped out by the fire. The lone, yellow stone Water Tower of 1869 loomed eerily near the intersection of North Michigan and Chicago avenues. Today, its fake battlements, crenellations, and turrets recall Disneyland rather than a real part of a vibrant and serious city. It serves now as a tourist information center, and even amid the amazingly varied architecture of central Chicago, it appears to be an anachronism.

In the years following the fire, many remarkable future builders flocked to the city that sprawled for miles along the western shore of Lake Michigan and inland along the branches of the Chicago River. Creative and brilliant minds such as engineer William Le Baron Jenney and MIT- and Paris-trained future architect/philosopher Louis Sullivan were joined by ingenious architects and engineers from diverse parts of America and Europe: Dankmar Adler (from Denmark), William Holabird (from New York), John Wellborn Root (from Georgia), Frank Lloyd Wright (from Wisconsin), Henry Hobson Richardson (from Louisiana via Boston and Paris), Daniel H. Burnham (from New York), and Martin Roche (from Ireland), among others. These pioneering men created the foundations of modern architecture and construction during the 1880s and 1890s in Chicago.

It's difficult to figure out precisely who did what, as they worked for and with one another, living in each other's pockets, shifting partnerships, arguing the meaning of what they did as well as how best to do it. Jenney and Adler were essentially engineers uninterested in decoration; with the exception of Richardson's Romanesque motifs, Sullivan's amazing ornament, and Wright's spatial and ornamental forms, these builders did not have distinct, easily discernible styles. It becomes an academic exercise to try to identify their individual efforts.

Philosophically, the Chicago architects sought to express the soul of American civilization, an architecture pragmatic, honest, healthy, and unashamed of wealth and commerce. Sullivan, a philosopher, romantic, and prolific writer (his most famous book on architecture, *Kindergarten Chats*, is a Socratic dialogue), originated and propagated the ideas that "form follows function" and "a building is an act." Sullivan believed that in order to create an architecture of human satisfaction, social purpose and structure had to be integrated.

The skyscraper was born here. The "curtain wall," a largely glass exterior surface that does not act as a "wall" supporting the building but is supported on the floors from within, originated here. Modern metal-frame, multistory construction was created here. The Chicago Window—a popular window design used in buildings all over America (until air-conditioning made it obsolete) consisting of a large fixed-glass panel in the center, with a narrow operable sash on each side—was developed here. In light of the fire that inspired the building boom, Chicago builders also discovered how to fireproof the metal structures that supported their buildings, which would otherwise melt in fires and bring total collapse: they covered the iron columns and beams with terra-cotta tiles that insulated the structural metal from heat.

THE CHICAGO SCHOOL'S greatest clients were wealthy businessmen and their wives. The same lack of inhibition that led Mrs. Potter Palmer and Mrs. Havemeyer to snap up Impressionist paintings that had been rejected by French academic opinion (and that today are the core of the Art Institute collection) led sausage magnates to hire young, inventive local talent to build their mansions and countinghouses. Chicagoans may have been naive, but history has vindicated their taste.

Although they started building in the 1870s, nothing of note remains from before 1885. The oldest important structure is Richardson's massive granite Italian Romanesque–inspired Glessner House, with its decorative interiors derived from the innovative English Arts and Crafts movement. The only Richardson building left in Chicago, the Glessner House is considered by some his highest creation; Wright was influenced by its flowing interior space. The building is at 1800 South Prairie Avenue in the Prairie Avenue Historic District.

Downtown, Richardson designed a wholesale building for Marshall Field that was later demolished. An addition to the Field store in the same architectural vocabulary, done by Burnham in 1893 and now part of the Marshall Field block, stands at the corner of Wabash and Washington streets. Burnham completed the block in 1902–07 but in the airy, open, metal-frame Chicago Window style.

In 1883 Jenney invented the first "skyscraper construction" building, in which a metal structural skeleton supports an exterior wall on metal shelves (the metal frame or skeleton, a sort of three-dimensional boxlike grid, is still used today). His earliest surviving metal-skeleton structure, the Second Leiter Building of 1891, stands at the southeast corner of State and Van Buren streets in the Loop. The granite-face facade is extremely light and open, suggesting the metal frame behind. The building looks so modern that it comes as a shock to realize it is more than a century old.

At 209 South LaSalle Street, the Rookery Building of 1886, a highly decorated, structurally transitional building by Burnham and Root, employs load-bearing walls (brick, terra-cotta, and stone) on the two major street facades and lots of iron structure (both cast-iron columns and wrought-iron beams) elsewhere. Here the decoration emphasizes the structural elements—pointing out, for example, the floor lines. Specially shaped bricks are used to create edges at the window openings and to make pilasters. This freestanding square "doughnut" was unusual at the time. A magnificent iron-and-glass skylight covers the lower two stories of the interior courtyard, which was renovated in 1905 by Frank Lloyd Wright, who designed light fixtures and other decorative additions.

The nearby Marquette Building of 1894, at 140 South Dearborn Street, by Holabird and Roche, seems to be a prototype for the modern office building, with its skeleton metal frame covered by decorative terra-cotta and its open, cellular facade with Chicago Windows. The marble lobby rotunda, a veritable hymn to local history, has Tiffany mosaic portraits of famous Native American leaders and Père Marquette.

The most advanced structure from this period, one in which the exterior wall surface is freed of all performance of support, is Burnham's Reliance Building of 1895, at 36 North State Street. Here the proportion of glass to solid is very high, and the solid members are immensely slender for the era. The white terra-cotta cladding brightens the street. Most critics consider the Reliance the masterpiece of the Chicago School's office buildings. The building was transformed in 1999 into the hip Hotel Burnham.

TO APPRECIATE FULLY the giant leap taken by the architects of the Reliance, look at Burnham and Root's Monadnock Building of 1889–92, at 53 West Jackson Boulevard. Its 16 stories are supported by conventional load-bearing walls, which are 6 ft thick at the base. Although it is elegant in its stark simplicity, its ponderousness contrasts sharply with the delicate structure and appearance of the Reliance Building. The Monadnock Building may have been the swan song of conventional building structure in Chicago, yet its very verticality expressed the aspirations of the city.

The impetus toward verticality was an essential feature of Chicago commercial architecture. Verticality seemed to embody commercial possibility, as in "The sky's the limit!" Even the essential horizontality of the 12-story, block-long Carson Pirie Scott store is offset by the rounded corner tower at the main entrance.

Jenney's Manhattan Building of 1890, at 431 South Dearborn Street, with its variously shaped bay windows, was the first tall building (16 stories) to use metal-skeleton structure throughout; it is admired more for its structure than for its appearance. Both it and the equally tall Monadnock would never have come into being without Elisha Otis's invention of the elevator, which was already in use in New York City in buildings of 9 or 10 stories.

The Chicago School created new decorative forms to apply to its powerful structures, and it derived them largely from American vegetation rather than from classical motifs. The apogee of this lush ornament was probably reached by Sullivan in his Carson Pirie Scott and Company store of 1899–1904, at State and Madison streets. The cast-iron swirls of rich vegetation and geometry surround the ground-floor show windows and the entrance, and they grow to the second story as well, with the architect's initials, LHS, worked into the design. (A decorative cornice that was originally at the top was removed.) The facade of the intermediate floors is extremely simple, with wide Chicago Windows surrounded by a thin line of delicate ornament; narrow vertical and horizontal bands, all of white terracotta, cover the iron structure behind.

Terra-cotta plaques of complex and original decoration cover the horizontal spandrel beams (the beams that cover the outer edges of the floors, between the vertical columns of the facades) of many buildings of this era, including the Reliance and the Marquette. Even modest residential and commercial structures in Chicago began to use decorative terra-cotta, which became a typical local construction motif through the 1930s.

Adler and Sullivan's Auditorium Building of 1887–89 was a daring megastructure sheathed in massive granite, and its style derives from Romanesque forms. Here the shades of stone color and the rough and polished finishes provide contrasts. Built for profit as a civic center at South Michigan Avenue and Congress Street, facing Lake Michigan, the Auditorium Building incorporated a theater, a hotel, and an office building; complex engineering solutions allowed it to carry heavy and widely varying loads. Adler, the engineer, devised a hydraulic stage lift and an early air-conditioning system for the magnificent theater. Sullivan freely decorated the interiors with his distinctive flowing ornamental shapes.

In the spirit of democracy and populism, Adler wanted the Auditorium to be a "people's theater," one with lots of cheap seats and few boxes. It is still in use today as the Auditorium Theater, and Adler's belief in the common man was upheld when thousands of ordinary Chicagoans subscribed to the restoration fund in 1968. The rest of the building is now Roosevelt University.

FRANK LLOYD WRIGHT, who had worked for a year on the Auditorium Building in Adler and Sullivan's office, remained in their employ and in 1892 designed a house for them in a wealthy area of the Near North Side of town. The Charnley House, 1365 North Astor Street, built of long, thin, yellowish Roman brick and stone, has a projecting central balcony and shows a glimmer of Wright's extraordinary later freedom with volumes and spaces. The Charnley House, with its exquisite interior woodwork and the exterior frieze under the roof, has now been completely restored. Soon after the Charnley House project, Wright left Adler and Sullivan to work on his own.

Wright's ability to break apart and recompose space and volume, even asymmetrically, was given full range in the many houses he built in and around Chicago. What became typical of American domestic "open plan" interiors (as opposed to an arrangement of closed, boxlike rooms) derived from Wright's creation, but they could never have been practical without the American development of central heating, which eliminated the need for a fire in each room.

Wright was the founder of what became known as the Prairie School, whose work consisted largely of residences rather than buildings intended for commerce. Its principal characteristic of horizontality was evocative of the breadth of the prairies and contrasted with the lofty vertical shafts of the business towers. Like his teacher Sullivan, Wright also delighted in original decorative motifs of geometric and vegetable design.

The opening of the Lake Street El railway west to the new suburb of Oak Park presented Wright with an enormous opportunity to build. In 1889 he went to live there at 951 Chicago Avenue, where he created a studio and a home over the next 22 years. Dozens of houses in Oak Park, of wood, stucco, brick, and stone, with beautiful lead- and stained-glass windows and carved woodwork, were designed or renovated by him. He became almost obsessively involved with his houses, wanting to design and control the placement of furniture and returning even after his clients had moved in. For Wright a house was a living thing, both in its relationship to the land and in its evolution through use.

Yet Wright's masterpiece in Oak Park is not a house but the Unitarian Unity Temple of 1906, at Kenilworth Avenue and Lake Street, a short walk from the Oak Park Avenue El stop. Strict budget limitations forced him to build it of the daring and generally abhorred material poured concrete, with only the simplest details of applied wood stripping. Nevertheless, Wright's serene creation of volume and light endures to this day. It is lighted by high windows from above and has operable colored-glass skylights inserted into the "coffers" of the Roman-style "egg-crate" ceiling, intended for ventilation as well as light. His window and skylight design echoes the designs applied to the walls, the door grilles, the hinges, the light fixtures; everything is integrated visually, no detail having been too small to consider.

Unity Temple was built on what became known as an H plan, which consisted of two functionally separate blocks connected by an entry hall. The Unity Temple plan has influenced the planning of public buildings to the present day. Restored to its original interior greens and ochers, Unity Temple is well worth a pilgrimage to Oak Park.

One of the most famous of all Wright's houses is on the South Side of Chicago. The Robie House of 1909 is now on the University of Chicago campus, at 5757 South Woodlawn Avenue. Its great horizontal overhanging rooflines are echoed by the long limestone sills that cap its low brick walls. Wright designed everything for the house, including the furniture. Because of a resurgence of interest in Wright's career, his stock has soared: a single lamp from the Robie House sold at auction for $750,000.

Complex political reasons caused Eastern architects to take the lead in planning the World's Columbian Exposition of 1893 at Midway Park in South Chicago. These architects brought the influence of the international Beaux Arts style to Chicago. A furious Louis Sullivan prophesied that "the damage wrought to this country by the Chicago World's Fair will last half a century." He wasn't entirely wrong in his prediction—the classicist style vied sharply over the next decades with the native creations of the Chicago and Prairie schools, all the while incorporating their technical advances. But the city fathers succumbed to the "culture over commerce" point of view, so most of the museums and public buildings constructed before World War II in Chicago were built in classical Greek or Renaissance style.

MANY OF THESE public buildings are fine works in their own right, but they do not contribute to the development of 20th-century architecture. The most notable of them, the Public Library of 1897, at 78 East Washington Street, by Shepley, Rutan, and Coolidge, has gorgeous interiors of white and green marble and glass; it now serves as the Chicago Cultural Center.

In 1922 an important international competition offered a prize of $100,000 for the design of a Tribune Building that would dominate the Chicago River just north of the Loop. Numerous modernist plans were submitted, including one by Walter Gropius, of the Bauhaus in Dessau, Germany, the world's leading modern design center. Raymond Hood's Gothic design—some called it Woolworth Gothic—was chosen. The graceful and picturesque silhouette of the Tribune Tower was for many years the symbol of Chicago until general construction resumed following World War II. More important, the Tribune Building moved the center of gravity of downtown Chicago north and east, prompting construction of the Michigan Avenue Bridge and opening the Near North Side to commercial development along Michigan Avenue.

One architect dominated the postwar Chicago school, influencing modern architecture around the world: Ludwig Mies van der Rohe. The son of a stonemason, Mies was director of the Bauhaus from 1930 until Nazi pressure made him leave in 1937. On a trip to the United States he met John Holabird, son of William, who invited him to head the School of Architecture at the Armour Institute, later the Illinois Institute of Technology. Mies accepted—and redesigned the entire campus as part of the deal. Over the next 20 years he created a School of Architecture that disseminated his thinking into architecture offices everywhere.

Whatever Mies owed to Frank Lloyd Wright, such as Mies's own open-plan houses, his philosophy was very much in the tradition of Chicago, and the roots of Bauhaus architecture can be traced to the Chicago School. Mies's attitudes were profoundly pragmatic, based on solid building techniques, technology, and an appreciation of the nature of the materials used. He created a philosophy, a set of ethical values based on a purist approach; his great aphorisms were "Less is more" and "God is in the details." He eschewed applied ornament, however, and in that sense he was nothing like Wright. All Mies "decoration" is generated by fine-tuned structural detail. His buildings are sober, sometimes somber, highly orderly, and serene; their aesthetic is based on the almost religious expression of structure.

The campus of IIT was built between 1942 and 1958 along South State Street between 31st and 35th streets. Mies used few materials in the two dozen buildings he planned here: light cream-color brick, black steel, and glass. Quadrangles are only suggested; space is never rigidly defined. There is a direct line of descent from Crown Hall (1956), made of black steel and clear glass, with its long-span roof trusses exposed above the level of the roof, to the great convention center of 1970, on South Lake Shore Drive at 23rd Street: McCormick Place, by C. F. Murphy, with its great, exposed, black-steel, space-frame roof and its glass walls.

Age requirements forced Mies to retire from IIT in 1958, but his office went on to do major projects in downtown Chicago, along Lake Shore Drive, and elsewhere. He had impressed the world in 1952 with his black-steel and clear-glass twin apartment towers, set at right angles to one another, almost kissing at the corner, at 860–880 North Lake Shore Drive. Later he added another, darker pair just to the north, at 900–910.

In 1968 Heinrich and Schipporeit, inspired by the 860 building and by Mies's Berlin drawings of 1921 for a free-form glass skyscraper, built Lake Point Tower. This dark bronze metal-and-glass trefoil shaft, near Navy Pier at East Grand Avenue, is a graceful and dramatic component of the Chicago skyline. It is one of the few Chicago buildings, along with Bertram Goldberg's Marina City of 1964— twin round concrete towers on the river between State and Dearborn streets—to break with strict rectilinear geometry.

Downtown, Mies's Federal Center is a group of black buildings around a plaza, set off by a bright red steel Alexander Calder stabile sculpture, on Dearborn Street between Jackson Boulevard and Adams Street. The Dirksen Building, with its courthouse, on the east side of Dearborn, was built in 1964; the Kluczynski office building at the south side of the plaza and the single-story Post Office to the west were added through 1975. The north side of the large Federal Plaza is enclosed by the Marquette Building of 1894, integrating the past with the present. The last office building designed by Mies, the IBM Building of 1971, is a dark presence north of the river, between Wabash and State streets.

Perhaps the most important spin-off of Miesian thinking was the young firm of Skidmore, Owings & Merrill (SOM), which blossomed after the war. Its gem of the postwar period was the Inland Steel Building of 1957, at 30 West Monroe Street, in the Loop. The bright stainless-steel and pale green glass structure, only 18 stories high, with exposed columns on the long facade and a clear span in the short dimension, has uninterrupted interior floor space. It is considered a classic.

SOM became the largest architecture firm in America, with offices in all major cities. In Chicago the firm built, among other works, the immensely tall, tapering brown Hancock Tower of 1965–70, with its innovative exterior crisscross wind-bracing, and the even taller Sears Tower (1970–75), with two of its nine shafts reaching to 1,450 ft, now the second-tallest structure in the world. SOM may have achieved the epitome of the vertical commercial thrust of the Chicago School.

Meanwhile, Mies's Federal Plaza started a Chicago tradition, that of the outdoor plaza with a focus of monumental art. These plazas are real, usable, and used; they are large-scale city gathering places, and they shape the architectural and spatial character of downtown Chicago.

A STRING OF PLAZAS, featuring sculptures by Picasso and Dubuffet and mosaic murals by Chagall, leads one up Dearborn and Clark streets to the Chicago River. The south-bank quays, one level down from the street, are a series of imaginatively landscaped gardens. Here one can contemplate the ever-changing light on the river and the 19th-century riveted-iron drawbridges, which prefigure Calder's work. Other monumental outdoor sculptures downtown include Joan Miró's *Chicago* and Claes Oldenburg's *Batcolumn.*

A Jean Dubuffet sculpture stands before the James R. Thompson Center (formerly the State of Illinois Building) of 1985, at the corner of Randolph and Clark streets. Here there are really two plazas: one outdoors, the other inside the stepped-back, mirrored-glass and pink-paneled irregular doughnut of a building. This wild fantasy is the work of Helmut Jahn, a German who came to Chicago in the 1960s to study at IIT. His colorful, lighthearted, mirrored Chicago buildings provide a definite counterpoint to the somber Mies buildings of the 1950s and 1960s, and they appear everywhere, influencing the design and choice of materials of the architecture of the 1980s.

Jahn's first important contribution to the Chicago scene was a sensitive addition to the Board of Trade in 1980. The Board of Trade was housed in an architectural landmark at 141 West Jackson Boulevard, at the foot of LaSalle Street, a jewel of art-deco design by the old Chicago firm of Holabird and Root in 1930. Murphy/Jahn's glittering addition echoed numerous features of the original structure. Both parts of the building have sumptuous interior atrium spaces. Marble, nickel, and glass motifs from the earlier edifice are evoked and reinterpreted—but not copied—in the high-tech addition. Within the new atrium, framed by highly polished chromium-plated trusses and turquoise panels, hangs a large art-deco painting rescued from the older building during renovation. This complex captures the spirit of Chicago architecture: devoted to commerce, it embraces the present without denying the past.

Next came Jahn's sleek, curving Xerox Center (1980) of white metal and reflective glass, at Monroe and Dearborn streets; it's now known simply as 55 West Monroe. Mirrored glass, introduced by Jahn, has become one of the favorite materials in Chicago commercial buildings. It acts as a foil to the dark Miesian buildings, especially along the river, where it seems to take on a watery quality on an overcast day. The elegant but playful high-tech United Airlines Terminal 1 (1987) at O'Hare Airport has been praised as a soaring technological celebration of travel, in the same splendid tradition as the 19th-century European iron-and-glass railroad stations that Jenney had studied.

Today, two disparate threads of architectural creation are weaving the modern tissue of Chicago, providing aesthetic tension and dynamism, just like the period following the World's Columbian Exposition of 1893. Chicago is a city with a sense of continuity, where the traditions of design are strong. Money and technology have long provided a firm support for free and original intellectual thought, with a strong populist local bias.

Chicagoans may talk of having a second-city mentality, but it seems certain through the history of architecture development in this city that they have a strong, enduring sense of self; perhaps being "second" has freed them to be themselves.

–Barbara Shortt

A practicing architect and an architectural historian, Barbara Shortt writes frequently on architecture and travel.

BOOKS AND MOVIES

Books

Chicago has been celebrated and vilified in fiction and nonfiction, as well as on film. For the flavor of the city a century ago, pick up a copy of Theodore Dreiser's *Sister Carrie*, the story of a country innocent who falls from grace in Chicago. Upton Sinclair's portrayal in *The Jungle* of the meatpacking industry's squalor and employee exploitation raised a public outcry. *The Pit*, Frank Norris's muckraking 1903 novel, captures the frenzy (yes, even then) of futures speculation on the Board of Trade.

More recently, native Chicagoan Saul Bellow has set many novels in the city, most notably *Humboldt's Gift* and *The Adventures of Augie March*. Richard Wright's explosive *Native Son* and James T. Farrell's *Studs Lonigan* depict racial clashes in Chicago from the black and white sides, respectively. The works of longtime resident Nelson Algren—*The Man with the Golden Arm, A Walk on the Wild Side,* and *Chicago: City on the Make*—show the city at its grittiest, as does playwright David Mamet's *American Buffalo*. On a lighter but still revealing note, two series of detective novels use a current-day Chicago backdrop: Sara Paretsky's excellent V. I. Warshawski novels (the 1991 movie *V. I. Warshawski* starred Kathleen Turner) and the Monsignor Ryan mysteries of Andrew Greeley. Greeley has set other novels in Chicago as well, including *Lord of the Dance*.

Chicago was once the quintessential newspaper town; the play *The Front Page,* by Ben Hecht and Charles MacArthur, is set here. Local reporters have penned some excellent chronicles, including *Fabulous Chicago,* by Emmett Dedmon; and *Boss,* a portrait of the late mayor Richard J. Daley, by the late Mike Royko. For a selection of Royko's award-winning columns, check out *One More Time: The Best of Mike Royko.* Lois Wille's *Forever Open, Clear and Free* is a superb history of the fight to save Chicago's lakefront parks. Books by Studs Terkel, a great chronicler of Chicago, include *Division Street: America* and *Chicago.* Jack Schnedler's *Chicago* (Compass American Guides) provides a fine

overview of the city as well as practical information.

Architecture buffs can choose from a number of excellent guidebooks. Ira J. Bach, former Director of City Development, is the author of *A Guide to Chicago's Public Sculpture*; this is currently out of print but worth looking for in a library. James Cornelius revised *Chicago on Foot,* by Ira J. Bach and Susan Wolfson; the book contains dozens of walking tours that concentrate on architecture. Franz Schulze and Kevin Harrington edited the fourth edition of *Chicago's Famous Buildings,* a pocket guide to the city's most important landmarks and notable buildings. The *A.I.A. Guide to Chicago,* edited by Alice Sinkevitch, is an exhaustive source of information about local architecture. The pocket-size *Chicago: A Guide to Recent Architecture,* by Susanna Sirefman, covers everything from office buildings to the new airport terminal. Finally, David Garrad Lowe's *Lost Chicago* is a fascinating and heartbreaking history of vanished buildings; it has some terrific, rare photographs.

Movies

Chicago has been the setting for films about everything from gangsters to restless suburbanites. Classic early gangster flicks include *Little Caesar* (1930), with Edward G. Robinson, and *Scarface* (1932), starring Paul Muni and George Raft. The theme is carried out on a lighter note in *The Sting* (1973), George Roy Hill's charming Scott Joplin–scored movie that stars Paul Newman and Robert Redford as suave con men. *Carrie* is the 1952 adaptation of Dreiser's novel about a country girl who loses her innocence in the city; Laurence Olivier and Jennifer Jones are the stars. Lorraine Hansberry's drama about a black Chicago family, *A Raisin in the Sun,* became a film with Sidney Poitier in 1961.

As Elwood and Jake, respectively, Dan Aykroyd and the late John Belushi brought wild energy and cool music to the screen in *The Blues Brothers* (1980). *Ordinary People,* the Oscar-winning 1980 film, starred Mary Tyler Moore in a drama about an affluent and agonized North Shore family. John Hughes directed 1986's

Ferris Bueller's Day Off, in which Matthew Broderick and a couple of his high-school friends play hooky and tour Chicago for a day, taking in everything from the Board of Trade and a Cubs game to a parade in the Loop; the film has wonderful scenes of the city. In *About Last Night* (1986), which is based on the David Mamet play *Sexual Perversity in Chicago*, Demi Moore and Rob Lowe go through realistic modern dating games with the help (and hindrance) of hilarious friends played by Elizabeth Perkins and Jim Belushi. Brian De Palma's *The Untouchables* (1987) stars Kevin Costner as Eliot Ness and Robert De Niro as Al Capone in a gangster tale with a 1920s Chicago background. *Eight Men Out* (1988)—with John Cusack, John Mahoney, and Charlie Sheen—depicts baseball's infamous Black Sox scandal, when members of the Chicago White Sox took bribes to throw the 1919 World Series against the Cincinnati Reds. Kurt Russell and William Baldwin play firefighter brothers in *Backdraft* (1991), which has some sizzling special effects. In the action thriller *The Fugitive* (1993), Harrison Ford pulls off one narrow escape in Chicago's St. Patrick's Day parade. Steve James's *Hoop Dreams* (1994), a documentary, is a powerful look at a couple of inner-city teens who dream that basketball will be their ticket out. In the romantic comedy *While You Were Sleeping* (1995), Sandra Bullock plays a CTA clerk who saves a man from death on the El. *My Best Friend's Wedding* (1997) is a romantic comedy starring Julia Roberts, who tries to break up the wedding of Dermot Mulroney and Cameron Diaz. *Return to Me* (2000) pairs David Duchovny and Minnie Driver. The plot is a bit far-fetched, as Duchovny's character falls in love with the recipient of his late wife's heart, but comic moments help it along. In *High Fidelity* (2000), John Cusack is a record store owner struggling with his past and present romantic life. *The Road to Perdition* (2002) stars Tom Hanks and Paul Newman in a 1930s gangster drama.

INDEX

NOTES

NOTES

NOTES

NOTES

NOTES

Fodor's Key to the Guides

America's guidebook leader publishes guides for every kind of traveler.
Check out our many series and find your perfect match.

Fodor's Gold Guides

America's favorite travel-guide series offers the most detailed insider reviews of hotels, restaurants, and attractions in all price ranges, plus great background information, smart tips, and useful maps.

Fodor's Road Guide USA

Big guides for a big country—the most comprehensive guides to America's roads, packed with places to stay, eat, and play across the U.S.A. Just right for road warriors, family vacationers, and cross-country trekkers.

COMPASS AMERICAN GUIDES

Stunning guides from top local writers and photographers, with gorgeous photos, literary excerpts, and colorful anecdotes. A must-have for culture mavens, history buffs, and new residents.

Fodor's CITYPACKS

Concise city coverage with a foldout map. The right choice for urban travelers who want everything under one cover.

Fodor's EXPLORING GUIDES

Hundreds of color photos bring your destination to life. Lively stories lend insight into the culture, history, and people.

Fodor's POCKET GUIDES

For travelers who need only the essentials. The best of Fodor's in pocket-size packages for just $9.95.

Fodor's To Go

Credit-card–size, magnetized color microguides that fit in the palm of your hand—perfect for "stealth" travelers or as gifts.

Fodor's FLASHMAPS

Every resident's map guide. 60 easy-to-follow maps of public transit, parks, museums, zip codes, and more.

Fodor's CITYGUIDES

Sourcebooks for living in the city: Thousands of in-the-know listings for restaurants, shops, sports, nightlife, and other city resources.

Fodor's AROUND THE CITY WITH KIDS

68 great ideas for family days, recommended by resident parents. Perfect for exploring in your own backyard or on the road.

Fodor's ESCAPES

Fill your trip with once-in-a-lifetime experiences, from ballooning in Chianti to overnighting in the Moroccan desert. These full-color dream books point the way.

Fodor's FYI

Get tips from the pros on planning the perfect trip. Learn how to pack, fly hassle-free, plan a honeymoon or cruise, stay healthy on the road, and travel with your baby.

Fodor's Languages for Travelers

Practice the local language before hitting the road. Available in phrase books, cassette sets, and CD sets.

Karen Brown's Guides

Engaging guides to the most charming inns and B&Bs in the U.S.A. and Europe, with easy-to-follow inn-to-inn itineraries.

Baedeker's Guides

Comprehensive guides, trusted since 1829, packed with A–Z reviews and star ratings.

At bookstores everywhere.   www.fodors.com/books